A Natural Paradise

Sarasota Jungle Gardens is a natural paradise, with cool jungle trails that wind through lush tropical vegetation, thousands of palms, tropical flowers, ferns and many more exotic species of tropical trees. It's also an animal and camera safari. Some of nature's most fascinating creatures: Spider and Squirrel Monkeys, Leopards, Crocodiles, Alligators, Emus, Wallabies, Iguana, Snakes, Lemurs, a Giant Land Tortoise, Flamingos (that are free roaming and may eat out of your hands), Koi Carp, Tropical birds and much more may be seen and photographed.

The informal gardens are breathtaking. An open garden, touched by lakes, a charming gazebo and manicured lawns are complete with stately palms and tropical plants. Truly a wonder and featured four times daily is the bird and Reptile Shows.

The Flamingo Cafe serves delicious sandwiches, snacks and beverages, and the Shell Museum is one of the most complete on the West Coast.

Kids will be delighted when they discover the Kiddie Playground with new state of the art playground equipment, haunted trees, tree houses, swings, sandbox and a petting area with miniature donkeys and other animals.

All of this is available to you. Sarasota Jungle Gardens has been entertaining visitors and local residents since 1939, come and join the fun.

Don't Miss

Botanical Gardens

Bird & Reptile Shows

Childrens Jungle Playground

Gift Shop

New Birds of Prey Area

(941) 355-5305

2 blocks off US 41
3701 Bayshore Rd, Sarasota

Siesta Beach

Go Native.

The Tasting Room • Locals simply fall in love here. Featuring the area's most innovative menu, extraordinary beer/wine list, single-malt scotch, small-batch bourbon and the very best Martini on the Suncoast! For lunch. For dinner. For happy ever afters.

J.D. Ford, Purveyor of Fine Wines & Spirits • A Sarasota favorite. Voted "Sarasota's Favorite Place to Buy Wine" (Sarasota/WWSB "Best of the Best), best wine values on Florida's Gulf Coast with many hard-to-find brands. Enjoy weekly wine tastings, educational programs, wine club and more!

Enjoy it all in the Historic Hillview/Osprey Shopping District - Sarasota's friendliest neighborhood.

1925 South Osprey Avenue, Sarasota • 362-WINE

Brian Johnson (AC/DC) & Jerry Wexler (ATLANTIC RECORDS)

The Difference.

Bruce Tassinare is *the* expert in Sarasota Real Estate.

Bayfront condos, waterfront estates, historic properties and investments properties - Sarasota is renowned for its unique residences and extraordinary lifestyles. Finding the perfect property is what Bruce does best. As a Certified International Property Specialist, Bruce Tassinare will make the difference. Call anytime.

BRUCE TASSINARE
Realtor®
Residence telephone
(941) 955-3333
Office telephone
(941) 951-6660
1801 Main Street, Sarasota

Michael Saunders & Company Licensed Real Estate Broker

Sarasota Bayfront

"Join us for an unforgettable waterfront dining experience"

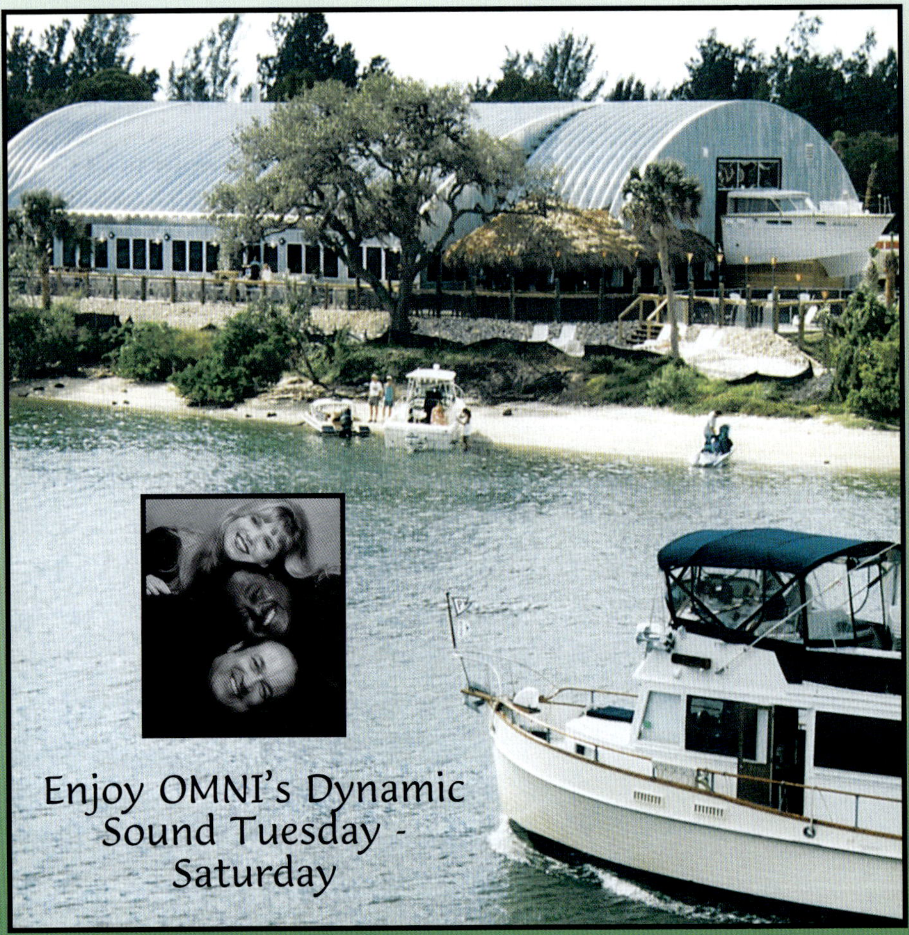

Enjoy OMNI's Dynamic Sound Tuesday - Saturday

- Tiki Bar & Swimming Pool
- Dock Space Coming Soon!
- Ask About Our 1-2-3 Club
- Enjoy our Sunday Brunch Buffet
- $8.95 Early Bird Specials

**1310 Old Stickney Point Road
Siesta Key, Florida
Phone: (941) 312-9111 • Mile Marker #62**

Table Of Contents

- 12 Acknowledgments
- 14 1999 "Season" Events
- **17 Welcome**
- 19 Convention & Visitors Bureaus
- 20 Chambers of Commerce
- **25 Information Station**
- 27 Area Maps
- 33 Important Phone Numbers
- 33 Tourist Information
- 34 Newcomer Information
- 35 Area Stats and Facts
- 36 Airport Information
- 37 Buses/Trolley
- 39 Accommodations Guide
- 46 Post Offices
- 47 Public Servants
- 48 Health Care
  - 51 Human Services
  - 52 Pets in Paradise
- **55 History**
  - 58 Manatee County History
  - 61 Sarasota County History
- 62 Sarasota School of Architecture
- 64 Sarasota Circus History
- 66 Venice History
- **71 Modern Times**
  - 73 Business
  - 78 Weather
- **85 Family Life**
  - 86 Purchasing A Home
  - 89 Real Estate Faces & Places
- 90 Neighborhoods
- 97 Schools
- 101 Higher Education
- 103 Libraries
- **109 Local Fun**
  - 111 Area Family Attractions
- **143 Sports & Recreation**
  - 145 Adult Recreation Centers
  - 146 Archery
- 146 Artificial Reefs
- 146 Aviation
- 146 Baseball
- 148 Basketball
- 149 Beaches
- 155 Bicycles
- 155 Billiards
- 155 Boating
- 157 Bowling
- 157 Canoes
- 158 Cheerleading
- 158 Community Sports Programs
- 158 Cricket
- 158 Croquet
- 158 Diving Instruction (Scuba)
- 159 Exercise/Fitness/Nature Trail
- 159 Fishing
- 164 Football
- 165 Frisbee Golf
- 165 Golf
- 172 Gymnasiums
- 172 Horseback Riding
- 172 Ice Skating
- 172 Judo
- 172 Kayaking
- 172 Lawn Bowling
- 172 Parasailing
- 174 Mountain Climbing
- 174 Personal Training
- 174 Pistol and Rifle Ranges
- 174 Playgrounds
- 175 Polo
- 175 Racquetball
- 175 Running Clubs
- 175 Sailing
- 175 Shelling
- 176 Shuffleboard
- 176 Skate Rentals
- 176 Skate Rinks
- 176 Snow Skiing
- 176 Soccer
- 176 Softball
- 177 Swimming
- 177 Tennis
- 178 Trap and Skeet
- 178 Volleyball
- 179 Watersports/Windsurfing
- 179 Yoga
- **181 The Arts**
  - 183 Art Agencies
  - 185 Crafts
- 187 Dance
- 188 Design
- 188 Education and Art Instruction
- 193 Film
- 195 Movie Theaters
- 197 Video Rentals
- 199 Area Fountains
- 199 Galleries
- 208 Gardening Arts
- 210 Music
- 216 Photography
  - 216 Poetry
  - 216 Theater
- **221 Shopping**
  - 223 Antique Districts
  - 223 Thrift Stores
- 224 Book Stores
- 228 Delectable Delights - Food
- 234 Flea Markets
- 236 Home Essentials
  - 238 Music, Music, Music
  - 240 Unusual Finds
- **257 Restaurant Guide**
  - 311 By Cuisine
  - 315 By Services
- 320 2000

Side Bar Contents

- 12 Credits
- 36 Rail Service
- 37 Trolly Service
- 52 Pelican Man Bird Sanctuary
- 62 Historical Groups
- 73 Networking
- 81 Hurricane Guide
- 89 Buying a Home
- 97 School Listings
- 112 Field Trips - Local Animal Info
- 156 About the Sun
- 158 Fishing Regulations
- 164 Golf Guide
- 174 Challenging Sports
- 183 1999 Festivals
- 223 Shopping Center Listings

Publishers
Steve and Kimberly Rabow

Author/Editor
Steve Rabow

Design
Kimberly Rabow

Production
Kimberly Rabow
Rosie White

Research Director
Barbara Viehmeyer

Research Team
Beth Evans
Barbara Miller
Susan Overstreet
Jan Thomas
Sharma Williams

Sales Staff
Sondra Guelfi
Diane Shane

Principle Photography
© Bill West

Color & Film
Coastal Printing

Printed By
Coastal Printing

Advertising Rates
(941) 927-1771

Rabow
Communication Arts
P.O. Box 15332
Sarasota, FL 34277
tel (941) 927-1771
fax (941) 922-5628
e-mail rabow@acun.com

Written, produced
and printed locally!

1999 - Eighth Edition
© 1999 Rabow
Communication Arts

All rights reserved.

A Legal Note About The Guide: Although this book is intended for use by active explorers and/or persons interested in pursuing some of the finer things life has to offer, The Publisher shall in no way be held responsible or liable for any information errors, mishaps, accidents or injury through the use of this book – we have enough problems of our own, thank you very much.

Preparing For The Next Millennium

We feel pretty lucky. *The Guide*, which you are holding, represents about as true an American "Mom and Pop" entrepreneurial success story as you can get. Imagine a couple - okay, admittedly not an ordinary couple (on their first date they "knew" and, thus, were married a year later) - who decided that what the Suncoast *really* needed was a comprehensive guidebook to help locals, visitors and newcomers explore the many treasures to be found in our area. So, silly them, they gave up the guaranteed world of paychecks and insurance coverage to become publishers. (For those who would likewise follow such a heady notion, please insert reality check here.) Eight years later, which included numerous attempts by various "personalities" and major publishing houses to replicate their efforts, there remains only one true guidebook to the area. This is it.

Year-by-year, we have been consistently surprised about how much actually changes around these-here parts. We have also been surprised by the number of residents who continue to buy updated editions each season. To keep them coming back for more, we make adjustments and improvements on an annual basis with the hope that each edition of *The Guide* is more "user-friendly" than the last.

1999 (8th edition) has some significant upgrades: you will note that, in addition to the basics, many listings now include Zip Codes, Fax Numbers, E-Mail and Internet Addresses. Perhaps even more impressive is that this edition is in full-color. An investment to be sure, but one which should help us to tell the story of how truly impressive this community is. And one which should position ourselves for the next century of guidebook publishing. Hey, wait a minute...that means a hundred more...uh, about that guaranteed paycheck...

Again, we can't do it without your support - our sincere thanks for your purchase and/or advertising participation.

More Questions About The Area?
Visit our website, www.exploreflorida.com, or send specific area questions to rabow@acun.com – we'll do our best to help you!

1999 Photo Gallery - Bill West
After 10 years in the New York area shooting advertising and corporate photography for Fortune 500 companies, Bill West recently relocated to Sarasota. (The sun, the sea, the friendly people – you had to ask?!) Bill specialized in some rather esoteric turn-of-the-century photographic techniques. You may have seen his work in Sierra Club Guides, Wilderness Magazine and the New York Times. A collection of his nature photography hangs in the Senate Offices in Washington, D.C. and in numerous private collections around the country.

Send Our Kids To College
Buy a dozen copies for your friends. *The Guide* is available in bookstores, finer hotels/resorts, retail outlets, restaurants, supermarkets and attractions throughout the state of Florida. To order by Mastercard, Visa, American Express or Discover, call (941) 954-3990 or send $14.95 (please add $3.00 for shipping/handling, Florida residents must add 7% sales tax: $1.26/book) to Steve Rabow's Guide Book, P.O. Box 15332, Sarasota, FL 34277.

Other Publications From Rabow Communication Arts
Sarasota Downtown Quarterly Guide
Sarasota Family YMCA Quarterly Guide
Die Freundliche Seite Floridas (German guide to Florida's west coast)
Sample copies are free, send $3.00 shipping/handling per title to: Rabow Communication Arts, P.O. Box 15332, Sarasota, FL 34277.

A LONG VIEW OF LONGBOAT © BILL WEST

1999 SEASON EVENTS & HAPPENINGS

Everyone loves a good party, but around here you are apt to find a purpose behind the pizazz. Most of the people behind the biggest events and parties don't get paid for their work; maybe they'll get a mention and a photograph in the newspaper's social column. Still, they raise hundreds of thousands of dollars for charities each year.

Now, when it comes to giving a party, few do it better than **Sandy Loevner**, Executive Director of Florida Winefest & Auction – one of the area's important annual fund-raising events with proceeds going directly to local charities. In 1996 this single event netted $500,000. Not bad for a weekend of wine and food. But, as Sandy tells us, these parties are not simply about "having a good time", nor do they involve just a simple weekend of work:

"Sarasota is full of benefits for all types of causes – civic, art, human services, etc. There are over 50 black-tie events alone in the Sarasota area each year – this doesn't count the numerous luncheons, roasts & toasts, casual buffets, dances, galas, dinners, and get-togethers. It seems that a new event is created each month that was not held the previous year.

Volunteers who run these events make it look easy – that is why the events are fun and make millions of dollars each year for hundreds of charities. The general public never sees the computers that run into the nights, the bags of bulk-mail sacks (so that postage is given at a special rate to save money), or the long hours that make these events possible. Dinners are put on the tables late, meetings are started at 7 a.m. frequently so that volunteers can meet before their paid work day starts – and volunteers work after their normal work day to volunteer their time, creativity, and energy. *Time is the key.* If these volunteers were paid, there would be no money left to give to the charities. Giving of yourself and your time is a gift of love for others. And if we don't, who will?"

The following social calendar is only a smattering of the many activities happening in our area during 1999. You will find specific concert/theater/performance/sports schedules located throughout *The Guide*.

Jan. 8 /Feb. 14 - Sarasota Visual Art Center, Latin American Art International 346-7509
Jan. 17 - United Cerebral Palsy Telethon, broadcast live on WWSB, Channel 40 from Sarasota Main Plaza. 957-3599
Jan. 21/30 - Manatee County Fair - Just say moo! 722-1639
Jan 21/Feb. 7 - Manatee Players "Cabaret", 748-5875
Jan. 24 - Arts Day Downtown. 365-5118
Jan. 24 - Sarasota Concert Band, Van Wezel, 955-6660
Jan. 30 - Anna Maria Flavors of the Isle, 778-1541
Jan. 30 - Ringling Museum - Baroque Bash, 359-5700
Jan. 30/31 - Antique Show, Sarasota County Fair Grounds, 365-0818
Feb. 5 - 1st Friday Downtown Sarasota Stroll, 951-2656
Feb. 6 - Scottish Festival, Sarasota County Fair Grounds, 365-0818
Feb. 6/7 - Anna Maria Island Bridge Street Festival, 778-1541
Feb. 6/13 - Ringling Museum - Project Black cinema, 359-5700
Feb. 6 - 21st Annual Fishing College - Angler heaven. 745-7020
Feb. 8-14 - American Express Invitational, Prestancia. 1-800-387-9991
Feb. 9-14 - Greek Glendi - Music, food, fun. 355-2616\Feb. 11-13 - Mennonite Quilt & Craft Show - 955-8919
Feb. 12/14 - Bluegrass Festival, Sarasota County Fair Grounds, 365-0818
Feb. 13-14 - 20th Annual Terra Ceia/Rubonia Mardi Gras - Mardi Gras '70s Style. Kazoo marching band and more. 722-5048
Feb. 13/15 - Selby Gardens Spring Plant Fair, 366-5731
Feb. 14 - Sarasota Music Archive, Carole Sparrow Music Recital 955-5890
Feb. 14 - Say "I Do" Ceremony - A chance to say your vows once again, this time at sunset, on Siesta Beach.
Feb. 17 - St. Patrick's Day Downtown Sarasota, 951-2656
Feb. 19/20 -Volunteer Center Garage Sale, Sarasota County Fair Grounds, 365-0818
Feb. 19/20 - Venice Snowbird Art Fest 488-2236
Feb. 19/21 - Sarasota Festival of the Arts, Main Street - 951-2656
Feb. 19/21 - Sarasota Shell Show at Municipal Auditorium. She sells sea shells. 359-3353
Feb. 20/21 - Cortez Fishing Festival - Fabulous Cortez. 794-0280
Feb. 20 - Annual Porcelain Show and Sale - 953-7638
Feb. 21 - Sarasota Concert Band, Van Wezel, 955-6660
Feb. 25/28 - Ringling Museum Medieval Fair, 359-5700
Feb. 25/28 - Italian Feast & Festival - Venice Airport. 493-6344
Feb. 26/March 25 - Sarasota Visual Arts Center - Winter Members' Exhibit 365-2032
Mar. 1-28 - Design Showcase. 953-4252
March 3-4 - 22nd Annual Antique Show - A fave rave. 955-0935
March 7 - Sarasota Music Archive, the Life & Music of John McCormack 955-5890
March 7 - Sarasota Concert Band, Van Wezel, 955-6660
March 11/28 - Manatee Players "You Can't Take It With You", 748-5875
March 13 - Venice St. Patrick's Day Parade 488-2236
March 18/19, Sailor Circus, 361-6350
March 19, American Cancer Society, Serendipity Ball, 365-2858
March 20 - Cardinal Mooney Dinner/Auction - 379-2647
March 12-20 - Sarasota County Fair - Fairgrounds. 365-0818
March 13/14 - Hunsader Farms Spring Festival
March 13/15 - Spring Plant Fair, Selby Botanical Gardens
March 13/14 - Green Bridge Festival - Entertainment, ethnic foods and children's scholarship art contest. 795-7427
March 14 - Sarasota Music Archive, Opera "Cavalleria Rusticana 955-5890
March 14 - 26th Annual Cardinal Mooney High School Telethon - fundraising on WWSB, Channel 40. 379-2647
March 24/26, Sailor Circus, 361-6350
March 26/April 8 - Sarasota Visual Art Center - Power of the Pixel 3, 366-2032
March 27/28 - Antique Show, Sarasota County Fair Grounds, 365-0818
April 1/3, Sailor Circus, 361-6350
April 2 - 1st Friday Downtown Sarasota Stroll, 951-2656
April 2/May 2 - Sarasota Visual Art Center - The 2nd Florida Arts Invitational, 349-0531
April 3 - Selby Gardens 17th annual Orchid Ball, 366-5731
April 3 - Venice Easter Egg Hunt 488-2236
April 10 - Ringling Museum Children's Art Festival, 359-5700
April 17, Ringling Museum Croquet Soiree, 359-5700
April 18 - St. Armands Circle sit & Shop (Florida Winefest)
April 21/25 - Florida Winefest & Auction - The best. 952-1109
April 24/25 - Shrine Circus, Sarasota County Fair Grounds, 365-0818
April 26 - Sarasota Concert Band - Free Concert on Siesta Beach - 955-6660
May 1 - Manatee Community College Outdoor Pops Concert Under The Stars, Bradenton, 753-0850
May 6/23 - Manatee Players "Crazy For You", 748-5875
May 7 - Barefoot Beach Ball to benefit Girls, Inc. 366-6646

May 8- Manatee Community College Outdoor Pops Concert Under The Stars, Venice, 483-5988
May 9 - Mother's Day Garden Tour - sponsored by Children's Haven and Selby Gardens. 355-8808
May 14-15 - Relay for Life. Luminaries light up the night in honor or in memory of someone touched by cancer. 365-2858
May 15 - 9th Annual MCC "Evening Under The Stars."Pops Concert, The Florida West Coast Symphony. 753-0850
May 15/16 - Antique Show, Sarasota County Fair Grounds, 365-0818
May 21 - Casual Day '98 sponsored by United Cerebral Palsy. Call 957-3599 to register your company.
June 4 - American Cancer Society - "In the Pink & All That Jazz", 365-2858
June 12/13 Venice Fine Craft Fair, 488-2236
July 1 - Sarasota Boat Parade and Block Party
July 2 - Powerboats on St. Armands
July 4 - Palmetto 4th of July - Day-long, party-on. 723-4570
July 17 - Selby Gardens Summer Plant Fair, 366-5731
July 17 - Snooty the Manatee's Birthday Party - South Florida Museum in Bradenton. Great for the kids. 746-4132
July 23/24 Venice Christmas In July Sidewalk Sale, 488-2236
Aug. 7 - American Cancer Society Bachelor Ball, 354-2858
Aug. 7 - Selby Gardens Annual Summer Children's Day, 366-5731
Sept. 10/11 Venice Island Daze, 433-2236
Sept. 11, St. Armands Circle, Classic Antique auto Show
Sept. 11/17 - Selby Gardens Free Week, 366-5731
Sept. 19 - Hillbilly Hoedown, Sarasota County Fair Grounds, 365-0818
Oct. 9/10 Sarasota Downtown Fall Festival, 951-2656
Oct. 16/17 - St. Armands Circle 11th Annual Art Festival
Oct. 24/25 - Antique Show, Sarasota County Fair Grounds, 365-0818
Oct. 30 Venice Halloween Parade, 488-2236
Nov. 6 - Sarasota Blues Festival. 365-2787
Nov. 6 - St. Armands Circle Corvette Show
Nov. 6 - Snooty Gala, black tie event to support manatee education, 746-4131
Nov. 6 - Bluesfest, Sarasota County Fair Grounds, 365-0818
Nov. 6/7 Venice Art Fest '99, 488-2236
Nov. 7-8 - Art Fest '99 - Downtown Venice. 484-6722
Nov. 12/14 - Selby Gardens Fall Plant Fair, 366-5731
Nov. 28/29 - Antique Show, Sarasota County Fair Grounds, 365-0818
Dec. 1- Venice Christmas Walk, 488-2236
Dec. 1- Jan. 3 - Selby Gardens Holiday Celebration
Dec. 3 - Christmas Night on St. Armands Circle
Dec. 3/4 - Selby Gardens by Candlelight, 366-5731

Sandy Loevner

Sandy has been involved in fund-raising events in Sarasota for 20 years - in fact, it is highly doubtful that anyone else locally has been on more boards or has worked directly with as many not-for-profit organizations in the area. Sandy's extraordinary organizational skills (including her amazing ability to mobilize an army of volunteers) have benefited such groups as The American Cancer Society, Critical Care Center at Sarasota Memorial, The American Heart Association, Parent Child Center, Longboat Key Art Center, African Vision Fund, Sarasota Arts Council, Special Olympics, Hospice, Safe Place and Rape Crisis, United Way, Florida Winefest and Schoenbaum Human Services Center...to name just a few.

Welcome

EXPLORE AND ENJOY

You have in your hands the key which will open the door to "The Cultural Side of Florida" – Sarasota, Bradenton, Venice and the surrounding island communities.

It's important to keep in mind that this is an exploring guide. As such, we are not abrasively critical. We like to think of ourselves as reflective of the choices available, not dictative as to what is "cool and hip" or not. We'll leave that job, to others much more "cool and hip" than we are, thankfully.

In truth, we remain respectful of the reader's ability to make decisions about spending time and money. What you'll find here are plenty of possibilities, and if we are doing our job you should make some exciting discoveries – everything fun to see and do within our sophisticated and artistic tropical haven, nestled here on the Gulf of Mexico.

The Guide has been specifically designed to make the first-time visitor feel like a long-time resident. Concurrently, *The Guide* should make the lifetime "local" feel like one of our tourists, enriched with fresh insight. In fact, a year has not gone by without hearing from many long-time residents who tell us how many places and different things they discover in *The Guide* - places and things they knew absolutely nothing about before.

This 1999 edition is our eighth annual Suncoast celebration. Please patronize our advertisers and mention "Steve Rabow's Guide" when you do; these supportive folks make this (hopefully) important resource possible.

And now an important editorial comment: what is true with our weather is also true within this resort community – things change quickly and often without warning. We do our darndest to make sure that all of the information in The Guide is accurate at printing time, but life goes on so...

Rabow Rule #1 – always call ahead. All numbers provided are within the 941 area code unless otherwise noted.

Now get out there, explore and enjoy yourself!

Our Convention and Visitors Bureaus

SARASOTA COUNTY

Dear Visitor:

If you're a visitor to the Sarasota area, and if you're unable to find what you need in the "Official Guide Book," which is unlikely, we invite you to stop by the Visitor Information Center, located on North Tamiami Trail (US 41) at 6th Street.

The visitor center offers a variety of brochures and pamphlets on places to stay, to shop, attractions to visit, plus helpful information for folks moving to the community.

The visitor center is a distinctive edifice designed by architect Victor Lundy in 1957. The oriental design of the building, with its blue ceramic title roof, explains why everyone in Sarasota refers to it simply as, the Pagoda.

Inside the Pagoda you will find a dedicated staff of volunteers and professionals standing by to answer any question you may have about Sarasota and the gulf coast islands. Even if you don't have a question, stop by and say hello. The welcome mat is always out.

Kevin Lawler, Executive Director
Sarasota County Convention and Visitors Bureau
655 N. Tamiami Tr. 34236
Phone: 957-1877 or 1-800-522-9729
Fax:951-2956
E-mail:scvb@netsrq.com
Internet: www.sarasotafl.org

BRADENTON AREA CONVENTION & VISITORS BUREAU

SARASOTA VISITORS CENTER © BILL WEST

Dear Visitor:

You have made, or are about to make, several wise decisions, for which I congratulate you.

First, you have, just by thumbing through this guide to the Sarasota/Bradenton area, indicated an interest in the best that Florida has to offer in a vacation experience. After the crowd-crush of much of Florida, this area is an alternative you'll enjoy; near enough to those "other" attractions, yet removed from the chaos of it; up to our hips in culture, history, and elegance, yet more laid back than most Florida destinations.

Secondly, you may have already decided to come here, or, better, you may already be here, which really shows how smart you are! We hope you enjoy our island lifestyle.

Finally, you've had the good sense to buy this guide book. On the slim chance that Steve Rabow has not included everything you need to know about Bradenton and Florida's gulf island beaches, please call us. The Convention and Visitors Bureau office is in the Manatee Convention and Civic Center at One Haben Blvd., Palmetto, Florida 34221; call 729-9177. Our Tourist Information Center is located at I-75, Exit 43 Ellenton, open 7 days week. Enjoy!

Larry White, Executive Director
Bradenton & Florida's Gulf Island Beaches Convention & Visitors Bureau
Phone 729-7040 or 1-800-4-MANATEE, Fax:729-1820
E-mail:gulfisl@bhip.infi.net; Internet: www.floridaislandbeaches.org

Sophisticated Sarasota

Sarasota gained its renowned international reputation as a distinctive resort destination through Chicago socialite Mrs. Potter Palmer during the early 1900s. John Ringling (of Ringling Bros. circus fame) helped to secure a continuing spotlight on the area by making Sarasota his winter headquarters. Today, Sarasota's discerning consumer base possesses one of Florida's highest per capita incomes. *The Economist* magazine ranks Sarasota as the 7th best city in the nation for private sector job growth. *Money* magazine ranks Sarasota as the 14th best place to live in the nation.

SELBY ORCHID © BILL WEST

OUR CHAMBERS OF COMMERCE

First, keep in mind that unless you are from Australia, Argentina or Antarctica, *everyone* from out of state is a "Northerner." Most everyone here is from somewhere else and – amazing as it seems – most everyone here is genuinely nice. This is especially true of the local residents.

Born here or relocated from the north, the "locals" are some of the friendliest people you will ever meet. In fact, we are proposing an official slogan for the area: "Sarasota, Bradenton and Venice - where people reek of friendliness!"

This happy attitude is put into practice through our local Chambers of Commerce whose members spend uncountable hours on networking, promotion and development; an important vision of community growth, nurtured through the act of sharing.

ANNA MARIA ISLAND CHAMBER OF COMMERCE

Dear Suncoast Newcomer/Visitor:

Anna Maria Island is an arc of seven-and-a-half miles of white sand beach connecting the Gulf of Mexico, Tampa Bay, Intercoastal Waterway and Anna Maria Sound. Three small cities calling Anna Maria Island home boast modern fire, police and emergency facilities while maintaining a congenial air of unhurried tropical living.

This sub-tropical island offers year-round beach weather and gentle seasons. Surrounded by warm water, the island is cushioned from extreme, prolonged cold fronts. Typically, in the summer months of May through September, thunderheads roll in from the mainland toward the Gulf of Mexico bringing brief cooling downpours, closely followed by a reappearing "tropical" sun.

Unspoiled by high-rise concrete buildings often found in congested coastal communities, the skyline of Anna Maria Island offers sea, sky and a new 150 foot stabilized and restored beach front. Towering pines and palms, abundant bird life, including pelicans and sea gulls that soar against rich blue skies, dunes and natural deep-rooted vegetation all celebrate the pristine sands and beaches of Anna Maria Island.

Island recreational options extend from beach walking, shelling, swimming, boating, fishing and cycling to attending any of the annually scheduled cultural celebrations. Tennis courts and a variety of educational, health oriented and "just for fun" classes for all age groups are available at the Island Community Center. Three public beaches, three fishing piers, three boat launching sites and two parks continue the list of never-ending vacation opportunities.

More than 1,000 rooms are available on the island, offering accommodations to fit every budget. Choices range from quaint beach motels and cottages, resorts to rental condominiums with a wide selection of amenities. Truly, the "Old Florida" flavor sought and found by seekers on Anna Maria Island has been retained. Come experience the island ambiance – our Island Paradise can be your Vacation Paradise.

Mary Ann Brockman
Executive Director; Anna Maria Island Chamber of Commerce
Phone: 778-1541 Fax: 778-9679
E-mail: amicc@netsrq.com
Internet: www.annamariachamber.org

GULF COAST LATIN CHAMBER OF COMMERCE

Dear Sarasota/Manatee County Newcomer/Visitor:

The Hispanic population is growing at an astonishing pace across the nation and this is also true for our beautiful suncoast area of Sarasota and Bradenton. Hispanic business is the fastest growing business sector in the country and our chamber is a prime example of this economic growth. Hispanic purchasing power hit $350 billion in 1997 and by the year 2025 Hispanics will represent the largest majority in the United States.

According to the latest figures, there are approximately 30,000 to 40,000 Hispanics in the bi-county area, and whereas most of these were migrant workers involved in agricultural endeavors, a new and very progressive class of entrepreneurs is starting to open businesses and settle in our area.

We would like to welcome you to our fast-growing community. Our quality of life, beautiful environment and beaches, tremendous economic development initiatives and increasing business opportunities are some of the great incentives as to why so many people and businesses are re-discovering us and want to move here.

If you are relocating your business here please call us to help you answer any questions you may have, especially in reaching our fast-growing market. Our mission is the promotion, development and dissemination of information, trends and opportunities available in the Latin community in our area, and we are here to serve you. Call me personally at (941) 758-1711 for anything we might be of help to you or your business.

Yours Truly, Alex Chavez, President
Gulf Coast LATIN Chamber of Commerce

The Charm of Anna Maria Island

Anna Maria was initially developed by Charles Roser, the Ohio baker who also developed the Fig Newton. Roser sold his recipe to the National Biscuit Company in 1910 for a reported one million dollars and soon became one of our pioneering "snowbirds" – moving to St. Petersburg and opening the Anna Maria Beach Co., directly responsible for many of the city's most significant structures. A strictly-enforced zoning code retains the rustic charm; condominium developments and large-scale commercial construction is banned, making the north end of the island one of the most popular "escape" destinations for tourists and locals alike. Over the past few years many of our international friends have discovered this wonderful hideaway – many languages are spoken here.

Luxurious Longboat

Highly regarded as some of the most sought after real estate in the area, the 12 mile-long barrier island community of *Longboat Key* is divided in half; the southern half lies within the jurisdiction of Sarasota County, the northern half within Manatee County. Locals will tell you that the two halves are very different from each other. Original rustic charm can still be found on the northern end while the southern section is now home to a number of internationally respected resorts. Winter months bring an explosion of seasonal visitors, more than doubling the resident population. A $2.5 million expansion of the Longboat Key Center for the Arts is taking place which will only add momentum to this already monumental destination.

P.O. Box 3311 Sarasota, 34230
Phone: 758-1711 Fax: 739-8763
Email: InfoRed@compuserve.com

LONGBOAT KEY CHAMBER OF COMMERCE

Dear Longboat Key Newcomer/Visitor:

A vacation on Longboat Key is a true "get-away-from-it-all." Located in the heart of the Florida Suncoast, its exclusive resorts and dining establishments are nationally and internationally recognized.

The natural beauty that is inherent to the island is surpassed only by its quiet relaxed atmosphere. Breaking the routine of daily life is what vacations are all about.

Longboat Key visitors enjoy some of Florida's finest accommodations. They range from small family-owned gulfside motels and cottages to luxurious, all inclusive AAA Four-Diamond, Mobile Four-Star resorts, hotels and condominiums.

Some provide their guests with every activity available under the warm Florida sun. Amenities may include championship golf or tennis, health clubs, whirlpools, saunas, steam baths, fitness centers, swimming pools, and, of course, direct access to some of the most beautiful beaches in the world. The smaller, family-owned motels offer a very relaxed, informal atmosphere and generally lower pricing.

Dining on Longboat Key can be an incredible culinary adventure. You will find restaurants of every style and description on the island, from rustic beach bars frequented by the natives to fine restaurants with national...even international reputations. The selection of food available is just as diverse. Obviously, seafood is the premier selection. But, if seafood isn't on your list of personal preferences, you won't be disappointed. Beef, pork and poultry are also well represented.

Because Longboat Key is a resort town, most diners dress casually and comfortably. Generally, restaurants will not require a tie or jacket, but it's wise to ask when you make reservations.

For more information on Longboat Key's restaurants, accommodations, exclusive shops, sparkling turquoise waters and white sand beaches, contact us anytime.

Sincerely, Gail Loefgren
Executive Director; Longboat Key Chamber of Commerce, 6854
Gulf of Mexico Drive,
Longboat Key, Florida 34228
Phone: 383-2466 Fax: 383-8217
E-Mail: director@longboatkeychamber.com
Internet: www.longboatkeychamber.com

MANATEE CHAMBER OF COMMERCE

Dear Manatee County Newcomer/Visitor:

Manatee County enjoys the privilege of being one of the most beautiful and pleasant places to live or visit in the entire United States. Our warm sunshine, sandy beaches, sparkling Gulf Coast waters and friendly people combine to provide our citizens and visitors with the best in personal and professional lifestyles.

Historically, we were called the "friendly city." It's easy to understand why. There is a unique spirit shared by the citizens in our network of communities. The executive, the service technician, the person working the register

SARASOTA AT NIGHT © BILL WEST

at the local grocery – all share the same smile that tells everyone we are proud to call Manatee County home.

Our weather is unparalleled anyplace in the world. There is the Gulf of Mexico with its warm waters and crystal white sand beaches providing year-round recreation as well as a quiet place to watch spectacular Florida sunsets. Our roots in agriculture and fishing can be readily seen in lush farms and groves and quaint fishing villages. While preserving our past, Manatee County has grown into a dynamic, diversified community.

Today, Manatee County offers unlimited opportunities to fulfill your dreams; entrepreneurs and established businesses are supported by a community that knows the value of hard and honest work and the rewards it provides. Our community has grown to encompass a full spectrum of service and business opportunities. Most of all, it is our people - diverse, unpretentious, honest and aware of the fact that what we share together is what makes this a very special place.

We invite you to share the vision, the dream, and the excitement of what our county can offer whether you are visiting or looking for that special place to raise a family or start a business.

As the president of the Manatee Chamber of Commerce, I invite you to stop by our offices at 222 10th Street West, in downtown Bradenton, directly across from the South Florida Museum and Bishop Planetarium, for a variety of important newcomer information. We can provide you with material about the best places in the area with which to do business and point you in the direction of where to find the many services necessary for your smooth transition. If you're vacationing, we have numerous brochures on places to visit.

Living and working in Manatee County is living at its finest...we wouldn't have it any other way!

Sincerely,
Robert P. Bartz President; Manatee Chamber of Commerce
Phone: 748-3611 Fax: 745-1877
E-Mail: chamber@manatee-cc.com
Internet: http://www.manateechamber.com

GREATER SARASOTA CHAMBER OF COMMERCE

Dear Sarasota Newcomer/Visitor:

Sarasota has long been known for its natural beauty and cultural attractions. The blue-green waters of the Gulf of Mexico, the glorious sunsets and miles of sugar-white sandy beaches enchant visitors from all over the world. It is also nationally known for its theater, opera and ballet companies which have given Sarasota a reputation as one of the finest cultural communities in the South.

If you are looking for a dynamic and distinctive new environment for your business, for your personal relocation, or just for temporary relaxation, Sarasota is eager to welcome you. We are proud of our county and the way it has flourished economically, without sacrificing the quality of life and natural beauty that drew so many of us here.

As a Chamber of Commerce we represent area businesses and in that capacity have a special responsibility to serve the entire community. We welcome your inquiries about Sarasota and its business environment and invite you to visit our office in downtown Sarasota.

Sarasota has established itself as an extraordinary destination – a world-class community rapidly becoming one of Florida's most desirable locations...truly a place like no other.

Modern Manatee

Manatee County has always been a fabulous place to explore, although things have changed a bit since Hernando DeSoto landed here in 1539 in search of El Dorado, the lost city of gold. Located between the booming St. Pete/Tampa market and "cultural capitol" Sarasota, the *Bradenton/ Manatee County* area now boasts one of the fastest population growth rates in the United States. The new community of Lakewood Ranch which, just a few years ago was farmland with a single paved road in east Manatee County, is now an exploding 5,500 acre residential town. Bradenton is hot! hot! hot!

World Class Beaches

Siesta Beach was awarded the #1 spot for having the whitest, finest sand in the world in the 1987 "Great International White Sand Beach Challenge," conducted by Woods Hole Oceanographic Institution in Massachusetts. In their August 1994 issue, *Conde' Nast Traveler* proclaimed *Siesta Beach* as having the "best sand in America."

Venice Beach has the distinction of being the "shark tooth capitol of the world" – the extremely popular Shark's Tooth & Seafood Festival is held the second week in August.

Caspersen Beach is the longest beach in Sarasota County, located on the island of Venice.

We sincerely hope you enjoy your "Sarasota experience" and if the Greater Sarasota Chamber of Commerce can assist you in any way, please feel free to call upon us.

Sincerely,
David L. May, President; Greater Sarasota Chamber of Commerce
1819 Main Street, Suite 240, Sarasota 34236
Phone: 955-8187 Fax: 366-5621
E-Mail: saracham@ix.netcom.com
Internet: www.sarasotachamber.org

SIESTA KEY CHAMBER OF COMMERCE

Dear Siesta Key Newcomer/Visitor:

When you visit Florida you must come and experience Siesta Key, with the "World's Finest, Whitest Sand." Take a barefoot stroll on Siesta Key's beautiful beach and enjoy the feel of the white, sugary-soft sand.

Accommodations range from exclusive condominiums to romantic beach hideaways. Siesta Key offers dining experiences - from gourmet to casual. Unique shops provide a marvelous variety appealing to all lifestyles and pocketbooks.

Two bridges link Siesta Key to the mainland, allowing it to remain an uncomplicated, natural paradise - yet never sacrificing the amenities of comfort.

Come and see us soon, we'll be waiting to greet you for a visit or a lifetime!
Paul Ralston, Executive Director; Siesta Key Chamber of Commerce
Phone: 349-3800 Fax: 349-9699
E-Mail: siestakey-chamber.com
Internet: www.sarasota-online.com/siesta

VENICE AREA CHAMBER OF COMMERCE

Dear Venice Newcomer/Visitor:

Each and every year more and more people choose the greater Venice area as the place to raise their families, retire and grow their business.

Our parks and beaches provide outstanding recreational opportunities for our residents and visitors. The city's historic streets are alive with shops and restaurants.

The cultural arts include a community theatre, an art league, opera and theater guilds, dinner theatre, ballet company and symphony orchestra.

Our fourteen miles of white sand beaches provide us with an array of prehistoric sharks' teeth and fossils. Venice is proud to boast that we have earned the title of the Sharks Tooth Capital of the World.

Welcome to the place that we call home. We hope that you will find what we have found - a quality of life that is second to none.

Sincerely,
Beth E. Dilley, President, Venice Area Chamber of Commerce
Phone: 488-2236 Fax: 484-5903
E-Mail: vchamber@venicechamber.com
Internet: www.venicechamber.com

Information Station

WHAT YOU HAVE IN YOUR HANDS RIGHT NOW IS CALLED A "BOOK."

Popular cultural commentators are predicting that such things will soon go the way of the hat. You remember hats don't you? It wasn't long ago, in geologic terms at least, that no *proper* person left the house without one.

Conveniently, on the heels of the Ice, Stone and Industrial periods, we have entered The Information Age: a communication revolution which, if we don't consume ourselves out of existence in the process, should provide the next social and economic steps for continued prosperity.

A wake-up call for shopaholics and couch potatoes alike, we think the Internet is somewhat more fascinating than CB radios. Or 8-Track tapes. We, in fact, enjoy the notion of accessing the entire world from a desktop, contacting anyone, anytime, from world leaders to old flames.

And are you ready for something called Automated Fabrication – generating three-dimensional solid objects from disk files? Maybe this means that hats will make a comeback.

Maybe books won't really have to be replaced by portable screens. And maybe there's a bridge we'd like to sell you, just to the north.

Adventuresome map-makers of yore, once lured by plotting undiscovered territories, are now full-time employees at biotechnology companies. It won't be long before a single drop of your blood will produce a map illustrating the new world – the human genome – more knowledge about yourself than you ever really wanted to know.

We welcome these inspired innovations with kidlike glee but we never lose sight of the fundamental truth: access is the key.

While perhaps not exactly earth shattering, this chapter will provide you with fundamental access to the area's most essential services.

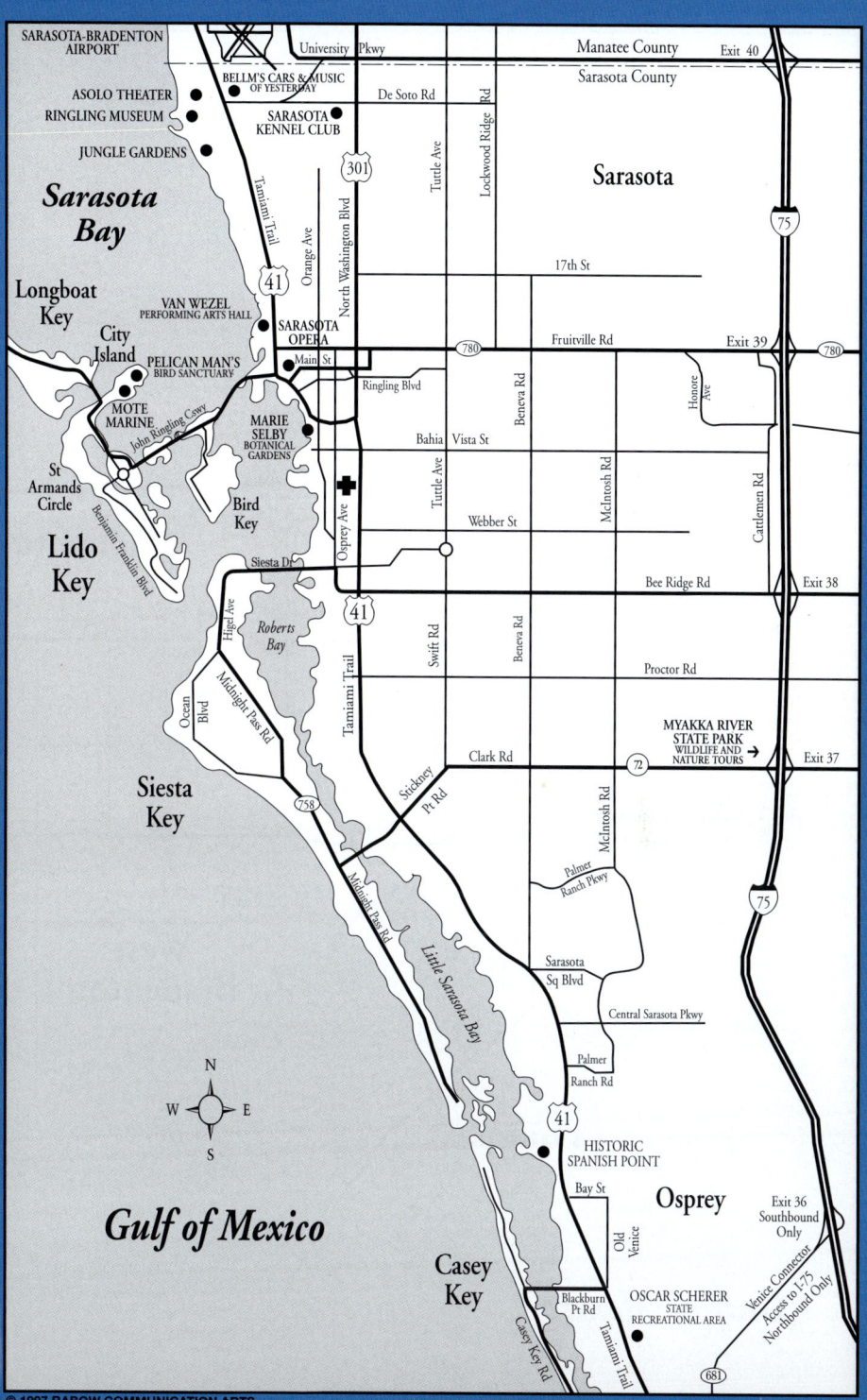

WEST BRADENTON

EAST BRADENTON

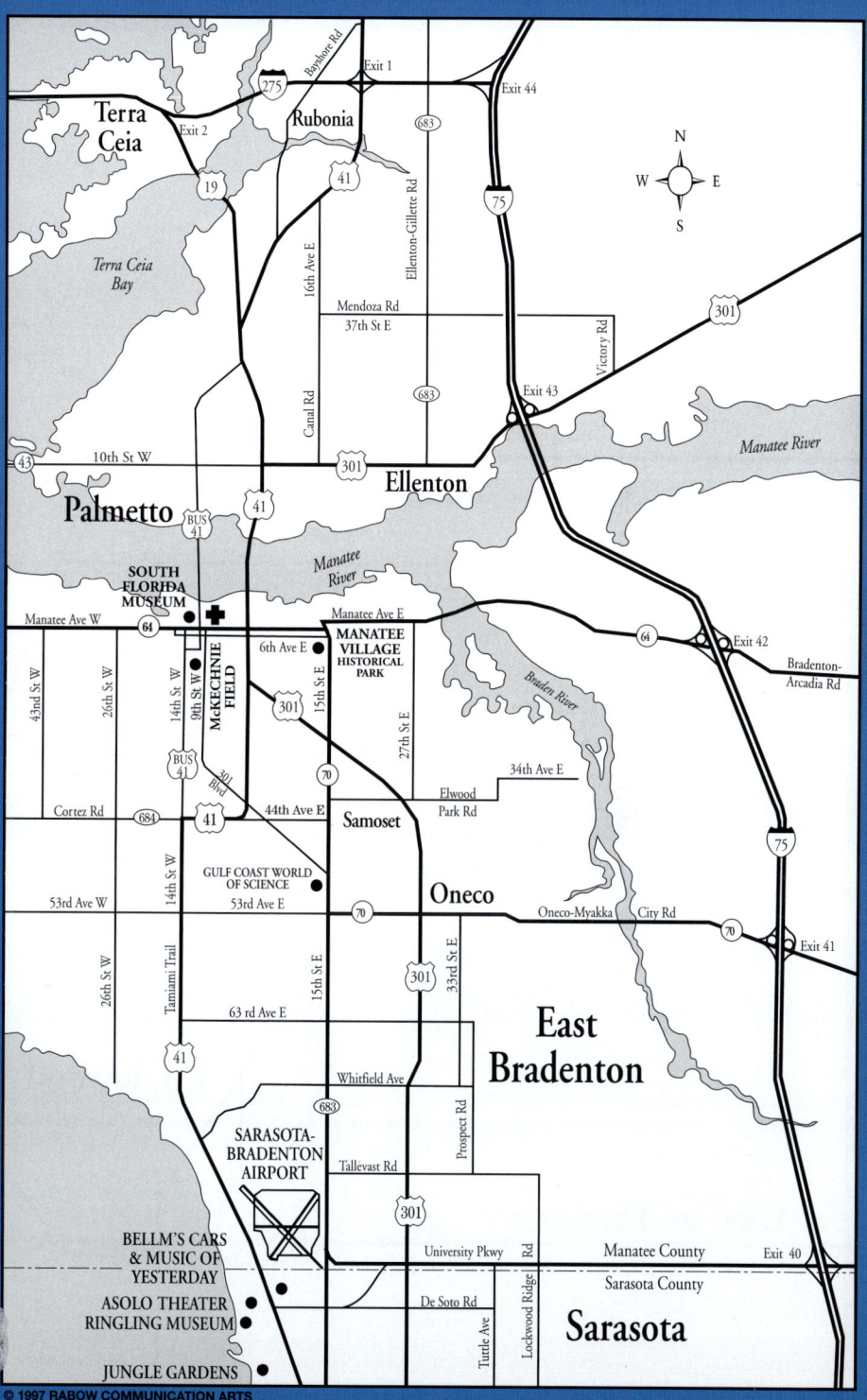

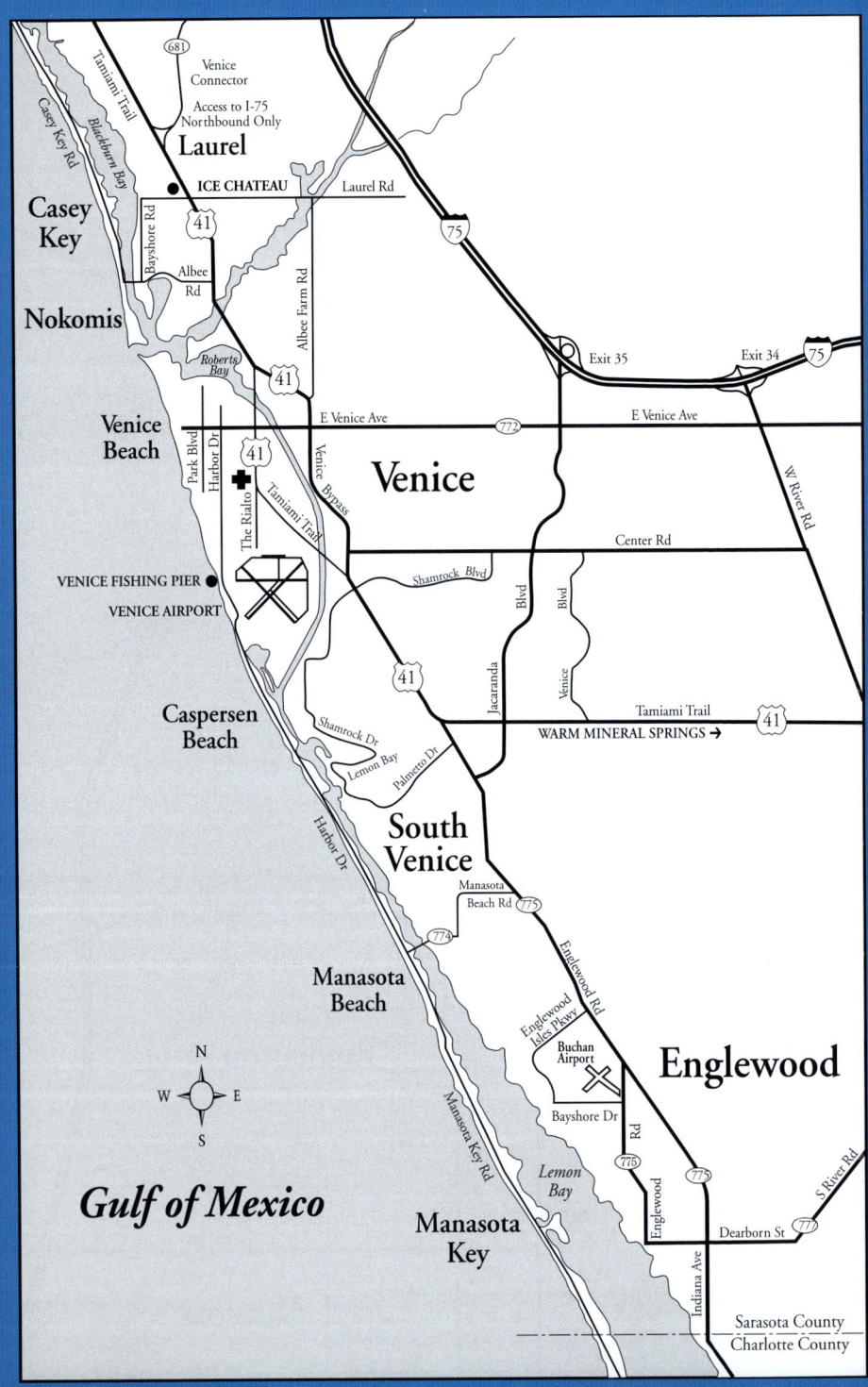

Some Professionals Provide Technical Expertise In A Full Range of Services.

Other Professionals Provide Exceptional Personal Service and Attention.

WE DO BOTH.
— Experience the Difference —

CERTIFIED PUBLIC ACCOUNTANTS

Accounting • Auditing • Tax Return Preparation
Income Tax Planning • Estate Tax Planning
Other Taxation Services

Management Consultation • Financial Planning
Mergers & Acquisitions • Litigation Assistance
Micro-Computer Consulting

One Sarasota Tower	Center Park
2 N. Tamiami Trail, Ste 604	153 Center Road
Sarasota, Florida 34236	Venice, Florida 34292
(941) 365-0620	(941) 497-5600
FAX (941) 955-9990	FAX (941) 497-0234

THE CPA FIRM THE OTHER ACCOUNTANTS DEPEND ON

George V. Famiglio, Jr. CPA, PFS*, MT, CRP•

CERTIFIED PUBLIC ACCOUNTANTS' WITH MASTERS DEGREES IN TAXATION

Tax Planning and Preparation
Tax Returns for All States
Canadian/International Tax Matters
Business Sale & Acquisition Analysis
Asset Protection Planning
IRS Negotiations / Late Returns
Financial Planning / Estate & Trust Planning

SMALL BUSINESS - ACCOUNTING / PROFIT MANAGEMENT
ADMITTED TO PRACTICE - U.S. TAX COURT

George V. Famiglio, Jr.
& Associates
A PROFESSIONAL ACCOUNTANCY CORPORATION

957-0775

1634 Main Street Sarasota, FL 34236
Established 1971 - Member of AICPA / Tax Division and FICPA

•Not awarded by government; information available upon request

Emergency

Police/Fire/Ambulance/Poison
911
Hearing Impaired (TDD) Emergency
Fire/Police/Medical
911 (Sarasota County)
742-5800 (Manatee)

Hearing Impaired (TDD) Non-Emergency
366-0727 (Sarasota County)
742-5800 (Manatee)

Non-Emergency - Important Numbers
Police
316-1199 (Sarasota)
746-4111 (Bradenton)
488-6711 (Venice)
778-4711 (AnnaMaria)
778-6311(BradentonBeach)
778-0791 (Holmes Beach)
316-1977 (Longboat Key)
Sheriff
951-5800 (Sarasota County)
747-3011 (Manatee)
Florida Highway Patrol
751-7647 (Bradenton)
483-5911 (Venice)
CrimeStoppers (cash rewards up to $1000!)
366-TIPS (Sarasota County)
747-COPS (Manatee)
U.S. Marshal's Service
1-813-228-2146 (Tampa)
Ambulance
951-5800 (Sarasota County)
485-8111 (Venice)
Search and Rescue
1-813-896-6187
Coast Guard Station
794-1261 (Cortez)
Florida Marine Patrol
1-800-342-5367
FBI
955-3325
Poison Information Center
748-2121/1-800-282-3171
Hurricane/Emergency Evacuation Info
(PLEASE NOTE: DO NOT CALL 911)
361-6844 (Sarasota County)
748-4501 ext. 3526 (Manatee)
366-0727 (TDD only)
American Red Cross
379-9300 (Sarasota)
792-8686 (Bradenton)
486-8402 (Venice)
Access Center Help Line

741-3117 (Bradenton)
24-Hour Crisis Line/
917-7760 (Sarasota)
First Call For Help
366-5025 (Sarasota)
751-6793 (Bradenton)
485-1880 (Venice)
YMCA Youth & Family Services/Shelter
955-5596
Boys & Girls Club of Sarasota County
366-7940
Family Resources Inc. (Manatee)
741-3575
Girls, Inc. of Sarasota County
366-6646
Goodwill
355-2721
The Salvation Army
364-8845
SHARE
953-3287
Safe Place & Rape Crisis
365-1976
United Way
366-2686 (Sarasota)
748-1313 (Bradenton)
488-1122 (Venice)
All Faiths Food Bank
379-6333
Animal Control
316-1081 (Sarasota/Venice)
742-5933 (Bradenton)
Humane Society
955-4131 (Sarasota/Venice)
747-8808 (Bradenton)
Pelican Man Bird Sanctuary
388-4444
Wildlife Rescue Services
750-9453
To report wildlife violations
1-800-282-8002
Passports
951-5231

Tourist/Event Information
Important Phone Numbers
Visitor Centers
957-1877 (Sarasota County)
729-7040 (Manatee)
Manatee County Arts Hot Line
745-ARTS (2787)
Ticketmaster (Tampa)
1-813-287-8844
24-Hour Sarasota Herald-Tribune Infoline
953-INFO (Sarasota)

951-NEWS (Manatee)

Sarasota County Area Transit
Bus Schedule Information
  316-1234

Manatee County Transit Bus Schedule
Information
  747-8621

AAA Club Emergency Road Service
  362-2220

AAA Club Travel Information
(ask for Christine)
  362-2222

Sarasota/Bradenton International
Airport Info
  359-5200

Greyhound Bus
  955-5735 (Sarasota)
  747-2984 (Bradenton)

Amtrak
  1-800-872-7245

Newcomer Information Important Numbers

Florida Residence/Domicile
  951-5231 (Sarasota)
  749-1800 (Bradenton)
  492-3181 (Venice)

Auto Tags and Registration
  362-9888 (Sarasota & Venice)
  748-8000 (Bradenton)
  951-5600 (Venice)

Drivers License
  361-6217 (Sarasota)
  741-3010 (Bradenton)
  483-5995 (Venice)

Voter Registration
  951-5307 (Sarasota)

Absentee Ballots
  749-7181 (Bradenton)
  492-3060 (Venice)

Telephone (GTE)
  1-800-483-4200

Florida Power and Light Co.
  917-0708

Peace River Electric Co.
  722-2729 (Bradenton)

Peoples Gas System
  366-4277 (Sarasota)
  746-1888 (Manatee)

Water and Sewer
  378-6100 (Sarasota)
  792-8811 (Bradenton)
  486-2626 ext. 242 (Venice)

Garbage Collection and Special Pick Up
  378-6188 (Sarasota)
  795-3421 (Bradenton)
  485-3311 ext. 242 (Venice)

Recycling
  316-7575 (Sarasota)
  795-3421 (Bradenton)
  378-6188 (Venice)

Taxes
  951-5620 (Sarasota/Venice)
  748-8000 (Bradenton)

Occupational License
  362-9888 (Sarasota)

School Board
  927-9000 (Sarasota)
  741-7200 (Manatee)

Newspapers
  Sarasota Herald-Tribune (N.Y. Times)
    365-6060 (Sarasota)
  Manatee AM Edition
    742-6100 (Bradenton)
  Venice AM Edition
    486-3000 (Venice)
  Bradenton Herald (Knight/Ridder)
    748-0411

Cable Television
  Comcast Cablevision
    371-6700 (Sarasota/Bradenton)
  Time-Warner Cable
    748-1822 (Bradenton)

Hunting, Fishing and Boating Licenses
  951-5600 (Sarasota)
  748-8000 (Bradenton)

Florida Council of Churches
  1-407-839-3454

Volunteer Services
  953-5965 (Sarasota)
  746-7117 (Bradenton)
  488-5683 (Venice)

Retired Senior Volunteer Program (RSVP)
  748-6974

Manatee County Government Elder Helpline
  742-5818

Senior Friendship Centers
  955-2122 (Sarasota)
  493-3065 (Venice)

SARASOTA COUNTY	MANATEE COUNTY
1997 Population: 311,043	242,417
Median Age: 48.9	44.0
Females: 53.2%, Males: 46.8%	52.3%, 47.7%
Newborn - 15 years: 13.5%	17%
15 years - 24 years: 8.5%	9%
25 years - 44 years: 23.6%	25%
45 years - 64 years: 22.4%	21%
65 years and over: 32%	28%
Average Single Family Home Price: $118,000	$97,000
Per Capita Income: $29,486	$27,295
Average Household Income: $45,400	$30,128
Land Area: 571.75 Sq. Miles	741.2 Sq. Miles
Water Area: 50.6 Sq. Miles	151.6 Sq. Miles

Your full-service entertainment and communications company.

- Cable Television service
- Home Theater pay-per-view
- High Speed Internet access via Comcast@Home
- Local, cost-effective cable network advertising & production
- Web page hosting, design & Internet advertising services
- 24-hour classified television advertising

Tel: (941) 371-6700 Sarasota
Tel: (941) 484-0602 Venice
Tel: (941) 625-6000 Port Charlotte
5205 Fruitville Rd., Sarasota, FL 34323

www.insarasota.com

COMCAST®
EVERYTHING YOU CONNECT WITH

Sarasota/Bradenton International Airport

Information: 359-5200; www.srq-airport.com

Sarasota Bradenton International Airport (often called SRQ – the universal destination code you'll find on your luggage tags) is the main gateway for vacationers, business people, and residents alike. The airport is not simply important to us because of the amount of traffic it brings to our area (approximately 1.7 million passengers each year), it is also one of the most attractive and contemporary air facilities in Florida. Frequent airport users have rated SRQ as one of the best in the U.S. for convenience, cleanliness, employee courtesy and design.

A commitment to the arts and the environment – so prevalent within the Sarasota/Bradenton area – is reflected by SRQ. Works of art produced by some of the area's brightest talent adorn the walls and passageways. You'll also find a stunning salt water aquarium exhibit, presented by Mote Marine Laboratory, and a fabulous life-size manatee waterfall display.

SRQ has U.S. Customs Port-Of-Entry status, a full-time customs agent processes international charter passengers, private aircraft and cargo.

The contribution SRQ makes to our community cannot be understated. The airport generates over $950 million annually into the area.

Airlines Serving Sarasota/Bradenton International Airport

Air Sunshine	1-800-435-8900
American Eagle	1-800-433-7300
American Trans Air	1-800-225-2995
Continental Airlines	1-800-525-0280
Comair	1-800-221-1212
Delta Airlines	1-800-221-1212
Northwest Airlines	1-800-225-2525
TWA	1-800-221-2000
USAir	1-800-428-4322

Airport Car Rental Agencies

Alamo	1-800-327-9633
Avis	1-800-331-1212
Budget	1-800-527-0700
Dollar	1-800-800-4000
Hertz	1-800-654-3131
National	1-800-227-7368

Airlines Serving Southwest Florida International Airport

Air Canada	1-800-435-8900
America West/Cont. Exp.	1-800-525-0280
American Airlines/Eagle	1-800-433-7300
American Trans Air	1-800-225-2995
British Airways	1-800-428-4322
Canada 3000 Airlines Ltd.	1-941-768-3000
Canada Airlines Int.	1-800-426-7000
Continental Airlines	1-800-525-0280
Com Air	1-800-354-9822
Delta Airlines	1-800-221-1212
LTU International Airlines	1-800-888-0200
Midwest Express	1-800-452-2022
Northwest Express/KLM	1-800-225-2525
Spirit Airlines	1-800-772-7117
TWA	1-800-221-2000
United Airlines	1-800-241-6522
USAir/USAir Express	1-800-428-4322
ValuJet Airlines	1-800-825-8538

Rail Service

Amtrack does not provide "Choo-choo-direct" service to our area but their shuttle bus will pick you up in Sarasota, Bradenton or Venice and take you to the train in Tampa or Orlando. It's fun!

Information:
1-800-872-7245
www.amtrak.com

Rail freight service is provided by *CSX Transportation* and *Seminole Gulf Railway.* Neither provide public transportation, both are strictly freight bearing. CSX connects with Port Manatee's railroad; Seminole Gulf is a shortline railway, bringing primarily construction materials and paper products to the area.

Florida Gulf Coast Railroad Musuem

A wonderful trip to nowhere, and back. Really. Ride on an authentic antique railroad through northern Manatee County. A "must do" for families who have never been on a train before.

Information: 776-9656

Airlines Serving Tampa International Airport

Air Aruba	1-800-882-7822
Air Canada	1-800-776-3000
AirTran	1-800-247-8726
America West Airlines	1-800-247-5692
American Airlines	1-800-443-7300
British Airways	1-800-247-9297
Carnival Airlines	1-800-824-7386
Cayman Airways	1-800-422-9626
Comair, Inc.	1-800-354-9822
Condor	1-800-524-6975
Continental Airlines	1-800-525-0280
Delta Airlines	1-800-325-1999
GulfStream International	1-800-992-8532
KIWI International Air	1-800-538-5494
Martinair Holland	1-800-366-4655
Midway Airlines	1-800-446-4392
Midwest Express Airlines	1-800-452-2022
Northwest Airlines	1-800-225-2525
Reno Air	1-800-736-6247
Spirit Airlines	1-800-772-7117
Trans World Airlines	1-800-221-2000
United Airlines	1-800-241-6522
USAir/USAir Express	1-800-428-4322
ValuJet Airlines	1-800-825-8538

SARASOTA - TAMPA EXPRESS (shuttle van, door to door) 727-1344

Getting Around

The automobile, of course, is the most popular method of local transportation. However, our area boasts of some wonderful alternatives including an amazingly inexpensive bus system (50 cent fares), extensive trolley routes along with comprehensive taxi and limousine services.

Some area bike routes are in place, others are being developed. Bicycles are recommended for beach and neighborhood riding, but avoid US 41 and heavily congested roads whenever possible – keep in mind that many drivers are not only driving in unfamiliar territory, they are also driving unfamiliar rental cars. Also, many "seasonal" drivers are somewhat "seasonal" themselves. Florida has liberal drivers license renewal laws – you'll see many of our elderly retirees on the road. And so, with all due respect, it pays to drive defensively.

You'll find a general map of the area on pages 27 - 30 of *The Guide*.

For detailed street maps, stop by any real estate office or major bank; they should have a healthy supply of complimentary maps or pick up one of the outstanding local map books available at House of Maps located behind Gulf Gate Mall - 924-8998. Tell them we sent you.

Catching the Bus

Sarasota County Area Transit (SCAT)
Bus Information: 316-1234

Manatee County Area Transit
Bus Information: 747-8621

Our bus systems can get you just about anywhere you want to go in the area. Both systems offers friendly telephone information assistance Monday - Saturday, 5:30 a.m.- 7:00 p.m. Just tell them where you are and where you want to go and they'll let you know how to do it by bus.

Open Air Trolleys

Siesta Key Trolley

2 trips daily, 7 days a week to Siesta Key and Sarasota areas. Tours feature local attractions including beaches, restaurants, shopping and historical tour. Pick-ups at hotels, condominiums and restaurants. All-day on and off boarding pass $5 adults/children. Children under 3 free. *Information:* 346-3115

Anna Maria Trolley

Operates Tuesday through Saturday. All-Day On & Off Boarding Pass, $5. Children under 3 free. Call for information and reservations.
Information: 346-3115

Greyhound Bus Lines

Leave the driving to them.
General Information:
1-800-231-2222

Sarasota Terminal
575 N. Washington Blvd.
Information: 955-5735

Bradenton Terminal
3028 1st Street West
Information: 747-2985

Venice Terminal
225 Tamimami Tr.
Information: 485-1001

SIESTA BEACH © BILL WEST

TIVOLI BY THE SEA IS SIESTA KEY'S CROWN JEWEL

Superb accommodations, amenities and service on Siesta Key's world renowned white sand beach. Visit us at Tivoli – your "Vacation home away from home."

Call for rates today.
Tel (941) 349-5544, Fax (941) 349-5545, email: sj3227@yahoo.com
625 Beach Road, Siesta Key, FL 34242

ACCOMMODATIONS GUIDE

In a subtropical resort setting such as ours, there are accommodations to fit any mood, desire or economic condition for business, pleasure, romantic weekend getaways or the inevitable multifamily reunion. For complete accommodation listings, we strongly recommend calling the Sarasota Convention & Visitors Bureau (local: 957-1877; toll free: 800-522-9799) www.sarasotafl.org or the Bradenton Area Convention & Visitors Bureau (local: 729-9177; toll free 800-4-MANATEE; www.floridaislandbeaches.org). Both are staffed by friendly professionals who look forward to helping you find the perfect place for the perfect getaway.

On pages 42-44 you will find recommendations to some of the area's most comfortable home-away-from-homes.

ARGUS
PROPERTY MANAGEMENT, INC.

For the finest in Resort Rentals.

Gulf & Bay Club Bayside
1200 Siesta Bayside Drive • Siesta Key, FL 34242
Phone (941)346-3499 • Fax (941)349-6156

Siesta Beach House
5950 Midnight Pass Road • Siesta Key, FL 34242
Phone/Fax (941) 349-2233

Siesta Gulf View
420 Beach Road • Siesta Key, FL 34242 • Phone (941) 349-0900 Fax (941) 349-2105

Sunset Royale
711 Beach Road • Siesta Key, FL 34242 • Phone/Fax (941)349-6260

Sea Shell
6500 Midnight Pass Road • Siesta Key, FL 34242
Phone (941) 349-1191 • Fax (941) 349-5263

Crystal Sands
6300 Midnight Pass Road • Siesta Key, FL 34242
Phone (941) 349-7007 • Fax (941) 346-1963

Bahia Vista Gulf of Venice
1555 Tarpon Center Drive • Venice, FL 34285
Phone (941) 484-4855 • Fax (941) 488-5414

PHONE/FAX 1-800-349-6156 • WWW.ARGUSMGMT.COM • EMAIL: ARGUSMGMT@AOL.COM

Gulf & Bay Club Bayside

Siesta Beach House

Siesta Gulf View

Sea Shell

Crystal Sands

Bahia Vista Gulf of Venice

When you are considering making your vacation spot your Florida Home, call Argus Realty Group.
Phone/Fax 1-800-349-6156

Key to Accommodations

$ - Under $50/night
$$ - $51 - $75
$$$ - $76-$100
$$$$ - Over $100

AX - American Express
CB - Carte Blanche
DC - Diner's Club
DS - Discover
ET - Enroute
MC - Master Card
V - Visa
BF - Beach Front
BW - Walking distance to Beach
GV - Gulf View
BV - Bay View
LF - Lakefront
BY - Babysitting Service
BN - Banquet Service
BB - Bed & Breakfast
BI - Bicycles
BS - Bus Stop
BT - Boating
CT - Cable TV
CA - Children's Activities
CN - Concierge Service
EF - Efficiencies
F - Fishing
FC - Fitness Center

Banyan House Historic Bed & Breakfast
484-1385; e-mail: vnc@gte.net
www.banyan.qpg.com
519 Harbor Dr. S., Venice
Number of Rooms: 9
$$$/$$$$-MC-VS-WB-BB-BI-CT-EF-F-FC-FL-MI-P-RF-RT-W

Beach Inn
778-9597; 800-823-2247
e-mail: beachinn@aol.com
www.thebeachinn.com
101 66th St., Holmes Beach
Number of Rooms: 14
$$/$$$/$$$$-MC-V-BF-WB-GV-B-BS-CT-CN-FL-HP-LA-RF-RT-TS

Betts House Historic Bed & Breakfast
747-3607; e-mail:tizart@aol.com
http://members.aol.com/Bettsbnb
1523 1st Ave. W, Bradenton
Number of Rooms: 2
$$-DS-MC-VS-BB-BT-F-FL-G-M-RT (Art studio on premises.)

Best Western Midtown
955-8401
(800) 722-8227; fax 954-8948; e-mail:
bestwestern@earthlink.net
1425 S. Tamiami Tr., Sarasota
Number of Rooms: 100
$$-AX-CB-DC-DS-MC-VS-BI-BS-CT-CN-F-GP-IM-P-SB

Best Western Royal Palms
365-1342; fax 955-8066; email:
bestrooms@aol.com;
www.travelweb.bestwestern.com
1701 N. Tamiami Tr., Sarasota
Number of Rooms: 37
$$-AX-CB-DC-DS-MC-V-BS-CT-EF-HP-IM-RT-SB-WP

Best Western Siesta Beach Resort
349-3211; fax 349-7915
(800) 223-5786
5311 Ocean Blvd., Sarasota
Number of Rooms: 53
$$-AX-CB-DC-DS-ET-MC-V-WB-BS-CT-EF-GP-HP-LA-PE-RT-SB-TS-W-WP

Blue Water Beach Club
778-6688; fax 778-5765
6306 Gulf Dr., Holmes Beach
Number of Rooms: 29
$$$$-MC-VS-BF-GV-CT-MI-P-SB

Capri International Motel
349-2626
e-mail: capri@ix.netcom.com
6782 Sara Sea Circle,
Siesta Key
Number of Rooms: 11
$$$-MC-V-CT-RF-SB-WP

Captiva Beach Resort
349-4131
(800) 349-4131
e-mail:
robert@captivabeachresort.com
www.captivabeachresort.com

6772 Sara Sea Circle,
Siesta Key
Number of Rooms: 20
$$-AX-MC-V-WB-BI- BS-BT-CT-F-LA-MI-P-RF-SB

The Colony Beach & Tennis Resort
383-6464; Fax 383-4981
(800) 426-5669
e-mail: colonypl@ix.netcom.com
www.colonybeachresort.com
1620 Gulf of Mexico Dr.,
Longboat Key
Number of Suites: 234
$$$$-AX-DC-DS-MC-V-BF-GV-BY-BN-BI-BS-BT-CT-CA-CN-F-FC-GR-GP-IM-IS-IT-LM-L-MI-MR-PL-P-RF-TN-TP-VP-WP

Coquina On The Beach Resort
388-2141; fax 388-3017
e-mail: coquina@earthlink.net
1008 Ben Franklin Dr.,
Lido Beach
Number of Rooms: 34
$$$$-AX-DC-DS-MC-V-BF-CT-LA-PA-P

Crescent View Beach Club
349-2000; fax 349-9748
(800) 344-7171; www.sarasota-online/charteronee/crescent.htm
6512 Midnight Pass Rd.,
Siesta Key
Number of Rooms: 27 $$$$-AX-CB-DC-DS-MC-V-BF-WB-GV-CT-CN-F-LA-MI-P-RF-W

The Cypress Bed & Breakfast
955-4856; fax n/a
www.bbonline.com/fl/cypress/
621 Gul Stream Ave. S,
Sarasota
Number of Rooms: 4
$$$$-AX-DS-MC-V-BV-BB-BI-BS-BT-CT-CN-F-FL-GP-RT-W

Duncan House Bed & Breakfast
778-6858
email:Duncanbb@aol.com
www.duncanhousebb.com
1703 Gulf Drive, Bradenton Beach
Number of Rooms: 6
$$$$/$$$-AX-MC-VS-WB-BB-BI-CT-EF-FL-HP-MI-PE-P-RF-RT

Gulf and Bay Club Bayside
346-3499; fax 349-6156
e-mail: argusmgmt@aol.com
www.argusmgmt.com
1200 Siesta Bayside Dr.
Siesta Beach
$$$$-WB-BV-LF-CT-F-FC-FL-LA-MI-P-RF-TN

Half Moon Beach Club and Resort Hotel
388-3694; fax 388-1938; e-mail:
info@halfmoon-lidokey.com
www.halfmoon-lidokey.com
(800) 358-3245
2050 Ben. Franklin Dr.,

Lido Beach
Number of Rooms: 85
$$$$-AX-CB-DS-MC-V-BF-BN-BI-BS-CT-L-MR-P-RF-R

Harley Sandcastle Resort
388-2181; fax 388-2655
1540 Ben Franklin Dr.,
Lido Key
Number of Rooms: 179
$$$$-AX-CB-DC-DS-MC-V-BF-GV-BN-BI-BS-CT-CA-GR-IM-IS-LA-LM-L-MR-P-RF-R

Harrington House Beachfront B&B
778-5444; 1-888-828-5566
e-mail:
harhousebb@mail.pcsonline.com
www.harringtonhouse.com
5626 Gulf Drive, Holmes Beach
Number of Rooms: 18
$$$$-MC-V-BF-WB-GV-BB-BI-BS-CT-FL-HP-RF-RT-TS

Hathaway Arms
924-3363
1-800-431-0774; e-mail:
hatarms@gte.net
www.hathaway-arms.com
1681 Stickney Point Rd., Sarasota
Number of Rooms: 180
$$$$/$$$-AX-DC-DS-MC-V-WB-BY-BI-BS-CT-CN-FL-GP-IM-LA-MI-PE-P-RF-RT-WP

Hilton Longboat Key Resort
383-2451; fax 383-7979
(800) 282-3046
4711 Gulf of Mexico Dr.,
Longboat Key
Number of Rooms: 102
$$$$-AX-CB-DC-DS-MC-V-BF-BY-BN-BI-BS-BT-CT-CN-IM-IS-LM-L-MR-RT-R-SB-SH-TN-WP

Holiday Inn - Airport Marina
355-2781
7150 N. Tamiami Tr., Sarasota
Number of Rooms: 180
$$-AX-CB-DC-DS-ET-MC-V-BV-BY-BN-BS-BT-CT-F-HP-IM-IT-LA-LM-L-M-MR-PE-RT-R-SH-WP

Holiday Inn Downtown By the Bay
365-1900; fax 365-1900
e-mail: leerelelo@aol.com
1 N. Tamiami Tr., Sarasota
Number of Rooms: 100
$$/$$$-AX-CB-DC-DS-MC-V-GV-BV-BY-BS-BT-CT-CN-GP-IT-LA-M-MR-P-R-WP

Holiday Inn Express
924-4900; fax 923-7774
6600 S. Tamiami Tr.,
Sarasota
Number of Rooms: 130
$$$-AX-CB-DC-DS-MC-V-WB-BY-BS-CT-FC-FL-IS-IT-LA-MR-PA-P-RF-R-TS

Holiday Inn - Lido Beach
388-5555; fax 388-4321
e-mail: hilido@gte.net

233 Ben Franklin Dr., Lido Key
Number of Rooms: 140
$$$$-AX-CB-DC-DS-MC-V-BF-GV-BN-BS-CT-CN-GP-IM-LA-L-MR-R-WP

Holiday Inn-Longboat Key
383-3771; fax 383-7871
(800) 465-4436
e-mail:
holidaylongboat@mindspring.com
4949 Gulf of Mexico Dr.,
Longboat Key
Number of Rooms: 146
$$$/$$$$-HM-AX-CB-DC-DS-MC-V-BF-BN-BI-BS-CT-CN-FC-GR-IM-IS-LA-LM-L-MI-P-R-RF-SB-TN-W

Holiday Inn-Venice Resort
485-5411; fax 484-6193
(800) 237-3712
e-mail:odysseys@sprynet.com
455 U.S. 41 By-Pass N.,
Number of Rooms: 160
$$$-AX-DC-DS-MC-V-BN-CT-GP-LA-LM-L-MR-P-R-SB-W-WP

Hyatt Sarasota
953-1234; fax 952-1987
1000 Blvd. of the Arts, Sarasota
Number of Rooms: 297
$$$$-AX-CB-DC-DS-MC-V-BV-BY-BN-BS-BT-CT-CN-F-FC-GR-GP-IM-LA-L-M-MR-P-R-SH-TS-VP

Inn at the Beach Resort
484-8471; fax 484-0593
(800) 255-8471
101 The Esplanade, Venice
Number of Rooms: 46 $$$$-AX-DC-DS-MC-V-WB-GV-BS-CT-F-IS-LA-MI-P-RF-WP

Little Gull Cottages
383-8818; fax 383-1110
5330 Gulf of Mexico Dr.,
Longboat Key
Number of condos: 16
$$$$-MC-V-BF-BV-BI-CT-F-FL-GR-LA-MI-PL-P-RF-TS

Radisson Lido Beach Resort
388-2161; fax 388-3175
(800) 441-2113
e-mail: radlido@compuserve.com
www.radisson.com/sarasotafl
700 Benjamin Franklin Dr.,
Lido Key
Number of Rooms: 116
$$$$-AX-CB-DC-DS-MC-V-BF-BN-BB-BI-BS-BT-CT-F-IM-IS-LA-L-MI-MR-P-RF-R-SH-TS-WP

The Resort at Longboat Key Club
383-8821; fax 383-5396
(800) 237-8821
www.longboatkeyclub.com
301 Gulf of Mexico Dr.,
Longboat Key
Number of Rooms: 232
$$$$-AX-CB-DC-MC-V-BF-GV-BY-BN-BI-BS-BT-CT-CA-CN-FC-G-GP-IM-IS-IT-LA-LM-L-MI-MR-P-RF-R-SH-TN-TP-TS-VP-W-WP

Key to Accommodations

FL - Free Local Calls
GR - Game Room
G - Golf
GP - Golf Packages
HP - Heated Pool
IM - In-room Movies
IS - In-room Safe
IT - International Services
LA - Laundry
LM - Live Music
L - Lounge
M - Marina
MI - Microwave in room
MR - Meeting Rooms
PE - Pets Okay
PL - Playground
P - Pool
RF - Refrigerator in-room
RT - Remote control TV
R - Restaurant
SB - Shuffleboard
SH - Shuttle Service
TN - Tennis
TP - Tennis Packages
TS - Trolley Stop
VP - Valet Parking
W - Whirlpool
WP - Weekend Package Available

Key to Accommodations

$ - Under $50/night

$$ - $51 - $75

$$$ - $76-$100

$$$$ - Over $100

AX - American Express
CB - Carte Blanche
DC - Diner's Club
DS - Discover
ET - Enroute
MC - Master Card
V - Visa
BF - Beach Front
BW - Walking distance to Beach
GV - Gulf View
BV - Bay View
LF - Lakefront
BY - Babysitting Service
BN - Banquet Service
BB - Bed & Breakfast
BI - Bicycles
BS - Bus Stop
BT - Boating
CT - Cable TV
CA - Children's Activities
CN - Concierge Service
EF - Efficiencies
F - Fishing
FC - Fitness Center

Runaway Bay
778-6779; fax 778-7504
(800) 346-7340
1801 Gulf Drive N., Anna Maria Island 34217
Number of Rooms: 120
$$$$-C-MC-V-WB-GV-BV-BY-BI-BS-CT-F-FC-LA-MI-MR-P-RF-SB-TN

Sara Sea Inn An The Beach
349-3244; fax 349-4999; e-mail: sarasea@gte.net
www.sarasea.com
6760 Sara Sea Circle, Siesta Key
Number of Rooms: 28
$$-AX-DS-MC-V-WB-CT-LA-MI-P-RF-SB-W

Sarasota Surf & Racquet Club
349-2200; fax 349-2203
(800) 237-5671; e-mail: ssrc5900@aol.com
5900 Midnight Pass Rd., Siesta Key
Number of Rooms: 189
$$$$-MC-V-BF-GV-BY-BS-CT-FC-FL-LA-MI-MR-P-RF-TN-TP

Sea Club II Weekly Condominium Rentals
349-0760; fax 346-5207
(800) 626-0258
5955 Midnight Pass Rd., Siesta Key
Number of Rooms: 39
$$$-WB-BT-CT-F-FL-LA-M-MI-P-RF

Sea Horse Beach Resort
383-2417; fax 387-8771;
e-mail: sresort@aol.com
3453 Gulf of Mexico Dr., Longboat Key
Number of Rooms: 35
$$$/$$$$-DS-MC-V- BF-GV-BS--F-LA-MI-RF

Sea Shell Condominiums
349-1191; fax 349-5263
(800) 624-9276
6500 Midnight Pass Rd. Siesta Key 34242
Number of Rooms: 41
$$$$-MC-VS-BF-WB-GV-BS-CT-FL-LA-MI-P-RF-TS

Shorewalk Vacation Villas resort
794-9800; (800) 926-9255; e-mail: svvillas@aol.com
4601 46th St. C. W. Bradenton
Number of Rooms: 175
$$$-AX-DS-MC-VS-LF-BY-BI-BS-CT-CA-CN-F-FC-GR-GP-IT-LA-MI-PL-P-RF-SB-TN-W-WP

Siesta Beach House
349-2233; fax 349-2233
e-mail: argusmgmt@aol.com
www.argusmgmt.com
5950 Midnight Pass Rd., Siesta Key
Number of Rooms: 43 $$$$-WB-CT-FL-HP-LA-MI

Siesta Dunes Beach Condominiums
346-0210; fax 346-3215
6200 Midnight Pass Rd., Siesta Key 34242
Number of Rooms: 100
$$$$BF-BS-CT-FL-LA-MI-P-RF-TN-W

Silver Sands Motel & Apartments
383-3731; fax 387-3095
(800) 245-3731;
e-mail: silversandssurf@mail.pcsonline.com
www.silverresorts.com
5841 Gulf of Mexico Dr. Longboat Key
Number of Rooms: 38
$$$-AX-DC-DS-MC-V-BF-GV-BV-BT-CT-F-LA-MI-P-RF-SB-TN

Silver Surf Resort
778-6626; fax 778-4308
(800) 441-7873;
e-mail: silversandssurf@mail.psconline.com
www.silverresorts.com
1301 Gulf Dr. North
Bradenton Beach
Number of Rooms: 50
$$-AX-DC-DS-MC-V-WB-BV-BV-CT-FL-LA-MI-P-RF-SB

Sunset Beach Resort
778-7900; fax 778-0485
2201 Gulf Dr. N
Bradenton Beach
Number of Rooms: 14
$/$$/$$$-AX-DC-DS-MC-V-BF-GV-CT-CN-EF-FL-HP-LA-MI-RF-RT-SB-TS

Tivoli By The Sea Vacation Rentals
349-5544; fax 349-5545;
e-mail: sj@gte.net
625 Beach Rd., Siesta Key 34242
Number of Rooms: 35
$$$/$$$$-BF-GV-BS-CT-FL-GR-LA-MI-P-RF-TN-TS

Turtle Beach Resort
349-4554; fax 312-9034;
e-mail: grubi@ix.netcom.com
9049 Midnight Pass Rd.
Siesta Key 34242
Number of Rooms: 10
$$$$-AX-DC-DS-MC-VS-WB-BV-BI-BS-BT-CN-F-FL-LA-M-MI-PA-P-RF-R-W-WP

Radisson
LIDO BEACH RESORT

Radisson Lido Beach Resort
Sarasota, Florida

The perfect place to relax.

The difference is genuine.℠

Experience the Award Winning service and deluxe accommodations of our tropical beachfront resort. Located directly on Lido Beach, just a short stroll to renowned St. Armands Circle, the Radisson Lido Beach Resort is your perfect vacation getaway. With 300 feet of private beach, heated pool, watersports, beachfront Tiki bar and full service restaurant, we are the perfect place to relax.

700 BENJAMIN FRANKLIN DRIVE • SARASOTA, FL 34236
(941) 388-2161 • FAX (941) 388-3175

For reservations call 1-800-333-3333, visit us
at www.radisson.com or contact your travel professional.

At the Inn at the Beach Resort, we offer the friendly, personalized service only an intimate resort can provide. Our guest rooms and suites are set amidst Award winning tropical landscaping and winding brick walkways. All of our guest rooms feature a refrigerator, microwave, in-room safe, ceiling fans and 60 channel remote television. Whether relaxing by our heated pool or watching the sunset, we are the perfect hideaway for that next relaxing getaway.

725 West Venice Avenue, Venice, Florida 34285
(941) 484-8471, US Toll Free 800-255-8471 Fax (941) 484-0593

A MESSAGE FROM POSTMASTER PETER FERNANDEZ

"Our friendly and courteous postal employees invite you to their post office and welcome you to our beautiful community. We are confident you will experience the ultimate in customer satisfaction from our Sarasota postal employees." The Main Post Office offers a number of unique services, including a full-service "Lobby Director" who is available to answer your questions and to help you use the United States Postal Service most effectively; the only philatelic window for stamp collectors in Manatee and Sarasota Counties; and a full-time Customer Relations Coordinator (800-275-8777) who is available to assist new businesses.

SUNSET © BILL WEST

Our Post Offices

Okay, so maybe they don't have to worry about the "sleet and snow" part. Still, the folks who gather and deliver our mail face plenty of obstacles, including seasonal traffic, an influx of snowbirds with alien "attitudes" and a consistent unpredictability found within the subtropical forces of nature. For them, every day is an adventure. For us, and thanks to them, every day becomes Christmas.

The United States Postal Service in Sarasota has a total of twenty locations throughout the area that local business, residents, and tourists can utilize to meet their mailing needs. Sarasota Postmaster Peter Fernandez has made it as convenient as possible for all customers to use the Main Post Office located at 1661 Ringling Blvd. in Downtown Sarasota with a recent permanent change in business hours – 7:30 a.m. - 6:00 p.m. Monday - Friday; 9:00 a.m. - 1:30 p.m. Saturday.

For a complete listing of the postal facilities and directions to the location nearest you in Manatee and Sarasota Counties call – 1-800-275-8777. Here are some of the many services provided by the Main Post Office:

1. Stamps by FAX. Orders FAXED prior to 8:30 a.m. will be delivered the same day.

Zip Codes	FAX #
34231, 34238, 34241, 34242	925-2460
34232, 34233, 34240	927-3741
34239,	951-7502
34234, 34235, 34236, 34237, 34243	331-4253 34230

2. Stamps-by-Mail: call for a supply of Postage Paid envelopes: 1-813-877-0663
3. Express Mail and Priority Mail Pick Up Service.
4. Zip Code Information.
6. Open until midnight on Income Tax Day – April 15th
7. A Postal Customer Council for businesses who use the Postal Service. For membership information call.

Our Public Servants

Democratic Party
6360 Tamiami Tr. S; Sarasota
924-4977

Republican Party of Manatee County
Information:745-7101

The League of Women Voters
Location: 340 Tuttle Ave. S; Sarasota 34237
Information:921-9778

Explaining how government works while providing mechanisms to make it work well is what *The League of Women Voters* is all about. **Nancy Babigan,** of our local chapter, has kindly compiled the following anatomical rendering of our local government skeletal system:

"Sarasota County is governed by a Board of County Commissioners of five members elected from five districts within the county. Each commissioner is elected for a term of four years. There is an appointed county administrator. This commission meets every Tuesday.

Other county officials elected for four year terms are: the Clerk of the Circuit Court; the Sheriff; the Property Appraiser; the Tax Collector; and the Supervisor of Elections.

As Sarasota County is a Charter County, it has a Charter Review Board whose duty it is to review the operation of the county government on behalf of the citizens and recommend the changes for the improvement of this charter. This board consists of ten members, two elected from each of the five districts for four year terms.

The Sarasota-Manatee Airport is governed by an Airport Authority of four nonpartisan members elected from Sarasota County and four nonpartisan members elected from Manatee County. Each member serves a term of four years. The Airport Authority has an appointed executive director.

The Sarasota County School Board consists of five members each serving four year terms. These board members must live in their own districts, but are elected by the county at large in partisan elections. The superintendent is an appointed position.

Sarasota Memorial Hospital, as a nonprofit hospital, is governed by a Public Hospital Board. Two members each are selected from the Northern, the Central, and the Southern Districts, and three are selected at large in partisan elections to serve four years.

Sarasota County has four municipalities within its boundaries, each with its own governments:

Longboat Key has a town commission with five nonpartisan district commissioners and two at large members from whom the mayor is selected. Their term runs two years. There is an appointed city manager.

The city of North Port has a city commission of nonpartisan members elected to fill five seats for a term of three years. One member is chosen as chairperson, rather than a mayor. The city manager is appointed.

The city of Sarasota is governed by a commission of five nonpartisan members elected by district for terms of four years. The mayor is selected from these five commissioners. There is an appointed city manager.

The city of Venice has an elected mayor and a city council of six members elected in nonpartisan elections for three years. The city manager is an appointed position."

Heidi Godman

Heidi Godman joined News 40 more than a decade ago and today is one of the Suncoast's most familiar faces. She earned her Bachelor of Science degree in Journalism from West Virginia University and has since become an accomplished medical reporter. She loves reporting the latest in advanced medical procedures, showing viewers the future of medicine. Several Suncoast physicians use her work as an educational tool for their patients. In addition, Heidi was the first television reporter ever to accompany Sarasota Police on a dangerous crack house raid, and brought viewers the exciting story. Heidi co-anchors FIRST NEWS AT FIVE, a 5:00 p.m. weekday newscast on WWSB, Channel 40. She lives in Venice with her husband Jay, a writer, and their young son, Christopher.

Health Care

WWSB, Channel 40 anchor/reporter **Heidi Godman** provides news stories and topical reports about our area's health care providers for News40:

"The Suncoast is known for many things: beautiful beaches, cultural arts and an upscale lifestyle. However, we're quickly gaining a new, national reputation as a medical mecca. The area's six hospitals boast state-of-the-art equipment, and some of the best minds in the international community. Much of this is the result of our large senior population. With so many older patients battling heart disease, stroke, cancer and Alzheimer's's disease, hospitals have had to build outstanding facilities and programs to meet their needs.

Recently, though, our hospitals have taken those programs a step further. The Suncoast now ranks 15th in the country for open heart surgery expertise. And it's the Suncoast that now attracts some of the most advanced research in the world. Studies underway right now focus on robotic heart surgery, tiny pills that quadruple a cancer patient's chance for survival, and injections that virtually eliminate the debilitating side effects of stroke. Our doctors are constantly involved in futuristic clinical research, paving the way for the new drugs, treatments and surgical techniques of the 21st century.

© SARASOTA MEMORIAL HOSPITAL

As a health reporter, I've had the great privilege to tag along on many of these medical adventures into the future. Whether I'm standing inches away from a patient's beating heart, or watching the world's most high-tech brain surgery, I'm impressed not only by the expertise and pioneer spirit of these

Suncoast doctors, but also by their devotion to the comfort and care of the patients and their families.

Take an army of world-class medical experts and put them in a small, closeknit, beautiful community; what you have is the Suncoast's vastly talented collection of doctors who offer a caring hometown style."

SARASOTA

Columbia Doctors Hospital of Sarasota
5731 Bee Ridge Road
342-1100
www.doctorsofsarasota.com
Physicians Referral:
1-800-257-0944
AC/CA/CN/DI/GE/NU/OB/OP/PA/PN/RE/UR

Doctors Hospital is a tax-paying facility with six facilities in our area. As a member of the nation's largest health care company, Doctors is connected to a significant nationwide network system for physician referral. The 168-bed hospital offers an intimate level of health care and prides itself on a state-of-the-art building completed in 1995. A wide range of medical and surgical services are offered, including an obstetrics unit with all private suites. The facility's Level 1 newborn nursery requires that unexpectedly small or sick infants must be transferred to another hospital, depending on the infant's condition. The hospital offers a wound care center, a diabetes management center, and an emergency/chest pain center with all Board Certified physicians.

Sarasota Memorial Hospital
1700 South Tamiami Trail
917-9000; www.smh.com
Physicians Referral: 917-7777
AC/CA/CN/DI/IF/GE/NE/NU/OB/OH/PA/PC/PN/RE/SA/SP/UR

Sarasota Memorial Hospital is Sarasota County's only full-service hospital. It has the most sophisticated medical equipment and services in the county. The hospital is known for its advanced diagnostics and treatment, as well as its clinical research. Ninety percent of Sarasota Memorial's physicians are Board Certified. It is licensed for 885 beds and staffed by 550 medical staff members.

Sarasota Memorial is the only hospital in Sarasota County that offers open-heart surgery. It is among the top 15 hospitals in the United States in the number of open-heart surgeries performed annually.

The hospital offers a Level 3 neo-natal intensive care unit, a prenatal unit for high-risk pregnancies, a large critical care unit and a pediatric emergency room.

Ranked among the top 10 hospitals in the United States for the number of joint replacements performed annually, Sarasota Memorial is also in the top percentile nationally of rehabilitation outcomes, as measured by Functional Independence.

It measures the lowest average charge per day and per stay – as well as the shortest length of stay – of any rehabilitation department in the nation.

The cancer program at Sarasota Memorial is among the 22 percent in the United States accredited by the Commission on Cancer of the American College of Surgeons. It is the first nonacademic hospital in the nation to develop a clinical research service and has conducted more than 80 clinical trials in the past eight years.

The hospital is the first in the world to convert its imaging services to an electronic digital format, increasing speed and accuracy of results for physicians and patients.

Sarasota Memorial offers a Health Resource Network with Registered Nurses who may be reached 24 hours a day, seven days a week. They will answer health care questions at no charge. The network may be reached at 917-7777.

Area Hospital Codes

AC	Acute Care General Hospital
CA	Inpatient Cardiac Catherization
CN	Cancer Programs
DI	Diabetic Care
IF	Intensive Residential Psychiatric/ Substance Abuse Treatment Facility
GE	Gerontology Services
NE	Neonatal Intensive Care Unit
NU	Neurological/ Neurosurgery
OB	Obstetrical Services
OH	Open Heart Surgery
OP	Outpatient Surgery
PA	Psychiatric Treatment (adults)
PC	Psychiatric Treatment (children adolescents)
PN	Prenatal Care
RE	Comprehensive Rehabilitation Services
SA	Substance Abuse
SP	Sports Medicine
UR	Urology Services

Area Hospital Codes

- **AC** Acute Care General Hospital
- **CA** Inpatient Cardiac Catherization
- **CN** Cancer Programs
- **DI** Diabetic Care
- **IF** Intensive Residential Psychiatric/Substance Abuse Treatment Facility
- **GE** Gerontology Services
- **NE** Neonatal Intensive Care Unit
- **NU** Neurological/Neurosurgery
- **OB** Obstetrical Services
- **OH** Open Heart Surgery
- **OP** Outpatient Surgery
- **PA** Psychiatric Treatment (adults)
- **PC** Psychiatric Treatment (children adolescents)
- **PN** Prenatal Care
- **RE** Comprehensive Rehabilitation Services
- **SA** Substance Abuse
- **SP** Sports Medicine
- **UR** Urology Services

© BLAKE MEDICAL CENTER

BRADENTON

Blake Medical Center
2020 59th St. West, 34209
792-6611
Physicians Referral:
1-800-530-1188
AC/CA/CN/DI/GE/NU/OB/OH/OP/PN/RE/SP/UR

Blake Medical Center is the only area hospital to be rated as one of America's top 100 hospitals for 1996 and 1997. The Joint Commission on the accreditation of Health Care Organizations has also recognized Blake by awarding its highest honor - "Accreditation with Commendation" - on three consecutive surveys. Blake medical Center is a 383-bed acute-care, full service, medical center and leading provider of quality, affordable healthcare.

Manatee Memorial Hospital
206 2nd St. East
746-5111; 1-800-816-4145
Physicians Referral: 745-7575
AC/CA/CN/DI/GE/NE/NU/OB/OH/OP/PA/PC/PN/RE/SP/UR

Opened in 1953, Manatee Memorial Hospital is a 512-bed, full-service, acute care facility on the banks of the Manatee River. Recent distinctions include Accreditation with Commendation from the agency that rates the nation's hospitals, the Joint Commission for Accreditation Organizations; and "Best Hospital Facility in Manatee County" award for the fourth year in a row in the *Bradenton Herald* readership survey. Manatee Memorial has the area's only Level II Neonatal Intensive Care Unit and the acclaimed MOMM's Place for post-partum mothers and babies. The Manatee Heart Center, Pediatrics Center, Family BirthPlace, Manatee Center for Women's Health, Life Management Center and Emergency Care Center – all within the hospital; and Florida Home Health, two FirstCare walk-in clinics and rehabilitation services at The Fitness Center at Health Park East - in locations throughout the community - offer patients a continuum of medical care. Manatee Memorial provides a wide variety of programs, classes and support groups and a free speaker's bureau.

VENICE

Bon Secours Venice Hospital
540 The Rialto 34285
485-7711
Physician Referral: 483-7600
AC/CA/CN/DI/GE/NU/OP/PA/RE/SA/SP/UR

Bons Secours Venice Hospital is a 342-bed facility offering South County residents general medical and surgical services, including emergency room services, cardiac and cancer services, drug and alcohol treatment. Bon Secours Venice Hospital does not offer obstetrics services. All doctors are Board-Certified. Bon Secours is a Catholic not-for-profit health system. The system also offers home health, assisted living and a nursing and rehabilitation center. The hospital prides iitself on its large community involvement and support, including a volunteer program 1000-strong.

President of The Schoenbaum Human Services Center, **Dr. Kay Glasser**, shares her perspective: "There are many cities which may boast of their climate, of their cultural/arts facilities (or both). But what good would they be as places to visit if, at the same time, they did not offer a safe and secure environment which is essential if these attractions are to be enjoyed day and night? Sarasota has something that no other community in the State of Florida has – the Schoenbaum Human Services Center."

Kay Glasser

Human Services

The Schoenbaum Human Services Center of Sarasota
1750 17th Street; Sarasota
365-4545

The Human Services Center of Sarasota is known as "the Campus for Caring" – a facility consisting of 13 connecting buildings which house 15 nonprofit human services agencies. Its mission is to promote the quality of life of Sarasota by helping individuals and families maintain productive and self-sustaining lives. In effect, this is "one-stop shopping" for a range of preventive and treatment services for thousands of troubled individuals and families. This unique facility is totally the product of volunteer efforts over a period of 12 years, involving both public and private philanthropy (but no Federal tax dollars, thank you!) This has meant rent-free office space for the 16 agencies, and the dollars thus saved are available for the provision of additional services and programs. The Center welcomes visitors.

American Cancer Society – Cancer control through research, education and direct services. 365-2858

Children's Haven & Adult Center – Community based employment services 951-6518 and living services. 355-8808.

Coastal Recovery Centers, Inc. – Comprehensive drug rehabilitation and mental health services. 953-0000

Child Protection Center, Inc. – Prevention, intervention, and treatment of physical and sexual abuse. 365-1277

Consumer Credit Counseling Service of the Florida Gulf Coast, Inc. – Provides non-profit consumer credit education, confidential financial counseling, and debt reduction programs to all segments of the community regardless of the ability to pay. 365-5116

Domestic Violence Intervention Project – Counseling and education programs for people who abuse their partners and want to change. 957-1416

First Call For Help of United Way of Sarasota County, Inc. – Information/referral and financial assistance to those in crisis situations. 366-5025

Gulfcoast Legal Services – Free legal advice/representation for low income individuals. 366-1746

Pets in Paradise

Be sure to visit *Pelican Man's Bird Sanctuary* on City Island in Sarasota, a place where you can visit birds whose injuries prevent them from returning to their natural habitat. There are approximately 300 birds in residence including herons, cormorants, owls, osprey and, of course, pelicans! Local legend and national folk hero Dale Shields gave up his worldly possessions to dedicate his life to rescuing birds in distress, contributing over 100,000 volunteer hours to his cause.

Since he began in 1981, he has helped rescue over 50,000 birds. Currently the Sanctuary involves over 300 volunteers who help to rescue over 5,000 birds each year, returning 60% back to the wild. The Pelican Man's Sanctuary is open the public, free, from 10 a.m. - 5 p.m. seven days a week. Donations are appreciated. Information: 388-4444

Human Services Planning Association of Sarasota County, Inc. – Working to enhance health and human services delivery, the Human Services Planning Association provides needs assessments, forums and facilitation services for better collaboration and community problem-solving. 361-6045

Juvenile Alternative Services Program – Provides services for first time offenders. (Ages 7-18 years). 366-9660

Family Counseling Center – Offers therapy for individuals and families with marital, family relationship and child behavior problems. 955-7017

Safe Place & Rape Crisis Center (SPARCC) – Provides free services to victims of spouse abuse and rape. Services include 24-hour hotline, counseling, advocacy and shelter. 365-1976

Sarasota County Public Health Unit – Direct medical care, immunization, screening diagnosis, treatment and other health services. 954-2922

Severely Emotionally Disturbed Network (SEDNET) – A multi-agency network for the severely emotionally disturbed and at-risk children/youth and their families. Facilitates the coordination of services as provided by education, mental health, the Department of Children and Families, and the Department of Juvenile Justice within the seven-county area of District 8 in the State of Florida. 361-6397

Suncoast Workforce Development Board, Inc. – Responsible for the administration and fiscal management of the following programs: The Federal Job Training Partnership Act; Jobs, ETC; School-to-Work; WAGES or Welfare-to-Work; and High Skills/High wages. 361-6090

Volunteer Center of Sarasota – Assists individual and group volunteers to match their interests and skills with the appropriate not-for-profit agencies to solve community problems. The Center also co-sponsors the Human Race, a fund-raising event to benefit the not-for-profit community. 953-5965

Pets in Paradise

Reality check time. What you are about to read may seem scary, but don't fret. Pets are just as popular in our area as anywhere else in the nation. Taking extra precautions will become part of your regular schedule; it comes with the territory.

If pets had a vote as to where their families ended up moving, mountain states like Colorado would replace Florida paws down. The reason? Humans are attracted to Florida largely because of the subtropical climate. Pets, on the other – er – hand have a problem: fleas! Pets love Colorado because fleas don't live in the mountains. Instead, they have to deal with ticks and Lyme disease, fortunately, not a problem here.

For families moving to our area, it's important to understand how your new environment will affect your pet. **Dr. David Smith** of *Bay Road Animal Hospital* shares his expertise on the itchy subject of fleas, and other pet pests:

"All pets can live comfortably in our tropical environment. A few precautions can prevent flea problems. Fleas are with us all year 'round. Treating the house and yard along with your dog or cat can curtail these pests.

Advantage and *Frontline* are new flea control products that will completely eliminate adult fleas for four weeks at a time from your pet. Ask your vet about these remarkable products.

**David J. Smith
VMD**

Dr. David Smith received his Doctor of Veterinary Medicine from the University of Pennsylvania and has been practicing in Sarasota for over 20 years.

Owner of *Bay Road Animal Hospital, Crossings Animal Hospital, Longboat Key Animal Hospital* and *All About Pets* pet supply store, Dr. Smith can be seen weekly on BLAB Channel 36 on "All About Pets" where he answers questions from viewers about their Pets in Paradise.

Worms of all types abound in our warm humid climate. A simple pill once a month will control heartworm, roundworms, hookworms and whipworms. This only leaves the tapeworm. Tapeworm comes from the ingestion of fleas. Good flea control can go a long way in controlling tapeworm.

The Bay Road family of pet hospitals provide two full-service veterinary care facilities and one outpatient clinic. Surgery, medicine, clinical laboratory, bacteriology, X Ray, bathing, boarding, grooming, dentistry and emergencies for dogs, cats, birds, and exotics are provided at our hospitals. We also have an acupuncturist on staff for treatment of pet animals."

Basic pet rules for Sarasota and Manatee

Rabies shots must be given at four months of age. Unique to this area is the requirement of rabies booster shots which must be given yearly. Folks coming into town, used to the three-year booster, might think the reason for this is simply an easy way to raise money in tags every year. We have a large local raccoon population where rabies is prevalent. (Again, don't panic. But it's a good idea – and should be common sense – to keep your family and friends from feeding wild raccoons by hand.) Foxes and bats are also culprits, but not squirrels, rats or smaller animals. Because of our 365 days-a-year "outdoor weather" there is more chance for domestic animals to interact with the wild animal population. Tourists, who think feeding wild raccoons brie & caviar sandwiches will bring them closer to nature only help these critters to lose their fear of people and pets.

Here are some *musts* for Happy Suncoast Pets:
• Heartworm preventative every month.
• Flea control every month to kill pests before they bite.
• Full vaccinations, including Rabies yearly, due to large raccoon population.

If your pet is hurt, or you find a wounded wild animal (except alligators which are handled by the Florida Game and Fresh Water Fish Commission in Lakeland, there are a number of local services available:

Animal Services of the Sarasota Sheriff's Dept.
5407 Pickney Ave., Sarasota 34233,
316-1081
Picks up stray, trapped and injured domestic and wild animals.

Alligators
(941) 648-3200
Alligators are ONLY handled by the Florida Game and Fresh Water Fish Commission in Lakeland. NEVER attempt to feed, play with or handle an alligator!

Bay Road Animal Hospital
1712 Bay Rd., Sarasota, 366-2275
Domestic and wild animals are treated here, full-service pet treatment facility and care available. The best.

Bayshore Animal Hospital
1511 Florida Blvd., Bradenton,
756-5544
Wild animals are treated here, injured and orphaned.

The Cat Woman's Shelter
2120 Princeton St., Sarasota
953-2280; fax 953-3311
A haven for unwanted, injured and neglected animals that the world has abandoned. At press time over 200 cats and kittens, 10 dogs and five baby raccoons live there, waiting for a good home. Visitation available for those interested

in adoption. Adoption hours 10 a.m. to 5 p.m., 7 days a week. Sarasota's only no-kill and cageless shelter. Funded by private donations.

Crossings Animal Hospital
5309 Fruitville Rd., Sarasota, 378-1236
Full-service pet treatment facility and care available.

Florida Marine Patrol Hotline
(800) 342-5367 (Tampa District Office)
Call this number to report sightings in injured or distressed marine life, including manatees.

Humane Society
2331 15th St., Sarasota
955-4131; fax 955-3715
This private, nonprofit corporation has served Sarasota County for 45 years through the generous support of individual donations. Shelter tours are happily arranged for any size group. (This is a great place to find a pet for your home, highly recommended.)

Longboat Key Animal Hospital
5530 Gulf of Mexico Dr.
383-8816; fax 383-8817
Domestic and wild animals are treated here, full-service pet treatment facility and care available.

Palma Sola Animal Clinic
6116 Manatee Ave. W., Bradenton, 794-3275
Accepts all injured/orphaned wildlife. Veterinary services for domestic animals.

Pelican Man's Bird Sanctuary
1708 Ken Thompson Pkwy, Sarasota
388-4444; fax 388-3258
Open 10:00 a.m. - 5:00 p.m. every day; takes all kind of injured wildlife with special emphasis on seabirds. Admission is free, donations are appreciated.

Mote Marine Laboratory
1600 Ken Thompson Parkway, Sarasota
388-4441
Works with sheriff's department and Marine Patrol in response to strandings of live sea turtles and in response to marine mammal strandings.

Racing Dog Rescue Project
P.O. Box 18153, Sarasota
379-FAST (3278); fax 359-2391
Founded in 1993, the RDRP is a non-profit 501(C)3 organization which promotes adoption of greyhounds. In the past four years it has placed over 450 greyhounds in the tri-county area. Greyhounds make wonderful pets; highly recommended.

TLC for Wildlife
6109 Carlton Ave., Sarasota
924-0273
Accepts any kind of wildlife.

Wildlife Education & Rehabilitation
Anna Maria Island, 778-6324
Call to deliver an animal to this service on Anna Maria Island.

Wildlife Rescue Services, Inc.
Bradenton, 750-9453
Call for 24-hour ambulance service for sick and injured birds and animals.

ANOLE © BILL WEST

History

MYAKKA © BILL WEST

SWAMPS AND ALLIGATORS AND MOSQUITOES...OH MY!

Sherman, set the Way-Back machine to the mid 1500s. It was a time when Europeans began to hear stories of an "island named Bimini" - what would later be known as the west coast of Florida.

Today, it may seem somewhat strange that anyone would actually have wanted to leave family and friends to wade around in yucky swamps infested with mosquitoes and alligators.

Talks of a subtropical paradise - spread through Europe by Columbus and the men of his time - inspired groups of dreamers, explorers, soldiers and thieves to find their way here.

Oh yes, there was also that popular rumor of the day. "Some sort of Fountain of Youth this turned out to be!"

But the truth, of course, is a bit stranger than that.

The Europeans were successful in conquering the natives, thereby writing the most tragic chapter in our area's history. They, in turn, were ultimately conquered themselves without ever recognizing that what destroyed them was even more valuable than any imagined treasure they so desperately sought: the very land around them.

Also, our early pioneers didn't actually leave the warm family hearth to brave the Florida wild – most had no families, no money, no property. They braved the conditions because they had no choice.

They squatted in the wilderness on government-owned property and no one bothered them. No doubt, some were an hour ahead of the posse.

All in all, however, undeniably a hardy breed.

Like many people who call the Suncoast home, WWSB Channel 40 anchor/reporter **Linda Carson** and her husband are not native Floridians. "After living all over the country we chose to make Sarasota our permanent home because of the beauty and lifestyle," explains Linda. "Now we are fascinated as we explore its history and learn about those who were here before us. The Suncoast has an amazing story to tell of the people who molded it. Indians, and pioneers, art collectors and circus performers, fishermen and farmers, builders and dreamers, environmentalists and philanthropists. The Suncoast was also molded by natural phenomenon...hurricanes and storms, droughts and floods. And much of its special character comes from the wild creatures that make this their home. World and national events, wars, economic booms and busts, and advancing technology have also left their mark. All these forces have come together to create this special place we call Paradise."

Linda Carson

Our History

Some say Florida has no history. Humbug! (Or, maybe the word is Palmetto!)

Thousands of years ago mammoths roamed the Florida marshes. The first inhabitants were Indians with tribes in our area dating back 6,000 years. They left evidence of their presence that we still find today – stone tools and weapons, piles of discarded shells called middens, and burial mounds which now are grassy mounds found along the shoreline and inland.

We can boast a fascinating history from about 1500 of intrepid pioneers who braved a most hostile environment to settle in what has become an internationally famous resort. Florida was named after *Pascua Florida*, the traditional Spanish feast of flowers held during Easter by Juan Ponce de Leon, who landed near St. Augustine in 1513. The Spanish and other Europeans came to our gulf coast shores but

Manatee County Historical Highlights

Cortez - For those interested in Vernacular Architecture (built without the help of an architect and using local materials), Cortez is Florida's only remaining early fishing village. There are overbuilt by and for "fishing folk" in this official Manatee County Historic District. To get there take Cortez Road to 119th Street and turn south, drive to the docks and park your car – the best way to see Cortez is by walking around this pre-turn of the century village. Before you leave, stop by the Star Fish Co. at 124th and dock side and pick up some very fresh fish or smoked mullet (a local delicacy!)

Information:
794-1243

---

never established permanent settlements here. The diseases they brought with them decimated the native population.

Spain sold the territory to the United States in 1821 and Florida became a state in 1845. Through about 1850 we were a wild frontier with coastal areas populated seasonally. Fishing was the primary occupation. The 19th century was marked by three major turf wars between the Seminoles and the white settlers from Georgia and north Florida. Invasions these days are limited to a seasonal encroachment by "snowbirds."

Manatee County History

The beautiful acreage that comprises Manatee County has harbored human life as far back as 1000 A.D. The first inhabitants were the Timucan Indians – farmers, fishermen, and, as it turned out, fighters fierce in the defense of their land. The Timucan tribe had undisputed control of their territory for more than 500 years, until the first Europeans appeared on the scene.

Early Exploration

Ponce de Leon first arrived on the west coast of Florida in 1521 to start a settlement which was to be used as a base for Spain's trading activities. Legend has it that Ponce de Leon searched for a mythical "Fountain of Youth." Whether this is so, we don't know, but we do know that he didn't find anything he expected in the Manatee area. Thwarted in his colonization by area Indians, Ponce de Leon left Manatee County forever.

In 1539, Spain sent another emissary to try to establish a west coast trading center. Hernando DeSoto and his conquistadors landed in the Manatee area at Shaw's Point (Congress declared Shaw's Point a national monument in 1934).

DeSoto's massive forces accosted the Indian population. He enslaved the indigenous people and demanded to be guided to El Dorado, a city the conquistadors believed to be carved from and paved with gold. After numerous expeditions failed to reveal the location of the "Golden City," DeSoto wearied of the chase. He sent his sailing ships back to Cuba and set off on foot for the Mississippi River.

Each spring, a week-long gala celebration is held to commemorate DeSoto's landing. However, in 1994 the annual "DeSoto Celebration" was rechristened "The Florida Heritage Festival at Bradenton," reflecting a sensitivity to the atrocities associated with his name.

Josiah Gates The First Settler

A peaceful lull of 300 years passed before further settlement by "civilized" man was attempted. In 1842, Josiah Gates became Manatee County's first permanent settler. Gates, who ran a hotel in Fort Brooke (now Tampa), sailed down the west coast of Florida with his brother-in-law. He came searching for the bountiful land which he had heard much of from the fishermen who supplied seafood for his restaurant.

Knowing that this coastal territory would soon be opened to settlers, Gates surveyed the lush acreage and selected a suitable site to build a homestead.

The Armed Occupation Act of 1842 allowed any American citizen to homestead a quarter section of land (160 acres) in the southwest Florida region. The Act also provided military protection to residents living there five consecutive years. Garrisons were established all along the coast as the years went by, encouraging further settlement of the area by people who had formerly been fearful because of the lack of security precautions.

In January of 1842, Josiah Gates moved his family to present-day Manatee County. He was soon followed by enterprising pioneers who recognized, as he did, the value of the beautiful, fertile land.

Hector and Joseph Braden

Two prominent early settlers of the Manatee region were Hector and Joseph Braden, brothers from Tallahassee. Both men were successful in business: Hector was an attorney; Joseph was a graduate physician although he never practiced. The collapse of the Union Bank in Tallahassee in 1837 depleted the fortunes of many wealthy men, including the Braden brothers.

In an attempt to regain their former prosperity, the brothers turned south to the bountiful Manatee land. The acreage settled by the Braden brothers included the territory now known as Braden Creek. Altogether, the two amassed holdings of more than a thousand acres.

Strong sturdy homes capable of withstanding Indian attacks were built on their beautiful land. Joseph's home was truly his castle -- Braden Castle was constructed of a highly durable shell-based material and the exterior walls were more than 20 inches thick. It was fortunate for all of the area residents that Joseph Braden had the foresight to provide such protection, for one day they would need it.

The Gamble Mansion

Major Robert Gamble contributed much to the development of the land surrounding Bradenton and has long been a familiar name in Manatee County. When he arrived in the summer of 1842, he too was trying to recover from financial failure (his father was the organizer of the Union Bank). Gamble came to Manatee with the thought of raising sugar cane. He brought farming implements, stock and more than one hundred slaves to the area, transforming the wilderness into rich farm land.

Gamble liked to think he had "the best blood in Virginia" (his family's home state) in his veins – he was accustomed to the pleasantries of civilized life. After living in a simple wooden house for a number of years, Gamble began constructing a mansion befitting a man of his stature. It was modeled after his father's Tallahassee home, except, instead of clay, the building material contained a mixture of lime, water, shell and sand. Some architectural experts surmise that a portion of sugar or cane juice was added to the formula which helped to harden it and prolong its resistance to the elements.

The Gamble Mansion became a symbol of its time – colonial in appearance with its verandas and its eighteen wide columns, yet sturdy enough to hold off outside attackers.

Just after the Civil War, Major Gamble sheltered Judah P. Benjamin in the mansion – the ex-Secretary of State for the Confederacy was fleeing from government authorities. Benjamin stayed there a few weeks until it was deemed safe for him to continue his flight to Cuba and, finally, to England.

The mansion stands today much as it did in the mid-1800s thanks to the United Daughters of the Confederacy which purchased the ruined mansion in 1925 and caringly reconstructed it in authentic period design as a tribute to early Florida. It is now operated by the Florida Park Service and one of the south's few remaining confederate shrines.

Progress Opens Up A New Era

The years following the Civil War were devoted to recovering from the loss and destruction of the war. By 1878, when the first official post

---

Manatee County Historical Highlights

New Manatee River Hotel

Location:

309 10th Street,

Bradenton

Built for $850,000 during the 1925 land boom by the Van Seringer Company of Cleveland, the pyramid roof corner towers are an easily identified Bradenton landmark.

Iron Block Building

Location:

530 12th Street,

Bradenton

Moved from its original site on Manatee Avenue and restored to its original 1896 splendor, you'll be impressed by its pressed metal facades.

MANATEE HISTORY © BILL WEST

Manatee County Historical Highlights

Fuller Building
Location:
450 12th Street,
Bradenton
Built in 1905 for the Manatee River National Bank, this three-story Renaissance Revival wonder features decorative tiled parapet and native yellow rock. The addition was built in 1906.

Carnegie Library
Location:
1405 4th Avenue W.,
Bradenton
This 1918 structure houses the state of Florida's first County Historical Records Library. This is a great place to discover more local historical highlights.

office was opened, things were looking up for the community established as Braidentown. Confusion surrounds the first name given to that town, whether a postal clerk misspelled it or a government official misread it, must be left to speculation. At any rate, with an official name, Braidentown began growing and developing into a "modern" town.

A steady program of construction was initiated that lasted through the 1800s. The first pier was built then at the foot of Main Street (12th Street West).

Manatee County entered the 20th century growing by leaps and bounds. The first bridge was built between Palmetto and Braidentown while the Seaboard Air Line Railroad extended rail service to the area. In 1903 Braidentown was incorporated, Judge A.T. Cornwall was elected as its first mayor and the "i" and "w" in the city's name was dropped. The spelling changed to "Bradenton."

After the Great Depression and the ordeal of World War II, Bradenton and the surrounding area found itself once again back on the road to prosperity. Tourists flocked to the area and land sales increased. As the demand for tasteful, inexpensive housing increased, mobile home parks sprang up throughout the county.

All through the following decades Manatee County continued to grow in both population and affluence. Construction skyrocketed – businesses were moving in as fast as buildings could be erected to house them. Today, Manatee County reflects its rich heritage of courageous pioneers, enterprising businessmen and involved citizens in its tremendous popularity as both a vacation spot and permanent home. The great strides taken in technological development coupled with sincere environmental concern allow Manatee residents and visitors alike to enjoy the convenience of modern life in a beautiful, natural setting.

Manatee County Historical Commission
604 15th St. E., Bradenton
741-4075
The Manatee County Historical Commission is a nonprofit corporation, dedicated to preserving the pioneering spirit and heritage of the early settlers of the area. It welcomes donations of money or artifacts. Volunteers are always welcome.

Thanks to Manatee County Historical Commission for information on Manatee Village Historical Park.

Sarasota County History

A few Sarasota County Historic Highlights

Some of the few remaining remnants of 19th century Sarasota history are found downtown. The Bidwell-Wood House at 849 Florida Avenue was built in 1884 and is notorious as the site where the plot to assassinate Sarasota's first postmaster, Charles Albee, was hatched. This violent episode ended years of contention between local farmers and groups of land speculators who, after the Civil War, tried to circumvent the 1862 Homestead Act by terrorizing early settlers. With no organized system to dispense justice, frontier law ruled.

John Hamilton Gillespie arrived from Edinburgh, Scotland, in 1886 to help manage the Florida Mortgage and Investment Company's colony which had arrived the previous December. Gillespie built one of Florida's first golf courses in what is now downtown Sarasota.

By the winter of 1910, Sarasota had a population of less than 1,000, but a visit from Bertha Honore Palmer, a wealthy Chicago civic and social leader, was the catalyst that would help change the little town from a sleepy fishing village to a cosmopolitan city. Her declaration that Sarasota Bay was more beautiful than the Bay of Naples caught the attention of the press and visionaries who led the residents away from their frontier past.

Bee Ridge Community

Named for its bee swarms, Isaac Alderman Redd first settled the area following Florida's Seminole Wars. The town was platted by one of Mrs. Potter Palmer's companies. Her Bee Ridge Hotel opened in 1914 and the new town boasted a railway station, an apartment house, barbershop and store.

The most striking examples of Sarasota's past are landmark homes and commercial buildings which were built during the real estate boom of the '20s. Growth, which normally would have taken decades, was compressed into a few short years in a frenzy of development. Between 1923 and 1926, the town sprouted high rise hotels, theaters, banks, palatial private residences and housing developments.

In these boom years, builders capitalized on our Spanish heritage and many examples of this style of architecture can be found throughout the county.

The Ringlings

John and Charles Ringling, of the famous Ringling Brothers Circus, were major early builders/developers promoting the merits of Sarasota all over the world. Among the impressive reminders are the John and Mable Ringling home, the Ringling Art Museum and the Ringling School of Art and Design. John Ringling also developed Lido Key and built the first bridge linking the islands to Sarasota's mainland.

Theater Arts District

In the heart of the downtown Theater Arts District is the newly restored Sarasota Opera House on Pineapple Avenue, built as the Edwards Theater in 1925 by the city's first mayor.

The Florida Studio Theatre and Theatre Works buildings are both worth a visit, not only for their cultural contributions, but for their historical significance. The Florida Studio Theater building is the original Woman's Club and the Theatre Works' building was originally the Palm Tree Playhouse.

As you drive down Palm Avenue, you will see many rehabilitated early structures in use today as restaurants, art galleries and offices. Continu-

---

Manatee Village Historical Park

Location: Manatee Avenue & 15th Street East, Bradenton;

Information: 741-4075

Imagine this spot 90 years ago. You're in the Village of Manatee. Florida, minus air-conditioning and interstates, is a frontier. The pioneers in this small, but growing settlement on the Manatee River, have carved a center of commerce in their corner of the 5,500 square of mostly wilderness known as Manatee County. The huge county was eventually divided into the counties of Manatee, Sarasota, Hardee, Highlands, Okeechobee, DeSoto, Charlotte and Glades.

Historical Groups

Genealogical Society of Sarasota
Information:
378-0085
Studies in the history of individual family decedents.

Gulf Coast Heritage Association/Historic Spanish Point
Location:
500 N. Tamiami Trail, Osprey 34229
Information:
966-5214
The association preserves, interprets and promotes Historic Spanish Point.

ing south on Pineapple, we come to Burns Court and Herald Square, built by Sarasota's most prominent modern developer, Owen Burns.

Municipal Auditorium

The Florida land bust came in the last months of 1926 when the frantic activity stopped and growth came to a virtual standstill. While the country was in the grip of the Great Depression, the Works Progress Administration (WPA) financed several significant structures, among them, the Municipal Auditorium. Built in 1937, the original Art Deco facade was covered by a 1970s "renovation." Locally designated as a historic structure, the building has been restored to its original appearance with current cause for celebration being the return of the *Hazzard Fountain*, a gift to the city by Mr. and Mrs. Robert P. Hazzard in December of 1940 and missing in storage since the early 1970s.

Sarasota County Department of Historical Resources

Located at 701 Plaza de Santo Domingo, built in 1941 as the public library, it is now the depository of Sarasota County's historical collection. Acting in the public trust, this government agency engages in activities supporting the identification, evaluation, preservation, protection, development and interpretation of Sarasota County's historic resources.

Sarasota Visitor's Information Center

Located at U.S. 41 and Sixth Street, designed by Victor Lundy and built in 1957, this building received national attention for its use of plate glass walls, massive roof and blue tiles imported from Japan by Karl Bickel.

Historic Schools

Several schools built during the 1920s are still in use. Sarasota High School, built in the Collegiate Gothic style, Southside School on South Tamiami Trail and Webber Street and Bay Haven Elementary School on West Tamiami Circle are built in the Mediterranean Revival style. All have served Sarasota students for more than sixty years.

Sarasota Opera House

This beautiful restored building downtown on Pineapple Avenue opened in 1926 as the Edwards Theater. The name was changed to Florida Theater in 1936 and was the site of the world premier of Cecil B. DeMille's *The Greatest Show on Earth* on January 31, 1952.

Sarasota School of Architecture

During the 1950s, Sarasota again began to grow, prosper and modernize. A group of imaginative architects attracted national attention with their contemporary and environmentally oriented style which became known as the Sarasota School of Architecture.

Examples of this style are scattered throughout the area – private residences, schools – the Sarasota High School addition, Riverview High School, Brookside Middle School, Venice-Nokomis High School, Brentwood and Alta Vista Elementary Schools – and commercial buildings, the Summerhouse Restaurant on Siesta Key and the Sarasota Herald-Tribune Building, to name a few.

Design statements by Ralph Twitchell, Paul Rudolph and other members of the Sarasota School of Architecture made its mark on our landscape from 1941 to 1965. The most concentrated wealth of examples can be found in Lido Shores, developed on New Pass in the 1950s by Phillip Hiss. At the time it was a new, almost revolutionary, form of architecture.

Many of the original houses built during this period have been removed, altered or compromised. However, those examples which have survived are now being meticulously restored by their owners and anyone with a love for aesthetics, design and history will clearly appreciate their efforts. Of course, it doesn't hurt to have a national spotlight on your home either: in 1995 John Howey published "The Sarasota School of Architecture" (MIT Press). In an area known for the arts you can understand why a lucky (or astute) few can find cultural comfort by dwelling in a modern masterpiece.

SARASOTA'S HISTORIC NEIGHBORHOODS
Gillespie Park
When the city of Sarasota was platted in 1886, the Gillespie Park area was designated an experimental farm to promote agriculture in the new city. The effort failed because the soil was unsuitable for farming, but beginning in 1913, residential subdivisions were platted in the area. The real estate boom of the 1920s brought many people to the neighborhood who built middle class homes of excellent quality and craftsmanship.

A focal point of the Gillespie Park neighborhood is the historic park named after J. Hamilton Gillespie, one of Sarasota's early prominent citizens. The city created the park on ten acres of undeveloped land purchased for that purpose in 1924. Gillespie Park was developed with special emphasis on recreation for children and, in 1926, won an award in the National Playground Beautification Contest. An oasis of trees and green open space, Gillespie Park now provides tennis courts, picnic pavilion, playground recreational facilities, and features a lovely meandering pond.

Laurel Park
(bounded by Main Street on the north and Gulfstream Avenue on the south, between U.S. 301 and Orange Avenue.)

The history of this downtown neighborhood dates to the late 1800s when it was included in the original town plat. Most of the homes were built in the Craftsman Bungalow and Mediterranean Revival Styles between 1900 and 1926 by circus performers, city officials and downtown business owners.

Now Laurel Park, with an active neighborhood association working for improvements and conservation districts, is coming to the attention of young professionals, artists and families who are purchasing and restoring its charming old houses.

Bungalow Hill
(bounded by Hudson Bayou on the north and Bahia Vista on the south, between Orange and Osprey Avenues)

When the city of Sarasota cast a speculative eye on the Bungalow Hill subdivision in 1915 with thoughts of annexation, the "Bungalow Hillers" responded by incorporating as an independent municipality and called their little town, Sarasota Heights. They had no intention of paying the high city taxes when they knew it would be many years before they would benefit from infrastructure provided by the city.

This very successful subdivision was platted in 1921 and called Bungalow Hill because it sat on a hill overlooking Sarasota Bay and most of the structures were the popular Craftsman Bungalow Style.

Many significant early houses still remain in this lovely, quiet neighborhood. Rigby/LaPlaza Subdivision is a locally designated historic district on Osprey Avenue between Alta Vista and Bahia Vista Streets.

McClellan Park
(bounded by Hyde Park Street on the north and Cunliff Lane on the south, between Osprey Avenue and the Sarasota Bay)

Historical Groups

Historic Preservation Coalition

Mailing address: Rt 2, box 695, Arcadia 33821

Information: 322-1850

A coalition of 14 preservation organizations working togethertho increase public awareness of the importance of historic preservation and to protect these resources.

Historical Groups

Historical Records Library of Manatee County

Location:
1405 4th Ave. W.,
Bradenton 34205
www.clerkofcourts.com

Information:
741-4070

Hours: 8:30 a.m. - 5:00 p.m. Monday - Friday

Opened in 1979, it was the first county archival library of its kind in the State of Florida. Houses county historical records, open to the public.

An arched entrance with pergolas on Orange Avenue leads to Sarasota's first suburban community. Katherine and Daisy McClellan's plans for an exclusive residential area began with the purchase of 57 acres on Sarasota Bay early in 1915.

The McClellan Park neighborhood is interesting because of the wide variety of architectural styles that reflect its long growth period – Craftsman Bungalow Style, Spanish style and Tudor Revival houses, and houses built in the '40s, '50s and '60s.

Of special interest is the McClellan Park School which is surrounded by Oval Drive between Osprey Avenue and McClellan Parkway. Built in 1915 to serve as the clubhouse for the subdivision, the Craftsman-style wood frame building rests on an Indian mound. Many street names in this area reflect this heritage.

Granada
(bounded by Siesta Drive on the north and Bay Road on the south, between Osprey Avenue and Tangier Terrace)

Lucky Charley Tyson of Lebanon, Tennessee, came to town in 1924 and began buying up undeveloped acreage along Siesta Drive from Osprey Avenue to the bridge. Local folks shook their heads and wondered that anyone would pay so much money for all that palmetto scrub.

His keen judgment and hard work paid off. A year later, his beautiful Granada was, according to the contemporary press, "a beehive of energy, a picture of artistic merit."

This lovely quiet neighborhood now contains an interesting variety of styles – excellent examples of Craftsman bungalows and elegant Spanish styles.

Granada was a favorite of prolific architect, Thomas Reed Martin, who chose it for his home and office in his later years. Referred to as the "father of Sarasota architecture," Martin designed more than 500 structures throughout the county from 1910-1949.

Indian Beach/Sapphire Shores
(bounded by Indian Beach Drive [27th Street] on the south and the Ringling complex on the north, between U.S. 41 and Sarasota Bay)

During the 1920s land boom, wealthy New Yorkers bought choice waterfront lots in the new Indian Beach Subdivision which was promoted as the "ultra-exclusive residential area" on beautiful Sarasota Bay.

As you travel Bayshore Road and its cross streets, you will see many beautiful preserved important historic homes, both large and small in this neighborhood.

It is also in this neighborhood that you will find the preserved, palatial homes of three early Sarasota movers and shakers side by side on Sarasota Bay – John Ringling, Charles Ringling and their good friend, Ralph Caples – and the Ringling Museum.

SARASOTA CIRCUS HISTORY AND THE RINGLINGS

No clowning around, we take the circus very seriously. The notion of Sarasota as "The Athens of the Gulf Coast" was put in place by John and Charles Ringling who moved the winter quarters of the Ringling Brothers and Barnum & Bailey Circus from Bridgeport, Connecticut to Sarasota in 1927. The Ringlings were convinced that this area was prime for growth. At one time they owned tens of thousand of acres here and planned to build a casino to attract tourists.

The crash of 1929 and the following Great Depression put an end to their dreams of development. However, their influence continues to play a significant role in the area:

The John and Mable Ringling Museum of Art
Combines a world class art collection, circus memorabilia and gardens filled with majestic statues of antiquity. The palatial Ca'd'Zan, located on the grounds of the museum, was their home. As a collector of Italian baroque and renaissance art (including huge paintings by Paul Rubens) John Ringling built the museum which he left to the State of Florida.

Lido Key
John Ringling's dream location for a resort community was once a series of unconnected islands. Just before the crash of 1929, Ringling filled the areas between the islands and built a causeway reaching from the mainland thus opening up the newly formed Lido area.

St. Armands Circle
Designed by John Ringling as part of the Ringling Estates subdivision and dotted with his numerous Italian baroque statues, it is now a shopper's mecca. Ringling built the original wooden causeway to provide automobile access to his development. The modern causeway is named after him.

Courthouse Subdivision
Designed by Charles Ringling, the Courthouse Subdivision was platted on land which had been part of John Hamilton Gillespie's nine-hole golf course. It extended from Links Avenue to School Avenue and from Main Street to Golf Street and Adams Lane. Ringling provided some of the land for the Dwight James Baum designed courthouse which opened in 1927. His Charles Ringling Hotel, later the Sarasota Terrace Hotel, now the county administration building at 101 South Washington Boulevard, opened in 1926.

THE TRADITION CONTINUES

No question about it, without the Ringlings things would be much different around here. However, the Ringling legacy is only one part of our circus heritage.

Currently there are 15 circus companies with headquarters in Sarasota County. You'll find more circus people living here, both active and retired, than in any one place in the world.

Part of the 1952 circus film "The Greatest Show on Earth" was filmed in Sarasota, which, of course, must explain why it won an Academy Award for Best Picture of the Year – after seeing the film, no other explanation comes to mind.

The National Circus School of Performing Arts
Information: 924-7054 *Fax:* 924-1621
This new addition to Sarasota's long love affair with the circus was established in October 1998. Continuing the circus heritage established by John Ringling, schools for drama, ballet, art, opera, instrumental and choral music are being planned at publication time with classes scheduled to begin in January, 1999.

Sarasota Sailor Circus
2075 Bahia Vista, Sarasota 34239
Tickets: 361-6350
Prices: $6.00 or $7.00, depending on seat; reservations a must!
1998 Performance Schedule:
7:15 p.m. March 18-20, 24-26, 31, April 1 andl 3
Matinee : March 21
Founded in 1943, the Sarasota Sailor Circus is the only extra curricular after school three-ring student circus in the United States sanctioned

Historical Groups

Historical Society of Sarasota County
Information:
364-9076
Their purpose is to create a public awareness of the historical heritage of Sarasota County. The Society encourages collection, preservation, research in and interpretation of materials relating to the area's history.

Historical Groups

Sarasota Alliance For Historic Preservation

Information: 957-1115

A nonprofit community organization dedicated to the preservation of Sarasota's historic resources. Special events throughout the year including annual Historic Homes Tour every February, this year on the 5th from 11 a.m. to 5 p.m. Call for details.

by a school board. Participants (grades 3-12, all attending Sarasota County public or private schools) perform at professional level acts. "Sailor Circus" name comes from a time when Sarasota High School athletes had to travel by boat to play compteting teams in Tampa Bay.

OTHER HISTORICAL POINTS OF INTEREST

U.S.S. Sarasota

A Naval attack transport, the U.S.S. Sarasota, was built in California in 1944. She was named after the County of Sarasota and served in the southwest Pacific during World War II. During the war, the ship transported troops, defended itself against air attacks, came to the aid of wounded ships and took part in assaults and landings on Ie Shima, Okinawa and the Philippines.

After the surrender of Japan, the U.S.S. Sarasota served as part of the Magic Carpet Fleet which transported servicemen back to the United States and supplied the occupation forces in Japan. After almost two years of service, she was decommissioned in California in 1946. The ship was recommissioned in 1951, operated in the Mediterranean and was used in training exercises in the Atlantic Ocean and the Caribbean.

She dropped anchor in Sarasota in 1951 and again in 1953. On both occasions the officers and crew demonstrated a wartime landing and beachhead operation by staging a mock invasion of Lido Beach, coming ashore in assault boats.

The U.S.S. Sarasota was decommissioned in 1955. In 1983 she was sold as scrap.

The wood and brass official model of the U.S.S. Sarasota, built to a precise one to 48 scale – four feet tall and eleven and a half feet long – was moved to Sarasota in 1989 from Washington, D.C. where it was on display in the Navy Museum. Davi and Valenti Movers transported the model to Sarasota at no cost. The model is now on permanent display in the lobby of the Sarasota County Administration Building, 101 S. Washington Boulevard, through the hard work and dedication of a few local residents and the support of many local organizations.

History of Venice

Venice was first settled in the 1870s by Robert Rickford Roberts who established a 121 acre homestead on the south end of the bay which was named for him. In 1882, he sold some of his property to Frank Higel who established a citrus operation and whose descendents dominated the Venice area until the mid-1910s.

Originally called "Horse and Chaise" because of a carriage-like tree formation that marked the spot for fishermen, the city acquired its more elegant name in 1888. That was the year the city acquired its first post office "Venice" – a name suggested by Frank Higel and adopted by the city as its own, after the canal city in Italy.

Mrs. Bertha Palmer, with a portion of the magnificent fortune inherited from her late husband and owner of Chicago's famed Palmer House Hotel, purchased 140,000 acres of wild Florida frontier land. She built *The Oaks*, an elegant winter residence in nearby Osprey which attracted notice in northern newspapers of the time. Mrs. Palmer successfully lobbied to have the railroad line extended to Venice in 1911. The importance of this event cannot be overstated as it placed Venice on the path of progress and new development.

Just five years later, noted New York physician, Dr. Fred Albee, came to Venice with a dream. He wanted to build a "model city," and

Historical Groups

Venice Archives and Area Historical Collection

Location:

351 S. Nassau St., Venice

www.venice-florida.com

Information:

486-2487

Government agency to collect and preserve historical and archaeological material relating to the Venice area.

commissioned John Nolan to create what may have been Florida's first master planned community. Albee envisioned agriculture, industry, commerce, housing and recreation harmoniously coexisting. During the real estate boom of the 1920s, and thanks to a cash infusion by the Brotherhood of Locomotive Engineers (BLE) of Cleveland, Ohio, the plans began to turn into reality. Homes and businesses featuring graceful Italianate architecture were constructed, and the town became home for many of the retired members of the wealthy union. By June 1926, the three-story Venice Hotel (now Park Place) was completed by the BLE and the $1 million per month development of a model city had begun. The New York architectural firm of Walker and Gillette was hired to ensure that all construction would conform to the "northern Italian" theme designed to give the community its unique character. By 1927, the City of Venice was incorporated.

But hard times were just around the corner. The Great Depression left Venice and most other Florida cities in desolation. Venice was a virtual ghost town with more than 200 commercial and residential structures, 141 apartments, 10.5 miles of paved streets, 15 miles of sidewalks, seven miles of underground storm drains, 13 miles of water pipes and a water treatment plant. The real estate operations of the BLE went into receivership and most of the unsold land reverted to Albee and other creditors.

Venice began its economic recovery in 1932 when the Kentucky Military Institute (KMI) rented the Venice Hotel (now Park Place) and the San Marco Hotel (now Venice Centre Mall) as winter quarters for its cadets.

In 1933, Dr. Albee purchased the Park View Hotel (later demolished for a post office) and established the Florida Medical Center as a successful teaching hospital. In 1942, the U.S. government began construction of the Venice Army Air Base on property south of the city. The base trained fighter pilots throughout World War II and was a major influence on the development of the city.

In the 1960s The Corps of Engineers initiated work on the Intracoastal Waterway as a way of moving freight through the state. The happy result was the increase in pleasure boating in Venice and across Florida.

The 1960s also saw the arrival of the famous Ringling Brothers and Barnum & Baily Circus. In 1968 the circus founded the Clown College in Venice, renowned as one of the most prestigious training schools in the world for professional clowns. Clown College left the area in

Historical Groups

Time Sifters
Archaeology Society
Information:
924-2446
Meetings and lectures of archealogical historical interest; a chapter member of the Florida Anthropological Society.

Venice Historic and Preservation League
Information:
485-6062
Historical and preservation society concerned with the history and resources of the Venice area.

Warm Mineral Springs Archaeological Society
Information:
484-4037
Provides lectures, classes and exploration of local "finds."

1994. At press time negotiations were underway to bring the Florida Military Aviation Museum on the property that housed the circus.

Venice has evolved into a charming and lively town, an outstanding example of a planned Florida community with a wealth of "northern Italian" style structures populated by a warm and caring population.

Heritage Park
This linear park occupies the landscaped median of Venice Avenue from west of the downtown business district to the Gulf of Mexico. The stately live oaks and Canary Island Date Palms that line the street are prominent features of this 52 acre open space. This promenade is one of the many attractive green spaces and parks throughout the Venice plan.

Veterans Memorial Court
Located at the western end of the park, this court is dominated by a massive granite monument which honors veterans of all wars.

Air Base Court
This scale replica of the main entrance gate to the Venice Army Air Base dramatizes the tremendous impact that the building of the base by the U.S. Army had on the community. During World War II, more than 20,000 pilots and service personnel were trained at the base – the servicemen outnumbered the residents. After the war, many servicemen stationed at Venice returned to become the civic leaders of the 1950s and 1960s.

Indian Court
Long before the Spanish arrived, the west coast of Florida was inhabited by the Calusa Indians, formidable warriors and fishermen who prospered because of the rich marine life along the coast. In the early 1700s, Creek related tribes from the Carolinas moved into Florida and displaced the Calusa. During the 1800s the U.S. Army sought to displace the Seminoles leading to the three Seminole Wars. The court highlights Seminole chief Billy Bowlegs and his tribe's resistance to the army.

Archaeological Court
During the last ice age Florida was home to many species of giant mammals including the woolly mammoth, giant camel and giant sloth. Numerous fossils have been found throughout the Venice area including those of a complete woolly mammoth estimated to be 14 feet high and 20 feet long found during the 1920s. Canal and lake excavations have unearthed many finds for amateur paleontologists.

Pioneer Court
During the second half of the last century settlers arrived in the Venice area and sustained themselves through fishing, cattle ranching and citrus growing. The relief on this monument pays tribute to their industry as well as their determination. By the turn of the century they welcomed winter visitors, and the area's thriving tourist and retirement industry had begun.

Heritage Court
This court acknowledges the efforts of Dr. Fred Albee, John Nolen, and the Brotherhood of Locomotive Engineers in creating the city of Venice. Dr. Albee owned the land, John Nolen created the city plan, and the BLE built the city according to the Nolen plan after purchasing the land from Albee. The court contains the only known plaque to a city planner.

HISTORIC NEIGHBORHOODS OF VENICE

Venezia Park Historic District
Consists of structures on Harbor Drive South, Sorrento, Salerno, Nassau and Palermo Place near Venezia Park)

Listed on the National Register of Historic Places on December 18, 1989, this neighborhood of medium and large homes surrounds Venezia Park, a large trapezoidal-shaped park. The area is characterized by low density single-family dwellings that were built in the mandated "northern Italian" or Mediterranean Revival architectural style. Homes are detached one- and two-story structures, each with a separate auto park and, in many cases, servants' quarters.

Edgewood Historic District
(Consists of structures on Groveland and Myrtle Avenues east of Bypass 41)

Listed on the National Register of Historic Places in 1989, this neighborhood has smaller lots and more modest homes than other residential areas in Nolen's plan. Because the architectural guidelines were not strictly enforced, this district contains bungalows and structures of frame vernacular construction, as well as Mediterranean Revival or Mission style structures.

Apartment District
(Consists of structures on Armada Road, Menendez Court and Palmetto Court)

Listed on the National Register of Historic Places in 1989, this district consists of multi-family Mediterranean Revival apartment blocks built according to the comprehensive plan of John Nolen. This medium density area was designed around Palmetto Park which provides open space and recreation for the apartment residents. This area provided the community with an alternative to single family residences. This diversity of housing types was an important element in Nolen's plan. Granada Apartments, with its romantic courtyard, is an excellent example of the multi-family units constructed during the 1920s.

Eagle Point
(Located at the north entrance to Venice, west of U.S. 41 on Roberts Bay)

Listed on the National Register of Historic Places, this property was originally owned by Bertha Honore Palmer. Built in 1911 as an elite hunting and fishing resort, it welcomed governors and corporate executives to its secluded surroundings. When converted to a residential community in 1989, it was the oldest continuously operated business in Sarasota County. The clubhouse, guest cottage, water tower, and several small utility buildings have been restored for use by the residents of the development.

Downtown Historic Area
(Located between business 41 on the east, Tampa Avenue on the north, Harbor Drive on the west, and Miami Avenue on the south)

This area was designated in the John Nolen plan as the commercial center of the city. Numerous two-story business structures were constructed during the 1920s, many with rental apartments above the store fronts. In addition, two three-story hotels were built north of Tampa Avenue by the Brotherhood of Locomotive Engineers. Both structures have been restored and converted to new uses. One is a retirement residence known as Park Place and the other is a condominium with shops on the first floor and residences on the upper floors known as the Venice Centre Mall.

Local History Books

Master Sarasota historian Jeff LaHurd has published a definitive, yet continuing, collection of fascinating books on local history including *Quintessential Sarasota; Sarasota, A Sentimental Journey; Lido Casino, Lost Treasure on the Beach; Sarasota, Then and Now; Come On Down, Pitching Paradise;* and the soon to be published *Aristocrat of Beauty, The Story of the John Ringling Towers.*

Titles are available at all right-thinking area bookstores.

Local History Books

Also worth noting:
The Ringling Legacy by Pat Ringling Buck – grandniece of John and Charles Ringling; *The Sarasota School of Architecture* by John Howey (MIT Press).

HISTORIC STRUCTURES

Venice Train Depot
(Located on East Venice Avenue, west of the Intracoastal Waterway)

Using heavy timbers from their own sawmill, the Brotherhood of Locomotive Engineers built this Mediterranean Revival-style railroad depot in 1927. Listed on the National Register of Historic Places, it is the only remaining depot in Sarasota County. Federal funds have been programmed by the Florida Dept. of Transportation for the purchase and restoration of this building.

Hotel Venice
(200 N. Nassau Street, now the Park Place Retirement Residence)

This 100-room Italian Renaissance palace rose up in a sea of sand and scrub pine. Listed on the National Register of Historic Places in 1984, it was the first Venice building to be so designated. Restored to its original grandeur, the building is now an adult congregate living facility.

Triangle Inn
351 S. Nassau Street

This important structure gets its name from the triangular lot it was designed to fit when it was built in 1927. This outstanding example of Mediterranean Revival style architecture has a prominent tower and green concrete roof tile. In the process of restoration, it will be the home of the Venice archives and historical collection.

Thanks to the following for assistance with our history lesson:
Manatee County Chamber of Commerce; Nancy Wilke of the Sarasota Alliance for Historic Preservation; Ann Shank, historian at the Sarasota County Dept. of Historical Resources; Dorothy Korwek, chairperson of the City of Venice Historical Commission; Venice Hospital.

HISTORIC TOUR OF VENICE

Historic Transportation Inc.
Reservations: 488-2521
Prices: $7.00, adults; $5.00 children 6-12; 5 and under free
An 1 hour 15 min. tour of the City of Venice including 100 year area history, unique buildings, circus influence, air base impact the and development of the south Venice area - all from an antique fire truck, now converted to an open-air bus. Fascinating, informative and fun. Reservations a must.

Modern Times

DOWNTOWN ARCHITECTURE © BILL WEST

IT'S AN ATTITUDE THING.

People who live here year-round know that the real attraction of the area is the consistent quality of life, clean environment, support of the arts and a basically comfortable Midwest pace.

People who live here year-round think (okay, *know*) that it doesn't get much better than this.

Naturally, we will always have our little challenges. Road construction, thunderstorms and April 15th are some of the expected ones.

It's been said that how we deal with the unexpected is what defines our character and who we are as individuals. So do us all a favor - including yourself - keep your chin up.

Five ways you can do your part in maintaining the homeostasis:
1) Relax.
2) Smile.
3) Have fun.
4) Think about the alternative – life in Los Angeles.
5) And (at least while you are here) enjoy yourself.

Tools of The Trade

Human Resources
The regional labor force is somewhere near 290,000 and the prime working age group (18-44) accounts for around one-third of the population. Florida is a right-to-work state which means highly competitive wage rates. There are a number of direct ways in which business, labor and government interact.

Free Advice
The Small Business Development Center of the University of South Florida and both the Greater Sarasota Chamber of Commerce and Manatee Chamber of Commerce are now offering free business counseling to area business people in need of advice on developing business plans, advertising, financing and other steps to starting a small business. In Sarasota, USF management counselor **Bill Manck** offers help; call **955-2508, ext. 248**. In Manatee County, schedule an appointment with USF management counselor **Jim Parrish** at **748-4842**

Comcast@Home in Sarasota
5205 Fruitville Rd., Sarasota; 1-888-793-4800 (toll free)
Sarasota is the second city in the nation to receive the Comcast@Home service, one of the few multi-megabit residential services being offered for sale in the world. The fastest Internet access commercially available – not through telephone lines but through high speed cable modems – delivering information hundreds of times faster than traditional dial-up phone modems thanks to a new $50 million fiber optic network which was installed in Sarasota County and parts of Manatee County. Thanks to Comcast, local business and residents are now on the cutting edge of the emerging Information Age. Check out *The Guide* in Cyberspace: http://www.ExploreFlorida.com.

Sarasota County Committee for Economic Development
1819 Main Street, Suite 240; Sarasota 34236
955-2508, Ext. 237; fax 951-7837
e-mail: frank@searchesmart.usf.edu; www.sarasotachamber.org
According to Executive Director, **Frank Tamberrino**, "The Sarasota County Committee of 100 is the professional economic development entity for Sarasota County. It works to: attract and retain quality jobs; solicit new business compatible with the assets and values of Sarasota County; promote Sarasota County's business image; assist expansion of existing companies; enhance Sarasota County's overall quality of life."

Manatee Economic Development Council
222 10th St. W, Bradenton 34205
748-4842, Ext. 27; www.manateechamber.com/edc
According to Executive Director, **Nancy Engel**, "The Economic Development Council is a division of the Manatee Chamber of Commerce. The council provides assistance to both relocating and existing companies. Services include confidential site and building searches, permitting and workforce assistance, an employee relocation program, demographic packages and international trade and supplier networks. The council focuses on helping companies grow in Manatee County."

SCORE – Service Corps of Retired Executives
222 10th St., Bradenton 34205
748-3411 (ask for SCORE)
The mission of this organization is to help people find the means and experience to get into business for themselves. We don't know of a better resource available for obtaining sage wisdom. Virtually all

---

Networking

Executive Network
Information:
378-0608
Every Tues. morning at the Waterside Room at the Quay

North Sarasota Business and Professional Women's Club
Information:
359-8191
Second Sunday of the month.

Palm Aire Jaycees
Information:
955-1421
Meets fourth Wednesday.

Power Network
Information:
365-3650
Every Weds.
12:00 p.m. Cafe Baci.

Professional Network
Information:
377-6000, ext. 214
Every Tues. 12:30 p.m. at Cafe Baci.

THE BUSINESS OF DOING BUSINESS

Richard Stern

According to **Richard Stern**, NEWS40 Business Commentator, it couldn't be a better time to be involved in doing business on the Suncoast. "Real estate is booming, both Manatee and Sarasota counties are experiencing some of the best new business growth statistics in their history while unemployment has reached record lows. The retail outlook is also rosy; Gulf Coast Factory Shops have changed its name to Prime Outlets and now includes 135 stores spread over 482,000 square feet. Sarasota Outlet Center has new owners who promise expansion and redevelopment. Gulf Gate Mall's walls came down, getting ready for their own make-over (Uptons, Old Navy, Bed, Bath & Beyond are promised) and two - yes two! - multi-screen movie/malls are planned for Bradenton. Things continue to expand here, quickly."

members have "been there, done that," and at least one member will know how to avoid the potential pitfalls associated with your own business quest. Best of all (and what immediately places this group into our permanent "Local Heroes" file) is the fact that there is never a charge for their expertise. Yep, a free lunch

Training Resourses

Manatee Community College
5840 26th St, W, Bradenton 34207
755-1511; fax, 753-0853; www.mcc.cc.fl.us

Over 8,000 students and an occupational-technical program which can be designed for individual companies.

Sarasota County Technical Institute
4748 Beneva Rd., Sarasota 34233
924-1365; fax 921-7902; www.careerscape.org

Over 45 full-time training programs including an Industry Services program with emphasis on customized employee training.

Business Numbers You Can Count On

Advertising Federation of the Suncoast	918-0133
Better Business Council	748-1325 (Bradenton)
	366-3144 (Sarasota)
	485-3510 (Venice)
Citizen Dispute Center	363-7833
Chambers of Commerce	778-1541 (*Ana Maria Isl.*)
	383-2466 (*Longboat Key*)
Chambers of Commerce	748-3411 (*Manatee Co.*)

ABEL, BAND, RUSSELL, COLLIER, PITCHFORD & GORDON
CHARTERED

ATTORNEYS AND COUNSELORS AT LAW

- General Civil Law Practice
- Property Acquisition And Development
- Banking Law
- Real Estate Law/Title Insurance
- Corporation And Business Law
- Corporate And Individual taxation
- Mobile Home Park Law
- Securities Litigation
- Pension And Profit Sharing Plans And IRA Distributions
- Construction Law And Litigation
- Intellectual Property Law
- Commercial Litigation
- Bankruptcy Law
- Probate
- Estate Planning
- Wills And Trusts
- Environmental Law
- Land Use And Zoning

Anthony J. Abate✦
Saralyn Abel
David S. Band
Kathryn Angell Carr*
Steven J. Chase**
Ronald L. Collier
Kathleen M.P. Davis
Kenneth D. Doerr
Cheryl L. Gordon
Scott E. Gordon*
Scott A. Haas
Benjamin R. Hanan
Mark D. Hildreth***
James F. Kiely
William R. Korp*
Kurt E. Lee
Barbara B. Levin
George H. Mazzarantani
Jan Walters Pitchford*
Malcolm J. Pitchford*✦
Jeffrey S. Russell*
Michael S. Taaffe****
David S. Watson
John W. West III

Of Counsel
Harvey J. Abel
Richard W. Cooney
Johnson S. Savary✦

*Board Certified
Real Estate Lawyer

**Board Certified
Civil Trial Lawyer

***Board Certified
Business Bankruptcy Law By The
American Board of Certification

****Board Certified
Business Litigation Lawyer

Florida Supreme Court
Certified Mediator
✦Civil Court

Huntington Plaza
240 South Pineapple Avenue ■ P.O. Box 49948
Sarasota, Florida 34230-6948
Phone (941) 366-6660 ■ Fax (941) 366-3999
www.abelband.com

Tandem Center
Suite 199 ■ 333 Tamiami Trail South
Venice, Florida 34285
Phone (941) 485-8200 ■ Fax (941) 488-9436
EMAIL: information@abelband.com

The hiring of a lawyer is an important decision that should not be based solely upon advertisements.
Before you decide, ask us to send you free written information about our qualifications and experience.

Outdoor Space Planning, Design & Installation

Creating Stunning Outdoor Spaces in Sarasota's Finest Neighborhoods

- **Phenomenal Gardens**
- **Design Service**
- **Pond & Waterfalls**
- **Natural Outdoor Environments**

941.923.0618
941.925.9668 fax
email: sandt@gate.net

Outdoor Architecture & Landscape Design

	955-8187 (*Greater Sarasota*)
	349-3800 (*Siesta Key*)
	488-2336 (*Venice*)
Florida Public Relations Association	739-4801
Gulf Coast Legal Services	746-6151 (Manatee County)
	366-1746 (Sarasota County)
Jobs & Benefits	741-3030 (Bradenton)
	361-6100 (Sarasota)
	483-5935 (Venice)
Lawyer Referral Service	1-800-342-8011
Small Business Development Center	955-8187
Sarasota Bradenton Venice Advertising Federation	918-0133
Sarasota/Manatee International Trade Club	358-8850
SCORE (Service Corps of Retired Executives Assoc.)	748-3411

American Business Women's Association

The mission statement of the American Business Women's Association (ABWA) is to bring together business women of diverse occupations and to provide opportunities for them to help themselves and others grow personally and professionally through leadership, education, networking support and national recognition.

The ABWA was founded in 1949 on the premise that working women, together, could determine their own futures. Those charter members who set new goals for women also realized that education was the key both for developing personal opportunities and for ensuring the success of future generations.

As local chapters developed throughout the country in response to this unique women's support system, ABWA became an important focus for women who saw their business roles changing. Today, ABWA members enjoy extensive national and local support systems with members representing virtually every occupational and professional category.

Within the tri-city area of Sarasota, Bradenton and Venice there are nine local chapters:

All Achievers
954-4730
Meets second Thursday of the month at Walt's Oyster Bar.

Ringling Chapter
924-1624
Meets second Tuesday of the month at Red Lobster.

Sun 'n Surf
488-8771
Meets first Wed. of the month at Village on The Isle.

Sunrise
351-2400
Meets second Wednesday of the month at the Waterside Room at the Quay

Sunset
922-7752
Meets third Thursday of the month, call for location.

Networking

Sarasota County Bar Association

Information:

366-6703

Dates and locations vary each month.

Woman's Network

Information:

388-2416

First Tues. of the month at Sarasota Main Plaza, 2nd floor conference room, 5:30 p.m.

Woman's Owner's Network

Information:

922-8639

Second Monday each month at 6 p.m. Call for location.

ONE SARASOTA TOWER © BILL WEST

LIVING IN PARADISE

Bob Harrigan

WWSB Channel 40 Chief Meteorologist **Bob Harrigan**, has been tracking hurricanes on NEWS40 for more than a decade. In fact, he flew into the eye of Hurricane Bertha in 1996 aboard a hurricane hunter aircraft. Bob received his Meteorological degree at the University of Kansas. Before coming to Sarasota he worked for the National Weather Service and taught several weather classes. Bob donates much of his time to area school children and volunteer groups such as MDA and UCP. "This is the best place in the country to do weather," explains Bob. "The chance for snow is zero percent!"

Living In Paradise

The subtropics. That's the ticket. What other climate conjures up such romantic, exotic and deeply lush images?

We have all the trappings of Gilligan's Island: wild parrots, wild chameleons, wild armadillos, wild possum, wild palm trees (some with wild coconuts), wild dolphin, wild bugs and, yes, sometimes even wild parties.

Okay, the parties and bugs don't thrill everybody, but you have to admit, they both can get pretty darn big around here. Still, when it comes to big, nothing is bigger than our sky. That's the thing you fall in love with the first time you cross the Ringling Causeway and head towards the Gulf of Mexico – it's the gorgeous puffy cumulus clouds that roll from the interior part of the state over to the coast every afternoon. It gives us spectacular skies, and big thunderstorms.

Late afternoon and early evening, those clouds move out onto the Gulf of Mexico creating some of the most extraordinary sunsets you've ever seen – you just can't beat the white sand beaches going up and down, north to south, as far as the eye can see – sunsets with a full range of reds, purples and oranges. Any given evening you can expect about 5,000 or so other friendly people on the beach sharing the sunset with you.

To the untrained eye, to someone who has never lived here, one might ask, Why would you want to live where the seasons never change?

The fact is, the seasons do change.

Just ask WWSB, Channel 40 Meteorologist **Bob Harrigan**:

"Why would you want to live where the seasons never change? The answer is why wouldn't you? The weather is perfect. Who would want to live anywhere else?

You don't have to shovel snow, rake leaves or scrape ice off your car. And if you want to see the leaves change color – or snow, for that matter – just take a quick road trip to North Carolina.

Sure it gets hot in the summer, but hey! we have afternoon thunderstorms to cool us off, unlike the Midwest where the heat goes on and on and on.

Hurricane season can be tricky, but the Suncoast is the least likely place to be hit by a major hurricane than all the U.S. coastline. In the 12 years I have been here the storms that had a direct impact on our coast came toward the tail end of the season, October and November and those were small storms, with the exception of Hurricane Georges. But even there we were lucky yet again.

I feel I am truly blessed to live and work in such a beautiful area. The white sandy beaches and the usually beautiful weather makes for a perfect place in paradise to live. That's why I've stuck around so long. Besides, where else would I see so many of my family and friends every year? Des Moines, Iowa? NOT! "

Monthly Temperatures

	High	Low	Gulf	Rainfall
January	72	51	60	2.3
February	74	57	65	1.5
March	77	57	65	4.3
April	81	59	72	1.0
May	87	68	80	2.5
June	89	73	83	5.0
July	92	75	86	6.2
August	91	74	86	5.4
September	89	73	85	3.9
October	85	68	78	4.5
November	80	69	73	1.3
December	73	59	66	1.9

Average Annual Temperature	71.9 Degrees
Average Summer Temperature	80.1 Degrees
Average Winter Temperature	61.5 Degrees
Average Rainfall	39.8"
Average Snowfall	0.0"
Average Relative Humidity	High 83% - Low 58%
Prevailing Wind	East
Elevation	18 Feet

Weather Words for the Wise

Tropical Disturbance

The first stage of unstable weather with the potential to develop into a hurricane.

Tropical Depression

Weather disturbance with significantly defined low pressure area; highest wind speed is 38 m.p.h..

Small-Craft Advisory

Small craft is advised not to venture in open sea, wind speeds are between 21 to 38 m.p.h.

Tropical Storm

Winds reach 39 to 73 m.p.h., low pressure area of storm has clearly defined rotating circulation.

Tropical Storm Watch

Announcement is made when tropical storm poses threat to coastal areas within a 36 hour window.

SARASOTA SUNSET © BILL WEST

Weather Words for the Wise

Hurricane
A tropical storm with a constant wind speed of 74 m.p.h. or greater.

Hurricane Watch
Announcement is made when hurricane conditions pose a threat to coastal areas within a 36 hour window.

Hurricane Warning
Announcement is made when it is believed that a hurricane is expected to slam into a specific coastal area.

However, hurricanes are often erratic (much like politicians) so this warning may not be issued until only hours before hurricane conditions are actualized.

It's best to *never* trust a hurricane to do what you think it will do – be prepared to leave the area – you can draw your own conclusion about politicians.

Summer
Before air conditioning, few people did much in the summer time. If you enjoy the heat, the summer is wonderful. The heat sends you looking for shade. The best thing to do between 10:00 a.m. and 2:00 p.m. is to nap on the beach and let the breezes lull you. There's an afternoon sea breeze that's created by the uniqueness of the Florida peninsula which allows for convergence winds to occur – winds created by the heat rising in the central part of the peninsula along with winds coming off the water onto the beaches. So, the only place to be before modern times was on the beach – that was the only place where one could find a breath of air. These days, however, you're more likely to find a crowd at the matinee in a comfy air conditioned theater. The light traffic flow reflects the fact that our northern friends are home, leaving our sun drenched beaches and balmy weather almost exclusively to the locals and foreign visitors on holiday, it's a time to relish the luxury of relative solitude.

Autumn and Spring
No matter how much you love the heat, by Labor Day, you are ready to move to Alaska. You'll see the changing angle of the sun and it looks like it ought to start getting cooler. By the middle of October, it does. It's then you'll spot your first "Snowbird" – easily recognizable by the Illinois or Ohio license plate. Much like up north, where the first robin of spring signals the promise of inevitable thaw, the first out-of-state license is a sure sign that the invasion of tourists will be upon us soon. The nights become amazingly comfortable. You can open up the windows and have the ceiling fans going and, pretty soon, it becomes glorious. Heaven-like. An ideal temperature is 72 degrees and it's 72 degrees at night from August through April so night times are just wonderful. Once you get into mid-October and November, the days become perfect all the way through June.

Winter
Between October and March it's "rag top" weather all the time. It never gets beyond 85 degrees in the afternoon. At night the temperature dips to the mid-50s which means your electric bill drops to near nothing. You can have your convertible top down all the time. Just don't forget your sunscreen. Weather-wise, a lot happens around here in the winter. Every three or four years we'll have a freeze. Crop damage can occur, but mostly it means you can wear that $150 sweater that you simply couldn't resist. Yes, you can buy sweaters in Florida. As a matter of fact, a few years ago, much to the delight of just about everybody, it actually snowed on Christmas Eve. It only snowed for five minutes, but it snowed!

Dangers In Paradise

The Sun
Florida may be "The Sunshine State" but this isn't entirely good news. Our biggest attraction may be hazardous to your health. There is an exploding rate of skin cancer, especially deadly Melanomas, associated with overexposure to the sun.

EVERYONE should wear sunglasses, even children. Try to find sunglasses that have been coated to absorb 99 to 100 percent of both UVA and UVB rays as well as most blue light. (Wearing sunglasses that lack UV protection is actually worse than wearing none at all, because dark glasses make the pupils dilate, so even more UV can enter the eye.) Wraparound styles give the best protection.

Dermatologists will tell you to use sunscreen on every part of your body not protected by clothing every day, even days which are cloudy. Choose a sunscreen labeled "broad spectrum" and apply it 20 minutes before going outside, then reapply every two hours. Even products labeled "waterproof" should be reapplied directly after swimming or heavy sweating.

Common sense should tell you to schedule outdoor activities in early morning or late afternoon, when UV radiation is much less intense.

Thunderstorms

Florida is the lightning capital of the world. We have more lightning strikes than anywhere in the United States. This makes for fabulous storm watching but "caution" is the word.

The National Weather Service has some basic safety rules worth following during a lightning storm:

- Go to a low place, such as a ditch.
- If you are traveling, stay in your automobile.
- Stay away from open water, bikes and motorcycles.
- Don't stand under telephone lines or isolated trees.
- Keep away from pipes, rails, clotheslines, metal fences and structural steel fabrications.
- Don't use metal objects, such as fishing rods, tennis rackets and golf clubs. Golfers wearing cleated shoes are particularly susceptible to lightning.
- Get into a car (not a convertible), home or large building.
- Stay indoors and don't use the telephone unless it's an emergency.
- Keep away from open doors and windows, fireplaces, radiators, stoves, metal pipes, sinks and plug-in appliances.
- Don't use the bath or shower.
- If you hair stands on end, it may mean that lightning is about to strike you; drop to your knees, bend forward and put your hands on your knees.

By the way, if you are caught out on a golf course be sure to remove your golf shoes and drop your clubs, except the #1 iron because – as everyone knows, even the Lord can't hit a #1 iron!!!

Waterspouts

You can sometimes see them in the summertime while sitting on the beach as you watch offshore thunderstorms. A curl of cloud will come out of the sky and meet the water, and in moments, a large spray of water will appear on the surface.

Waterspouts are tornados filled with water which slows their progress so they aren't extremely dangerous, although caution must be exercised. They often occur right off of our beaches and are spectacular to watch. They usually dissipate quickly if they make landfall.

Hurricanes

This is the deadliest weather. It is the process of heat transferring from the tropics to the north. We have two hurricane seasons here in Florida.

The first is in spring. These are storms which begin in the Yucatan basin, the Caribbean or in the Gulf of Mexico and blow up out of scattered thunderstorms literally overnight. These are small storms which may only cover 100 miles, but the danger in these storms is that they can develop with almost no advance warning.

Hurricane Survival Guide

Make a "family survival plan" and rehearse it at least every six months. Have a survival kit ready. It should include the following:

- A four week supply of prescription medications.
- A two week supply of nonperishable food and water.
- Blankets, sleeping bags, pillows and air mattress.
- Flashlights and batteries.
- Portable radio and batteries.
- Extra clothing, shoes and prescription eyeglasses.
- Personal hygiene items.
- A good book or two.

Hurricane Intensity

Category 1

- 74-95 mph. winds.

- Intensifying rain squalls and wind gusts damage limbs of trees.

- Outdoor objects can become airborne, and weak trees could be blown over.

- Mobile homes are evacuated.

Category 2

- 96-110 mph. winds.

- Flooding possible along low-lying and coastal areas.

- Some roofing material, door and window damage to buildings.

Category 3

- 111-130 mph. winds.

- Shingles can be blown off roofs.

- Terrain lower than 5 ft. above sea level may be flooded inland as far as 6 miles.

The second hurricane season occurs during the summer and fall – June 1 to November 30. These, historically, are storms that come off the coast of Africa and spend two weeks crossing the Atlantic, building in strength, moving into the Caribbean and then into the Gulf of Mexico. These storms can cover areas up to 300 miles and can turn a coastline area into a wasteland. Fortunately, we are provided with plenty of advanced warning about these storms. WWSB, Channel 40 and local radio keep us well informed.

It would be a smart move to locate your evacuation zone and level to determine if and when you should evacuate. Maps with zones are available at most major supermarkets. You can find them printed in your phone book and you'll find special "tracking maps" inserted in your daily paper at the beginning of Hurricane Season. If you are asked to evacuate, you will have 24 hours to do so. Your map will provide evacuation routes and shelters near you; practice driving to them and be flexible. It's impossible to tell in advance which roads may be closed.

During a hurricane, all mobile home residents will be required to evacuate, no matter what their location. Red Cross locations should only be used as a last resort. If ordered to evacuate, find a hotel, motel or home of a friend or relative in a safe location. Make plans for your pets - shelters do not allow animals. Clear your yard of all loose objects. Clean containers and your bath tub for storing water.

Remember: to bring important papers and identification, to let your friends and relatives know where you are going, to lock windows and doors, to turn off electricity at the breaker, to store valuables and irreplaceable items in your empty appliances, to pack dry clothes in plastic bags and to put plastic bags over TVs , lamps, computers, etc.

Experts are now predicting that we are entering a 10-20 year active hurricane cycle – not great news by any means – which means that we will see an ever increasing number of hurricanes with winds reaching over 100 mph. We were extremely lucky with Hurricane Georges (August, 1998). This Category 3 hurricane was headed directly for us. Only a few miles in the Gulf made the difference from our "close call" to serious tragedy. We cannot overemphasize the need to be prepared.

Close Calls

Unnamed Hurricane, October 1921
Passing west of Sarasota, this storm hit Tarpon Springs in northern Pinellas County. Damage in Sarasota was confined to the bayfront, where all piers were demolished or damaged by tides above 7 feet. Many small boats were lost and some waterfront homes were damaged. Losses were estimated at $200,000.

Unnamed Hurricane, September 1926
This hurricane, which entered Florida near Miami with winds above 130 mph, killed more than 300 and injured thousands. By the time the storm had traveled across the state, winds had dropped to 100 mph. Sarasota storm damage was estimated at $400,000. Many roofs were torn off in the Englewood area. Damage to citrus crops totaled $10 million in 10 Florida counties, including Sarasota and Manatee.

Unnamed Hurricane, September 1935
(a.k.a. "The Labor Day Hurricane")
The most intense hurricane on record, this deadly storm battered the Florida Keys with 200 mph winds, killing more than 400, before making a lazy curve northward into the Gulf of Mexico. Sarasota-area

damage was limited to broken windows, blown-down garages, uprooted trees and waterfront flooding. A fishing guide speculated in a newspaper article that flooding damage was lessened by a lower-than-normal tide.

Unnamed Hurricane, October 1944
Originating south of Grand Cayman Island, this hurricane moved north over Cuba before entering the west coast of Florida near Sarasota. Eastern Sarasota County was hardest hit, with barns and storage houses blown down by the storm's high winds. One of the largest celery-growing centers in the United States suffered extensive damage. Sarasota county citrus growers also took heavy losses. Eighteen people were killed in the storm, including nine seamen who drowned when their boat capsized off Bradenton. Winds in Venice were estimated at 120 mph, but there was no significant damage.

Hurricane Donna, October 1960
Donna, the last hurricane to hit Southwest Florida slammed into the Florida Keys with 120 mph winds and continued northward, where it wiped out Everglades City in Collier County. Sarasota suffered minor damage, such as power outages and fallen trees, but Punta Gorda was declared a disaster area. Donna uprooted massive trees and littered the streets with pieces of roofs and carports. All but five of the then-new Punta Gorda Isles community were damaged. Wind gusts up to 160 mph were recorded in Arcadia.

Hurricane Elena, September 1985
Elena epitomized hurricanes' reputation for unpredictability. The catagory-3 storm traveled northward through the Gulf of Mexico before stalling for two days off Florida's west coast. Sarasota's damage was limited to beach erosion and low-level flooding. Elena knocked out power and phone service to Anna Maria Island, Longboat Key and St. Armands Circle. Several homes on Anna Maria Island were damaged by rising water and 200 residents were temporarily marooned on the island due to flooding. Manatee County was declared a disaster area with losses exceeding $6 million.

Hurricane Georges, August 1998
Talk about close calls! This category 3 hurricane killed hundreds in Haiti, whipped Key West into a ghost town and was heading directly for us. Residents and businesses on the Suncoast spent countless hours in preparation. Duct tape, plywood and "D" batteries sold-out quickly, shelves which held canned goods and bottled water were empty in most stores, driving around town was quite a sight. Windows not covered with plywood were taped up with various creative "X" patterns. Amazingly, Georges stayed just far enough off our shores so as to only give us minor rainfall and sporadic gusts. Still, it was a major scare, reinforcing the need to be fully prepared for the next big one.

Hurricane Names - 1999

Arlene, Bret, Cindy, Dennis, Emily, Floyd, Gert, Harvey, Irene, Jose, Katrina, Lenny, Maria, Nate, Ophelia, Philippe, Rita, Stan, Tammy, Vince, Wilma.

Hurricane Intensity

Category 4

- 131-155 mph. winds.

- Terrain lower than 10 ft above sea level may be flooded, requiring evacuation of residential areas inland as far as 6 miles.

- Major beach erosion.

Category 5 - Run!

- Winds more than 155 mph.

- Complete roof failure on many residences and industrial buildings.

- Major damage to lower floors of structures less then 15 feet above sea level.

- Do not pass "Go" do not collect $200 JUST RUN!!

Additional information kindly provided by The Sarasota Herald-Tribune, The 1996 Florida Almanac and the Sarasota County Dept. of Historical *Resources*.

YOUR ONE-STOP destination FOR EVERYTHING YOU NEED TO KNOW ABOUT THE GULF COAST lifestyle...

Welcome home

To The Michael Saunders Real Estate Gallery!

The Gallery is the place to help you sort it all out. Have a cup of cappuccino at our Internet Cafe. Ask about local schools. Information on over 200 new communities and custom homes. What does a Master Planned Community

offer? Which golf courses are public, private or equity? The answers are here. How much does it cost per foot to keep a boat in a marina? Yes, we know that too. Are there Gulf-front homes available for seasonal lease? What is a maintenance-free single family home? Find the answers at The Gallery, an exciting adventure designed to assist you in the real estate marketplace.

Michael Saunders & Company
Licensed Real Estate Broker

100 South Washington Boulevard (U.S. 301), Downtown Sarasota
New Homes: 941-951-6500 • Rental & Resort: 941-951-6668 or
800-881-2222 • http://www.michaelsaunders.com

Family Life

CHILDRENS' FOUNTAIN © BILL WEST

LIKE ANYWHERE ELSE IN AMERICA, OUR COMMUNITY IS FILLED WITH DIVERSE NEIGHBORHOODS.

But what sets Sarasota, Bradenton and Venice apart is the abundance of sun, sand and sea which seems to cast an "I'm on vacation for the rest of my life!" induced attitude, even on those who live inland.

The vast amount of waterfront property and easy access to the various coastal comforts helps to reinforce our relaxed outlook on life.

Thus, most of us share a perpetual reason to celebrate.

Underscoring our day-to-day activities is the reassuring knowledge that a trip to the beach, whenever desired, is only a moment away. And there are, oh so many, other wonders.

Purchasing a Home on Florida's Gulf Coast

W. Andrew Vac, President of the Sarasota Association of Realtors shares his expertise in the pursuit of a home:

"It's hard to resist the charm of Sarasota. The area abounds with wonderful weather, inviting beaches, challenging golf courses, the best in art and cultural events, award-winning restaurants and world-famous shopping. And that's just a few of the reasons so many people love living and vacationing in our area.

The real estate market is very healthy. We have a wonderful mix of cozy neighborhoods, waterfront & golf course properties, condominiums and new home developments. Interest rates remain favorable and demand is high. In our Multiple Listing Service area, the median sales price for an existing single-family home is about $121,000, but the average price of all residential property is about $178,000. It is still possible to find an attractive three-bedroom/two bath home in the $125,000-$186,000 range. Sarasota is part of the Sarasota-Bradenton Metropolitan Statistical Area, where the median price for existing single-family homes is $96,900, according to October 1996 data.

It's easier than ever to find a Realtor and the house of your dreams. There are about 3,500 local Realtor members of the Sarasota Association of Realtors, Venice Area Board of Realtors and the Manatee County Board of Realtors. You can find a Realtor using the traditional ways of searching through property ad magazines, attending open houses, using the classified ads or getting a referral from friends. Technology is providing more options. All members of the Association have a resume page on an Internet website hosted by the Florida Association of Realtors (http://fl.living.net).

A Realtor's resume page gives specific information on the member's company, service area and specialties, professional experience and education. You can also see property information about the homes the Realtor has available. Currently, there are more than 100,000 properties in the state of Florida being showcased at this Internet location.

This website also contains information that is helpful to both buyers and sellers. For example, you might be wondering why you should contact a Realtor before buying a home.

Under the heading of Consumer Information, the Florida Association of Realtors reminds us that "buying a home calls for your informed decision based in part on the knowledge, judgment and guidance of

Mortgages the Easy Way...

FLEXIBLE • CREATIVE • PROFESSIONAL

Low Rates

Zero Point Programs

Loans from
$50,000 - $4,000,000

Programs to fit
all mortgage needs

(941) 373-0019

(877) 360-9802
Toll-Free

1 FIRST TOWN MORTGAGE CORPORATION

PENNY HILL

City Center Building • Sarasota

Welcoming You to the Community

Barbara Katz
GRI - Graduate Realtor Institute

- Graduate of Brooklyn College
- Sarasota resident for 25 years
- On the Board of the Jewish Community Center
- Founding Member and on the Board of the Wellness Community Southwest Florida Cancer Support Group

**ReMax Properties
2000 Webber Street
941/954-5454 or 800/281/6867**

a real estate broker or agent – particularly one who is a Realtor.

Unlike many real estate agents who are simply licensed by their state to do business, Realtors have taken additional steps to become members of their local Board of Realtors and have agreed to act under and adhere to a Code of Ethics.

This membership obligates them to be fair to all parties involved in this transaction, be it buyer, seller or cooperating agent. Be sure your real estate agent is a Realtor.

Realtors do more...much more...than you may think:

• A Realtor can help you determine how much home you can afford. Often a Realtor can suggest ways to accrue the down payment and explain alternative financing methods.

• A Realtor, in addition to knowing the local money market, also can tell you what personal and financial data to bring with you when you apply for a loan.

• A Realtor is already familiar with current real estate values, taxes, utility costs, municipal services and facilities, and may be aware of local zoning changes that could affect your decision to buy.

• A Realtor can usually research your housing needs in advance through a Multiple Listing Service -- even if you are relocating to another city.

• A Realtor can help familiarize you with the closing process.

• A Realtor shows you only those homes best suited to your needs -- size, style, features, location, accessibility to schools, transportation, shopping, and other personal preferences.

• A Realtor often can suggest simple, imaginative changes that could make a home more suitable for you and improve its utility and value.

• A Realtor, though generally acting as an agent for the property owner, is bound and obligated by the Code of Ethics to give fair treatment to all parties in the transaction.

• A Realtor is sensitive to the importance you place on this major commitment you are about to make. Count on this real estate professional to facilitate negotiation of an agreement satisfactory to both seller and buyer.

If you see a home as one of your most important investments, the Realtor you work with could be one of your most valuable resources. As a home buyer, you can expect the commitment, integrity and expertise that you'll find in Realtors. It is the business of a Realtor to work with you by understanding your home buying needs and showing you properties that fit your lifestyle and budget."

Home Sweet Home Phones

Home Builders Association of Sarasota Co.	379-3306
Home Builders Association of Manatee Co.	749-7035
fax 746-2339 e-mail hbaeo@gte.net	

Sarasota County Board of Realtors, Inc.	923-2315
fax 923--191	
Manatee Asssociation of Realtors	747-1818
fax 745-2978	
Venice Area Board of Realtors	484-0614
fax 484-1974	
Florida House Foundation	927-2020
Anna Maria Island Chamber of Commerce	778-1541
Longboat Key Chamber of Commerce	383-2466
Manatee County Chamber of Commerce	748-3411
Sarasota Chamber of Commerce	955-8187
Siesta Key Chamber of Commerce	349-3800
Venice Area Chamber of Commerce	488-2236

Real Estate Places and Faces

Coldwell Banker Residential Real Estate, Inc.
3322 Bee Ridge Rd., Sarasota
927-3990, fax 378-8245, www.coldwellbanker.com

Full service real estate company featuring a complementary real estate buyer's guide and a 24-hour information home hotline. Ranked #1 in America by Real Trends. Local knowledge of the market and 20 Offices in West Central Florida to service you.

Barbara Katz, RE/MAX Properties
2000 Webber St., Sarasota
954-5454/1-800-281-6867, fax 954-5455, www.homes/fl.com

Concerned about moving? With Barbara you have a friend who will fully introduce you to the community. On the Board of Directors of the Sarasota Jewish Community Center and West Florida Wellness Community Center, Barbara is an active member of the community who listens to her clients. Her love for the area is reflected in her sales approach.

Anthony K. Ngai, A.I.A, Architect
921-0821, fax 927-9805

A recipient of the National Award of Excellence for his architectural work, Tony Nagi, Architect, adds Sarasota to his impressive list of residential design studio locations – San Francisco, Los Angeles, Honolulu and London. Mr. Ngai's design portfolio includes over 45 residences ranging in size from 1,800 square feet to 18,000 square feet. Tony brings a new level of international sophistication to our area, he is currently designing and remodeling in Sarasota's Cherokee Park area.

Chris McDivitt
316-6518, fax 388-4117

Chris has been the #1 real estate agent in Sarasota County and #1 RE/MAX agent in Florida numerous years. She is a CRS, GRI, Broker-Salesman, a member of the RE/MAX Hall of Fame and RE/MAX Platinum Club and recipient of the RE/MAX Lifetime Achievement award. Hard work, attention to detail and care for her clients' interests have resulted in over 80% of her business being repeat customers or referrals from satisfied buyers or sellers. Chris' strong in-depth knowledge of her market, a comprehensive national referral and marketing network and full-time professional staff contribute to her success.

Michael Saunders & Co.
1801 Main St., Sarasota
951-6600, fax 366-8210

Michael Saunders & Company is beginning a third decade as the

---

Buying a Home in Paradise

According to the Sarasota County Board of Realtors, in 1997 the average single family residential sales price was $121,000. Thanks to Florida's Homestead Exemption, homeowners are relieved from paying taxes on the first $25,000 of their home's appraised value. This should be good news for the budget minded, and these days who isn't? From location and price – to proximity – to life's little necessities (such as schools and shopping) – to life's major necessities (such as waterfront views and golf course vistas) – you're sure to find the perfect formula to match your personal lifestyle.

The median price for a two-bedroom, single family home in our area is about $96,900.

Buying a Home in Paradise

Since our area is home to the first golf course in America, you can reasonably expect that we take our golf communities very seriously.

Club homes within *Golf and Tennis Communities* offer owners easy access to their favorite pastimes. Other amenities include swimming pavilions, professional croquet courts, club house and family activities. Play where you live, live where you play! Some outstanding examples of these communities include Venice Golf & Country Club and University Park.

Range:
$100,000 - $5 million.

luxury market leader, and is the largest independently-owned real estate brokerage in west central Florida. The firm is rated in the Top Ten statewide by Florida Trend, and is the number one female-owned business in Sarasota, and in the Top-5 statewide. The company recently opened The Michael Saunders Real Estate Gallery, 100 S. Washington Blvd., Sarasota – a unique, multimedia, one-stop real estate shopping facility.

Tangerine Development
201 Gulf of Mexico Drive, Longboat Key
383-2833, fax 383-9466

Development and Construction Management of luxury single family homes and condominiums. Specializing in high-end waterfront communities. Noted (and much appreciated) for their work in the revitalization of Downtown Sarasota (Sarabande, Tessera, Mandarin Park and Palm Avenue Villas).

Bruce Tassinare
1801 Main St., Sarasota
951-6600, fax 366-8210

Whether you're buying or selling a home, condo or investment property, the Realtor you choose to work with will make a significant difference. Bruce Tassinare has built lasting friendships and professional relationships with his clients and customers, he is uniquely qualified to assist you with knowledgable and honest representation in any real estate transaction. He has achieved the rare designation of "Certified International Property Specialist."

University Park
On University Parkway, 1.8 miles west of I-75 (Exit 40)
351-7777, fax 355-6002, www.universitypark/fl.com

A gated community or private neighborhoods, meticulously designed with great attention to detail. Spectacular homes with sweeping golf course views, Braden River Trail, Fitness Park, world class tennis and more. Awarded "Best Community Design in America" by National Association of Home Builders. 27 holes rated "4-stars" by Golf Digest (only 4-star rating in Sarasota.) Croquet too.

Our Neighborhoods

Anna Maria Island Township
Northernmost point of Anna Maria Key, accessible by way of Gulf Drive. Seaside resort features fishing piers, yacht basin, Bayfront Park and beautiful beach front. Local ordinance prohibits condominiums so the area retains a village feel, rather than a resort or vacation spot. Outstanding views of lower Tampa Bay, the Sunshine Skyway Bridge and Egmont Key. Many international visitors have landed here.

Anna Maria Key
The northern most point of area's barrier islands, surrounded by the Gulf of Mexico and Palma Sola Bay. Includes Bradenton Beach, Holmes Beach and Anna Maria Island communities, each has its own government and police force. Connected to mainland by SR 684 at Bradenton Beach and SR 64 at Holmes Beach; south to Longboat Key by SR 789.

Arcadia
Once the second most important city on Florida's west coast (back when the railroad came straight through) then the Cracker Cowboy Capitol of the state for citrus farmers and cattle handlers (haircuts, a

When it's important, delicate, irreplaceable, high value, sentimental or one of a kind...

...only one mover can provide the special moving skills and professionalism that clients demand.

DAVI & VALENTI
DELUXE · WORLD WIDE
MOVERS

Call the Professionals for a FREE, No obligation consultation.
(941) 355-2936 or (941) 355-2961 (local)
Local, Long Distance, International Movers and Storage.
Fax (941) 351-3883   800-282-7674

The official movers of the U.S.S. Sarasota and Sarasota Ballet.

Since 1979   1755 University Parkway West   ICC/MC52793

shave and a good time once a month), now a respectful collection of very neat (as in "hip") shops, bed and breakfast inns and 15 antique stores downtown. Take Clark Road (SR 72) east. Well beyond Myakka River State Park but well worth the drive. Beautiful and historic.

Bird Key
Island community surrounded by Sarasota Bay. Very private and strictly residential – no commercial buildings. Located off John Ringling Causeway between downtown Sarasota and St. Armands Circle. You'll love their causeway traffic light. Not.

Bradenton
Peninsula community surrounded by Sarasota Bay to the south, Palma Sola Bay to the west, Tampa Bay to the northwest, Manatee River to the north and Braden River to the east. County seat and largest of county municipalities with miles of sandy beaches. Downtown was incorporated in 1878. Friendly small town flavor is being maintained even with current growth and development. Home of Bishop Planetarium/South Florida Museum, Tropicana and DeSoto Square Mall.

Bradenton Beach
Southern end of Anna Maria Key, can be reached from mainland across Cortez Road (SR 684) and from north end of Longboat Key (SR 789). Seaside resort community featuring Coquina Public Beach, Coquina Bayside Park, Bradenton Beach Fishing Pier, rock jetties and beautiful beach front.

Casey Key
Island community surrounded by Gulf of Mexico and Little Sarasota Bay. Access from U.S. 41 by way of Blackburn Point Road to the north and Nokomis drawbridge to the south. Small shopping areas, marinas, various types of extraordinary residences – from the stately to the understated – and motels. Well worth a sunset visit but be warned: some of the palatial residences may provoke spontaneous drooling.

Cortez Village
Peninsula village located directly east from Bradenton Beach on the mainland at Cortez Road and 123rd Street West, Bradenton. Established in the 1880s as a fishing village, the area is still a thriving fishing community. The Cortez Festival held annually on the third Saturday in February. Some scenes in the modern film adaptation of Charles Dickens' *Great Expectations* with Robert De Niro, Gweneth Paltrow, Anne Bancroft and Ethan Hawke were shot here (this is where Hawke's character *Finn* grows up).

Ellenton
North of the Manatee River, site of Gamble Plantation and Prime Outlets, a major discount outlet mall with over 135 shops.

Holmes Beach
Middle section of Anna Maria Key, access from mainland by way of Manatee Avenue (SR 64). Seaside resort features public fishing pier, various shopping centers, public tennis courts and beautiful beach front. Very popular for weekend picnics and family get-togethers.

Lakewood Ranch
East of I-75, north from University Parkway to SR 70. Manatee County's newest town, still under development but moving quickly. Now home to one of the state's top-rated golf courses and polo clubs, only a few years ago this was farmland with a single paved road. The first elements of shopping, banking and recreation are in place for the 5,500 acre planned community with more amenities on the way.

Buying a Home in Paradise

Condominium life offers the convenience "maintenance free" comfort – no lawns to mow! And choices? From downtown waterfront views, to barrier islands, to inland self-contained communities, many of which offer luxurious, first class amenities. Some sparkling examples of fabulous condo living include Hidden Bay in Osprey; on Siesta Key, Crystal Sands, Palm Bay Club and Tivoli-by-the Sea Resort.

In the downtown area a "must look at" are the properties developed by Tangerine Development Company.

Range:
$80,000 -
$2 million.

Laurel
Unincorporated area located 15 miles south of Sarasota, 5, miles north of Venice, was named by the Blackburn family in 1903 because of the abundance of beautiful laurel trees; landmark post office is still in operation. Today the woods are gone but you'll find some neat thrift stores here.

Lido Key
Island community surrounded by Gulf of Mexico to the west, Sarasota Bay to the east, New Pass to the north, Big Pass to the south. Connected to St. Armands Key by three roads, making Lido Key feel part of the same neighborhood. Absolutely fabulous beach, popular resorts and "to die for" sunset views. Lido Shores (located on the north end of the key) was developed by architect visionary Phil Hiss in the 1950s, the neighborhood offers outstanding examples of Sarasota School of Architecture.

Longboat Key
Distinctively maintained 10 1/2-mile long barrier island community surrounded by the Gulf of Mexico to the west and Sarasota Bay to the east. Popular resort, residential community, restaurants and shops. The island is divided between Sarasota County and Manatee County at the 4200 Block of Gulf of Mexico Drive; located just north of Lido Key and St. Armands Circle, just south of Anna Maria Key. A popular hideaway for tourists and host of the annual *Florida Winefest & Auction* (3rd largest event of its kind in the U.S.) and *Stone Crab Festival.*

Newtown
Established in the mid-1920s primarily as a black neighborhood, it still serves our African American community which represents about 5% of the county's population. The northern tip of Sarasota's city limits to Dr. Martin Luther King Jr. Way.

Nokomis
Just north of Venice on U.S. 41, includes island community Casey Key reached by a drawbridge across the Inland Waterway. Nokomis Beach area includes several restaurants, small shopping areas, marinas and various types of residences and motels.

North Port
Boomtown. Florida's fastest growing municipality (93 percent from 1980-90). This 72-square mile city was incorporated in 1959 with a population of 23 residents. Currently, only 7 percent developed, but the boom is on. Population projections necessitate new schools and services. A big part of Florida's southwestern explosion.

Osprey
Geographic center of Sarasota County; located 2 miles south of Sarasota Square Mall on U.S. 41. Home of Historic Spanish Point and Oscar Scherer State Recreation Area (both well worth a visit) and an upscale shopping district. Bald Eagles can often be seen in this area, the extremely rare Scrub Jay can be seen at Oscar Scherer State Park.

Palmetto
Located just north of Bradenton across the Manatee River; quiet community with a feeling right out of the 1950s which, in our book, is a high compliment. Once the site of Palmetto's first settlement, the area now includes restored buildings, parks, shops and a library. Inevitably a bedroom community for St. Petersburg/Tampa, now is a good time to explore (especially riverfront!) Namesake movie, with Woody Harrelson and Elisabeth Shue, simply did not do justice.

Pinecraft
The large mix of Amish and Mennonite families gives this special neighborhood its unique charm. You'll often see bearded men in traditional broad-brimmed hats pedaling around on three-wheeler bicycles. Amish farmers settled here in the late 1920s, followed by the less conservative Mennonites in the mid-30s. From just north of Swift Road to just north of Beneva Road on both sides of Bahia Vista Street in Sarasota. Loved by locals as *the* place for homemade pies and baked goods. Old Farmers market happens at The Fifties Diner every Saturday.

St. Armands Circle and St. Armands Key
Island community built by John Ringling, gateway to Lido Key and islands north (Longboat Key, Anna Maria Key). St. Armands Circle is a tourist mecca with over 150 boutiques, shops, galleries and restaurants. Circus Ring of Fame is located at center of circle walkway. Access from mainland on Ringling Causeway (SR 780); from Longboat Key by way of Gulf of Mexico Drive (SR 789).

Sarasota-East
Mainland east of Beneva Road; significant (meaning very large and prestigious) residential communities such as Lakewood Ranch, The

SIESTA KEY © BILL WEST

Meadows, Laurel Oak, Berkshire Estates, Country Woods Estates, Bent Tree Village, Brentwood Estates, Sunrise Gulf Club Estates, Fox Fire West... to name just a few. However, the farther east you go the more it looks like farm country – wait a minute – it is farm county out there. Moo! But, all kidding aside, this is where the major growth is, mini-cities are springing up all around I-75. Also, numerous industrial parks and new malls are developing. A great place for families.

Sarasota-West
Mainland west of Beneva Road to the Gulf of Mexico; U.S. 41 is significant (meaning very large and prestigious) thoroughfare with enough shops, boutiques, restaurants, malls and services to keep you occupied for years. And that's exactly the idea. Residential and lush, yet maintaining a cosmopolitan feel. To many, this *is* Sarasota.

Siesta Key
Island community surrounded by the Gulf of Mexico to the west, Sarasota Big Pass to the north, Roberts Bay to the east and Little Sarasota Bay to the South. Access from U.S. 41 by way of Siesta Drive to the north, Stickney Point Road to the south. Area's most popular beach for obvious reasons – distinguished for having won the "finest, whitest sand in the world" title in international competition. (Miss this and you've missed the whole point!) Entire community embraces a relaxed "beach" lifestyle. Northern end of the key is more "active" and includes Siesta Village; southern end is more "laid-back." See it all. Life *is* a beach.

Venice
Like its namesake, this community is surrounded by intercostal waterways to the north, east and south. Unlike the Italian version, the Gulf of Mexico hugs the entire west end. U.S. 41 follows the outskirts of the intercostal waterway, Business 41 goes across the bridges and into downtown. Our kind of place - warm, friendly natives, campus-like high school, strong community commitment from local business, "Shark Tooth Capital of the World;" relaxed, honest, no pretence. Location of two world-famous restaurants: Sharky's on the Pier and The Crow's Nest.

Educational Offerings

No matter what your age, interest or intellectual level, our area has a school to suit your needs. Our public schools are equipped with the latest advances in computer/audio/visual learning tools. You will also find active support from various parent, business and community groups who contribute countless hours in the pursuit of educational excellence.

PUBLIC SCHOOLS - ELEMENTARY THROUGH HIGH SCHOOL

We seem to be in the midst of a student population boom. As more new families move to the area, new schools are being built to meet the growing demands. Currently, students are required to attend the public school within the district of their family residence. There are some exceptions to this rule. Most involve admission to special purpose schools. Our schools provide a wide variety of programs for gifted and differently-abled students, vocational education and several innovative school-wide programs which allow for an interdisciplinary approach to learning.

Manatee County

A message from Marianne Lorentzen, School Board of Manatee County: "The Manatee County school system has a total enrollment of 32,000 students and consists of 26 elementary schools, six middle schools, four high schools and a Vocational/Technical school. The School Board of Manatee County has committed to "focusing on the learner." The direction to student success is for a carefully designed curriculum that specifically identifies core competencies and key skills that students must know to be successful learners and future workers. High expectations are being set for all students. Technology and concurrent technology training, including career/vocational education, is considered an obligation of the school district. Emphasis has been placed on the need for open communication and involvement with parents, businesses, and others in the community. For example, new processes for interviewing principal candidates involve parents and staff in the selection of site administrators. High schools offer Honors and Advanced Placement courses. In addition, Dual Enrollment courses are conducted with Manatee Community College. Students have access to numerous extracurricular clubs, sports activities and endeavors in the arts." For further information contact the School Board of Manatee County Public Information Office at 741-7615.

Sarasota County

A message from Dr. Thomas H. Gaul, former Superintendent of Sarasota County Schools: (Ed. Note: Dr. Gaul donned a cowboy hat, spurs, and headed to Texas to head the Round Rock School district. The search for a new Superintendent was initiated at publication time.)

"The love of learning and the feeling of confidence and accomplishment are gifts every child deserves. Sarasota County wraps these gifts to all public school children in one of the finest education packages in the state of Florida. In fact, in a recent nationwide survey by *Money Magazine,* Sarasota County School District was rated one of the top 100 districts in the country. Another publication, Expansion Management magazine, ranked Sarasota's public schools number one in Florida and in the top 20% nationally, based on characteristics most valued by business and industry. But Sarasota is not a school system that rests on its laurels. Hundreds of educators, classified staff, business leaders, community members, parents and students worked together in early 1996 to develop a strategic plan called the Campaign for Excellence, which will enable the school district to continue its

---

Sarasota Area Public Schools

Alta Vista Elementary
2589 Alta Vista St.,
Sarasota 361-6400
(Barry Napshin)

Ashton Elementary
5110 Ashton Rd., Sarasota
361-6440
(John Zoretich)

Bay Haven School of Basics Plus
2901 W Tamiami Circle,
Sarasota 359-5800
(Marilyn Highland)

Booker High School/The Sarasota Visual and Performing Arts Center
3201 N Orange Ave.,
Sarasota 355-2967
(Janice Gibbs)

Booker Middle School
2250 Myrtle St.,
Sarasota 359-5824
(Andrew Jones)

Emma E. Booker Elementary
2350 Dr. Martin Luther King Jr. Way, Sarasota
361-6480
(Gwen Riegell)

Brentwood Elementary
2500 Vinson Ave.,
Sarasota 361-6230
(Sandra Russell)

Brookside Middle
3636 S. Shade Ave.,
Sarasota 361-6472
(Jeff Hradek)

Cyesis Program
4650 Beneva Rd.,
Sarasota 361-6240
(Lorraine Colby)

Fruitville Elementary
601 Honore Ave.,
Sarasota 361-6200
(Janis Komara)

Gocio Elementary
3450 Gocio Rd., Sarasota
361-6405
(Page Dettmann)

Gulf Gate Elementary
6500 S Lockwood Ridge Rd., Sarasota
361-6499

Sarasota Area Public Schools

Lakeview Elementary
7299 Proctor Rd.,
Sarasota 361-6571
(Janice Coleman)

McIntosh Middle School
701 S McIntosh Rd.,
Sarasota 361-6520
(Robert Hagemann)

Oak Park School
7285 Proctor Rd.,
Sarasota 361-6428
(Brenda Meiners)

Phillippi Shores Elementary
4747 S Tamiami Tr.,
Sarasota 361-6424
(Carlotta Cooley)

Preschool
2926 Hyde Park St.,
Sarasota 361-6046
(Sonia Alberts)

Riverview High School
1 Ram Way, Sarasota
923-1484
(Arthur Williams)

Sarasota County Technical Institute
4748 Beneva Rd.,
Sarasota 924-1365
(Steve Harvey)

Sarasota High School
1001 S Tamiami Tr.,
Sarasota 955-0181
(Daniel Kennedy)

Sarasota Middle (6-8)
4826 Ashton Rd.,
Sarasota 361-6464
(Linda Nook)

Southside Elementary
1901 Webber St.,
Sarasota 361-6420
(John Spielman)

Tuttle Elementary
(Pre K-5)
925 N Brink Ave.,
Sarasota 361-6433
(Nancy Dubin)

Wilkinson Elementary
3400 Wilkinson Rd.,
Sarasota 361-6477
(William Muth Jr.)

preeminence into the 21st Century. Through this plan, the students will be provided a world-class curriculum, strong instructional leadership, safe and orderly schools, high expectations for all, creative learning environments, and quality home/school partnerships.

The academic programs in Sarasota County schools are outstanding. Students regularly outscore their peers statewide and nationwide on the National Achievement tests for Math and Reading, the Scholastic Aptitude Test (SAT) and American College Testing Programs (ACT), and other nationally normed tests. A variety of recognition programs honor students for their superior achievements, including the Renaissance Program for those with a 3.0 or higher grade point average, and the Disney Dreamers and Doers program, which salutes students who demonstrate curiosity, confidence, courage and constancy.

In partnership with the YMCA, hundreds of minority students are encouraged yearly to attain higher academic levels and career opportunities through The Black Achievers Program. The YMCA also works with targeted children ages 3-5 and their parents to help prepare the youngsters for kindergarten.

Sarasota's innovative curriculum offers students the opportunity to participate in programs designed to meet their individual talents. The district offers many magnet schools, as well as schools that specialize in specific areas, such as a highly acclaimed visual and performing arts high school, a program for teen parents, and a school offering exceptional education for students with intellectual, physical or emotional challenges.

Students who thrive on high level academics, acceleration and enrichment have the opportunity to participate in special classes in their schools or attend a centralized school for the gifted. A technical institute trains young adults in a variety of careers, including the health professions, child care, culinary arts, horticulture, cosmetology, agriculture and business. An organized School-to-Work Program helps to create work-ready graduates by providing them with the opportunity to apply skills they have learned in the classroom to real job situations.

The Sarasota County School District is a pioneer in incorporating leading-edge technology and distance learning into the classroom. Students and teachers use computer-based communication, such as E-mail, the internet, and video conferencing to enhance both teaching and learning.

Sarasota County School District's mission - to prepare students to achieve the highest learning standards by engaging a high quality staff, involved parents and supportive community - guides the system's daily and yearly planning. It is the vision of the Sarasota County School District that all students will lead productive, responsible and healthful lives as they enter the next millennium."

For additional info, please contact The School Board of Sarasota County, 1960 Landings Blvd., Sarasota, FL 34231, 927-4000.

P.A.L.S. (Partnerships and Alliances Linking Schools)
1960 Landings Blvd., Sarasota
927-4009

P.A.L.S. provides recruitment, training, recognition and coordination of volunteers and business partnerships for the benefit of all students and schools throughout Sarasota County. Its efforts promote partnerships and alliances linking schools with the community.

What Is Cardinal Mooney High School?

CARDINAL MOONEY IS...

- Coeducational and offers a college preparatory curriculum.
- The only Catholic High School serving students in Sarasota, Manatee & Charlotte counties.
- Accredited by the Southern Association of Colleges & Schools.
- Located at 4171 Fruitville Road, just 3 miles east of downtown Sarasota and minutes from I-75.

Serving God in The Community

Cardinal Mooney High School is committed to providing a quality education in a Catholic environment for those who desire it. We are dedicated to the development of the whole person in an atmosphere characterized by a strong sense of family and centered in Gospel values. In all that we do, we strive to instill in our students a sense of discipleship and moral responsibility thus providing our community with young Christian leaders dedicated to social justice and service.

For more information or to schedule a tour of the school please call 371-4917.

Under the auspices of the Diocese of Venice, Cardinal Mooney High School's open admission policy states that no individual shall be subject to discrimination on the basis of race, color, or national origin.

Private School Spotlight

Cardinal Mooney High School
4171 Fruitville Rd., Sarasota 34232
379-2647, fax 371-6924

The only diocesan secondary school serving Sarasota and Manatee counties, Cardinal Mooney High School is committed to providing a quality education in a Catholic environment for those who desire it. They are dedicated to the development of the whole person in an atmosphere characterized by a strong sense of family and centered in Gospel values. In all that they do, they still strive to instill in their students a sense of discipleship and moral responsibility, thus providing our community with young Christian leaders dedicated to social justice and service.

Julie Rohr Academy
4466 Fruitville Rd., Sarasota 34232
371-4979, fax 379-5816

Julie Rohr Academy is a private school which services students from two-years old through eighth grade. The school seeks to provide its students with a motivating, challenging, creative, and enjoyable learning climate in a safe, warm, family atmosphere. JRA also offers a strong performing arts program which gives its students

Strong Academic and Arts Programs

2 Years through 8th Grade

Art • Music • Phys. Ed.
Computers • Karate • Drama
Foreign Language

School Hours: 8:30 a.m. - 3:30 p.m.
Extended Services Available

Julie Rohr ACADEMY

4466 Fruitville Rd. • Sarsasota, FL 34232
(941) 371-4979

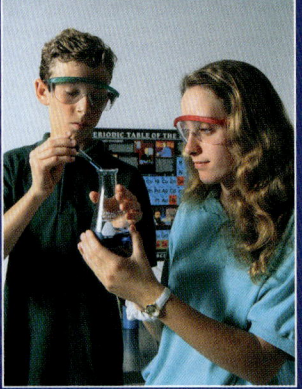

New Gate School

The Montessori Foundation's
National Lab School for Students
in Preschool (15 months) — Eighth Grade
High school set to open soon.

An international,
coeducational,
college-preparatory school

- Age 15 months - 8th grade
- 5 acre campus
- Warm, supportive atmosphere
- Montessori approach
- International studies
- Enriched science & mathematics
- Computer skills
- Phonetic-based reading approach
- Children's literature & poetry
- Research-oriented curriculum
- Nature study & gardening
- Practical life skills
- Critical thinking
- Spanish
- Fine arts, music & dance
- Community service programs
- Physical education & sports
- Extended day programs
- Summer camp
- Weekly open house

5237 Ashton Road
Sarasota, Florida
922-4949

the opportunity to learn how to handle themselves in front of the public and develop a positive self image.

New Gate School
5237 Ashton Rd., Sarasota 34233
922-4949, fax 922-7660

New Gate was founded in 1984 as an independent, non profit, international school. The Montessori Foundation selected New Gate to serve as a national laboratory school and center for educational innovation and curriculum development. Today we have an enrollment of 195 students, preschool (15months+) through the 8th grade. Their community of students, faculty, and families is founded on kindness and respect. They work in partnership, share strong common valudes and prepare young men and women both for college and life.

The Out-of-Door Academy
444 Reid St., Sarasota 34243, 349-3223, fax 349-8133
5950 Deer Dr. (9-12), Sarasota 34240 fax 907-1251 (high school)

The Out-of-Door Academy, founded in 1924, is Florida's second oldest coeducational, independent school, and is accredited by the Florida Council of Independent Schools. Prekindergarten through grade 12, The Out-of-Door Academy has an outstanding college preparatory curriculum and excellent Athletic and Fine Arts programs. Renowned for its small class size (student/teacher ratio is 10:1) and devoted, caring faculty with exceptional educational credentials, The Out-of-Door Academy offers students the personal attention necessary to achieve their academic goals, to foster independent thought and to instill a true love of learning. The Out-of-Door Academy serves 600 students from an area encompassing Bradenton to Boca Grande/Port Charlotte.

Prekindergarten through eighth grades are located on the beautiful Siesta Key campus and the new high school campus is located on University Parkway, one mile east of Interstate 75, in Lakewood Ranch. An after-school care program and transportation are available. Qualified students are admitted regardless of race, religion, or ethnic origin. Financial Aid is available. Voted "Best of the Best" in 1997 and 1998 by *WWSB, Channel 40 and Sarasota Mag.*

Higher Education

MANATEE COUNTY

Manatee Community College
5840 26th St. W.,
Bradenton 34207
755-1511, fax 727-6140 www.mcc.cc.fl.us

Designated by the state as a "Center for Excellence for Computer Education," the college offers university parallel, technical, occupational, noncredit and continuing education courses. Enrollment 8529. Degrees: AS, AA, certificate programs.

ODA
College Prep School

Pre-K through Grade 12
Founded 1924

The only private school
voted
"Best of the Best"
in 1997 and 1998

349-3223

Sarasota Area Private Schools

The Achievement Center
1999 Lincoln Dr.,
Sarasota 365-3330
Elementary - High School
T/S ratio - 1:3
College Prep

Cardinal Mooney High
4171 Fruitville Rd.,
Sarasota 379-2647
Catholic High School

Concordia Lutheran School
5651 Honore Ave.,
Sarasota 922-8164
Lutheran School
Pre-K - Middle School

Faith Christian School
2105 Worrington St.,
Sarasota 921-7210
Elementary - Middle
T/S ratio - 1:15
Christian environment

Fielding Academy
5020 Feilding Ln.,
Sarasota 924-0429
Junior High School
T/S ratio - 1:4
College Prep/Enrichment

Incarnation School
2911 bee Ridge Rd.,
Sarasota 924-8588
Elementary - Middle
T/S ratio - 1:15
Catholic environment

Julie Rohr Academy
4466 Fruitville Rd.,
Sarasota 371-4979
Elementary - Middle
T/S ratio - 1:11
College Prep/Enrichment

McClellan Park School
1700 Seminole Dr.,
Sarasota 955-4574
Elementary - High School
T/S ratio - 1:14
College Prep/Enrichment

The Out of Door Academy
444 Reid St., Siesta Key
349-3223
Elementary - High School
T/S ratio - 1:10
College Prep/Enrichment

Manatee Technical Institute
5603 34th St. W.,
Bradenton 34210
751-7900, fax 751-7927

Short and long term vocational and technical courses (day and evening hours) for adults and high school students. The adult school offers classes for high school credit, graduates who want to continue or refresh skills, and GED testing.

SARASOTA

Eckerd College, Sarasota PEL Center
2050 Oak St., Sarasota 34237
957-3397, fax 957-4334
www.eckerd.edu

Sarasota Offers Bachelor's Degree for busy adults through program for Experienced Learners (PEL). Flexible evening and weekend classes and 8-week terms. Small classes and personal attention. Offers credit for experiential learning.

Goshen College
3737 Bahia Vista Street,
Sarasota 34232
951-6424, fax 365-6329
e-mail: jm2051@aol.com

Goshen College is a four-year national liberal arts school located in Goshen NY, owned and operated by the Mennonite church. The Sarasota Extension offers classes across the age span, particularly to adult learners. Both non-credit and credit courses are available.

Keiser College
332 Sarasota Quay,
Sarasota 34236
954-0954, fax 366-5545
www.keisercollege.cc.fl.us

This branch campus of an accredited independent junior college is located in the Sarasota Quay, the main campus is in Ft. Lauderdale. Associate Degree offered in Business Administration, Accounting, Paralegal, Health Service Administration, Computer Network Administration, Computer Programming, Medical Assistant, Hospitality Management and Computer Graphics.

New College
5700 N. Tamiami Trail,
Sarasota 34243
359-4200 (General information)
359-4269 (Admissions)
e-mail: ncadmissions@sar.usf.edu
www.newcollege.usf.edu

New College of USF is the honors college of the State University System of Florida. An undergraduate, residential college, New College of USF offers liberal arts education for the intellectually curious, academically talented student. Seven percent of the 1998 entering first year students were National Merit finalists. Faculty-student ratio is approximately 1:12, and the average class size is less than 20. Tuition for the 1998-99 academic year is $2,403 for Florida residents and $10,390 for non-residents. From 1993-95, *Money Guide: Best College Buys* ranked New College of USF No. 1 in the nation. More than 13 percent of the college's graduates have earned the Ph. D, a percapita "Ph.D. production" in the top 10 of all colleges. Enrollment 600.

Ringling School of Art & Design
2700 N. Tamiami Trail,
Sarasota 34234
351-5100, fax 359-7517

Ringling School of Art and Design, founded in 1931, is a private, accredited college of professional visual arts offering B.F.A. degrees in Computer Animation, Fine Arts, Graphic and Interactive Communications, Illustration, Interior Design and Photography. A variety of noncredit art programs for adults and youths are offered year-round as well. Exhibitions by nationally and internationally known artists and other educational programs are open to the public in the School's Selby Gallery. Enrollment 806. Degrees: BFA

Sarasota County Technical Institute
4748 Beneva Rd., Sarasota
924-1365 x283, Admissions or x340/339, Part-time programs fax 921-7902, www.careerscape.org

SCTI is a ready resource to business and industry for qualified, entry-level employees and training to update current employees in the latest medical, business,

TECHNICAL & VOCATIONAL SCHOOLS

agribusiness and industrial techniques and technology. SCTI designs programs to meet individual and unique business needs. Over 14,000 adult and high school students enroll yearly at SCTI to learn from certified, experienced instructions in well-equipped labs/classrooms and acquire the decision-making skills demanding by employers. SCTI graduates consistently achieve high scores on their respective State licensing exams. (Currently 92-100% pass rate campus-wide.) Eighty-four percent of recent graduates are working in their new career, attending college or entering the military. Programs include initial career preparation (choose from over 50 options), part-time supplemental or continuing education.

University of Sarasota
5250 17th St.,
Sarasota 34235
379-0404, fax 379-9464
www.sarasota.edu

Accredited master's and doctoral degrees in business, education, counseling, psychology, and human services administration. Designed and scheduled for working professionals. Selected offerings at University of Sarasota's Tampa Bay Campus. Enrolment 1,300. Degrees: MBA, MAEd, EdD, PsyD, DBA, MA

University of S. Florida at Sarasota
5700 N. Tamiami Trail,
Sarasota 34243
359-4200 (General information)
e-mail ncadmissions@sar.usf.edu,
www.newcollege.usf.edu

Upper level and graduate programs in professional studies, such as Business, Education and Engineering. Enrollment 1744. Degrees: BA, BS, MS, MA, MBA, M. Ed.

USF at Sarasota, located on the historic bayfront campus on Sarasota Bay, offers junior, senior and graduate level programs in the Colleges of Arts and Sciences, Business, Education, Engineering and Nursing. Continuing Education courses are also available. USF at Sarasota is a regional campus of the University of South Florida, located in Tampa. Other USF regional campus are located in St. Petersburg, Lakeland, Tampa and Ft. Myers.

VENICE

Manatee Community College South Campus
8000 S. Tamiami Trail, Venice
493-3504 www.mcc.cc.fl.us

Designated by the state as a "Center for Excellence for Computer Education," the college offers university parallel, technical, occupational, noncredit and continuing education courses. Degrees: AS, AA, certificate programs

Libraries

MANATEE COUNTY

Central Library
1301 Barcarrota Blvd. W.,
Bradenton, 748-5555
Monday - Thursday
9:00 a.m.- 9:00 p.m., Friday, 9:00 - 5:00p.m., Saturday 10:00 a.m.- 5:00 p.m. Closed Sunday.
Full-service library with 300,00+ volumes; extensive reference and genealogy departments; outreach programs; adult learning materials; Eaton Room features Manatee County historical archives including 25,000+ negatives of Manatee County history.

Sarasota Area Private Schools

The Prew Academy
7201 State Road 72,
Sarasota 921-7739
Middle - High School
T/S ratio - 1:10
College Pre/Enrichment

Sarasota Christian School
5415 Bahia Vista St.,
Sarasota 371-6481
Elementary - High School
T/S ratio - 1:23
500 Students
20 Denominations

St. Martha's Catholic
801 N. Orange Ave.,
Sarasota 953-4181
Elementary - Middle
T/S ratio - 1:20
Catholic environment

The Tabernacle Christian
4141 DeSoto Rd., Sarasota
365-1050
Elementary - Middle
T/S ratio - 1:19
Christian environment

The Westcoast School
403 N. Washington Blvd.
365-7543
Elementary - High School
T/S ratio - 1:13
Christian environment

West Florida Christian
4311 Wilkinson Rd.,
Sarasota 921-6311
Elementary - High School
Christian environment

Bradenton Area Public Schools

Abel Elementary
7100 Madonna Pl.,
Bradenton 751-7040
(Teressa Haskins)

Anna Maria Elementary
4700 Gulf Dr. N,
Holmes Beach
778-1125
(James Kronus)

Ballard Elementary
912 18th St. W,
Bradenton 741-3313
(Altamease McPherson)

Bashaw Elementary
3515 Morgan Johnson Rd., Bradenton
741-3307
(Tim Kolbe)

Bayshore Elementary
6120 26th St. W,
Bradenton 751-7000
(Tom Levengood)

Bayshore High School
5323 34th St., W,
Bradenton 751-7012
(Doug Gorham)

Braden River Elementary
10850 State Rd. 70,
Bradenton 751-7012
(Ronnie Moore)

Braden River Middle
6201 River Club Blvd.,
Bradenton 751-7080
(George Douglas)

Daughtrey Elementary
515 63rd Ave. E,
Bradenton 751-7023
(Judy Laurent)

Haile Middle School
9501 State Road 64 E.,
Bradenton 714-7240

Harlee Middle School
6423 Ninth St. E,
Bradenton 751-7027
(Bill King)

Johnson Middle
2121 26th Ave. E,
Bradenton 741-3344
(Gary Hocevar)

King Middle
600 75th St. NW,
Bradenton 741-3183
(Jo Ann Forston)

SELBY LIBRARY © BILL WEST

Braden River Library
4915 53rd Ave. E. (SR 70),
Bradenton, 727-6079
Monday/Wednesday/Friday 10:00 a.m. - 6:00 p.m., Tuesday/Thursday 12:00 noon - 8:00 p.m., Saturday 10:00 a.m. - 5:00 p.m.

Public library with 17,000 volumes; children's programs and special events.

Historical Records Library of Manatee County (Carnegie)
1405 4th Ave. W, Bradenton
741-4070
Monday - Friday
8:30 a.m. - 5:00 p.m.

Opened in 1979, it was the first county archival library of its kind in the State of Florida. Carnegie Library houses county historical records, open to the public.

Island Branch Library
5701 Marina Drive,
Holmes Beach, 778-6341
Tuesday/Thursday,
10:00 a.m.- 6:00 p.m.
Wednesday 10:00 a.m.- 8:00 p.m.
Friday/Saturday 10:00 a.m. - 5:00 p.m.
Closed Sunday

Full-service public library with 38,000 volumes, children's programs and special events throughout the year.

Palmetto Branch Library
923 6th St. W., Palmetto
722-3333
Monday - Wednesday
9:00 a.m. - 5:00 p.m.
Friday/Saturday 9:00 a.m. - 5:00 p.m.
Thursday 9:00 a.m. - 8:00 p.m.
Closed Sunday

Public library with 35,000 volumes, children's programs and special events throughout the year.

Rocky Bluff Branch Library
7042 U.S. Highway 301 N., Ellenton, 723-4821
Tuesday/Thursday/Friday
10:00 a.m. - 6:00 p.m.
Wednesday noon - 8:00 p.m.
Saturday 10:00 a.m. - 5:00 p.m.

Store-front public library with 5,000 volumes, children's programs.

South Manatee Library
6081 26 St. W., Bradenton
755-3892
Monday/Tuesday
9:00 a.m. - 8:00 p.m.
Wednesday - Saturday
9:00 a.m. - 5:00 p.m.

Full-service public library with 35,000 volumes, children's programs and special events throughout the year.

Talking Books Service for the Visually Impaired
6081 26 St. W., Bradenton
742-5914
Monday-Friday 9:00 a.m. - 5:00 p.m.

Services the visually and physically impaired in Manatee and Sarasota counties. Doctor's certification necessary to qualify for service.

SARASOTA

Arthur Vining Davis Library
Mote Marine Laboratory,
1600 Thompson Pkwy, Sarasota
388-4441
Monday - Friday 8:00 a.m.- 5:00 p.m.

Scientific research library specializing in marine and environmental subjects open to the public.

The Environmental Library
1331 1st St., Sarasota 34236
316-1181
Monday - Thursday
9:00 a.m. - 9:00 p.m.
Friday-Saturday 9 a.m.-5 p.m.
Sunday 1-5 p.m.

Extensive collection of environmental publications and videos including 5,000 books, 5,000 government documents an 75 current journal subscriptions on ecology, conservation, waste management, recycling, water resources, wetlands and more. Environmental newspaper archives and children's section.

Gulf Gate Library
7112 Curtiss Ave., Sarasota
316-1213, TTD: 925-2751
Tuesday Thursday and Friday
9:00 a.m. - 5:30 p.m.
Monday and Wednesday
9:00 a.m. - 9:00 p.m.
Saturday 9:00 a.m.- 5:00 p.m.

Public library with 70,000 books, popular children's programs, reference section, large print books, books on tape, instructional movies and videos.

The John and Mable Ringling Museum Of Art Library
5401 Bay Shore Road, Sarasota
359-5743
Wednesday and Friday
1:00 p.m.- 5:00 p.m.

Open to the public for art research, collection is non-circulating.

Jonas Kamlet Library of The Sarasota Opera
61 N. Pineapple Ave., Sarasota
366-8450

The Jonas Kamlet Library resources are available to all who seek information about opera. Located on the ground floor of the newly renovated Pavilion addition to the Opera Complex, the Library contains a large general collection of written material about opera singers, performances and history as well as opera librettos, music scores and recordings and videos. Pre and Post Season video Opera Salons are presented on large screen video with surround sound. These presentations are free to the public and consist of a discussion of the opera along with the video showing.

Bradenton Area Public Schools

Manatee Area Vocational and Technical Center
560334th St. W,
Bradenton 751-7900
(Napoleon Mills)

Manatee Elementary
1609 Sixth Ave. E,
Bradenton 741-3319
(Ozell Ackerman)

Manatee High School
902 33rd St. Ct. W.,
Bradenton 714-7300
(Pat Lucas)

Miller Elementary
4201 Manatee Ave. W,
Bradenton 741-3300
(Chuck Banks)

Moody Elementary
5425 38th Ave. W,
Bradenton 741-3170
Enrollment: 679
(Judy Joachim)

Oneco Elementary
5214 22nd St. Ct. E,
Bradenton 751-7018
(Bil Lance)

Orange Ridge/Bullock Elementary
400 30th Ave. W,
Bradenton 741-3325
(Fran Padgett)

Palma Sola Elementary
6906 Fifth Ave. NW,
Bradenton 741-3179
(Doug DeGruchy)

Prine
3801 Southern Pkwy,
Bradenton
751-7006
(Phil Joachim)

Samoset Elementary
1720 33rd Ave. E,
Bradenton 741-3337
(Greg Kunka)

Seabreeze Elementary
3601 71st St., W,
Bradenton 741-3190
(Michael Sicord)

Southeast High
1200 37th Ave. E,
Bradenton 741-3366
(Ralph Heath)

Stewart Elementary
7905 15th Ave. NW,
Bradenton 741-3176
(Jackie Sexton)

Sugg Middle
3801 59th St. W,
Bradenton 741-3157
(Judy Bills)

Bradenton Area Public Schools

Tara Elementary
6950 Linger Lodge Rd.
Bradenton 751-7660
(Tom Wailand)

Wakeland Elementary
1812 27th St.
Bradenton 741-3358
(Brian Flynn)

Witt Elementary
200 Rye Rd.
Bradenton 741-3628
(Myra Russell)

Bradenton Area Private Schools

St. Stephen's Episcopal
315 41st St. W,
Bradenton 746-2121
Elementary - High School
T/S ratio - 1:15 - 1:9
College Prep/Enrich

West Coast Junior Academy
1112 49th Ave. E,
Bradenton 755-9667
Elementary
T/S ratio - 1:10 - 1:13

HIBISCUS © BILL WEST

Longboat Key Library
555 Bay Isles Road, Longboat Key
383-2011
9:00 a.m. - 4:00 p.m. Nov 1 - May 31
9:00 a.m. - 12:30 p.m.
June 1 - Oct. 31.
Closed Saturday afternoon.

Subscription library with offerings of biographies, fiction, nonfiction, books on tape, large print and children's books.

Ringling School Of Art and Design Verman Kimbrough Memorial Library
2700 N. Tamiami Trail, Sarasota
359-7587
Monday - Thursday
8:00 a.m. - 10:00 p.m.
Friday 8:00 a.m.- 4:30 p.m.
Saturday 2:00 p.m.- 6:00 p.m.
Sunday 2:00 p.m. - 10:00 p.m.

Open to the public, specializing in art and design reference books.

Sarasota Music Archive
265 S. Orange Ave., Sarasota
955-5890
Monday - Friday 10:00 a.m. - 3:00 p.m.

An extraordinary collection of over 300,000 recordings, books, audio and video tapes, scores, sheet music, magazines and memorabilia. Archive resources include the equipment to play every type of recording in existence. Educational services available to researchers and the community. Lectures, programs; a priceless treasure of music.

Selby Public Library
1331 1st St., Sarasota 34236
316-1181 (Recorded)
Reference Desk: 316-1183,
TTD: 316-1190
Monday-Thursday 9:00 a.m. - 9:00 p.m. , Friday and Saturday 9:00 a.m. - 5:00 p.m. , Sunday 1:00 - 5:00 p.m.

171,000 volumes plus 400 periodicals serves community in variety of ways including extensive youth programs from preschool to high school; story time; family films; cultural art series and much more. Books-on-tape, CDs, videos, reference and on-line services – all available 68 hours a week! According to Head Librarian Liz Beatrice there are now ten-times as many people using Selby at the new location as were using their old facility last year, there's now around 30,000 visitors each month.

University Of South Florida at Sarasota / New College Cook Library
5700 N. Tamiami Trail, Sarasota
359-4300,
Reference Desk: 359-4301
Monday - Thursday 8:00 a.m. - 1:00 a.m., Friday 8:00 a.m. - 11:00

p.m., Saturday 10:00 a.m. - 11:00 p.m., Sunday Noon - 1:00 a.m.

245,000 volumes, open to public; serves as research center for college studies; Internet and on-line CD ROM database on education, science, psychology, social science, art, humanities, law, medicine, engineering, business and general periodicals plus media center. The best library hours in the area, a wonderful place to spend the evening.

VENICE

Francis T. Bourne Jacaranda Library
4143 Woodmere Park Blvd., Venice, 486-2723,
TTD Number: 486-2004

Monday, Wednesday 9:00 a.m. - 5:00 p.m., Friday and Saturday, 9:00 a.m.- 8:00 p.m. Tuesday and Thursday, closed on Sunday.

Newest library in the Sarasota County Public Library system, dedicted to a library and school advocate for over 15 years. Its 12,500 sq. feet contain over 41,000 volumes as well as a superior collection of videos. The library has seasonal adult and youth programming. Internet access and informational CD ROM, public access computers for word processing and desktop publishing. ADA equipment available for the physically disadvantaged. Volunteers provide nearly 12,000 hours of service annually.

Venice Public Library
300 S. Nokomis Ave., Venice
486-2338
Reference Desk: 486-2341,
TTD Number: 486-2342
Monday - Thursday 9:00 a.m. - 9:00 p.m. , Friday and Saturday, 9:00 a.m. - 5:00 p.m.
Sunday 1:00 p.m. - 5:00 p.m.

Very popular public library serving the Venice community; now expanded to 25,000 sq. ft. with new genealogy center and low vision resource center; outstanding selection of special youth programs from preschool through young adult; teen volunteer summer program; fall and winter lecture series; book review program; in-library and out reach program plus exhibits and music events. Volunteers give over 25,000 hours to the library.

Venice Area Public Schools

Garden Elementary
700 Center Rd., Venice
486-2110
Enrollment: 656
(Mark E. Cook)

Laurel/Nokomis School
(PK-8)
1900 E. Laurel Road, Nokomis
486-2171
Enrollment: 1500
(Wendy Katz)

Pine View School for the Gifted (2-12)
1 Python Pass,
Osprey 486-2001
Enrollment: 1,441
(Steve Largo)

Taylor Ranch Elementary School
2500 Taylor Ranch Tr., Venice 486-2000
Enrollment: 615
(Robert Earley)

Venice Area Middle
1900 Center Rd., Venice 486-2100
Enrollment: 1330
(Gary Wetherill)

Venice Elementary
301 Bahama St.,
Venice 486-2111
Enrollment: 687
(Emile Quinn)

Venice High School
1 Indian Ave.,
Venice 488-6726
Enrollment: 2,422
(Daniel Parett)

Venice Area Private Schools

Epiphany Cathedral
316 Sarasota,
Venice 488-2215
Elementary - Middle
T/S ratio: 1:20 - 1:35
Catholic Environment

Venice Christian School
1936 Venice Ave E.,
Venice 488-2228
Elementary
Christian Environment

Local Fun

BEACH FUN © BILL WEST

DECISIONS...DECISIONS...

Botanical gardens where rare species from the Amazon are preserved...

Marine aquariums where research programs provide essential oceanographic information on a daily basis...

Art museums widely hailed as "important" on an international level...

But wait, there's more!

Antique cars, ancient Indian burial mounds, miniature horses, major league baseball, dolphins in the gulf, alligators in the wild, peacocks in suburbia, snowbirds on ice, a beach where you can find prehistoric sharks teeth and the largest indoor amusement park in Florida...

These are just some of the highlights offered here for you and your family.

Who needs Mickey? We have Snooty! And Mo! And Hugh! and Buffett! (Each a local manatee celebrity.)

Scott Dennis has been with WWSB, Channel 40 since 1985. His work has been honored by the Florida Sportscasters Association with awards for "Best Series" and "Best Live Sportscast". In 1989, Scott was promoted to Sports Director, and then in the summer of 1995 Scott moved into the news department as Co-Anchor of FIRST NEWS AT FIVE. He was promoted again in January 1999 as Co-Anchor of NEWS40 AT SIX and NEWS40 AT ELEVEN. Scott graduated from Sarasota's Riverview High School and received his Bachelor of Science Degree in Broadcast Journalism from the University of Florida. He lives in Sarasota with his wife, the ever-so-fabulous Gilda, who works for NEWS40 as Executive Producer.

According to NEWS40 Anchor **Scott Dennis**, "For a great time, the Suncoast offers plenty of possibilities. Families and friends will find more than enough choices, from simple pleasures such as shark-tooth hunting on the beach to more involved entertainment like a 3-hour kayak tour. You're bound to find any number of memorable activities which will add to the quality of your life and those you "share the fun" with. In fact, there's almost too much to see and do here. Luckily, this section of 'The Guide' is your ticket to the very best."

Albritton Fruit Co. Trolley Tours
5947 Clark Center Ave., Sarasota 34238
925-7155 (ask for Vivian), fax 925-1098
Tours: Mondays Only at 10 am and 3 pm
Reservation Required
Adults: $5.00
Children under 12, accompanied with an adult: Free

For the first time in fifty years you can take a tour of the 1,000 acre historic Albritton citrus groves and their original 1948 grove store – see it all in an authentic reconditioned trolley. Free samples of juice, homemade fudge and ice cream too.

Trolley service provides direct pickup/drop-off at various locations around Siesta Key, call for specific locations and details.

Allyn Museum of Entomology
3621 Bay Shore Rd., Sarasota 34234
355-8475, fax 355-8475

Not really worth going out of your way for (unless you are a butterfly/moth specialist) but worth a quick visit if you are in the neighborhood – if you are visiting Sarasota Jungle Gardens this is located just next door. The museum has one of the largest collections of moths and butterflies in the Western Hemisphere, 600,000 of each. Unfortunately it is only open to researchers. However, they do have a nice display at the entrance, that's why we can only recommend a quick but colorful visit.

Field Trip: Alligators

Alligators can be found throughout Florida. They live in rivers, lakes, canals and even in some water hazards on golf courses.

For the most part, alligators are more afraid of you than you are of them.

But NEVER get close to an alligator – we shouldn't have to tell you not to "play" with alligators.

The biting pressure of a Great White Shark is 1,700 pounds per square inch; a 12-foot alligator is about 3,200 pounds – and they are not known for their table manners. Trust us, this is the not kind of dental work you want to see up close.

Aquatel Resort
1220 Mill Creek Rd.,
Bradenton 34202
746-6884
Rates: Half Day canoe rental - $10.00; Full Day canoe rental - $16.00; Overnight rental (24-hours) - $25.00; Boat Launch area - $3.00.

Canoeing on the Manatee River for the whole family. Seeing manatees in the wild is not guaranteed, but there are plenty of them in the river.

Manatee County Audubon Society
795-2762

Sarasota County Audubon Society
364-9212

Each local Audubon Society offers a wealth of knowledge about local and migratory birds. Best of all, each offers special programs, day trips and overnight tours – a great excuse for families and friends to get outdoors. Call for schedules and exciting activities.

Balloon Safaris, Inc.
2359 S Tamiami Trail, 3104,
Sarasota 34239
492-9792, fax 492-9792
Location: 45 minutes south of Sarasota via US-41 or I-75, shuttle van will meet you just south of Venice and carry you to the launch site.

Cost: $149/per person - Visa/Master Card accepted.

Tired of looking at birds from below? This is an adventure you'll remember for the rest of your life! You'll be floating in air, coming within inches of towering pine trees below in a 7-story hot air balloon. Pilot Jim Henry is southwest Florida's most experienced balloonist. Flights begin at dawn and last approximately 45 minutes. A complimentary champagne picnic breakfast is served right after your flight. Sightings of boar, deer, owls, alligators, rabbits, eagles and even the rare Florida panther are possible. Elegant gift certificates available.

Bay Lady Cruises (featuring "August" the potbellied pig!)
Osprey Marine Center, 480 Blackburn Point Rd, Osprey 485-6366
Rates: Adults - $9.50
Seniors (60+) - $8.50
Children (12 and under) - $6.50

2-hour sight-seeing tours daily at 1:00 p.m. on 40' fiberglass catamaran through Venice, Nokomis, Osprey and south Sarasota. Visit bird sanctuaries, manatee habitats and beautiful homes. Licensed for up to 49 people. Yes, August the potbellied pig will ride with you – the kids will love this! Also sunset cruises, Christmas-light sails and more. Call for reservations.

Bishop Planetarium (see: South Florida Museum)

Bucko's Museum
1923 Myrtle St., Sarasota 34234
355-7646

Not many folks know about this one. Essentially the knickknacks collected by Bucko over the years during his pursuit of used furniture (his massive furniture shop is connected to the museum). Rustic relics from everywhere including tools, farm equipment, odds and ends. With luck Bucko himself will escort you around. Every piece has a story. Never a charge, always amazing.

Caspersen Beach County Park
At the end of Harbor Drive,
Venice, 951-5572
A close look at marshes, mangroves and tidal flats on a 20-min. walk through this coastal hammock. Picnic tables are set up at the end of the trail, the two-mile stretch of beach is a great place to find shells and prehistoric sharks teeth.

Cortez Fleet
4330 127th St. (near Cortez Rd. at the bridge) Cortez 34215
794-1223, fax 795-2221
Fares: Adults - $15.00
Seniors - $13.00
Under 15 - $8.00.

Trips: Tuesday, Thursday and Sunday, 1:00 p.m. to 5:00 p.m. Beachcombing and shelling cruises to historic Egmont Key. Take a guided walking tour of historic Fort Dade. Walk the paved pathways that are being reclaimed by "the jungle," swim little used white sandy beaches, explore to your heart's content. Fun for all ages! A full bar and grill is available on board. Reservations are highly recommended. Four, six and nine hour deep sea fishing, 4 hour bay fishing and private charters are available. Parasailing 1400 ft. also available. See Anna Maria island as never before. (For information on deep sea fishing and parasailing trip prices, call 794-1223.)

Crowley Museum and Nature Center

16405 Myakka Road (Route 2), Sarasota 34240
322-1000
Admission: Adults - $3.00; Children - Free; Members - Free; Individual Membership - $15.00; Family Membership - $25.00.

185 acres of natural Florida with nature trails and a 2,000 ft. boardwalk through five different habitats and an observation tower overlooking the marsh. A pioneer Florida presentation includes a homesteader cabin, blacksmith shop, a Cracker house, sugarcane mill and a museum. Open to the public Thursday-Sunday 10 a.m. to 4 p.m. Call for special programs. Located 15 minutes east from I-75 and Fruitville Rd.

Desoto Memorial Dragstrip

State Road 64 E., Bradenton
748-1320 (Office open 9:30 a.m. - 5p.m. Mon - Fri.)
Test and Tune: Every Tuesday evening from 6:00 p.m. - 10:30 p.m. and Saturday mornings from 10:00 a.m. to 2:30 p.m. and Fri. night 6-11 p.m.

You can bring anything that moves and race it down the straight line drag strip - no speed limit! $5.00 admission, $10.00 to "drag" your vehicle, kids under 12 admitted free.

Drag Racing: Every Saturday from January 27 - December 7th $10.00 adults admission, kids under 12 admitted free. The rates to "drag" depend on how fast your hamsters can peddle.

DeSoto National Memorial

North end of 75th Street NW, Bradenton 34280
792-0458, fax 792-3094
www.nps.gov/des
Hours: 9:00 a.m.- 5:00 p.m.; Open daily year 'round except Thanksgiving, Christmas and New Year's Day. Admission: Free.

DeSoto National Memorial's mission is to commemorate Hernando DeSoto's landing in Florida and the significance of his expedition of the later history of North America. A 22 minute film entitled "Legacy of a Legend" is shown on the hour. This film depicts the four year, 4000 mile journey of DeSoto and his men throughout what is now the southeastern United States. A one-half mile self guiding interpretive trail leads through mangrove and coastal environments. The visitor center offers museum articles which relate to the DeSoto expedition. Also in the visitor center, a touch screen computer gives detailed information on the routes of DeSoto, Columbus, and other European explorers, other National Parks in Florida, and local area information. Camp Ucita is similar to the camp in which DeSoto and his men spent their first winter in Florida, from late December to early April, Park rangers dressed in period costume give demonstrations of black powder and crossbow weapons, as well as blacksmithing and cooking. The demonstrations are given several times each day, weather permitting. Please call in advance for current schedule. Upon advance requests, special films or demonstrations may be arranged for groups during the winter season.

Ed Smith Stadium

2700 12th St., Sarasota 34237
Information: 954-SOXX (7699)
"The Cadillac of Spring Training Facilities" is how they like to promote this baseball park and it's no wonder, this is simply one of the country's finest baseball training facilities. Spring training camp of

Field Trip: Alligators

Alligators are night dwellers, that's when they eat and, depending on the season, make whoopie. (Kids, don't ask how.) It's during this "whoopee" season that alligators will sometimes move out of their native swimming areas on to more populated venues for a night on the town. Not to worry, these little soirees into suburbia are usually rewarded with an all expense paid vacation into a professional 'gator trapper's net – a quick way to ruin one's love life.

Alligators are most dangerous to humans during mating season, from May to June, and when the eggs hatch, from late August to the end of September.

Field Trip: Alligators

The male alligator may wander great distances during mating season – sometimes five miles from a fresh water source. They CAN climb over fences. A six foot alligator can jump about five feet. We're sure you'll agree, alligators belong in the wild. You can help them stay there with one simple rule: NEVER FEED AN ALLIGATOR! Why? It's a violation of state law ($500 fine and/or 60 days in jail) and when you feed alligators they lose their fear of humans. That means, YOU could end up as their dinner date. Not very romantic.

the Cincinnati Reds and home of the Florida State League's Sarasota Red Sox.

For 1999 Spring Training information see pg. 147.

The Enterprise Sailing Charters
Marina Jack Marina, Bayfront, Downtown Sarasota
951-1833
Daily Sailing Schedule: Half day - $35.00 per person
Sunset (2 hrs.) - $20.00 per person
Reservations suggested, departure times vary with the seasons.

U.S. Coast Guard inspected and licensed custom 41' sailboat which will comfortably accommodate twelve people. A great way to enjoy the water, knowledgeable Captain. Charters available.

Emerson Point Preserve
Information: 749-3070

This 195-acre costal conversation park is located of Snead Island on the Southwest shore of Tampa Bay. The State of Florida and Manatee County have worked together to reconstruct wetlands and preserve the remains of a 1400 year old Native American Village. Visitors can enjoy a journey to the top of a sacred ceremonial indian mound, with interpretive signage and boardwalks to help guide the way. This area will soon be open to kayaking and canoeing (recognized by the Florida Canoe Trails Association) and "facilities" will be added.

Fallen Pine Ranch Miniature Horses
Location: Rainbow Ranch Acres (End of Fruitville Rd.), Sarasota
322-1897
Hours: By appointment only (late afternoon & weekends).
Admission: $3.50/per person.
Time it takes to see it all: 1 - 1 1/2 Hours.

Norm and Judy Middleton have been raising miniatures for 23 years and are primarily responsible for turning Florida into the second largest population of "minis" in the country. Several of their horses are "Top Ten" champions. They will personally guide you and your family on a tour of their pastures, filled with these very affectionate miniature horses. Be sure to bring plenty of carrots, apples and film. The "minis" won't eat the film, but they do love to be photographed.

Fat Cat Cruises
Location: 509 N. Tamiami Trail, Venice
362-7565

Enjoy a 2 hour picturesque sail through the Venice Inlet and into the Gulf of Mexico aboard the beautiful Hakuna Matata, the most spacious, comfortable catamaran in the area. Plenty of uncrowded deck space to move about under sun or shade. Cruise includes cold soft drinks. We specialize in private parties. Call for current schedule. Adults $20; Children over 10, $10; Kids under 10 are always free.

Florida House Learning Center
4600 Beneva Rd., Sarasota 34233
316-1200, fax 316-1203
Hours: 9:00 a.m. - 1:00 p.m. Tuesday and Thursday,
1:00 p.m. - 4:00 p.m. Saturday and Sunday

An "earth friendly" demonstration of conserving technology and design for living in southwest Florida, the Florida House Learning Center incorporates available "off-the-shelf" technology: affordable and cost effective methods of using resources efficiently while promoting economic viability. Essentially, this is where you can learn how to get more out of less, raise your environmental consciousness and find out how to incorporate a philosophy which embraces recycling and buying local whenever possible. Free admission.

Florida West Coast Symphony
Also: Florida String Quartet, Florida Wind Quintet, Florida Brass Quintet, New Artists Piano Quartet
709 N. Tamiami Trail, Sarasota 34236
Tickets: 953-3434, fax 953-3059

A message from **Gretchen Serrie**, Executive Director:

"Serving both Sarasota, Manatee, and Charlotte Counties, the Florida West Coast Symphony is the foremost presenter of orchestral and chamber music on the West Coast of Florida. In its 49th season, the Orchestra will present the finest musical masterpieces with world-class soloists in six, three-concert Masterworks Series performances: Friday evenings at Neel Auditorium in Bradenton and Saturday matinee and evenings at the Van Wezel Performing Arts Hall in Sarasota. The Englewood Series features the orchestra in three sunday afternoon performances at the Lemon Bay High School Fine Arts Center. The season also includes six Children's Concerts, two Family Concerts, and a wide variety of Pops Concerts. The Chamber Orchestra's Enchanted Evenings and Concert Lites Series offers lighter classics and solo showpieces in Boston Pops-style concerts in Holley Hall of the Symphony Center.

The Florida West Coast symphony has a national reputation for its focus on chamber music. Four resident ensembles, The Florida String Quartet, the Florida Wind Quintet, the Florida Brass Quintet and the New Artists Piano Quartet, present their own concert series in addition to more than 100 performances and workshops throughout Southwest Florida."

© FLORIDA WEST COAST SYMPHONY

The Sarasota Music Festival, often referred to as "the Tanglewood of the South," brings 120 of the finest young musicians from the U.S. and abroad to study with a faculty of 40 internationally acclaimed artists. Three weekends of concerts each June are one of the highlights of Sarasota's music season.

The Symphony's youth program, one of the most extensive in the nation, includes two orchestras, a wind ensemble, four string orchestras, a Young Artists Competition, and a Summer String, Wind, Brass and Percussion Program. Scholarships make this programs available to all interested children.

Gamble Mansion
Off U.S. 301, 1 mile West on Exit 43 off I-75, Manatee County, Ellenton
723-4536
Guided Tours: Thursday - Monday, 9:30 a.m., 10:30 a.m. and every hour from 1:00 p.m. - 4:00 p.m.
Admission: Adults – $3.00; Children (6 - 12 years) – $1.50; Toddlers (5 years and under) – Free.

Field Trip:
Alligator Facts

- The largest alligator ever recorded in Florida was a 17 feet five inches monster, killed in 1956 at Apopka.

- Adult alligators have no predator except man.

- Male and female alligators are the same color, there is no way to distinguish them externally.

- An alligator has very little strength when trying to open its jaws, and the mouth of even a very large alligator can be kept closed by holding the jaws together at the snout. Don't try it!

Site of the oldest building in Manatee County, the "Old South" brought back to life by the United Daughters of the Confederacy who bought this ruined mansion in 1925 and caringly reconstructed it with authentic period design, today operated by the Florida Park Service. Entrance to mansion is by guided tour only and will take 40 to 45 minutes.

Gamble Mansion Period Vocabulary

HOGSHEAD – A large barrel made of wood, used to store and ship sugar, molasses, tobacco and other farm products.

CISTERN – A structure for holding water. Rainwater could be collected and stored. Much needed good drinking water was scarce.

DOGTROT – An open corridor between parts of a building. Its name comes from a tradition that the dogs of the home sought the cool and shaded walkway to escape the heat of midday.

TABBY – Building material made from a mixture of sand, water and a cementing material called lime which was manufactured through the burning, crushing and sifting of oyster shells.

VERANDA – A porch with a roof that provided an outdoor place to enjoy cool parts of day and evening. Fans and incense helped to keep insects away.

SWEEP – A gravel area in front of a house where carriages could be driven to the doorstep and moved on without turning around. Usually the space was kept carefully swept or raked and clean.

PARLOR – A room for entertaining visitors; a young girl might sit here with her beau.

Gulf Coast WACO Biplanes
Dolphin Aviation Bldg., Sarasota/Bradenton Airport,
359-2246
Fares: $90 for 15 minutes (1 or 2 people), $160 for 30 minutes.
High above the beaches, you'll zoom around in an authentic factory built reproduction of the original 1935 Biplane. Seats two, plus the FAA commercially rated pilot. Call for reservations and don't forget to bring your camera!

GWIZ - Gulf Coast Wonder & Imagination Zone
Sarasota's "Hands-On" Museum
Airport Mall, 8251 15th St. East (Old Hwy. 301), Sarasota
359-9975 (Location will change in September, 1999 - call first)
Hours: Tuesday - Saturday 10:00 a.m.- 5:00 p.m.
             Sunday 1:00 p.m. - 5:00 p.m.
Admission: Adults - $3.00 , Children - $1.50, Under 2 - free.
Time it takes to see it all: 2 Hours.

Highlights: Over 60 interactive, hands-on exhibits including laser harp, reaction time exhibit, body bubble, laser oscilloscope, fossil dig, butterfly garden, live snakes and other reptiles, distorted house, anti-gravity mirror, echo tube, computer fun and games. Special weekly "happenings" every Saturday morning at 10:30 a.m. for children and families, field trips/birthday parties can be arranged by calling in advance. It is requested that one adult accompany every four children.

Historic Spanish Point
337 North Tamiami Tr., Osprey 34229
966-5214, fax 966-1335
Hours: 9:00 a.m.- 5:00 p.m. Monday - Saturday, Noon - 5:00 p.m. Sunday
Admission: Adults – $5.00; Children (6-12 years) – $3.00.
Seniors admitted for $3.00 on Monday. Children under 6 free.
Time it takes to see it all: 1-1/2 - 2 hours.

A pristine thirty-acre environmental, archaeological and historic site representing three important eras in the state's history.

Highlights: Prehistoric Indian mound and middens dating from 2150 BC, pioneer homestead buildings from the late 1800s, gardens from the estate of Mrs. Potter Palmer, 1911-1918.

The Visitors Center in historic Osprey School features special exhibits. Guided tours daily, call for tour times. Tram available Sat., Sun., Mon. for $1 extra, 48 hours prior reservation required.

Indian Mound Park
Take State Road 776 south to Orange Street and head west and follow signs to Lemon Bay, at the end of Winson St., 210 Winson Avenue, Englewood 34223
474-8919
Time it takes to see it all: 20 minutes

A five acre park with a very short (!) self guided tour featuring 22 educational stations placed along ancient Indian trails. See indigenous plants used by Indians for medicine, food and dyes. Site was occupied by Indians from approximately 1000 B.C. to 1350 A.D. Before you go call 316-1172 and request the 16-page Nature Trail Guide, provided free of charge from the Sarasota County Parks & Recreation Department.

J.P. Igloo
5309 29th St. E., Ellenton, 34222
723-3663 fax 722-1121

This 113,500 sq. ft. state of the art domed "igloo-like" all-ages sporting center, opening early 1999, will be Florida's premiere skating facility: two NHL size ice rinks, one USA Inline Hockey rink, a full-service pro-shop, Health & Fitness exercise facility, four birthday party rooms, full-service restaurant with catering capabilities, video arcade room, supervised child play area, broadcast facility, six conference rooms (on the second floor) and more! Olympic Ice Dance medallists head the Figure Skating coaching staff. Programs include hockey, regular and figure skating - all levels. Located adjacent to Prime Outlet Mall.

(Sarasota) Jungle Gardens
3701 Bayshore Road, Sarasota 34234
355-5305, fax 355-1222, e-mail sarasotajg@aol.com
Hours: 9:00 a.m. - 5:00 p.m. Daily
Admission: Adults – $9.00; Children (3-12 yrs.) – $5.00; Toddlers (3 and under) – Free; Friday Senior Special (62+) – $8.00. Annual Passes available (recommended for local kids!)
Time it takes to see it all: 2 - 2 1/2 hours.

Highlights: 10 acres filled with native and exotic plants, jungle animals, reptiles and birds, "kiddie jungle" where kids can pet animals and hold birds, shell and butterfly museums, impressive reptile and bird shows. Gazebo available for private weddings. Group discounts available.

Reptile Showtimes: 10:00 a.m. Noon, 2:00 p.m. and 4:00 p.m.

J.P. IGLOO

Ice & Inline Skating Complex

- 2 – 200'x85' NHL SIZE ICE RINKS
- 1 – 185'x85' FULL SIZE INLINE RINK
- Ice & Inline Hockey Programs (Youth & Adult)
- Figure Skating Programs (Group & Private)
- Learn-to-Skate Programs
- Conference Rooms (holds up to 80 people)
- Pro-Shop (Figure Skating, Ice & Inline Hockey)
- Public Skating   • Skate Rentals
- Birthday Party Rooms   • Concessions Area
- Broadcast Academy   • Health Center
- Group Ice Rental   • Broomball
- Full-Service Restaurant

(941) 723-DOME (3663)
5309 29th St. East/Ellenton, FL 34222
Just north of the Prime Outlet Mall
Interstate 75 & U.S. 301, Exit 43

Field Trip: Alligator Facts

- To estimate the length of an alligator, the distance in inches from the forward edge of the eye to the nose is roughly equivalent to the length of the alligator in feet. An alligator that appears to have a 10 inch space from the eyes to the nostrils is about a 10-foot alligator.

- In captivity, male alligators may live up to 50 years old; in the wild, 30 to 35 years is probably the maximum life span.

For more information, request a free copy of "Florida's Alligators and Crocodiles' from Florida Power and Light Environmental Affairs Department by calling: 1-800-552-8440.

Bird Showtimes: 10:30 a.m., 12:30 p.m., 2:30 p.m. and 4:30 p.m.

Known as "The Gardens," this attraction was once listed in the Sarasota city records as "an impenetrable swamp." In the early 1930s, a local journalist named David Breed Lindsay bought 10 acres of it, planning to develop the virgin subtropical jungle into a beautiful botanical garden. Exotic tropical plants, flowers and trees were added to the native flora as well as tropical birds, some of whom flew in freely.

A neighbor, Pearson Conrad, who operated a nursery provided many of the plantings, chartered the streams, and planned the lands or ponds. When people began to wander the jungle to see the exotic plants, trees and birds, the men decided an admission fee would be appropriate, and in 1936 one was established: 10 cents for children and 35 cents for adults. Four years later, Sarasota Jungle Gardens opened as a tourist attraction.

Today, The Gardens features a wide collection of animals: Rheas, Emus, Wallabies, Aldabra Tortoise, a pair of Asian Leopards, Ring Tail Lemurs, Squirrel and Spider Monkeys, a colony of Flamingos, other wild fowl and exotic birds, a farm zoo with goats, donkeys and chickens, and a collection of alligators, crocodiles, snakes, lizards and turtles. In addition, there are various areas of The Gardens referred to as: Tiki Garden, Garden of Christ, the Children's Jungle Playground, Bird pose area, the Jungle trails and Open Ponds and Gardens.

Kokopelli Kustomware
437 Burns Court, Sarasota, 34236
362-7990

This "paint it your way" contemporary ceramic studio and pottery place caters to all ages. Create your own dinnerware, ceramic tiles or personalize unique gifts from their selection of ready made items. No experience necessary. Great for birthday parties and fun get-togethers. Located in the historic Burns Court District of Downtown Sarasota.

Lake Manatee State Recreation Area
20007 State Rd. 64, Bradenton 34202
Fifteen miles east of Bradenton on State Road 64
741-3028, e-mail lmsra2@juno.com

This 556-acre recreation area extends along three miles of the south shore of Lake Manatee, a water reservoir for Sarasota and Manatee counties. The park is mostly mesic flatwoods and sand pine scrub with some depression marshes and xeric hammock. Recreational activities include camping, swimming, picnics and boating. No water-skiing or boats with more than 20 horsepower allowed - keeping things on the tranquil side.

LeBarge Sightseeing Cruises
U.S. 41 at Island Park Circle (Marina Jack Marina)
366-6116
Daytime Narrated Sightseeing Cruise: 2:00 p.m.- 4:00 p.m. daily.
Tickets: Adults – $15.00; Children (12 and under) – $5.00.
Romantic Sunset Cruise: 7:00 p.m. - 9:00 p.m. daily (depending on time of sunset) –$15.00 per person.

Highlights: Two hour, 25 mile trip on Sarasota Bay. Daytime cruise features running commentary on points of interest and wildlife, sunset cruise takes you out to the Gulf to see a spectacular Sarasota sunset and enjoy live entertainment. Food and drink prices are additional. Private charters are available. Call for cruise schedule.

Linger Lodge
7205 Linger Lodge Rd., Bradenton 34202

755-2757, fax 758-0718

RV Resort and restaurant with Old Florida scenery and a "collection of stuff" which will amaze you. Located on the Braden River with museum-like decorations - over 200 rattlesnakes adorn the restaurant (dead, thankfully), but you really have to see this place to believe it. Featured as the very first "Steve Rabow's Suncoast Treasures" story on WWSB, Channel 40. Well worth the drive!

Cortez Fleet Parasail

Seafood Shack Marina, 4330 127th St W., Cortez 34215
Reservations: 792-1900, fax 795-2221

Highlights: An hour of anticipation, 10-12 minutes of unforgettable adrenaline. You'll ride out to sea in an offshore racing hull, preparing to fly (just like Peter Pan) skyward, up to 600' in the air. Takeoffs and landings are soft, DRY and directly from the towing vessel. Coast Guard licensed crew swears there is no effort required whatsoever. We're still searching for our nerve, it's around here somewhere, maybe locked in the cabin. Call for reservations.

Major League Baseball

Does it get better than this? The Cincinnati Reds in Sarasota, The Pittsburgh Pirates in Bradenton and other clubs in the "Grapefruit League" who all take advantage of our state-of-the-art facilities. Michael Jordan may be doing other things, his loss. For a complete list of Florida "Grapefruit League" Spring Training teams, sites and phone numbers for ordering tickets see pg. 147.

1999 SCHEDULES

Cincinnati Reds 1998 Spring Training Schedule

Ed Smith Stadium
2700 12th St., Sarasota 34237
Tickets: 954-4464 or any Ticketmaster location

Individual Ticket Prices:

$10 Box Seats
$ 8 Reserved Seats
$ 5 General Admission

To order tickets by mail, include $2 per order for postage and handling and send order to 1090 N. Euclid Avenue, Sarasota, 34237

All games begin at 1:05 p.m. except *games which begin at 7:05 p.m. (All dates and times are subject to change. Please call ahead.)

Day	Date	Opponent
Thursday	March 4	Minnesota
Friday	March 5	Texas
Saturday	March 6	Boston
Monday	March 8	Pittsburgh
Tuesday	March 9	Texas*
Wednesday	March 10	Detroit
Thursday	March 11	Minnesota
Saturday	March 13	Philadelphia
Monday	March 15	New York Yankees*
Friday	March 19	Boston*

Kokopelli Kustomware
437 Burns Court 362-7990

- Sarasota's ultimate paint-it-yourself contemporary ceramic studio.
- Featuring a wide array of bisque pieces.
- Create (your own) dinnerware, ceramic tiles or personalize unique gifts for others.
- Everything non-toxic, dishwasher and microwave safe.
- Perfect for birthday parties, company events, field trips, showers, or get togethers.
- Located in the historic Burns Court district of downtown Sarasota
- Walk-ins and browsers welcome
- Certified Instruction

Hours: M-Sat 10-5, Sun 12-5
Evening appointments available upon request

**Field Trip:
The Brown Pelican**

If you've seen *Jurassic Park* you already know that current Speilberg theoretics place these magnificent creatures as direct descendents of rather repugnant carnivorous reptiles. (Say to yourself, "It was only a movie!") While it's true that pelicans have been on earth for over forty million years, these days their appetites most assuredly favor fresh fish.

Sunday	March 21	Texas
Wednesday	March 24	Tampa
Thursday	March 25	Pittsburgh*
Sunday	March 28	Minnesota
Tuesday	March 30	New York Yankees

1999 Pittsburgh Pirates Spring Training Schedule

McKechnie Field, Bradenton
748-4610 or any Ticketmaster location.
Individual Ticket Prices:
$8.50 Box Seats
$8.00 Reserved Seats
$5.50 Reserved General Admission (sold at ticket office only)

1999 introduces an $5 million facility upgrade - the team is happy. To order tickets by mail send check or money order to: Tickets-Pittsburgh Pirates, P.O. Box 1359, Bradenton, FL 34206. Add $2 to order for postage and handling. All games begin at 1:05 p.m.

Day	Date	Opponent
Friday	March 5	Detroit
Sunday	March 7	Philadelphia
Wednesday	March 10	New York Yankees
Tuesday	March 11	Tampa Bay
Friday	March 12	Minnesota
Sunday	March 14	Texas
Tuesday	March 16	Texas
Wednesday	March 17	Cincinnati
Thurssday	March 18	Philadelphia
Sunday	March 21	Tampa Bay
Monday	March 22	Boston
Friday	March 26	Minnesota
Thursday	March 27	Cincinnati
Tuesday	March 30	Toronto
Wednesday	March 31	Boston

1999 Baltimore Orioles Practice and Training Sessions

Twin Lakes Park, 6700 Clark Rd., Sarasota
Call 923-1996 for schedule.
Admission: Free

No scheduled games, but you can watch the big boys work on skills which might make their big bank accounts even bigger, while the minor league players try to make their mark, from Feb. 15th through the end of April. Skill, sweat and smiles.

Manatee Airboat Tours

12310 Manatee Ave. W., Bradenton
at Perico Harbor Marina (Leverocks & Galati Marine)
795-5353
Cost: $12.00 adults; $10.00 children

Take an exciting Florida wildlife and wilderness eco-adventure on the Bradenton area's only airboat tour through some of Florida's most beautiful waterways – rarely seen by visitors – including a trip to nesting grounds of the Roseate Spoonbill, Reddish Egret, Ibis, Sandhill Crane and the native Wood Stork. The airboat holds up to six people. Whooshh!! Call for reservations. Open 9 a.m. to 4 p.m. Trips hourly.

Manatee Village Historical Park

Sixth Avenue E. and 15th Street E., Bradenton 34208
749-7165
www.clerkofcourt.com

Hours: 9:00 a.m. - 4:30 p.m. Monday - Friday, 1:30 p.m. - 4:30 p.m. Sunday, Closed Saturday, Closed Weekends July and August.
Admission: Free
Group tours are available on request and at no charge.
Time it takes to see it all: 1-1/2 hours.

Manatee County was established in 1856. It encompassed approximately 5,500 square miles and contained what is now Manatee, Hardee, Highlands, Okeechobee, Sarasota, DeSoto, Charlotte and Glades Counties. This park includes Manatee Counties first Court House (1860), Stephen's House (1912), an historic church (1887), Wiggins Store (1903) and Bunker Hill School (1908), replica of Florida barn, smokehouse, sugar kettle, cane mill and Bat Fogarty boatworks.

Marie Selby Botanical Gardens (see Selby Gardens)

Marina Jack II
Marina Jack Marina, 2 Marina Plaza (Bayfront), Sarasota 34236
366-9255, fax 957-1291
Lunch Cruise (Mid-January through Mother's Day only)
Dinner (Year 'round)

Go back in time when shallow-drought steamers navigated Sarasota Bay. In the 1890s steamboats carried passengers, freight and mail between the young towns of Sarasota and Tampa. The Marina Jack II may look as if it steamed out of the last century, but the newly constructed paddle boat vessel is one of the area's most popular attractions for lunch and dinner, providing passengers with unusual bayfront views of the John and Mable Ringling mansion and art museum, the Van Wezel Performing Arts Hall, Indian mounds and the occasional waterfront home of a famous "personality." Meals are served in two lavishly appointed dining rooms, both decks of the 100-foot boat are fully enclosed and are fully climate controlled. The schedule fluctuates during the year, be sure to call ahead for current information.

Live entertainment on Dinner Cruise only. The boat is available for private parties, weddings, business gatherings or bloodthirsty buccaneer pirate raids of neighboring island communities.

Mote Marine Aquarium
1600 Ken Thompson Parkway (City Island), Sarasota 34236
388-4441/800-691-MOTE, fax 388-4312
www.mote.org
Recorded Information/Events:
388-2451
Hours: 10:00 a.m.- 5:00 p.m. daily.
Admission: Adults - $8.00 Students (4-17 years) - $6.00
Members - Free. Time it takes to see it all: 1-2 hours

Get up close and personal with a shark. Hold a prickly sea urchin. See a living reef. Displays at Mote Marine Aquarium explain more than 40 years of research conducted by Mote scientists, and encourage understanding and appreciation for aquatic environments. A highlight to any trip is the 135,000 gallon Shark Tank. The tank's underwater viewing area allows you to come eye-to-eye with various species of sharks and other fish, such as co-

Field Trip:
The Brown Pelican

- Pelican chicks are snow white as babies. They reach their adult coloration (white heads and brown bodies) during their third year.

- Healthy pelicans weigh four to eight pounds. Their wingspread is five to six feet and they can fly at speeds up to 35 miles per hour.

- Males and females look alike, but males may be distinguished by their slightly longer beaks and greater body weight.

- Pelicans quiver to assist in the metabolic process of food digestion.

- To cool his body a pelican will flap his pouch and pant like a dog.

bia, snook, and grouper. In Rivers, Bays and Estuaries, follow a drop of water as it flows downstream to the Gulf of Mexico. In the 30-foot touch tank, watch a conch crawl or feel a horseshoe crab walk across your hand. Knowledgeable guides are ready to answer questions about the creatures of the Gulf or the work of scientists at Mote. The 1999 Mote is twice the size of the original aquarium, built in 1980. Features include 10 new exhibits and three viewable research laboratories.

Ready to brave the waters? Board the Sarasota Bay Explorer for a relaxing one hour and 45 minute tour Sarasota Bay waterways. Cruise through rookeries to view nesting sea birds and see firsthand the fascinating creatures living in local grass flats.

Before leaving, stop by the Marine Mammal Visitor Center. Meet Mote's two resident manatees, Hugh and Buffett. Observe various turtles and hatchlings at the sea turtle display. Learn how a stranded animal is rehabilitate and how research at Mote helps to conserve and protect marine animals.

Mote is a great place to visit year-round. Call the Mote INFOLINE at 388-2451 to hear updates and news about special activities and educational opportunities.

Myakka River Queen at Snook Haven Restaurant & Fish Camp
5000 Venice Ave. East, Venice
485-7221
Hours: Friday/Saturday/Sunday - 3:00 p.m.
Admission: $6.00 - Adults, $3.00 children.

Take a one-hour leisurely narrated tour down the Myakka River on the Myakka River Queen. See "pre-Mickey" Florida! Private tours with brunch available.

Myakka River State Park/Wildlife and Nature Tours
14 miles east of U.S. 41 on State Road 72
(Clark Road), Sarasota
Tour Information: 365-0100
Ranger Station: 361-6511
Park Hours: 8:00 a.m. to sunset daily.
Time it takes to see it all: A lifetime.

Put this on your "must do" list! Here is what Florida looked like before the condos, shopping malls and Mickey arrived. Yes, you are sure to see alligators in the wild! We are proposing a new law whereby locals will be required to take a day off work at least once a year just to take advantage of this spectacular park: "Sorry boss, I feel too healthy to come to work today, I'm off to Myakka!"

Park Highlights: Over 28,875.5 acres of pristine area, wildlife trails, canoeing, biking, camping, wildlife museum, snack bar and highly recommended airboat rides and tram tours – each ride and tour takes about an hour and no walking is required.

Canoes and bicycles are available for rental, picnic tables are located near boat and tram tour rides. If you are planning to take one of the tour rides, getting there early is a good idea. No reservations are accepted. Group rates and charters are available.

Tour Highlights: Extremely knowledgeable and entertaining tour guides – ranger-guided walks Saturday mornings at 9:00 a.m.; "Gator Gal" (the world's largest airboat) alligators, deer, bobcat and bald eagles in the wild, plenty of fresh air.

Tour Fares: Adults – $7.00; Children (6-12 years) – $3.00;

Toddlers (5 and under) –Free
Winter Schedule (December 16 - May 31)
"GATOR GAL" BOAT TOUR
    10:00 a.m., 11:30 a.m., 1:00 p.m., 2:30 p.m.
LAND TRAM SAFARI TOUR – 1:00 p.m., 2:30 p.m. (In season only)
Summer Schedule (June 1 - December 15)
"GATOR GAL" BOAT TOUR
    10:00 a.m., 11:30 a.m., 1:00 p.m.
LAND TRAM SAFARI TOUR – Closed until December 16

Myakka River State Park is Florida's largest state park, famous for its panoramas of lakes, river, marshes, hammocks and prairies, and for its abundant wildlife populations. Deer, alligators and many species of wading birds are abundant, as well as thousands of waterfowl in the winter months. Ospreys, Bald Eagles and Sandhill Cranes are commonly seen. An Interpretive Center has exhibits of wildlife and plant communities on display. Park rangers provide guided walks and campfire programs according to seasonal attendance. During the winter, they offer bird watching for beginners. A 7,500-acre wilderness preserve resembles Florida as it looked before the arrival of Europeans. A limited number of visitors are allowed to visit this preserve each day on foot or by boat. All plant and animal life is protected in state parks. Intoxicants are not permitted in any area of the park.

A Brief History of Myakka River State Park

In the early 1920s, A.B. Edwards, a prominent resident and Sarasota's first mayor, launched a movement to set aside a natural area for recreation and preservation. Edwards persuaded the Florida Internal Improvement Fund to buy more than 17,000 acres (at 37.5 cents an acre!) from the A.C. Honore Estate. A few weeks after the purchase, Honore and Potter Palmer donated more than 1,900 acres to the state - a memorial to their mother Bertha Palmer. In the 1930s the Civilian Conservation Corps (one of many federal relief agencies established through President Roosevelt's New Deal, to help ease the Depression) brought around 200 men to make the 26,000 acres usable. From 1934 to 1941 the crew built roads, bridges, cabins, dug drainage ditches

© MYAKKA RIVER STATE PARK

**Field Trip:
The Cormorant**

Dark, sleek and streamlined, the Cormorant resembles a duck – a duck that dives! These birds are in constant search of food in gulf waters and can be seen diving in pursuit of their supper. When they become waterlogged, they sit on the bank or on pilings, preening and drying their feathers, wings outspread.

Not to be confused with the Anhinga, a large black bird (but not as large as the Cormorant) with a needle sharp bill which it uses as a spear to get freshwater fish. The Cormorant prefers to hang out on the salty gulf waters.

and planted over 100,000 trees. Everything constructed was done with native materials. On February 18, 1941 the park was dedicated, it opened to the public on June 1, 1942.

Myakka Safari Survival Suggestions
1. Bring binoculars.
2. Bring plenty of film for your camera.
3. Bring a picnic or charcoal for cooking outside; tables and grills are available in several picnic areas.
4. Bring blanket and lawn chairs.
5. Bring rain gear, sunscreen, mosquito repellant.
6. Get to the boat basin to buy tickets EARLY, at least an hour before launch time during Season.
7. Get to the Bird Walk about an hour before sunset and don't forget #1.

The Mystic Dolphin Island Cruise
5325 Marina Dr., Homes Beach 34217
Information/Reservations: 778-2761
Per Person Rates: $15.00 - First hr.; $5.00 - Each Additional hr. min. $40. Special rates sometimes available, call for details.
A 28' pontoon boat (12' of fully enclosed area) with restroom available for personalized cruises, max. Six persons per cruise. Highlights include "Dining with the Dolphins" for great dolphin watching, sight-seeing along numerous waterways, bird watching among the many sanctuaries, shelling and snorkeling (view scopes are available for anyone who would rather stay onboard) and water taxi service to the many bayside restaurants. Coolers welcome.

Natural Encounters
955-1438

Nature walks and excursions for the whole family available on a customized basis or as a class with other participants. Stresses active involvement – you can touch and examine at close range living animals and plants, walk at your own leisurely pace and explore a wide range of biological and ecological interests. Wildlife photography is permitted. Leader Bill Boothe is warm, personable and fun. He also has a B.A. in biology, a Masters degree in oceanography/marine biology and has worked for the Smithsonian. Perhaps, even more impressive was Bill's personal discovery of two previously unknown living species of shrimp. Short excursions start at a couple of hours, longer half-day and full day encounters are also available. Call for private arrangements, group rates and class schedules; be sure to get on the newsletter mailing list.

Oscar Scherer State Park
U.S. 41 in Osprey
483-5956, www.dep.state.fl.us/parks
Hours: 8 a.m. to Sunset
Admission: $3.25 per car load (up to 8 people)
Special Note: This park includes The Lester Finley Nature Trail, a special hiking trail constructed in compliance with the Americans with Disabilities Act.

Not as far of a drive as it is to Myakka, the entrance to this park is on U.S. 41. The park originally consisted of 462 acres of scrubby flatwoods and mesic flatwoods; South Creek, a blackwater stream, flows through this area. An additional 922 acres acquired in 1992 contain tracts of depression marshes, pine forests and additional flatwoods on the banks of a small tidal creek. The park is noted for its population of Florida scrub jays, which is a threatened species. (Some jays at the park will land on your outstretched hand!) Bald Eagles as well as bobcats, River Otters and alligators are often seen in the winter months as are many birds. The rare Gopher Tortoise, Gopher Frog and Indigo Snake are occasionally seen here. Pick up an animal identification booklet at the entrance.

Highlights: Self guided nature trail, voicebox information stations, freshwater lake swimming, picnic area, canoe rentals, campsites with water and electric hookup plus the very impressive Lester Finley Nature Trail for outdoor enthusiasts with disabilities – a sight impaired and wheelchair friendly hike with touch activated audio speakers which provide interpretive information.

Peacock Safari On Longboat Key
Location: Longboat Key Village Area – Follow sign to Longboat Key Art Center, take first left, drive around.

First, keep in mind that these wild peacocks are running loose among *PRIVATE HOMES*. You may NOT walk on anyone's lawn to feed them but you can see all you want from the car. In fact, many will come right up to the window to eat of your hand. Be *VERY* sensitive to the residents who live here, do not block driveways or interfere with their privacy. No one knows exactly how these peacocks got there but they have been roaming the area for at least 20 years. Current population is estimated between thirty and fifty, running wild in the suburban jungles of Longboat Key.

Pelican Man's Bird Sanctuary
1708 Ken Thompson Parkway, City Island, Sarasota 34236
388-4444, fax 388-3258
Hours: 10:00 a.m. - 5:00 p.m. daily, except Major Holidays
Admission: Free (Donations gratefully accepted)

The Sanctuary is home to birds whose injuries prevent them from returning to their natural habitat. There are approximately 250 birds in residence, including herons, cormorants, owls, osprey and, of course, pelicans! Local legend and national folk hero, Dale Shields, gave up his worldly possessions to dedicate his life to rescuing birds in distress, contributing over 100,000 volunteer hours to his cause. Since he began in 1981, he has helped rescue over 100,000 birds and, yes, he *CAN* talk to pelicans. As local officials became aware of his volunteer work to save our area wildlife, the city of Sarasota leased him the present location for his Sanctuary on City Island. The Sanctuary, a nonprofit organization, receives no financial support from federal, state, county or city governments. Mr. Shields' efforts are made possible through the contributions of sanctuary visitors and the organization's many members from every state in the nation and several foreign countries. Currently the Sanctuary involves over 300 volunteers who help to rescue over 5,000 birds each year, returning 60% back to the wild. On July 2, 1990 the Pelican Man was honored by President Bush as the 184th Point of Light in the 1000 Points of Light campaign. In 1992 he was honored as a recipient of a Sol Feinstone Environmental Award. "Liberty," an adult bald eagle, is a new permanent resident. Part of her wing had to be amputated but she's healed and adjusted to her new enclosure, built by local Eagle scouts.

Pelican Pete's Playland
3101 McCall Rd. S, Englewood 34224
475-2008, fax 475-7335, e-mail pelicanpete@ewol.com
Hours: Monday - Thursday 10:00 a.m.- 9:00 p.m.

Field Trip: Dolphins

Dolphins and porpoises thrive in the gulf waters. You will often see schools of them playfully tumbling in the salt water. Happy, happy, joy, joy.

Please note that none of them will respond to you as Flipper would – don't expect one to play catch with you or to save you from a sudden calamity.

Also, don't confuse these extraordinary creatures with the "dolphin" featured on many seafood restaurant menus; a saltwater delicacy fish (and no resemblance at all to our television buddy) menu "dolphin" is also commonly referred to as "Mahi-Mahi."

Field Trip: Egrets

The Great Egret, the Snowy Egret, and the Common Egret are all the same magnificent shore bird.

If you are confused, you should be.

Apparently this bird gets renamed every few years by ornitholo-gists so a new Field Guide Book would have to be written. Never call an ornitholo-gist stupid.

These birds once were hunted almost to extinction for their beautiful snowy white plumes.

Friday - Saturday 10:00 a.m.- 11:00 p.m.,
Sunday 11 a.m. - 6 p.m.

18-Hole Miniature Golf Course, four different Go-Kart tracks, train, four Hard Ball batting cages, two Soft Ball batting cages, complete video arcade. Parties and group rates available

Miniture Golf: $5.00 Adult; $3.50 Children under 13
           $1.25 Additional Round

Go-Karts: $2.25 Power Wheel Track (Ages 2-5); $2.50 Jr. Track;
         $3.65 Slick Track; $4.50 Gran National
     10-Ride Pass good for any track $34.00

Batting Cages (non-stop pitching)
     15 min.-$6.00; 30 min.-$11; 60 min.-$1

Train: $1.25 (1 parent free w/small child

Pirate City
1701 27th St. E., Bradenton 34205
747-3031, www.pirateball.com

This is where the Pittsburgh Pirates train their instructional and rookie leagues. Games are free to watch, call for schedule information. Be advised: No "facilities" are available.

Pirate's Cove
5410 14th Street West, Bradenton 34207
755-4608

Five acres jam packed with fun and excitement for the whole family. Open 7 days a week; closed on Christmas and Thanksgiving. Grand Prix Style Go-Carts, Bumper Boats, Laser Tag, Miniature Golf "Challenge Course;" 8 batting cages, video games, snack bar and some exciting things on the way.

Planet Fun
7250 Cortez Rd W, Bradenton
792-0555, fax 798-9258

Hours: Mon 10-9 (when school is <u>not</u> in session, closed on Mon when school is in session); Tues-Thurs 11-9, Fri-Sat 10-10, Sun 11-8

Cost: Parents: Always Free
          Toddlers: From $3.99
          Children over 23 months: From $5.99
          Fun Package: $9.99 includes
          Playstation, free video games, 6
          rides and 4 game tokens
          Birthday Party Packages: Any budget

Florida's largest indoor amusement park just for kids! Includes over 3 stories of indoor playground equipment called "Jellybean's Playstation" (also the largest in Florida - 5,000 sq. ft.) plus free Sega Genesis, Pico and Nintendo 64 games, an indoor roller coaster, $80,000 Italian jet ride, and a special tea cup: "The Space Drum Adventure." Toddler play are for children under 23 months. Four private birthday party rooms (with hostess) and kids rides throughout, a complete game room and full dinner/snack bar. Socks are required to play!

Ray's Canoe Hideaway
1247 Hagle Park Rd., Bradenton
747-3909, fax 957-3031, www.rayscanoehideaway.com

Rental rates are based on a 2 adult minimum, kids 12 years of age and under are an additional $2.00 each:
1/2 Day (up to 5 Hours) – $9.00/per person
Full Day (8:00 a.m. - Sunset) – $12.00/per person

24-Hour Rental – $15.00/per person
Launch your own boat – $3.00 for canoe; $3.50 power boat.

Canoe rentals on the upper stretch of Manatee River, about 6 miles below Lake Manatee Dam. (Closed Tues. and Weds.) Small store with bait, ice, drinks and snacks. Kayaks soon to be available. Camping information available.

Regal Cruises
P.O. Box 1329, Palmetto, 34220
721-7330, 1-800-270-SAIL, fax 723-0900, www.regalcruises.com
Affordable cruises are here! Reminiscent of the "Golden Age of Cruising" the 900-passenger, 23,000-ton Regal Empress (the former Caribe D) offers 4-nights to Mexico, 7-nights to western Caribbean and 10-nights to Panama Canal. "Home" is Pt. Manatee where a new terminal was built for this extraordinary ship. Elegant midnight buffet, poolside Trattoria, pizza parlour, six lounges, game room, children's activities, first run movies, Disco, ballroom dancing, Las Vegas style shows, fully equipped exercise room, professional massage, whirlpool, full-service beauty salon, piano bar, shuffleboard, bingo, "horse racing" and - of course - a floating casino, all in a warm, intimate friendly atmosphere. Every state room is outfitted with a private bath and wall-to-wall carpeting. How do you spell vacation? This is it.

The John and Mable Ringling Museum of Art
5401 Bay Shore Rd., Sarasota 34243
359-5700, recording 351-1660, fax 359-5745, www.ringling.org
Hours: 10:00 a.m.- 5:30 p.m. daily, 7 days a week
Admission: Adults - $9.00, Sr. Citizens (55 years and older) - $8.00, Children (12 & Under) - Free, Groups of 10 or more - $6.50 per person, Florida students and teachers with proper ID - Free.
Ticket includes admission to Art Museum, Ringling Home and Circus Museum. Saturdays admission free to art museum only.

© RINGLING MANSION

Most people think of John Ringling as simply a circus owner, albeit the largest circus on the planet at the time. But his passion for collecting art remains his legacy and this museum, located on the grounds of the Ringling home, his living memorial.

Apparently inspired by his card playing partner Stanford White, an architect and socialite (both Ringling and White were major shareholders of Madison Square Gardens) whose way of life included a keen knowledge of art, John Ringling took it upon himself to learn everything he could about the subject. A mountain of art magazines would be waiting at his is bedside for night reading. Ringling's jaunts to Europe turned into shopping sprees. Trunks full of old masters, 500 paintings worth $4 million dollars in his day, were the rewards of his efforts.

The John and Mable Ringling Museum of Art – the State Art Museum of Florida – holds one of the country's premier collections of baroque art. Within the collection are five world-renowned cartoons (designs for tapestries) by Peter Paul Rubens along

Field Trip: Great Blue Heron and Little Blue Heron

The Great Blue Heron is a very tall, long-necked grey bird of amazing grace and beauty. You'll see them standing motionless through shallow water in search of fish and small reptiles. Then again, you may see them trying to cross the street with school children – some are as big as your neighborhood eight year old, standing four feet high with a wing span of six feet.

The Little Blue Heron is actually born white and remains white its first year, blue and white the second year, eventually turning blue as it approaches its third birthday.

---

with other major Rubens works, early Italian and Northern European Renaissance paintings, and French, Dutch, Flemish and Spanish baroque highlights by such artists as Velasquez, Pietro da Cortona, Piero di Cosimo, El Greco and Poussin. Built by John Ringling in 1927-29, the estate with its treasures was a gift from him to the people of Florida at his death in 1936.

The Art Galleries are built around an Italian Renaissance-style courtyard in which an evolution of sculpture through many schools and centuries is traced in full-sized reproductions. It contains a bronze replica of Michelangelo's *David* which has become the symbol of the City of Sarasota. The West Galleries – a 1966 addition – exhibit the Museum's modern collection and special contemporary exhibitions.

Also on the 63-acre landscaped estate are John and Mable Ringling's Venetian mansion, Ca' d'Zan, built 1924-26; the Asolo Theater, an 18th-century Italian court playhouse; and the Museum of the Circus.

The Museum founder did not include any circus objects in his legacy, so the museum has acquired its collection of costumes, props, wagons and other circus memorabilia through purchases and contributions. Located in the center of the grounds is the Banyan Cafe where you can pause for a delicious lunch or refreshments under the shade of huge Banyan trees (call **359-3183** for reservations).

Three Museum Shops can be found, one in each of the main buildings: the Art Museum, the Ca' d'Zan, and the Circus Museum. The merchandise selection in each shop is tailored to match its venue. Admission to the shops is free.

Also not to be missed is Mable Ringling's Rose Garden, designed in the Italian wagon wheel style. It was created in 1913 making it one of the oldest rose gardens in the nation. In fact, the garden was planted first, before either the home or the museum was built. Her secret for keeping her roses so beautiful and full of life? Every two years she uprooted the old plants and replaced them with healthy new ones. (A helpful gardening hint: be sure to have circus trunks full of money!) When the state took over care of the Ringling estate in 1936, the garden began to decline. In 1991 the Ringling grounds supervisor organized a donation drive and a massive volunteer effort among the many local gardening clubs. Thanks to their efforts the Rose Garden is back...dare we say...in full bloom and well worth a leisurely walk.

An estimated 250,000 people visit the museum each year. John Ringling's cultural legacy provides the people of Florida and the world with a splendid and important museum for the public to enjoy – and we sincerely hope they do.

Rock & Glo Bowling
Galaxy Lanes, 1100 US-41 Bypass S., Venice 34292
484-0666, fax 484-6346

Okay, so maybe this is a bit odd. But it's not boring. Every Saturday night from 9 p.m. to midnight. Venice's Galaxy Lanes turns their bowling alley lights off and their disco lights on and the music gets weird (K.C. and the Sunshine Band?) and loud! A fascinating mix of bowling, limbo lines and dancing. WILD – and fun. $12.00

Royal Lipizzan Stallions of Austria
32755 Singletary Rd., Myakka City
322-1501/322-2539

Drive to end of Fruitville Rd., turn left on Verna, go one and a half miles to Singletary Rd., turn right and go three miles and look for sign. (Be sure to call ahead - reservations taken before 5 p.m.)

Training Sessions:
From the first weekend in January through the last weekend in March
3:00 p.m. - Thursday and Friday
10:00 a.m.- Saturday
Admission: Free (Group reservations call 322-2539)

These world famous horses travel much of the year, but when they are home they are sure to please the whole family. Yes, these are the horses featured in the 1960s Disney movie. Well, not the same ones exactly...

Sarasota Bay Explorers
1600 Ken Thompson Parkway (City Island), at Mote Marine Aquarium, Sarasota 34236
388-4200, fax 927-1519
Cruise Times : 11 a.m., 1:30 p.m., 4 p.m.
    Cruise Only - Adults - $24.00
    Cruise Only - Child - $20.00
    Cruise & Aquarium - Adults - $28.00
    Cruise & Aquarium - Child - $22.00
    Group Rates Available - Reservations Requested.
    Call for information on other cruises.
    Time it takes to see it all: 1 hour 45 minutes

A wonderful extension to a visit to Mote Marine Aquarium. This sea life encounter is sprinkled with fascinating historical tidbits and takes you on a tranquil cruise of Sarasota bay. You may see dolphins, manatees or osprey. You will discover the remarkable creatures living in the local grass flats. Short stop on an uninhabited island is included. Each trip is narrated by a marine biologist. Reservations requested.

Sarasota Classic Car Museum
5500 North Tamiami Trail, Sarasota 34243
355-6228, fax 358-8065
Hours: Open 9:00 a.m.- 6:00 p.m. daily.
Admission: Adults - $8.50
                 Children (6-12 years) - $2:50
                 Toddlers (5 and under) - Free
                 10% Seniors and AAA discount
                 Annual Pass: Adults $14, Children $9
Time it takes to see it all: 1-1/2 hours.
Tour of Cars Collection
Every hour on the half-hour beginning at 9:30 a.m.

Tour of Music Collection
Every hour on the hour beginning at 9:00 a.m.

Explore automotive history in this nation's third oldest automobile museum. Walk leisurely among many turn-of-the century horseless carriages, vintage and classic cars from the 50s & 60s and exotic automobiles from around the world. Visit the Chevy muscle car room and try your hand doing the twist with one of their docents. Tour the Great Music Hall - see the many music boxes, band organs, calliopes and player pianos that made the Gay 90s & Roaring 20s famous. Have fun in the antique penny arcade, play the old time games your grandparents played - a favorite for all ages. Private party space available too!

Sarasota County Parks and Recreation Rentals
316-1172, fax 316-1227, www.acun.com/parks

Conceptually, family reunions are wonderful ideas, unless they occur in your own house. Perfect for such get-togethers (or club cook-outs, company picnics and birthday parties) are the area parks which have shelters for rent starting at $20.00. A bargain, not to mention a great savings to your domicile and sanity.

**Field Trip:
The Manatee**

Extremely gentle by nature and perhaps the most unusual of all our native creatures, the manatee is an endangered species whose existence in the wild is seriously threatened by man. The manatee's seal-like body tapers to a flat, paddle-shaped tail, and two small forelimbs on the upper body have three to four nails on each flipper. Adult manatees move through the water primarily by the use of the tail.
The front flippers are used for steering and lateral movement or to crawl over water bottom.

Field Trip: The Manatee

The head and face of the manatee are wrinkled and the snout has stiff whiskers. Adults have been known to reach lengths of over 13 feet and weights over 3,500 pounds. Calves are three to three and onehalf feet long and weigh 60 to 70 pounds at birth. The current manatee population is estimated at around 1,200 animals.

They are often sighted in our area.

If you are a boater, please use extreme caution in "no wake" zones.

The manatee is slow, defenseless and, at this point, our responsibility.

Reservations can be made twelve months in advance, minimum two weeks notice required to allow for department authorization and payment processing. Please note: Shelter Rentals do not include exclusive use of our parks, you'll have to learn to share.

Arlington Park & Aquatic Complex
2650 Waldemere St., Sarasota 34239
316-1346

Air conditioned gym, locker rooms, showers. 7/10 mi. trail, duck pond, 50 meter pool, instructional pool, baby pool, playground, fitness center, 4 lighted hard based tennis courts, lighted racquetball/handball courts, multipurpose field, picnic areas with barbecue grills and tables.

Bee Ridge Park
4430 Lockwood Ridge, Sarasota 34231
316-1328

Basketball court, horseshoes, picnicking, play equipment, rest rooms, shuffle board softball fields, volleyball courts.

Blind Pass Beach
6725 Manasota Key road, Manasota Key 34223
474-8919

Play equipment, canoe launch, nature trail, large picnic shelter.

Carlton Reserve
1800 mabry Carlton Parkway, Venice 34292
316-1172

Picnicking, rest rooms, hiking, Nature trails: wet prairie trail (3/4 mi.), forested wetland trail (3/4 mi.), pine flatwoods/hammock trail (1/4 mi.). Environmental tours, bird watching (over 100 species).

Colonial Oaks Park
5300 Colonial Oaks Blvd., Sarasota 34232
316-1330

Basketball, Indoor Rental Space, Picnicking, Medium Shelters, Grills, Play Equipment, Garden Deck, Recreation Building, Tennis, Rest Rooms.

Dallas White Park
5900 Greenwood Avenue, North Port 34287
423-2786

Heated 25 meter pool, fitness center, restrooms/shower, wheelchair lift, boating, tennis, ball fields, play equipment, volleyball, picnicking, fitness trail

Englewood Recreation Center
101 N. Organge St., Englewood 34223
474-8919

Tennis courts, basketball courts, volleyball courts, multi-purpose field, picnicking, play equipment, shuffleboard, softball, restrooms, recreation building.

Fruitville Park
5151 Richardson Rd., Sarasota 34232
316-1172

Fitness/Nature Trail, Football/Soccer, Three Small Shelters Together, Picnicking, Play Equipment, Softball, Tennis, Volleyball, Grill, Rest Rooms.

Gillespie Park
710 N. Osprey Ave., Sarasota 34236
316-1331

Basketball, Picnicking, Large Shelter, Grill, Play Equipment, Tennis. Dogs on a leash are welcome.

Indian Mound Park
210 Winson Ave., Englewood
474-8919

Boat Ramp, Fishing, Fitness/Nature Trail, Large Shelter, Picnicking, Volleyball, Rest Rooms.

Lakeview Park
7150 Lago Street, Sarasota 34241
316-1172

Picnicking, canoe launch, fishing, petanque court, disc golf

Laurel Park
509 Collins Rd., Laurel
486-2753

Basketball, Picnicking, Large Shelter, Grill, Play Equipment, Softball, Tennis, Indoor Rental Space, Rest Rooms.

Lemon Bay Park
570 Bay Park Blvd, Englewood 34223
474-3065

Large picnic pavillion, nature trails, environmental exhibits, educational butterfly garden, daylily/rose garden, guided nature tours, scenic bay boardwalk, canoe launch, bald eagle habitat, community meeting rooms.

Longwood Park
6050 Longwood Blvd., Sarasota
316-1383

Basketball, Picnicking, Large Shelter, Grill, Indoor Rental Space, Recreation Building, Play Equipment, Softball, Tennis, Rest Rooms.

Manasota Beach
8570 Manasota Key, Englewood
474-8919

Boat Ramp, Fishing, Swimming, Picnicking, Large Shelter, Grill, Volleyball, Rest Rooms.

Newtown Estates
2800 Newtown Blvd., Sarasota 34234
316-1161

Basketball, Baseball, Indoor Rental Space, Large Shelter, Picnicking, Play Equipment, Recreation Building, Softball, Tennis, Rest Rooms.

North Jetty Park
1000 S. Casey Key Rd., Nokomis
486-2311

Concession Stand, Fishing, Horseshoes, Picnicking, Large Shelter, Grill, Swimming, Volleyball, Rest Rooms.

Pinecraft Park
1420 Gilbert Ave., Sarasota 34239
316-1346

Basketball, Canoe and Small Hand-Carried Boat Launch, Fishing, Horseshoes, Shuffleboard, Large Shelter, Grills, Picnicking, Play Equipment, Rest Rooms.

**Field Trip:
Manatee Facts**

• The average manatee is about 10 feet long and weighs about 800 to 2,000 pounds.

• It is not known if the birth rate is high enough to offset the 120 or so dead manatees recovered annually in Florida in recent years.

• Dives by manatees of up to 24 minutes have been reported, although the length of time between breaths usually ranges from about four minutes while resting to about 30 seconds during strenuous activity.

• Most females breed successfully by seven to nine years of age. The gestation period is about 13 months and the interval between births is three to five years.

**Field Trip:
Manatee Facts**

• Manatees have no natural enemies, except human behavior.

• Manatees spend about five hours a day feeding.

• Manatees consume about 4 percent to 9 percent of their body weight in wet vegetation.

• Manatees are neither territorial nor aggressive and individuals within a group do not dominate each other.

• Boat related mortality is probably the single greatest threat to the manatee.

Want to help? Join Save the Manatee Club, 500 N. Maitland Ave., Maitland FL 32751
Information:
(407) 539-0990

Shamrock Park & Nature Center
4100 W Shamrock Dr., Venice 34293
486-2706

Picnic pavilion, nature trails, environmental exhibits, guided nature tours, celestial observation events, Florida scrub jay habitat, pesticide free play equipment area.

Siesta Beach Gazebo or Shelter
Location: 948 Beach Rd., Siesta Key 34242
346-3207

Concession Stand, Fitness/Nature Trail, Football/Soccer, Picnicking, Medium/Large Shelters, Grill, Play Equipment, Softball, Swimming, Tennis, Volleyball, Rest Rooms.

South Lido Park
North end of Taft and South Blvd. of Presidents, Lido Key
951-5572

A great place to getaway, without going too far. Three nature trails (two for walking, one for canoes) plus volleyball and swimming. Free admission, daylight to dusk.

Turtle Beach
8918 Midnight Pass Rd., Siesta Key 34242
346-3207

Large Shelter, Grill, Boat Ramp, Picnicking, Canoeing, Fishing, Horseshoes, Play Equipment, Swimming, Volleyball, Rest Rooms.

Twin Lakes Park
6700 Clark Rd., Sarasota 34241
316-1172

Meeting Rooms, Dining Facility, Picnicking, Grill, Large Pavilion, Fishing, Tennis, Handball/Racquetball, Canoeing, Football/Soccer/Baseball, Rest Rooms.

Woodmere Park
3951 Woodmere park Blvd, Venice 34293
486-2780

Tennis courts, Basketball court, nature trail, picnicking, play equipment and tot lot, restrooms/showers, sand volleyball court

Youth Athletic Complex
2810 17th St., Sarasota 34234
316-1172

Baseball, Football/Soccer, Large Shelter, Picnicking, Play Equipment, Tennis, Rest Rooms.

Sarasota Institute of Lifetime Learning (SILL)
365-6404

The area's absolute best winter lecture series on topics of general interest (primarily intended for retirees to widen their horizons, but youngins should not be dissuaded from participating – this really is an extraordinary event) featuring discussions and workshops led by internationally renown experts, often former ambassadors or former U.N. representatives. Sarasota series takes place at Sarasota Square East AMC Theaters (outside mall); Venice series takes place at Venice Community Center. Complete series program booklet is available at all public libraries. Well worth attending!

Sarasota Kennel Club
5400 Bradenton Rd., Sarasota 34234
355-7744, fax 351-2207
Admission: $1.00

Greyhound racing rain or shine. We go every year and, knock on woof... uh, we mean "wood"... we're still ahead. Twin trifectas, Pick 3, Quinielas and Superfectas...bet the farm but keep enough for cab fare. Also live simulcast satellite betting on thoroughbred and harness horse racing from Miami area and Pompano Beach on year-round basis, along with major championships from around the country and Canada. Must be 18 years or older to enter.

Rain or Shine Greyhound Schedule:
    December 26 - April 10
    Matinee – Monday, Wednesday & Saturday 1:00 p.m.
    Nightly (except Sunday) – 7:30 p.m.

The Sarasota Kennel Club has two climate controlled clubhouses for your dining and entertainment pleasure; all-you-can-eat buffet and full bar. Social organization and business group packages available.

Sarasota Jungle Gardens (See: Jungle Gardens)

Sarasota Opera
61 N. Pineapple Ave.,Sarasota
(941) 366-8450, fax 954-1262, e-mail sarasotaop@aol.com,
www.sarasotaopera.org
The most challenging of all live art forms (combining acting, singing, dance, full symphonic orchestra, extravagant costumes, extraordinary sets, vivid lighting) and the most rewarding when done well. The Sarasota Opera has an international reputation for doing opera very well indeed. This is the place to discover the joys of opera, your first-

**Field Trip:
The Osprey**

Also called the fish eagle, the Osprey is a true raptor which swoops down on its prey with strong, powerful wings. Its talons are razor sharp.

The community of Osprey, just south of Sarasota is named for this bird, probably because the local police use similar tactics – swooping down on unsuspecting motorists who are paying too much attention to the wonderful collection of antique stores, instead of their speedometer.

time experience will not be your last. The Sarasota Opera celebrates its 40th season in 1999.

Sarasota Sailor Circus
2075 Bahia Vista, Sarasota 34239
Tickets: 361-6350
Prices: $6.00 or $7.00, depending on seat, reservations a must!
1998 Performance Schedule:
7:15 p.m. March 18-20, 24-26, 31, April 1 andl 3
Matinee : March 21
Founded in 1943, the Sarasota Sailor Circus is the only extra curricular after-school three-ring student circus in the United States that is sanctioned by a school board. Participants, all who attend public or private schools in Sarasota County, are in grades 3-12. Students perform at professional level in acts such as flying trapeze, high wire walking, teeterboard and other astounding feats. The name "Sailor Circus" comes from a time when Sarasota High School athletes had to travel by boat to play competing teams in the Tampa Bay area. 1999 marks the 50th anniversary of public performances, many special events are planned including spotlights on returning alumni.

Sarasota Ski-A-Rees
Directly behind Mote Marine Laboratory, City Island, Sarasota
388-1666
Event times: 2:00 p.m. - 3:00 p.m.
Dates: Every Sunday beginning the first Sunday in February through the week after Easter.
Admission: Free.

State and Southern Regional Ski Show Champions every year since 1990, this amateur ski show club gives it everything they've got, every week. These fully costumed and choreogrphed productions put other Florida attractions who promote the same (and charge admission) to shame. Stadium seating, no charge.

Shapes 2 Paint
502 N. Beneva, Ste. 410, Sarasota 34232
952-5253, fax 727-7301
Hours: Tues-Fri 10-6, Sat 10-5, Sun. 1-5

Ready to paint plastercraft, you pay by the piece and then spend as much time as you'd like painting and decorating - paint and sparkles included at no extra charge. This is a great place to take the kids for an afternoon of fun. Birthday Pizza Parties and group rates available.

Schomburg Farms
2504 24th Ave. E., Palmetto 34221
729-2884
Hours: Open seven days a week, 9:00 a.m. - 5:00 p.m.
Rates:$3.00 for petting zoo and pony ride
 $2.00 for just the pony ride
 1/2 Hour Trail Horseback Riding - $5.00 per/person
 1 Hour Trail Horseback Riding - $10.00 per/person
 Group rates available by request.

Horseback riding and petting zoo (goats, pigs, geese, mules, cows, rabbits, sheep, ducks) with pony rides available for the kids. You can pet emus and give them a kiss on the neck! Hayrides, picnic area and campfire areas available by reservation only. Birthday Party Special - $50 all day, access to everything plus three ponies for the entire day. Kid Heaven!

Tropical displays • Miniature rain forest • Learning Center • 20- dazzling display gardens • Museum featuring botanical prints

Selby Gardens is a world orchid and bromeliad center and an outdoor and under-glass museum of thousands of tropical plants, many of them rare and seldom seen.
Adults $8.00 Children 6-11 $4.00
Located on South Palm Avenue at US 41 on Sarasota's downtown bayfront.

MARIE SELBY Botanical Gardens

Call 366-5731 or 366-5730 for recorded information. $1 off admission with ad, maximim 6 adults.

Seafood Shack Showboat
4110 127th St. W., Cortez 34215
794-5048/1-800-294-5048, fax 794-8119

"Mississippi Style" sternwheeler, 110' long "Showboat" licensed for up to 324 passengers. Daily narrated sightseeing cruise. Charters and group rates available. Also: live entertainment, concession area and two cocktail bars. Carpeted and enclosed lower deck is heated and air-conditioned. Departure times and prices vary monthly. Call for current schedule.

(Marie) Selby Botanical Gardens
811 S. Palm Ave., Sarasota 34236
Recorded Information: 366-5730, fax 366-9807
Administrative Offices: 366-5731
www.selby.org
Hours: 10:00 a.m. - 5:00 p.m. daily (Except Christmas)
Admission: Adults – $8.00; Children (6 - 11) – $4.00; Toddlers (under 6) – Free; Groups of 20 or more – $7.00/person.
Time it takes to see it all: 1-1/2 hours.

Highlights: Living museum of more than 20,000 plants; world orchid center (about 6,000 on premises); 6,000 square-foot display greenhouse; many rare and endangered species; 9 acres of gorgeous grounds and boardwalk by the bay; offers continuing classes for children and adults throughout the year in a variety of horticultural related subjects.

For many Sarasota area visitors and new residents, the next step after getting the fabled sand in their shoes is to get some dirt under their nails. This semitropical locale offers unique opportunities and rewarding challenges to the accomplished home gardener and the novice

Local Fun

Field Trip: Sandpipers

These busy little birds leave thousands of tiny tracks on our beaches. They can be seen darting allover the shoreline in search of insects and small crustaceans. *The Sandpiper,* the movie, contained the Academy Award winning song, "The Shadow of Your Smile," in 1965. The Sandpipers were a vocal group who made the top ten hit list with "Guantanamera" in 1966. These sandpiper success stories never seemed to have had any impact on the nonstop eating habits of these birds whatsoever.

alike. Sandy soil, periodic salt spray, and alternating months of near drought followed by short-lived but torrential rains, combine to make this area a horticultural dreamscape of epic proportions.

Marie Selby Botanical Gardens, a nine-acre verdant respite on Sarasota Bay near downtown, serves year-round as a multifaceted resource for observing and learning about the plant life of this area and far beyond our coastal plains. It has been called "a supernova in the constellation of botanical gardens," by syndicated garden columnist Duane Campbell, and is known locally as the place to go for advice, demonstration and inspiration.

Marie Selby, widow of oil magnate and philanthropist William Selby, was an avid amateur horticulturist who bequeathed her bayside family home and grounds to Sarasota. When the Gardens opened to the public in 1975, Marie's own work provided the foundation for the highly respected institution that now attracts visitors and researchers from all over the world. This outdoor and under-glass museum has catalogued more than 20,000 living plants within its gardens and greenhouses, and 73,000 dried specimens in its herbarium. Selby Gardens is known for its extensive orchid center, an internationally-recognized rain forest canopy research center, and what is acknowledged as the world's most outstanding collection of epiphytes or "air" plants.

As part of its commitment to education, Selby Gardens offers a highly competitive international horticultural internship program. Students from South and Central America, the Far East, Europe, and Africa work shoulder-to-shoulder with America's best and brightest to examine threats to and explore solutions for maintaining the delicate balance of plants in natures.

In addition to providing a home for the plants themselves, Selby Gardens also presents rotating exhibits of artwork inspired by fascinating flora. With its colorful and exotic backdrops, classes in nature photography and watercolor are among the most popular offerings at Selby.

Selby's tranquil setting on Sarasota Bay serves as a romantic venue for private events of all kinds, including weddings throughout the year.

The Gardens staff is eager to assist you and answer your gardening questions.

Shark Teeth Hunting on Venice Beach
Location: Venice Beach
Venice is called "The Shark Tooth Capital of the World" for good reason, it's impossible to go there and NOT find sharks teeth on the beach. We're not talking about just one or two sharks teeth. We're taking about LOTS of sharks teeth, so many that the Venice Area Chamber of Commerce gives packages of them away FREE to folks who stop by. Here's why there are so many on Venice Beach: All sharks continually shed their teeth and grow new ones, as many as 24,000 in a ten-year period. Many of the teeth you will find here are prehistoric, sharks have inhabited the area for millions of years. After dropping to the bottom, their teeth wash up on shore with the waves and changing tides. You'll find a variety of grey, brown or black teeth, stained by the mineral deposits where they have been buried, finding a white tooth from living sharks is unusual. Types of shark teeth most commonly found include Bull, Dusky, Lemon, Mako, Tiger Shark, Sand Shark, Carcharodon and Extinct Mako. Teeth range in size from one-eighth inch to three inches or more (these are very rare.) Digging for teeth and prehistoric bones is illegal; however, you can sift the top layer of sand with a professional sifter, a wire mesh basket attached to a long handle or bring a colander from home. The teeth make great souvenirs and the kids will go wild. For a nifty hand sized field guide with photos and descriptions, send $3.50 (includes postage) to: "1990

Collectors Guide," P.O. Box 3250, Venice, FL 34293. For further information contact: Venice Area Chamber of Commerce at 488-2236.

Silent Sports of Florida
7660 S. Tamiami Tr., Sarasota 34231
922-4042, fax 921-5881

Mary Gordon leads a three hour kayak tour of Sarasota Bay filled with information about local waters, birds and history. Pace is suited towards individual groups. Call for details.

Smuggler's Cove Adventure Golf
2000 Cortez Rd. West, Bradenton 34207
756-0043
Hours: 9:00 a.m. - 11:00 p.m. daily
Single Play Prices: Adults - $6.25
                    Children under 12 - $5.25
                    Children 3 and under - Free
                    Special - Second Round is $1.00
All-Day Unlimited- Play Prices: Adults - $8.20
                    Children - $7.25
                    Children 3 and under - Free

Miniature Golf – 18-holes including caves and a sunken ship in a tri-level tropical garden setting.

Snook Haven Restaurant & Fish Camp
5000 Venice Ave. East, Venice
Information: 485-7221

	Canoe Rentals	12' Powerboat	14' Powerboat
3 Hours	$17.17	$36.38	$47.08
2 Hours	$14.98	$28.89	$38.52
1 Hour	$12.84	$21.40	$27.82

Supposedly this is where the first couple of Tarzan movies were filmed along with that 1940 semi-classic movie "Revenge of the Killer Turtle." Don't expect herds of charging elephants, roving bands of chimpanzees or, for that matter, any killer turtles either. But it is easy to understand the attraction for filmmakers, tourists and locals alike - this is primitive Florida with picnic tables! Canoes and powerboats are available for rent here which will put you in the middle of the Florida jungle very quickly. Home of the Myakka River Queen. Restaurant is also popular hangout for famlies on weekends (friendly "bikers invasion" every Sunday afternoon). Entertainment nightly, wide variety of musical styles. Fun and unforgettable.

South Florida Museum, Bishop Planetarium and Parker Manatee Aquarium
20f10th St. West, Bradenton 34205
746-4131, fax 747-2556
www. sfmbp.com
Weekly Schedule of Events: 746-STAR
Hours: 10 a.m. - 5:00 p.m. Tuesday - Saturday, Noon - 5:00 p.m. Sunday, 10:00 a.m. - 5 p.m. Monday. Open Mondays Jan.-April and during July
Daytime Admission: Adults – $7.50; Seniors (60+) – $6.00; Children (5-12) – $4.00; Toddlers (4 and under) – Free
Time it takes to see it all: 2 Hours

Admission includes two-story museum and Spanish Courtyard; new Parker Manatee Aquarium with "Snooty" the manatee and his new poolmate "Mo"; all afternoon planetarium presentations; and the new Wilson Environmental Classroom with the hands-on Discovery Place. Evening shows are a separate admission.

Field Trip: Seagulls

Ready for a bubble burst? There's no such thing as a seagull. Really.

There are at least forty-nine different kinds of gulls, not one of them is actually named "seagull."

We know what you're thinking: "Go tell that to Richard Bach!"

Most locals affectionately refer to these large scavengers as *"rats with wings."*

We assume they help our environment by helping themselves to our leftovers.

The South Florida Museum and Bishop Planetarium is a comprehensive facility dedicated to telling the story of Florida from "Astronomy to Zoology" through life size exhibits, dioramas and displays from the Museum's extensive collections. (New director, Dr. Peter Bennett plans a complete redoing of the museum, exciting changes are in the works.) Visitors can also learn about the diversity of Florida's natural resources from exhibits of fossils, shells and local wildlife. Snooty the world famous manatee is the official mascot of Manatee Count and a "must see" for visitors to the Museum. An orphaned West Indian Manatee named "Mo" joined Snooty (the world's oldest captive manatee) in 1998, together they share a state-of-the-art 60,000 gallon multi-level aquarium which allows above and below water viewing.

Snooping on Snooty
Born: July 21, 1948 in Miami Weight: 1,300 pounds Length: 9 feet Sex: Male Food: Snooty is a vegetarian sea mammal and eats 80 to 100 lbs. food of each day including lettuce, carrots and apples, plus monkey chow snacks and vitamins.

Snooty/Mo Educational Presentations: 12:30 p.m., 2:00 p.m., 3:30 p.m.

Starshows
Planetarium shows feature general astronomy, diverse planetary themes and seasonal sky shows with new shows introduced throughout the year. Call for show themes and schedules. *Starshow Showtimes:* 1:00 p.m. and 4:00 p.m. (included with daytime admission) *Skies over Florida:* Every Fri. and Sat. at 7:00 p.m. $3.00 adults; $1.50 children.

"Tonight" Show
This informative program, based in the evening sky, is offered every Friday and Saturday evening at 8:30 p.m. followed by Observatory Viewing (weather permitting) from 9:00 - 10:00 p.m.; admission to Tonight Show and Observatory is $1.00 per person.

Solar Observing
Saturdays 11:30 a.m. - 1:00 p.m., weather permitting. Admission is free with regular daily ticket.

Laser Lightshows and "Laser Fantasies"
Critically acclaimed as "one of the best laser light shows in the world." Features dynamic shows that change weekly; offering selections range from popular rock groups such as Pink Floyd, The Doors, U-2, The Beatles, Metallica and Pearl Jam to a wide mix of musical styles from Classical, Top-40, Big Band, Country (Garth Brooks), Psychedelic 60s/70s, Alternative and MORE! Evening shows change weekly are are held at concert volume.

Friday/Saturday Showtimes: 9 p.m. and 10:30 p.m.

Daily Matinee: 2:30 p.m. (included in daytime admission)

Saturday Morning Family Program
This educational and fun program is for children Pre-School through third grade and their parents, grandparents or other accompanying adult. Included is a Children's Starshow at 10:30 a.m. The program concludes at noon with time afterwards to see Snooty and explore the Museum. Program is free with regular admission price that day. Program changes monthly.

The Steigerwaldt/Jockey Fountain - Sarasota's Children's Fountain
Bayfront Park (enter at Ringling and U.S. 41)

Sarasota's first real tribute to children is a maze of water fountains shooting up from the floor of a thematic "Florida animal statuary" set within a Grecian style ampitheater. No kids? Go anyway. Never a

Steve Rabow's Guide Book Local Fun 139

SOUTH FLORIDA PLANITARIUM © BILL WEST

charge for what has to be the best entertainment away from the beach – a much appreciated gift. This is *the* place to take the kids when the summer sun hits a bit too hard, suntan lotion (and bathing suits) strongly recommended.

Sunshine Skyway Fishing Bridge
Off Exit 1A and 1B, on I-275 north of Bradenton
1-813-865-0668
Hours: 24-hours, daily

Cost: $3.00 per vehicle to drive out on the pier, $2.00 per person
What is now the world's longest fishing pier was once the south section of the original Sunshine Skyway bridge, which links the St. Petersburg area to Bradenton. The bridge was destroyed during a storm in May, 1980 when a phosphate tanker rammed into one of the supports. Thirty five people, who happened to be driving on the central section of the southbound span of the bridge, lost their lives when the bridge was hit and collapsed into the mouth of Tampa Bay. The Sunshine Skyway bridge has since been rebuilt and now spans 3,300 feet from shore-to-shore. The original south section is now home to the world's longest fishing pier (1-1/2 miles), open 24 hours a day and completely lighted. Unlike fishing from a boat, fisherman are not required to have licenses here.

© VAN WEZEL

Van Wezel Performing Arts Hall
777 North Tamiami Trail (U.S. 41), Sarasota 34236
Ticket Information: 953-3366

1995 was the 25th Anniversary year of this essential, and much loved jewel of our community. The City of Sarasota-owned Van Wezel, set on a hill above Sarasota Bay near downtown, offers a range of programs unequaled by any other local cultural organization. Where else can you see a major jazz vocalist, a Broadway play or musical, a classical pianist, a championship ice show

**Field Trip:
Sharks**

Here's an entire species that could use a good press agent – sharks have received an enormous amount of bad press. No doubt they are among nature's most efficient killing machines, honed by million of years of evolution into a brutal package of strength, speed and ultrasensitive senses. They are the ocean's scavengers, culling the sick and injured from the sea. But they also play a very important role in our daily lives and have great potential to help us in medicine and other areas of science.

and a nationally renowned symphony orchestra – all in the same week?

During the Van Wezel season, which runs from October through April, more than 130 performances are sponsored here by the Hall. And Van Wezel proudly plays host regularly to concerts, films, lectures and benefits presented by other local arts groups as well – the Florida West Coast Symphony, Sarasota Concert Band and Sarasota Music Festival among them.

When it was built in 1969, the Van Wezel was the only performing arts hall on Florida's west coast. Since it opened, hundreds of people have told the management that the primary reason they chose Sarasota over other Florida west coast cities for their retirement or second homes was the presence here of the Van Wezel Performing Arts Hall.

Free guided tours of Van Wezel Performing Arts Hall, conducted by members of the Sarasota Fine Arts Society, are available from mid-November through April. The tours run from 10:00 a.m. to noon and 2:00 p.m. to 4:00 p.m. Monday-Friday, except on matinee performance days.

1999 Van Wezel Performance Schedule

JAN. 2 Phylis Diller and John Byner
3 Roberta Peters
4 Legends of Motown - The Temptations & The Four Tops
5 Stars of the Paris Opera Ballet
8 Star of Magic Terry Evanswood
10 London City Opera "Die Fledermaus"
18 "Big"
19 "Big"
20 Billy Taylor's Jazz at the Kennedy Center from Sarasota
21 The Boston Pops
22 Robert Klein/David Brenner
23 Theatreworks/USA "Curious George"
25 Monsters of Grace: The Concert Version - Philip Glass
28 The Four Freshmen Tribute to Stan Kenton
29 Toronto Symphony Orchestra
30 Tom Chapin
31 "Plaza Suite" starring Lee Meriwether

FEB. 1 Big Band '99 - The Fabulous Dorseys
2 Moiseyev Dance Company
3 Moiseyev Dance Company
4 Mark Morris Dance Group
6 Urban Bush Women
9 Guy Lombardo's Royal Canadians with Al Pierson
9 Chamber Music Society of Lincoln Center
10 The American Boychoir
10 Radio Symphony Orchestra Berlin
11 Tango Buenos Aires
12 New York City Opera National Company "Madama Butterfly"
13 Paul Anka
15 The World Famous Glenn Miller Orchestra
16 Dixie Carter
19 The Peking Acrobats
21 Moscow Philharmonic Orchestra
22 "Two Pianos, Four Hands"
23 "Two Pianos, Four Hands"
24 "Two Pianos, Four Hands"
26 The Acting Company, "Tartuffe"
27 Russian National Ballet "Sleeping Beauty"
27 Russian National Ballet "Swan Lake"

28	Kathleen Battle "So Many Stars" with special guests
MAR 1	"Hit Me With A Hot Note" - the Duke Ellington Songbook starring Marilyn McCoo & Billy davis, Jr.
2	Denyce Graves, mezzo-soprano
3	Tony Bennet
4	Gordon Lightfoot
5	Ahmad Jamal
7	Yakov Kasman, piano
8	Vienna Choir Boys
9	Jerusalem Symphony Orchestra
11	Spoleto/USA Chamber Music
13	Theatreworks/USA "Ramona Quimby"
15	The Bayou to Bourbon Street - BeauSoleil avec Michael Doucet, The Dirty Dozen, and Geno Delafose & French Rockin' Boogie
16	Rich Little
16	Chanticleer
19	Murray Louis & Nikolais Dance
20	Orchestra of the Royal Opera House Covent Garden
21	Los Angeles Philharmonic
22	Les Ballets Trockadero de Monte Carlo
28	Gypsy Caravan - A Celebration of Rroma Music & Dance
30	Gala Closing Concert! Florida West Coast Symphony/Key Chorale
31	The Neville Brothers

Venice Fishing Pier
Harbor Drive and Center Rd., Venice

Stretched 750 feet over the Gulf of Mexico, this is one of the longest fishing piers on the west coast of Florida.

Highlights: Complete bathhouse facilities including showers, changing areas and concession shop with bait and tackle and beachcombing equipment and plenty of fish! fish! fish!

Venice Ice Pavilion
1266 U.S. 41 Bypass S., Venice 34292
484-0080, fax 484-3160

Who say's there's no winter in Florida? This brand-new regulation size rink offers public ice skating, youth hockey, adult hockey, freestyle, group classes, kids club, birthday parties, video game room, pro shop, rooms available for private parties, learn to skate program for kids and adults. Plus LASER TAG! Home to the Florida Suncoast Figure Skating Club, Gulf Coast Youth Hockey Association, Adult Hockey Leagues and The Special Skaters Society (designed for handicapped children); call for details. Open all year except Thanksgiving Day, Christmas Day and Easter Sunday. Skating sessions vary during week, weekends, and school holidays. Intermissions may occur during all sessions for ice resurfacing. Live D.J. during most weekend evening sessions. Call ahead for daily schedule and rates.

© WARM MINERAL SPRINGS

Warm Mineral Springs
12200 San Servando Avenue, Warm Mineral Springs, 34287
12 miles s. of Venice on U.S. 41 (Exit 34 off of I-75)
426-1692, fax 426-1231

Field Trip: Sharks

Of the 25 species of sharks in Florida waters, few are seen inshore. The species include lemon, bull, nurse, brown, mako and hammerhead.

Why save sharks? Much of what we know about human kidney function has come from studying sharks, their skin is used to make artificial skin for burn victims and sharks seem to posses the ability to resist cancer – if those mechanisms can be discovered it may be possible to reduce human suffering.

Hours: 9:00 a.m.- 5:00 p.m. daily
Admission: $7.00

The famed Fountain of Youth? An historic treasure to be sure. Florida's only warm springs is very popular with our international visitors because of its "health restoring" mineral water; the mineral content is actually many times higher than other famed international spas such as Vichy and Aix les Bains (France), Hot Springs (Arkansas) and Baden Baden (Germany). The water is consistently 87 degrees, about nine million gallons flow from the springs each day into a 2 1/2 acre lake. Full service spa (including massage hydrotherapy) and health studio available. Museum portrays history of early explorers. Restaurant on site, accommodations available. Bring your bathing suit, lockers provided. Very popular with European visitors and certainly well worth a visit, if for no other reason than just to listen to many diferent languages while enjoying this unique slice of "old Florida."

White Birds Bayou
3815 Tamiami Trail N., Sarasota 34239
351-8716. fax 355-4340
Hours: 10:00 a.m. - 10:00 p.m. daily

Miniature Golf – 18 holes in a mountain setting with waterfall and caves, snack bar.

First Game: Adults – $5.00 - Children under 12/Seniors - $4.50 ; Toddlers 3 and under - Free. Additional Games: $1.25 each.

Sports & Recreation

THE SUNCOAST IS RENOWN FOR OUR SPORTS AND RECREATION ACTIVITIES.

You'll find the obvious (Major League Baseball Spring Training, world class beaches, tennis, golf and fishing) along with the not-so obvious (Olympic windsurfing training, Little League World Series contenders and the highest number of Offshore Kilo Speed Run records set in on the planet.)

Name your sport and you'll find it here.

Well, okay maybe downhill skiing isn't a major Florida activity, but believe it or not you'll find that here too. Along with world-class ice skating.

(See what we mean?)

Both the active sport fanatic and sideline fan will enjoy a wide range of recreational fun – fishing, golf, tennis, diving, windsurfing – ours is a subtropical playground filled with year 'round challenges for the sport enthusiast.

And don't be surprised if you run into a major "name" sports figure either. Some of the world's finest athletes make it a point to stop in our area, often just to flex their muscles in the Florida sun.

Tony Cornish, Jr.. News40 Sports Director

Tony Cornish. Jr. joined WWSB, News40 as Sports Director in July 1998. Prior to joining WWSB, Tony served as Executive Producer and Sports Anchor for *SportsTalkLive!* -- a locally produced sports show seen weeknights on WBEK-TV (UPN affiliate) in Augusta GA, where he worked as a Sports Anchor. Tony attended the University of Central Florida where he majored in Communications. Tony has received several awards for his work in sports journalism, including Best Sportscaster of the Year from *Augusta Magazine* and, Best Sportscaster Award from the Georgia Associated Press. Tony has also been recognized by the National Academy of Television Journalists and is a member of the American Sportscasts Association. Tony and his wife Kelly have two children. They live in Sarasota.

Tony Cornish, Jr. may be a relative newcomer, but he knows a great sports town when he sees one: "Without question, the biggest dream for any Sports Director is to work in an area filled with plentiful recreational activities. Serious sports. The Suncoast seems to have it all, and some big names to prove it including Nick Bollettieri, Wayne Garett, Otto Graham, Monica Seles, Tripp Schwenk, Paul Azinger, Pee Wee Reese, Early Winn and - oh, baby! - Dick Vitale! World class beaches, world series baseball, world champion tennis, world renown golf, even the World Wrestling Federation, you'll find it all here. And, probably like you, I am going to try to see and do it all."

Recreation Centers

Adult Recreation Center
803 N. Tamiami Tr., Sarasota 34236
316-1125

Hours: Monday, Wednesday, Friday 9:00 a.m. - 4:00 p.m., Tuesday 11:00 a.m. - 4:30 p.m., Thursday 9:00 a.m. - 4:00 p.m. and 7:00 p.m. - 10:30 p.m., Monday and Wednesday evenings 6:00 p.m. - 10:00 p.m., Saturday 11:30 a.m. - 4:30 p.m., Sunday 1:00 p.m. - 5:00 p.m. Wide variety of regularly scheduled activities for seniors including dancing, yoga and the most difficult sport in the world - Bingo!

The Sport of People Watching: Local Superstars

Playground of the rich and famous? Not exactly.

Our area isn't on the "jet set's Top Ten" – and that's good news for artists, actors and sports figures who like to escape the spotlight glare, but who don't mind from us "little folk" the occasional stare. Keep in mind that they work hard for a living too – giving them their well deserved space is appropriate – but you'll be amazed at who you might see sitting next to you at your favorite restaurant.

The following is a list of some of the sports superstars who live here in the Sarasota, Bradenton and Venice area.

Venice Community Center
326 Nokomis Ave., Venice 34235
486-2311, fax 486-2304
Open 7 days a week. Located on seven beautifully landscaped acres. Along with a wide variety of regularly scheduled activities for seniors including dancing, bridge, yoga and bingo, its modern facilities are used for a myriad of purposes, including public service lectures and seminars sponsored by various clubs and businesses for the community's welfare.

Archery

Sarasota Archery Club
4570 17th Street, Sarasota 34235
377-7005

Artificial Reefs

Information about seven locations (they can fax or mail it to you)
742-5980

Aviation Instruction

Florida Flight Training
150 Airport Ave. E, Venice 34285
484-3771, fax 483-9022

Huffman Aviation
400 Airport Ave. E, Venice 34285
484-8183, fax 485-7401
e-mail: huffmanaviation2compuserve.com

Jones Aviation Service
1234 Clyde Jones Rd., Sarasota 34243
355-8100, fax 351-9700,
www.jonesav.com

Seaplane Flight Instruction
Sar/Brad Int. Airport
795-8890
e-mail: seaplanecfi@msn.com

Baseball

Since the early 1900s, Sarasota and baseball have been hand and glove. The first couple of decades saw small fields turned into makeshift diamonds. But in 1923 John Ringling helped to convince John McGraw, owner of the New York Giants, to come to Sarasota to practice during the spring. McGraw demanded that for him to bring the team a "big league" field would need to be built. Through public subscriptions it was, and The Giants came on Feb. 1, 1924 and played here through 1927. The Indianapolis Indians played at Payne Park from 1929 to 1932. The Boston Red Sox made their home there from 1933 to 1958; the Los Angeles Dodgers played there in 1959 and then the Chicago White Sox played there from 1960 until 1988 when Ed Smith Stadium was built. The White Sox continued to play in Sarasota until 1997. The Cincinnati Reds will play at Ed Smith Stadium for the first time in 1998, sharing the Suncoast sunshine with the Pittsburgh Pirates who play each spring in Bradenton.

Community Programs
Adult Baseball
758-2356

Babe Ruth Baseball
371-4539

Central Sarasota County Little League
371-1565

Manatee County Girls Soft Ball
3813 Highland Ave. W.,
Bradenton, 795-0861

Manatee County Little League - Bradenton
746-0172

Newtown Little League
953-4518

Sarasota County Athletic Program
316-1172

Sarasota County Little League
924-0209

BASEBALL "DREAM" CAMPS

The Baseball Academy
5500 34th St. W.,
Bradenton 34210
755-1000, fax 756-6891
www.bollettieri.com

Part of the Nick Bollettieri Tennis Academy sports empire – boarding and non-boarding programs combining outstanding academics with a professional caliber training program.

Baseball Fantasy Camp
2100 Constitution Blvd., Sarasota 34231
925-4855, fax 925-2394

For men and women, age 30 and older, with big league dreams, who would rather be in the game rather than watching from the stands. This Sarasota based company gives you a chance to play ball with The Seattle Mariners, the San Diego Padres, or The Milwaukee Brewers in the spring training complex of your favorite team. You get your own uniform and number too. Call for details. Bus trips and cruises.

Camp Bradenton (Fantasy Week)
412-323-5025
www.pirateball.com

A Bradenton "dream camp" where participants 30 years of age or older are coached, trained and play ball just like they're the big league. You even get to keep your very own uniform. Special rates to local residents who commute. Write or call for details: Pittsburgh Pirates, 600 Stadium Circle, Pittsburgh, PA 15212.

BASEBALL PROFESSIONAL LEAGUES

Professional Leagues - Florida Sites and Tickets

Atlanta Braves – Municipal Stadium, West Palm Beach
Tickets: (407) 966-3309

Baltimore Orioles – Ft. Lauderdale Stadium, Ft. Lauderdale
Tickets: (410) 685-9800

Boston Red Sox – City of Palms Park, Ft. Myers
Tickets: (941-) 334-4700

Cincinnati Reds – Ed Smith Stadium, Sarasota
Tickets: (941) 954-4101

Cleveland Indians – Chain O' lakes Park, Winter Haven
Tickets: (216) 241-8888

Detroit Tigers – Joker Marchant Stadium, Lakeland
Tickets: (941) 6603-6278

Florida Marlins - Space Coast Stadium, Melbourne
Tickets: (407) 633-9200

Houston Astros – Osceola County Stadium, Kissimmee
Tickets: (407) 933-5500

Kansas City Royals – Baseball City Sports Complex, Haines City
Tickets: (941) 424-2500

Los Angeles Dodgers – Holman Stadium, Vero Beach
Tickets: (407) 569-6858

Minnesota Twins – Lee County Sports Complex, Ft. Myers
Tickets: (941) 768-4270/768-4200

Montreal Expos – Municipal Stadium, West Palm Beach
Tickets: (407) 684-6801

New York Mets – St. Lucie Stadium, Port St. Lucie
Tickets: (561) 871-2115

New York Yankees – Legends Field, Tampa
Tickets: (813) 287-8844

Philadelphia Phillies – Jack Russell Stadium, Clearwater
Tickets: (813) 442-8496

Pittsburgh Pirates – McKechnie Field, Bradenton
Tickets: (941) 748-4610/747-3031

St. Louis Cardinals – Al Lang Stadium, St. Petersburg
Tickets: (813) 896-4641

Texas Rangers – Charlotte County Stadium, Port Charlotte
Tickets: (941) 625-9500

Toronto Blue Jays – Grant Field, Dunedin
Tickets: (813) 733-0429

PUBLIC DIAMONDS

Bradenton

Blackstone Park
2112 14th Ave. W, Palmetto
722-9053

G.T. Bray
3700 59th St. W. Bradenton
749-7174

Manatee County Fairgrounds
1303 17th St. W, Palmetto
722-1639

75th St. Park
75th St. W. and 40th Ave. W.
792-9005

The Sport of People Watching: Local Superstars

Paul Azinger
Golf Pro extraordinaire. '93 PGA Champion. Makes more birdies than a mother hen.

Wilson Alvarez
Tampa Bay Devil Rays Pitcher.

Nick Bollettieri
Tennis guru has taught the game's very best, now runs Bollettieri Sports Academy.

Tommy Frazier
Two Time National Champion as Nebraska's Quarterback.

Wayne Garett
Former Mets 3rd baseman - part of the '69 Miracle and all 'round great guy.

Otto Graham
NFL Hall of Fame quarterback for the Cleveland Browns.

Gene Lamont
Pittsburgh Pirates Manager.

The Sport of People Watching: Local Superstars

Mean Gene Okerland
The coolest "sports" announcer in the world. Period.

Pee Wee Reese
Nothing pee wee about this Baseball Hall of Famer.

Tripp Schwenk
Olympic swimmer, gold and silver medalst.

Monica Seles
The #1 tennis player in the world!

Dick Vitale The hippest sports announcer in the world. Period.

Early Winn
Baseball Hall of Famer and 300-game winner.

Tyrone Williams
Tommie Frazier's former teammate at Manatee High and Nebraska, now member of Super Bowl Champion Green Bay Packers.

24th St. East Park
Bradenton
742-5948

Sarasota

Bee Ridge Park
4430 Lockwood Ridge, Sarasota
316-1172

Glebe Park
998 Glebe Lane, Siesta Key
316-1172

Newtown Community Center
1845 34th St., Sarasota
316-1331

Newtown Estates
2800 Newtown Blvd. and Dr. M.L. King, Jr., Blvd., Sarasota
316-1161

Fairgrounds Park
185 South Pompano Ave., Sarasota

Fruitville Park
5151 Richardson Rd.,Sarasota
316-1172

Siesta Beach
948 Beach Rd., Siesta Key
346-3207

17th Street Park
4570 17th St., Sarasota
316-1172

Twin Lakes Park Facility
6700 Clark Rd., Sarasota
316-1194

Youth Athletic Complex
2810 17th St., Sarasota
316-1268

Venice

By Pass Park
1101 Gulf Coast Blvd., Venice
316-1172

Lemon Bay Park
316-1172

Chuck Reiter Stadium
250 Fort St., Venice
316.1172

Wellfield Park
1300 Ridgewood, Venice
316-1172

BASKETBALL

Community Programs

Jewish Community Center
378-5568

Newtown Community Center
316-1331

Newtown Estates Park
316-1161

Sarasota Boys and Girls Club
366-3911

Sarasota/Manatee Jewish Federation
371-4546

Manatee YMCA
792-7484

YMCA Euclid Branch
1075 S. Euclid Ave., Sarasota
955-8194

YMCA Evalyn Sadlier Jones Branch
8301 Potter Park Dr., Sarasota
922-9622

Public Courts Bradenton

Blackstone Park
2112 14th Ave. W., Palmetto

G.T. Bray
3700 59th St. W.

Public Courts Sarasota

Arlington Park Facility
2650 Waldemere St.

Bee Ridge Park Facility
4430 South Lockwood Ridge Rd.

Colonial Oaks Park
5300 Colonial Oaks Blvd.

Gillespie Park
710 N. Osprey Ave.

Longwood Park
6050 Longwood Blvd.

Newtown Community Center
1845 34th St.

Newtown Estates
2800 Newtown Blvd. and Dr. M.L. King, Jr., Blvd.

Pinecraft Park
1420 Gilbert Ave.

Pioneer Park
1121 Cocoanut Ave.

Potter Park
8587 Potter Park Dr.

Riverview High School
One Ram Way

Sevilla Park
1506 Central Ave.

Twin Lakes Park Facility
6700 Clark Rd.

Public Courts Venice

By Pass Park
1101 Gulf Coast Blvd.,
Venice

Challenger Park
71 South Olivia St.,
South Venice

Hecksher Park
450 West Venice Ave.,
Venice

Laurel Park
860 Forest Street,
Laurel

Pinebrook Park
1251 Pinebrook Rd.,
Venice

Shamrock Park & Nature Center
 4100 W. Shamrock Dr.

Woodmere Park
3951 Woodmere Park Blvd.

Public Beaches

Some areas are internationally recognized for their skyscrapers, bridges and architecture. Others are recognized for their art, music and contributions to science. With us, it's mainly one thing – world class waterfront!

Rabow Rule #3: At sunset you should be on any of our gulf beaches. It doesn't matter which one, just be there.

Photography hint: Place the subject (the sun or the person you are shooting) in either of the lower or upper corners of your viewfinder. This will give you a more interesting shot - instead of the same-ol' centered photo. A polarizing filter will help to eliminate glare and heighten colors.

For visitors and residents alike, it's our beaches that make spending time here something truly special. Our Parks and Recreation Department continues to do a wondrous job in the maintenance, preservation and protection of our treasured waterfront areas. Those accomplishments alone would be enough for a medal, but add the watchful eye of their lifeguards – keenly focused on those of us enjoying the sun and fun, and the whole department is elevated to the status of local hero.

There's plenty to be thankful for besides the emerald waters and snow white sand – you'll often find public lavatories, outside showers,

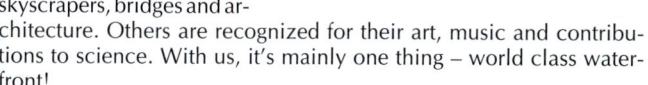
SIESTA RELAXATION © BILL WEST

> **Two words (and then a few more) about walkovers...**
>
> **"Use Them!"** Wooden walkovers have been built over sea oats and beach elder – essential vegetation necessary to protect our dunes and beaches.
>
> Please use walkovers whenever possible, avoiding any vegetation growing around and underneath them. You will help save our beaches for future generations.
>
> Thanks.

concession stands and, of course, REAL lifeguards at our beaches. (It's important to note that even though you can probably buy one in souvenir shops, a "lifeguard" tee shirt with a big red cross on it won't make you a hero at the beach no matter how much it cost you. Stick with Mickey or Snooty, okay?)

There's no fishing allowed off the public beaches and no barbecuing allowed on the beach. Many public beaches have grill facilities which are listed further on in this chapter.

If you are planning a weekend jaunt on any of our public beaches get there early, the earlier the better. Holidays are the busiest. The picnic tables during peak holidays are taken by 6 a.m., parking lots are completely filled by 10 a.m. and Season (February - April) is always busy, the rest of the year you should find plenty of space.

Bring along sunscreen and a hat or an umbrella so when you've had too much sun you can get out of the rays but still enjoy your day at the beach. You'll find concession stands that sell food and rent umbrellas and chairs listed further on in this chapter.

Our beaches are family oriented. If you are playing ball, respect the people around you. The same is true for radios: the lifeguards will not allow them to disturb others. If a lifeguard blows a whistle, be sure to glance in his or her direction – they may be blowing it at you.

Most beaches have restricted swimming areas. Only swimmers, no boats. If you plan to come to the beach by boat, be sure to land or anchor outside of the designated "swimming only" areas.

If you find yourself being swept out to sea in a rip current (strong current):

1. Remain calm.
2. Swim parallel to shore.
3. Once out of the current, swim to shore at an angle, not straight in.

If you find yourself in trouble:

1. Remain calm.
2. Call for help.
3. Follow the instructions of a rescuer.

SARASOTA COUNTY PARKS & RECREATION

Dune Restoration Program

It is important to understand that there is a natural balance to the ongoing cycle of dunes, beaches, and the "littoral drift" which is the movement of sand along the coast by currents. Even if man were not present, they would all still move, changing their appearance in response to the forces of nature. However, this balance can be upset when structures are built too close to the water, excessive foot or vehicle traffic occurs, and when abnormal tides or waves are caused by storms.

Beaches and dune systems are able to absorb enormous amounts of storm energy and thus play a major role in protecting our barrier islands, which in turn, protect the mainland of Sarasota and Manatee Counties. Dunes are often taken for granted but are very important to this process. They act as dikes to prevent high tides from flooding upland areas and also provide a reserve supply of sand that can be released naturally to replenish an active beach area at times of severe erosion. These systems are our best and most natural defense against the powerful actions of waves, winds, and tides. The goal is to enhance this natural occurrence through the establishment, protection and nourishment of dunes, enabling them to provide their fullest benefits.

NORTH MANATEE COUNTY BEACHES

Anna Maria Beach
located on the northern tip of Anna Maria Island on the Gulf of Mexico. Over three acres of undeveloped sandy beach; access from private residential streets; parking; public transportation drop off/pick up; no alcohol allowed unless it's been mixed with gasoline for your car's motor.

Anna Maria Bayfront Park
over 1,000 feet of sandy beach along the Tampa Bay side of Anna Maria Island; developed park includes over 150 parking places off Bay Blvd., restrooms, picnic tables, shelters, group facilities, handicap facilities, public transportation drop off/pick up.

Holmes Beach
14,400 feet of Gulf of Mexico sandy beach located off Gulf Drive from Beach Avenue to 27th Street. Parking, boating facilities, public transportation drop off/pick up.

Central Manatee County Beaches
Manatee County Beach – 900 feet of sandy beach on the Gulf of Mexico with access at Gulf Drive (State Road 789) and 40th Street (State Road 64) in the City of Holmes Beach. 120 parking places, restrooms, showers, picnic tables, lifeguard station, boating facilities, shelters, concession stand, group facilities, handicap facilities, public transportation drop off/pick up.

Palma Sola Causeway
3,000 feet of developed sandy beach on both sides and each end of causeway located at Manatee Avenue and Palma Sola Bay. Parking, restrooms, picnic tables, boating facilities, shelters, group facilities, public transportation drop off/pick up. Popular with boaters.

South Manatee County Beaches
Cortez Beach – 140 feet of undeveloped beach on the Gulf of Mexico located between 5th Street and 13th Street off Gulf Drive (State Road 789) in the City of Bradenton Beach. Parking, restrooms, showers, picnic tables, lifeguard station, boating facilities, shelters, concession stand, group facilities, handicap facilities, public transportation drop off/pick up.

Coquina Beach
over 5,000 feet of developed sandy beach on the Gulf of Mexico with access from Gulf Drive (State Road 789) at the southern end of Anna Maria Island, one mile south of 5th Street North in the City of Bradenton Beach. 1,350 parking places, restrooms, showers, picnic tables, lifeguard station, boating facilities, shelters, concession stand, group facilities, handicap facilities, public transportation drop off/pick up.

NORTH LONGBOAT KEY

Beer Can Island
2,000 feet of primitive sandy beach at the northern tip of Longboat Key, accessible by walking north from the street end of North Shore Road off of Gulf of Mexico Drive. Best to come by boat or walk to island at low tide. Limited parking, public transportation drop off/pick up.

North Longboat Key Beach
Undeveloped sandy beach extends from North Shore Road, south to the county line, accessible through residential street ends: Jay, Coral, Palmetto, Seabreeze, Broadway and Gulfside Roads. Parking only available on residential streets but they don't make it easy.

Beach Basics 101

"Baby powder" white sand beaches, year 'round sunshine, romantic flaming sunsets, friendly natives – it's only a matter of time before the rest of the world discovers our special paradise. So enjoy our beaches. Often. The Sarasota area is home to more than eight miles of the finest, whitest sand in the world – *Siesta Key* was awarded that distinction a few years ago in the Great International White Sand Beach Challenge by David Aubrey, a beach expert and director of coastal research at the Woods Hole Oceanographic Institution in Massachusetts.

Longboat Key contains 11 miles of white sand beaches however, there are very few public access points. *Lido Key* is a great place to bring the kids, you'll find a playground on the north end of the Key

Manatee County (*Anna Maria, Holmes Beach, Bradenton Beach and Longboat Key*) boats of 150 miles of white sand beaches.

Before you swim, know your Beach Flags.

At each of the lifeguard stands you'll see a flag. Here's what it means:

Green Flag It's safe to swim.

Yellow Flag Caution, there may be a current or rip tide.

Red Flag It's dangerous to swim, due to lightning, big rip tide or heavy surf.

Blue Flag Hazardous marine life: jelly fish, sting rays, red tide or the occasional (but rare) shark.

The yellow diamond shaped sign at lifeguard station will describe exact marine life sighted.

NORTH SARASOTA COUNTY BEACHES

Longboat Key Beach
Located along Gulf of Mexico Drive, this primitive sandy beach stretches over five miles from the county line south to the New Pass Bridge. However, access is limited to Bay Isles Road, Neptune Avenue and Buttonwood Drive where parking is likewise very limited.

North Lido Beach
77 acres of land including 3,000 feet of primitive sandy beach located on the north end of Lido Key on the west side of West Way Drive, a quarter mile west of John Ringling Blvd. Another access is available on Emerson Drive. Nude sunbathing was allowed here until 1986. No lifeguards - swift currents - be careful. Very limited parking; public transportation drop off/pick up.

CENTRAL SARASOTA COUNTY BEACHES

Lido Beach
15 acres of land including 3,100 feet of developed sandy beach on the Gulf of Mexico, located two and a half blocks southwest of Harding Circle, left on Benjamin Franklin Drive. 25-meter heated swimming pool with diving board, 400 parking spaces, restrooms, showers, lifeguard station, concession stand, meeting room, observation deck, public transportation drop off/pick up.

South Lido Park
100 acre park interacts with four significant bodies of water: The Gulf of Mexico, Big Pass, Sarasota Bay and Brushy Bayou. This park presents a unique opportunity to visitors to enjoy natural outdoor resources of Sarasota. The southern beach portion of the park offers expansive views of the emerging skyline of downtown Sarasota and the Gulf of Mexico. Parking, restrooms, showers, picnic tables, grills, playground equipment, volleyball court, fitness trail, handicap facilities. Lifeguard station open weekends from Memorial Day to Labor Day.

Siesta Key Beach Park
Widest, most popular beach in Sarasota County. About a half mile of developed, unique sandy beach located along the south side of Beach Road, west of the Midnight Pass Road intersection on the Gulf of Mexico. One of the most beautiful beaches found anywhere, officially rated as "The Whitest, Finest Sand in the World." Shallow water depth in the near-shore area together with year 'round lifeguard protection makes this one of the safest beaches in the county.

Plenty of parking with 800 spaces available – available if you get there early, that is. Restrooms, showers, picnicking, lifeguard stations, group size and small size shelters (for reservations call 346-3207), tennis courts, ball field, volleyball courts, concession stand, group facilities, handicap facilities, 20-station fitness trail, playground equipment and public transportation drop off/pick up.

The perfect beach? It just doesn't get much better than this. The grains of sand on Siesta Beach are so fine the beach itself is like powder.

The Upside – You'll have "happy feet," your toes will love trotting on this beach. It really is one of the most beautiful beaches in the world.

The Downside – The sand is so fine it gets into everything. Leave your valuable watches and electronics at home.

The Funnyside – Since the sand on Siesta Beach is actually 99% quartz, you may run into the occasional "new age hippie" who thinks the whole beach is one big cosmic tuning fork. Although not as prolific as they were in the early 80s, they are easy enough to spot. You'll see them dancing in the sun, like Aztec lunatics harmless, even when provoked.

But never mind all of that, Albert Einstein, Charlie Chaplin, Gloria Swanson and Hulk Hogan have reportedly walked on Siesta Beach. You should too.

OTHER SIESTA KEY BEACH ACCESSES

Shell Road
Old Stickney Point Road and Point of Rocks Road with limited parking, no facilities.

Turtle Beach
Quarter mile of developed sandy beach on the Gulf of Mexico located at the south end of Siesta Key, two and a half miles south of Stickney Point Road on Midnight Pass Road. Very popular for family outings and gatherings, its picnic shelters are used extensively for this purpose. For reservations call 346-3207.

LONGBOAT © BILL WEST

Parking, restrooms, showers, picnic tables, horseshoe courts, volleyball court, playground equipment and dune walkovers. No lifeguards. Boating facilities, group facilities, handicap facilities, public transportation drop off/pick up.

SOUTH SARASOTA COUNTY BEACHES

Palmer Point
Primitive sandy beach begins at the southern tip of Siesta Key and continues to the north end of Casey Key. Seclusion at its finest - no lifeguards, no facilities. You're on your own, playing on 24 acres including 2,400 linear feet of gulf beach frontage.

Nokomis Beach
Two tenths of a mile long, 1,700 linear feet of developed sandy beach

No! No! A Thousand Times No!

NO - Pets in our parks

NO - Fishing in swimming areas

NO - Glass containers

NO - Surfing in swimming areas (Dude!)

NO - Littering

NO - Crossing the vegetation except on walkovers

NO - Alcohol at Venice Beach or Anna Maria Beach

NO - Vehicles outside of parking lots

NO - Fires except in grills

NO - Games and sports outside of designated areas

on the Gulf of Mexico and 3,200 linear feet of Intracoastal waterway frontage located one mile west of Tamiami Trail on State Road 789 at the intersection of Casey Key Road. Family oriented beach popular for fishing and picnics. Parking, restrooms, showers, picnic tables, lifeguard station all year, boating facilities, handicap facilities.

North Jetty Park
Two tenths of a mile of developed sandy beaches on the Gulf of Mexico and Venice Inlet, located at south end of Casey Key. One of the most exciting surfing beaches on the west coast of Florida. Dude! Great fishing too. Lots of boats. Parking, restrooms, showers, picnic tables, lifeguard station all year, shelters (for rental information call 486-2311), concession stand, bait shop, group facilities, handicap facilities.

Venice Municipal Beach
875 feet of developed sandy beach, located a mile west of U.S. 41 on Venice Avenue West at the Gulf of Mexico. Wonderful spot to find prehistoric shark teeth and other fossilized material. If you are looking for live *Jaws*, there is a coral reef about a quarter-mile offshore. Parking, restrooms, showers, picnic tables, volleyball courts, lifeguard station all year, group facilities, handicap facilities, public transportation drop off/pick up.

Brohard Park Beach
Developed sandy beach between Venice Municipal Airport and the Intracoastal Waterway and Gulf of Mexico, connected to Caspersen Park Beach. Total beach area is three miles with 4,800 linear feet of shoreline along the Gulf of Mexico. 740 foot public fishing pier, great bird watching (visitors from Great Britain: we mean the kind with wings) parking, restrooms, picnic tables, snack bar and bait shop. No lifeguards on duty.

Caspersen Beach
Developed sandy beach on south side between Venice Municipal Airport and the Intracoastal Waterway and Gulf of Mexico, connected to Brohard Park Beach; southern two thirds of beach is primitive. One of the great shelling beaches in the area. 177 acres of land including 9,150 linear feet of gulf beach frontage. Parking, restrooms, picnic tables, nature trail, dune walkovers, handicap facilities. No lifeguards.

Manasota Beach
One quarter mile of developed sandy beach located on Manasota Key at west end of Manasota Bridge. Parking, restrooms, showers, picnic tables, boat ramp, small and large shelters (for reservations call 474-3065), lifeguard station all year, handicap facilities.

Blind Pass Beach
2,940 linear feet of undeveloped sandy beach located 3.6 miles south of the Manasota Bridge fronting both Lemon Bay and the Gulf of Mexico. Parking, restrooms, showers, picnic tables. No lifeguards.

Bicycles

TRACKS AND CLUBS

B.M.X. Bicycle Motorcross
Southwest District Parents
Council, Sarasota, 371-0895

BMX Track
Youth Athletic Complex
2810 17th St., Sarasota
957-4393

The Coastal Cruisers Bicycle Club
497-2736

Sarasota-Manatee Bicycle Club
351-7870

BICYCLE RENTALS

Anna Maria Island

Neumann's Island Beach Store
427 Pine Ave., Anna Maria
778-3316

Bradenton

Bradenton Bike & Kayak
5604 Cortez Rd.,
795-0701, fax 793-1703
e-mail: mredfish@aol.com

Ryder Bike Shop
1905 Cortez Rd. W.,
Bradenton 34207
756-5480

Wide World of Cycles
1118 8th Ave. W., Palmetto
722-8758

Longboat Key

Backyard Bike Shop
5610 Gulf of Mexico Dr,
383-5184

Sarasota Beach Service
4949 Gulf of Mexico Dr.
383-4466

Sarasota

Myakka River Outpost
State Rd. 72,
923-1120

Pedal N Wheels
2881 Clark Rd. 34231, 922-0481
4934 Fruitville Rd. 34232, 377-6662

Sarasota Bicycle Center
4084 Bee Ridge Rd. 34233
377-4505

Sarasota Schwinn Cyclery Inc.
3800 Osprey Ave. 34239
366-4144

Siesta Key

CB's Bait & Tackle
1249 Stickney Point Rd. 34242
349-4400, fax 346-1148

Siesta Sports Rentals
6551 Midnight Pass Rd. 34242
346-1797, fax 346-1954
e-mail: ggchapman@aol.com

Venice

The Bicycle Shop
336 Venice By-Pass S. 34292
488-4490

Billiard Parlors

Corner Pocket Lounge
2460 Stickney Pt. Rd., Sar 34231
922-3777

Gallery Billiards
925 Northgate Blvd.,
Sarasota 34234
355-5630

Livingston's Rack N' Roll
7113 S. Tamiami Tr.,
Sarasota 34231
925-7665

Monte Carlo Billiards
521 US 41 By-Pass N, Venice
484-8337

Sure Shot Billiard Lounge
1863 Tamiami Tr. S.,
Venice 34239, 497-4086

Boating

INSTRUCTION

Longboat Key Flotilla 82
1599 City Island Rd., Sarasota,
388-1982

O'Leary's Sarasota Sailing School
Island Park, Sarasota, 953-7505

BOAT RAMPS

Bradenton

Braden River Shores
E. Manatee Ave.

No! No! A Thousand Times No!

NO - Operation of vehicles outside of designated areas

NO - Skimboarding in guarded areas

NO - Destruction or removal of dune vegetation

NO - Disturbing sea turtles (in their nest or anywhere else)

NO - Spear fishing within 200 feet of swimming areas

NO - Operation of boats in swimming areas

NO - Scuba or skin diving without flags

Shedding some light on Sunlight

Sunlight consists of various wavelengths of electromagnetic energy, divided into visible light and ultraviolet light. Your eyes can't "see" ultraviolet light, but these are the rays responsible for "tanning," or if you are not careful, "burning." Your mother would tell you to use plenty of sunscreen, often. By now you should have learned never to argue with your mother. Also, drink lots of fluids, both before you go to the beach and while you're there. You'll do a lot of sweating at the beach and fluids will help prevent both dehydration and heat exhaustion. Oh, yes...men "sweat," women "glow."

Coquina Boat Ramp
(North and South)
SR 789, North of Longboat Pass

Kingfish Shores
R 64, west of Anna Maria Bridge,
Holmes Beach

Palma Sola Causeway Country Park
E. Manatee Ave.

Riverside Drive, Palmetto
State Rd. 64 - SR 64 and Braden Rd.

Warner's Bayou
Riverview Blvd. and Warner's Bayou, Sarasota

Causeway Park
420 John Ringling Causeway, Sarasota

Centennial Park
1059 N. Tamiami Trail

Ken Thompson Park/City Island
1700 Ken Thompson Pkwy.,
Lido Key

Pinecraft Park
420 Gilbert Avenue, Sarasota

Turtle Beac
8918 Midnight Pass Road,
Siesta Key

Venice

Higel Marine Park
1330 Tarpon Center Dr.

Marina Boat Ramp Par
215 E Venice Ave., Venice

Nokomis Beach
901 Casey Key Rd., Nokomis

Manasota Beach
8770 Manasota Beach Road, South Venice

RENTALS

Anna Maria

Bradenton Beach Marina
402 Church Ave.,
Bradenton Beach 34217,
778-2288, fax 778-2763

Bradenton Beach Sailboat Rentals
1325 Gulf Dr. N.,
Bradenton Beach 34217
778-4969, fax 778-1495

Captain's Marina
5501 Marina Dr., Holmes Beach
34217, 778-1977, fax 778-6617

Bradenton Area

Cortez Watercraft Rentals
127th St. W., Cortez, 792-5263

Jiggs Landing
6106 Branden River Rd.,
Bradenton 34203, 756-6745

Palma Sola Boat Rental
9915 Manatee Ave. W.,
Bradenton 34209, 778-4083

Longboat Key

Cannon's Marina
6040 Gulf of Mexico Dr. 34228,
383-1311, fax 383-5600
www.cannons.com

Sarasota Area

Club Nautico of Sarasota
2 Marina Plaza at Marina Jack
34236, 951-0550

Landings Marina, Inc.
1780 Phillippi Shores Dr. 34231
922-6100, fax 923-4055

O'Leary's Sarasota Sailing School
Island Park, Sarasota 34236
953-7505

Silent Sports
7660 Tamiami Tr S,
Sarasota 34231
922-4042, fax 921-5881

Siesta Key

All Water Sports
1504 Stickney Point Rd. 34242
921-2754

Anchor Down Resort
9004 Midnight Pass Rd. 34242
349-5556, www.sarasota.com/anchor

Mr. CB's Saltwater Outfitters
1249 Stickney Point Rd. 34242
349-4400, fax 346-1148

Siesta Key Marina
1265 Old Stickney Point Rd.
34242, 349-8880, fax 349-4326

Venice Area

Casey Key Marina
482 Blackburn Point Rd., Osprey
34229, 966-4000, fax 966-6393

Don & Mike's Boat & Ski Rental
520 Blackburn Point Rd., Osprey
966-4000

Osprey Marine
480 Blackburn Point Rd. 34229, Osprey, 966-5657, fax 966-5650

Snook Haven Restaurant & Fish Camp
5000 Venice Ave. E., Venice 34293, 485-7221 fax 484-3637
www.venicefla.com/snookhaven

VIP Boat Club of Venice
509 Tamiami Tr. N., Venice 34292, 488-2789

SALES

Gulfwind Marine
1601 Ken Thompson Pkwy. (City Island), Sarasota 34236, 388-4411 fax 952-9194
2005 N. Tamiami Tr., Sarasota, 366-9279
1485 S. Tamiami Tr., Venice, 485-3388 fax 484-7496

Bowling

Ebonite Recreation Centers
2750 Stickney Pt. Rd., Sarasota 924-2816

AMF Lanes
4208 Cortez Rd. W., Bradenton, 758-8838

7221 Tamiami Tr. S., Sarasota
e-mail: amf00203@amf.com
921-4447
e-mail: amf00204@amf.com

1100 Venice By-Pass S., Venice, 484-0666
e-mail: amf00205@amf.com

Rip Van Winkle Lanes
8154 N. Tamiami Tr., Sar. 34243, 355-7358

Sarasota Lanes
2250 Fruitville Rd., Sarasota 34237, 955-7629

Sarasota-Manatee County Bowling Association
753-9603

Sarasota Women's Bowling Association
371-6421

Bradenton Women's Bowling Association
756-4244

SAILBOATS DOWNTOWN © BILL WEST

Canoes and Kayaks

Aquatel Resort
4315 Aquatel Rd., Bradenton 34202, 746-6884

Econony Tackle
6018 Tamiami Tr. S., Sarasota 34231
922-9671, fax 922-8842
www.floridakayak.com

Feather Canoes
3080 N. Washington Blvd., Sarasota 34234
355-6736/953-7660

Island Style Wind & Watersports
2803 Tamiami Trail, N., Sarasota 34234
954-1009

Myakka River State Park
361-6511

Florida Fishing Rules and Regulations

African Pompano
24 inch minium, two per day.

Amberjack (Greater)
28 inch (at tail fork), bag limit 1.

Amberjack (Lesser)
14 inch (at tail fork) min.
20 inch max, bag limit 5.

Bluefish
12 inch minimum length (at tail fork), 10 per day.

Cobia
33 minimum length (at tail fork), bag limit 2 per day.

Flounder
12 inch minimum length (at tail fork), 10 per day.

Grouper
(black, gag, Nassau, red, yellowmouth and scamp) 20 inch overall, limit five aggregate per day.

Oscar Scherer State Park
483-5956

Pinecraft Park
1420 Gilbert Ave., Sarasota, 951-5572

Ray's Canoe Hideaway
2711 Hagle Park Rd NE, Bradenton 34202,
747-3909, fax 957-3031
www.rayscanoehideaway.com

South Lido Beach
190 Taft Dr. & 2201
Ben Franklin Dr., Lido Key
951-5572

Snook Haven Restaurant & Fish Camp
5000 Venice Ave. E.,
Venice 34293,
485-7221, fax 484-3687
www.venicefla.com/snookhaven

Venice Campground Inc.
4085 Venice Ave. E,
Venice 34292, 488-0850
www.campvenice.com e-mail:
mail@camapvenice.com

Wilderness Adventures
792-7272

Cheerleading, Ages 9 -14

Sarasota Ringling Redskins
953-6560

Sarasota Sun Devils
922-0812

Venice Vikings
497-7107

Community Sports Programs

The family that plays together stays together...or something like that. Here are some family oriented groups which provide area residents and visitors alike with our kind of family values – fun in the sun!

Manatee County Sports and Recreation Department
748-4501 ext. 3251

Sarasota County Parks and Recreation Department
316-1172

Sarasota/Manatee Jewish Community Center
582 McIntosh Road S.,
Sarasota, 378-5568

Manatee County Family YMCA
3805 59th St. W.,
Bradenton 34209,
792-7484 fax 794-1057

Frank Berlin Sr. Branch YMCA
1075 S. Euclid Av.,
Sarasota 34237, 955-8194

Main Plaza YMCA
1991 Main Street, Sarasota 34236,
366-6778

Evalyn Sadlier Jones YMCA
8301 Potter Park Drive,
Sarasota 34238, 922-9622

South County Family YMCA
701 Center Rd., Venice 34292,
493-9659
Web site for all Sarasota YMCA locations: www.sarasotaymca.org

Cricket

Fraternal Order of Eagles
Sarasota, 923-6788

International Cricket Club
365-1900 (SICC has games every Sunday, call for directions.

Croquet

Professional U.S.C.A. instruction/ public courts.
Call for details. 484-3206

DIVING INSTRUCTION

Dolphin Dive Center
6018 Tamiami Trail S., Sar. 34231,
924-2785, fax 922-8842

Florida Down Under
5215 Tamiami Trail S., Sar. 34231,
922-3483, fax 922-5118 e-mail:
info@fdu.com www.fdu.com

Ocean Pro Dive Shop
2259 Bee Ridge Rd., Sar. 34239,
924-3483

Scuba Quest Pro Dive Centers
www.scubaquestusa.com
3318 Manatee Ave. W,
Bradenton, 745-2511

1129 S. Tamiami Tr.,
Sarasota 34236, 366-1530

5770 S. Tamiami Tr.,
Sarasota South 34231, 925-7055

2375 S. Tamiami Tr.,
Venice, 497-5985

SeaTrek Diver's Inc.
105 7th St N, Bradenton Beach,
779-1506

Turner Marine Supply
826 13th Street W., Bradenton
34205, 746-3456, fax 747-8194

Exercise/Fitness/ Nature Trails

Arlington Park
2650 Waldemere St., Sarasota,
316-1346

Caspersen Beach
4100 Harbor Drive, S., Venice,
316-1172

Colonial Oaks Park
5300 Colonial Oaks Blvd., Sar.,
316-1330

DeSoto Park
end of 75th St. NW, Bradenton,
792-0458

Fruitville Park
5151 Richardson Rd.,
Sarasota, 316-1172

G.T. Bray Park
5502 33rd Ave. Dr. W., Brad.,
748-4501

Island Park
US-41 Bay Front. Sarasota,
954-4102

North Lido Beach
400 Ben Franklin Dr., Lido Key,
316-1172

Payne Park
2050 Adams Lane, Sarasota,
954-4884

Pinebrook Park
1251 Pinebrook Rd., Venice,
316-1172

Potter Park
8587 Potter Park Dr., Sarasota,
316-1172

Shamrock Park
3900 W. Shamrock Dr., Venice,
486-2706

Siesta Beach
948 Beach Road, Siesta Key,
346-3207

South Lido Beach
190 Taft Dr. and 2201 Ben
Franklin Dr., Lido Key, 316-1172

Woodmere Park
3951 Woodmere Park Blvd.,
Venice, 486-2780

Fishing in Paradise

For anyone who has ever dreamed of "catching the big one" this is the place to do it. One of the area's most knowledgeable fishing fanatics is **Capt. Jonnie Walker**, host of the weekly *Gone Fishin' with Capt. Jonnie Walker* segment on WWSB, Channel 40. We asked him where the fish are biting, and how to lure them in:

Fishing Knows No Season
"Along the Sarasota/Manatee Suncoast, there is something for everyone no matter what the time of year – whether it be fly fishing, walking the beaches looking for the shadowy Snook, or going to the deepest parts of the gulf for the wily Barracuda. From the simplest pole with just a hook and line to the more sophisticated fly rod and reel, there is fishing for everyone along the Suncoast.

No season is the *best* season for fishing in our area. Certain times of the year provide different types of fish. Sarasota County has an extensive artificial reef program in the bay and in the gulf which has enhanced the fishing in this area. In the bay there are six artificial reefs. These reefs not only provide structure for juvenile fish, but also attract larger fish such as Cobia, Bluefish, Pompano and many other bay species. In the gulf, there are five inshore reefs, which are within three miles of the beach, that attract Mangrove Snapper, Cobia, Grouper, Flounder and other exotic fish. There

Florida Fishing Rules and Regulations

Jewfish
Harvest is prohibited in Florida state waters.

King Mackerel
20 inch minimum length (at tail fork), 2 per person per day.

Mangrove Snapper
10 inch minimum, five per day. Total 10 snapper aggregate, only 5 of which can be mangrove snapper.

Permit/Pompano
10 inch minimum length, only one fish greater than 20 inch maximum (at tail fork) is allowed. 10 fish aggregate permit and pompano.

Redfish
18-27 inch slot limit, one per person per day. Season is now open for redfish all year long.

Florida Fishing Rules and Regulations

Red Snapper
14 inch min. length, 16 inch in Gulf, bag limit 4.

Seabass
8 inch minimum length (overall length).

Sheephead
12 inch min., 5 per day.

Snapper
Mutton - 16 inch. min., 10 per day.

Lane - 8 inch min., 10 per day.

School Master - 10 inch min., 10 per day.

Vermillion - 10 inch min, no bag limit.

(Queen, Blackfin, Cubera, Dog, Mahogany, Silk, Yellow Tail) - 12 inch min.

Total bag of 10 Snapper in aggregate of which only 5 can be Mangrove Snapper.

---

are twenty one offshore reefs that are located from 6 miles to 28 miles from the shore. These reefs are made from materials including railroad boxcars, concrete rubble and surplus army tanks. They attract a wide range of fish, not only those you find on the inshore reefs but also exotics such as Permit, Barracuda, Yellowtail and Tripletail.

Bay fishing
Bay fishing can produce a wide variety of fish. Some can be caught all during the year and others are seasonal and overlap each other. Spotted Sea Trout are the most plentiful and can be caught year round. Snook, the most popular, are not the easiest to catch, but when they do bite – hold on! During May, June and July, the Snook are in their spawning mode, and they congregate around the passes. This is the best time to catch them. After spawning, they move into the bays onto the grass flats. As the weather cools, they move to and up the rivers where they stay 'til around the first of September. I like to call them the "poor man's bonefish" because when they're on the grass flats, tailing and stirring up muds, you can sight cast to them just like bonefish. Flounder, Jacks (pound for pound - one of the strongest fighting fish around), Grouper, Mangrove Snapper, Lady Fish (also known as the "poor man's tarpon"), Bluefish, Sheepshead and Pompano are some of the other fish the bays produce.

The Passes also produce some fantastic fishing action with Pompano, Flounder, Snook, Redfish, and Bluefish to name a few.

Offshore
Offshore, the Cobia and Kingfish make their yearly migrations. They head North during the Spring run (March - April) and South during the Fall (October-November). Cobia being a very strong fish, are great on light tackle. They like to hang around structure and the near shore reefs provide such an environment. Usually when you have one on and bring him to the boat, others will follow. They are not real fast, but are very strong and run in size from just a few pounds to over 50 pounds. Most are in the 10 to 25 pound range. Kingfish on the other hand are one of the fastest fish in the water. They start showing up about the same time as the Cobia, but a little father on the gulf. They can be taken on trolled lures, but are much more fun caught the way I like to do it – which is with light tackle and live bait. Kingfish range in size from 10 to 50 pounds. The largest and most exciting sport fish on the West Coast of Florida has got to be the Silver King or better known as Tarpon. These high jumping, drag pulling giants start migrating up the beaches of Sarasota and Manatee counties in mid April and stay until the July 4th weekend. They range in size anywhere from 75 to 150 pounds, and will congregate in small schools (or pods) waiting to go to deeper water to spawn in mid July. During these few months, they feed ravenously and will take live baits and flies quite readily.

Bait and Lures
Artificial or live baits work well. Live bait is of course the best. Some are easy to catch yourself. You can catch sand fleas on the beach with your bare hands, or a cast net will catch you sardines and pinfish, which are both excellent baits. Shrimp, though, is the most common bait and can be purchased frozen or live from all bait and tackle stores. Artificial lures range from soft plastic jigs to wooden plugs. A lot of lures that are used in the north for Bass and Walleye are just as productive on Snook and Redfish along the Suncoast. Spoons and jibs that work on Bluefish along the upper East Coast, work just as good on Bluefish and Mackerel in our waters. Top water plugs are one of my favorite lures to use. There is something about seeing a fish making a push (a bulge in the water) toward your lure and having an explosion where your lure

used to be, that makes my knees shake every time.

You do not need elaborate tackle to fish the Suncoast. Eight to ten pound spinning tackle will land you just about any type of fish you may encounter in the bays and gulf. The trick to fishing the clear waters of Sarasota Bay is to use as little terminal (at the end of the line) tackle as possible. I personally like to tie 20# mono leader directly to my line with a surgeon's knot. A swivel can be seen by most fish very easily. On the end of the line, tie a very light 3/0 long shank wire hook. The long shank keeps toothy critters from biting through your leader. If weight is needed, use a small split shot sinker, adding another if necessary. Big fish can be landed on light tackle if you remember not to horse the fish to the boat, but to take your time and let the fish fight the rod, keeping your drag loose. As long as there are no obstructions for the fish to swim around, you have all the time in the world to enjoy the fight. Most fish are lost trying to get them to the boat too fast.

Finding Fish
People as me all the time where and how to find fish. The best way is to be observant – wathc what is going on around you. Watch the birds – they will tell you where a school of bait fish are. Watch the other boats around you. If they are not catching any fish, move. If they are catching fish, watch what they are doing – what bait is he using, how he has his line rigged, the speed of the retrieve. If you are in a boat, see if he is ancchored or drifting. And please be careful about getting too close. Tackle stores are a good source to found out what is biting. They are always talking ot the local guides and other fishermen. Just ask! But, as my dad always said, "I'll answer your questions, if you will listen to my answers."

Rules and Regulations - nag, nag!
A salt water license is required for all nonresidents unless you are fishing on a licensed charter boat or on a licensed fishing pier. It is up to you to check all local and state laws before venturing out to fish. There are size and bag limits on every species of sport fish. Practive "catch and release" – keep only what you will eat fresh and let the rest go. The best source of information about restrictions and identifying fish is the "Fishing Lines" magazine which can be found at most bait shops, tackle stores, or the county tax collectors offices."

Fishing Information
Sarasota County Licence Office
362-9898

Manatee County Licence Office
741-4807

Fishing Friends
Sitting on the beach soaking up the rays with your line in the water can be a very relaxing and enjoyable way to fish. But for the beginning angler, to learn about what tackle, the type of bait and where to fish, go with a professional. How to find the right licensed fishing guide to go with? Listen to what other people toel you or ask at the marinas, bait shops and tackle stores. There are some great guides in the area.

Head Boats
These are boats which go off shore and take up to 50 passengers, charges are based per person.

Cortez Fleet, Cortez
794-1223 fax 795-2221

Flying Fish Fleet, Sarasota
366-3373
www.flyingfishfleet.com

OFFSHORE CAPTAINS
These Captians take up to six people and charge for the boat

MANATEE COUNTY
Capt. Roy Best (Happy Hooker I)
792-7124

Capt. Phil Sheilds (Reef Reacher)
778-2727

Florida Fishing Rules and Regulations

Snook

24 inch minimum length, limit two per day total. Only one snook 34 inches or larger may be taken per day. Closed December 15th through January 31st, and June through August. Snook stamp required.

Spanish Mackerel

12 inch minimum length (at tail fork), ten per day.

Spotted Sea Trout

15 inch minimum, one fish over 20 inches, 5 per person, per day. Closed November and

Golf Guide

Sarasota is considered to be home of the first golf course in the United States, built in 1886 by Colonel J Hamilton Gillespie. Colonel Gillespie came to Sarasota to act as residential manager of the new colony of "Sarasota" – estab-lished by his father, Sir John Gillespie of Moffatt of Dumfriesshire, Scotland – which by then consisted of some 60 Scottish families. Colonel Gillespie, a veteran golfer in his home country, built a four-hole course along what is now Golf Street near Downtown Sarasota, just east of Osprey Avenue and north of Fruitville Road. A few years later the course was expanded to nine holes, the community has embraced golf as an important part of our recreational life ever since.

Capt. Joe Webb (Old Florida)
778-3885

SARASOTA COUNTY

Capt. Joe Bonaro (Rum Runner)
349-3119

Capt. Jerry Dotson (JerryRig II)
371-2399

Capt. Ed Hurst (Reel Freedom)
925-1871

Capt. Mark Liberman (The Teal)
955-4524

Capt. Tino Loyal (Cuda)
366-2832

Capt. Brian Martel (Midnite Son)
349-7677

Capt. Dan Morningstar (Fish Tail)
371-5029

Capt. Capt. Rob Roberts (War Bird)
922-1045

Capt. Bob Smith (Let's Go Fishing)
366-2159

Capt. Ned Van Deree (Triple Trouble)
484-3225

Capt. Jonnie Walker (Gone Fishin')
922-2287

BAY FISHING/LIGHT TACKLE/FLY FISHING

Normally three to four people and charter costs of the boat:

MANATEE COUNTY

Capt. Steve Baden (Gulf and Bay)
722-2370

Capt. Mark Bradow (Sidewinder)
747-2623

Capt. Calvin Brannen (Cane Patch)
748-8274

Capt. Tom Chaya (Dolphin Dreams)
778-4498

Capt. Mitch Cockrell (Fish-Hoek)
745-1361

Capt. Chuck Collins (Cap'n C's)
722-7080

Capt. Jonathan Davis (Sand Gnat)
729-4005

Capt. Rick Ehlis (Flats-Master)
792-5078

Capt. Rick Gross (Fishey Business)
794-3308

Capt. Tom Larkin (Daydreammer)
792-7533

Capt. Scott Moore (Primadonna)
778-3005

Capt. Jim O'Neil (Day Tripper)
794-5960

Capt. Todd Romine (Oscar II)
747-3866

Capt. Tom Smith (Flats Lady)
776-1187

Capt. Zack Zacharias (Dee Jay II)
795-5026

SARASOTA COUNTY

Capt. Meryl Lee Dunn (Game Fish-Her)
364-6316

Capt. Jeffri Durrance (Josi D)
371-4231

Capt. Rick Grassett (Snook Fin-Addict)
923-7799

Capt. Pete Greenan (Gypsy)
925-9483

Capt. Ed Hurst (Reel Freedom II)
925-1871

Capt. Mark Liberman (Teal II)
955-4524

Capt. Paul Lundquist (Yellow-Bird)
371-2435

Capt. Doug Mikesell (Back Country)
497-1357

Capt. Dan Morningstar (Fish-Tail)
371-5029

Capt. Brandon Nave (Grand-Slam)
966-4112

Capt. Bob Smith (Let's Go Fishing)
366-2159

Capt. Kelly Stilwell (Tide Tuit)
927-4366

Capt. Mark Schindle (Miss Adventure)
924-5490

Capt. Jonnie Walker (Bay Walker Too)
922-2287

Tackle and Bait Shops

ANNA MARIA ISLAND

Island Discount Tackle
3240 East Bay Dr.,
Holmes Beach 34217,
778-7688 fax 778-4999

BRADENTON

Turner Marine Supply
Franklin, Lido Key, 316-1172

Turtle Beach
8918 Midnight Pass Rd., Siesta,
346-3207

Venice Beach
101 The Esplanade, Venice,
316-1172

LONGBOAT KEY

Cannons Marina
6040 Gulf of Mexico Dr.
383-1311, fax 383-3600
www.cannons.com

SARASOTA

Economy Tackle
6018 Tamiami Tr. 34231,
922-9671; fax 922-8842

Hart's Landing
John Ringling Causeway 34236,
955-0011

Mr. CB's
1249 Stickney Pt. Rd. 34242,
349-4400; fax 346-1148

New Pass Bait Shop
City Island, 388-3050

Protection On The Water

The Marine Patrol
1-800-342-5367

The Sheriff's Marine Patrol
951-5800

U.S. Coast Guard
794-1261

**Wildlife Alert
(Reporting Violations)**
1-800-282-8002

Fishing Hot Spots

Longboat Pass – All around the bridge spanning Longboat Pass is a favorite spot for many local fishermen.

City Island – Bay fishing in the park makes for a great afternoon, also fish from the seawall into New Pass.

Saprito Pier – Just before you cross the Ringling Bridge this fishing pier is one of Sarasota's most popular spots. Fish from the pier, around the seawall or shore. Bait & Tackle shop located nearby.

Golf Guide

Golf Service Codes:

CR - Club Rentals
DR - Driving Range
LA - Lessons Available
LG - Lounge
RS - Restaurant

TEE SPOTLIGHT

University Park Country Club

7671 Park Blvd., Sarasota
359-9999

Ron Garl designed this 27-hole championship course, winner of the *Sarasota Herald-Tribune* "Readers Choice" award as the BEST GOLF COURSE four years in a row. Rated 4-stars by *Golf Digest* making it the highest rated in the area, one of the highest rated in the state.

New Pass Bridge – Located between Lido Key and Longboat Key, record catches have been made from this bridge and adjacent seawall. Plenty of parking and a Bait & Tackle Shop is nearby.

South Lido Park – At the southern tip of Lido Key, on the shore of Big Pass, this is a great place for family fishing fun. Shelters, grills, restrooms and shelling is all there, along with a very strong current and occasional undertow. Swimming should be done with caution.

Siesta Bridge – Northern bridge connecting Siesta Key to the mainland is very popular, with plenty of parking but no facilities.

Bay Island – On the Gulf side of Siesta Bridge with benches located around the seawall for your sitting pleasure.

North Shell Road – Shore fishing off Higel Avenue on Siesta Key into Sarasota Big Pass offers a nice family spot with white sand beach and swimming.

Stickney Point Bridge – Southern bridge connecting Siesta Key to the mainland, Bait & Tackle Shop nearby.

Point of Rocks – The only rock formation on Siesta Key, just south of Crescent Beach, is a fabulous place for fishing (but be very aware of swimmers in the area!) Great for snorkeling too. Lots of rocks and underwater caves, some coral too, so bring extra tackle. No parking, no facilities, but worth getting to anyway.

Turtle Beach Lagoon – A mile or so south of Point of Rocks, this is where you can fish from shore, seawall or pier with scads of parking, grills restrooms and a playground for children.

Old Midnight Pass – For the serious fisherman, at the southern end of Siesta Key (walk south from Turtle Beach about a half-mile) with great fishing from both Gulf and Bayside.

The Ultimate Fishing Trip – Tarpon Hunting in Boca Grande
The biggest fishing attraction in the area is tarpon fishing which, like everything else around here, is seasonal. In the spring and early summer the tarpon populate the beach areas up and down the coast and they cluster in an area known as Boca Grande just south of Sarasota County. Boca Grande is considered the tarpon capital of the world.

The tarpon is not good eating, but as a sport fish it has no peer. The fish run in large schools along the beaches and you cast a bait into their schools as they go by. They will invariably strike, but it is very difficult to bring one to boat.

Why? Because they are large, fierce fighters and have a hard palate.

Tarpon run up to 150 lbs. and break water many times when they are caught. They are called the "Silver King" because the flash of the sun on their silver sides is (literally) blinding.

Boca Grande Pass is a natural home for tarpon because it is one of the deepest points on Florida's Gulf coast with a steady current, bringing with it a wide variety of smaller fish, thus making life for the tarpon a relatively easy one.

Tarpon is an ancient species, one of the oldest fish to travel in the waters around here. You may bring one out of four or five strikes to the boat, if you are lucky and skillful, but the "Silver King" is always released to fight another day.

Football

COMMUNITY PROGRAMS

Flag Football
497-4246/746-3021

Sarasota County Athletic Program
316-1172

Sarasota Junior Football Assoc., Sun Devils
317-0620/923-8733

Sarasota Redskins
953-6560

Venice Vikings, Pop Warner Football
485-5875

LEAGUES

NFL - Tampa Bay Buccaneers
1-800-282-0683

Pop Warner Football League
Sarasota Sun Devils,
923-8733

Public Fields

Arlington Park
2650 Waldemere St., Sarasota

Fruitville Park
5151 Richardson Rd., Sarasota

G.T. Bray Park
5502 33rd Ave. Dr. W., Bradenton

Siesta Beach
948 Beach Rd., Siesta Key

Twin Lakes Park
6700 Clark Rd., Sarasota

Wellfield Par
1300 Ridgewood, Venice

Youth Athletic Complex
2810 17th St., Sarasota

Frisbee Golf

North Water Tower Park
4700 Rilma Ave., Sarasota
316-1172

There is no charge to play on the 18-hole course, but players need to provide their own equipment. Indeed, Frisbeers have special discs specifically designed for drives, approaching shots, and putts just like golf clubs. Most golf discs cost less than $10, available through Wright Life (907) 484-6932, credit card (800) 321-8833. In 1998 the Frisbee Golf World Championship took place in the area.

Golf

Col. John Hamilton Gillespie is credited from bringing the game of Golf to Sarasota in May, 1886 when he laid out what was probably the first practice golf course in Florida – two greens and one long fairway, which was on what is now Main Street. He was way ahead of the curve, so to speak. Now the Suncoast boats some of the most sophisticated and challenging courses in the United States. First, and still the best, as the pros like to say.

GOLF ASSOCIATIONS

Florida State Golf Association
5710 Draw Ln., Sarasota, 921-5695

GOLF COURSES – PUBLIC AND SEMI-PRIVATE

MANATEE COUNTY

Buffalo Creek Golf Course
8100 Erie Road, Palmetto 34222
Tee Times: 776-2611,
fax 723-4596; two-day advance.

Directions: Exit 43 off I-75, two miles east, left on Erie Road, when road takes sharp right, bear left and look for large white water tower.

18 Holes - Par 72 - Public
Course Record: 67 - Red: 5261, White: 6440, Blue: 7005

Head Golf Pro: Robert Conforte
General Manager: Becky Ross
Superintendent: Gary MacDougall
Architect: Ron Garl

CR-DR-RS-SB

Rabow Raves: Scottish links style course, secluded location with lots of wildlife.

Imperial Lakes Golf Club
6807 Buffalo Road, Palmetto 34221
Tee Times: 747-GOLF (4653),
fax 746-0157; two-day advance.

Directions: Exit 45 off I-75. 1/4 mile east

18 Holes - Par 72 - Semi-Private
Course Record: 65 - Red: 5270, White: 6067, Blue: 6658

Head Golf Pro: Tracy Lowry
General Manager: Patrick Walsh
Superintendent: Paul Neumann
Architect: Ted McAnlis

CR-DR-LA-LG-RS-SB

Rabow Raves: Excellent fairways and greens, best par 5 on the 9th hole.

Golf Guide

Golf Service Codes:

CR - Club Rentals

DR - Driving Range

LA - Lessons Available

LG - Lounge

RS - Restaurant

SB - Snack Bar

TEE SPOTLIGHT

Terra Ceia Bay Golf & Tennis Club

2302 Terra Ceia Bay Blvd., Palmetto

729-7663

Just a quick hop over the bridge will bring you in touch with beautiful views of Tampa Bay and the Sunshine Skyway Bridge.
Located right on Terra Ceia Bay.

Golf Guide

Golf Service Codes:
CR - Club Rentals
DR - Driving Range
LA - Lessons Available
LG - Lounge
RS - Restaurant

TEE SPOTLIGHT

The River Club
6600 River Club Blvd.,
Bradenton
751-4211

Ron Garl designed this 18-hole championship course which is every bit as challenging as it is beautiful. *Golf Digest* rated 3-1/2 stars, *Florida Sports Fan Magazine* rated as "One of the top 50 courses in the state."

Palm View Hills Golf Course
5712 28th Avenue East,
Palmetto 34221
No Tee Times: 722-2392

Directions: North on U.S. 41 to 49th Street East, one mile to 28th Avenue East, turn left.

18 Holes - Par 63 - Semi-Private
Course Record: 55 - Red: 3122, Blue: 3485

General Manager: Gary Hamilton
Architect: Dick Hamilton

CR-SB

Rabow Raves: Challenging.

Palmetto Pines Golf Club
Old Tampa Road, Parrish 34219
No Tee Times: 776-1375

Directions: 15 minutes north of Palmetto on Hwy. 301

36 Holes - Public
Rabow Raves: Four 9-hole courses to mix/match - creative golfing.

Terra Ceia Bay Golf & Tennis Club
2802 Terra Ceia Bay Blvd.,
Palmetto 34221
Tee Times: 729-7663, fax 729-8103; two-day advance.

18 Holes - Par 62 - Semi-Private
Red: 3276, White: 3823, Blue: 4092

Head Golf Pro: Rod Grizzel
General Manager: Dave Baites
Superintendent: John Garcia

CR-DR-LA-LG-RS

Rabow Raves: On Terra Ceia Bay with a view of Tampa Bay and Sunshine Skyway Bridge - beautiful courses and setting.

BRADENTON

Heather Hills Golf Course
101 Cortez Rd. West (U.S. 41 and Cortez Road), Bradenton
No Tee Times: 755-8888

Directions: Opposite DeSoto Square Mall

18 Holes - Par 61 - Semi-Private
Course Record: 54
General Manager: Rick Copeman
Superintendent: Rick Copeman

CR-LA-SB

Rabow Raves: Executive course, appealing for a short game.

The Links at Greenfield Plantation
10325 Greenfield Blvd., Bradenton
Tee Times: 747-9432

18 Holes - Par 72 - Public - 6,400

Head Golf Pro: Peter Dennis
General Manager: TBA
Superintendent: Dan Lomax
Architect: Chip Powell

CR LA DR RS

Manatee County Golf Course
6415 53rd St. W., Bradenton
Tee Times: 792-6773, fax 741-3506; two-day advance.

Directions: Take 53rd Ave. W. until 65th St. W., then turn right.

18 Holes - Par 72 - Public Course Record: 66 - Red: 5619, White: 6216, Blue: 6747

Head Golf Pro: Penny Porter
General Manager: Gary MacDougall
Superintendent: Herschel Pickens
Architect: Wayne Marshall

CR-DR-RS-SB

Rabow Raves: Perhaps the most rounds played on an 18-hole course in Manatee county; a very fair, well-maintained course.

Palma Sola Golf Club
3807 75th Street W., Bradenton
Tee Times: 792-7476, fax 792-3286; two-day advance.

Directions: Just north of Cortez Road on 75th Street W.

18 Holes - Par 72 - Public
Course Record: 62 - Red: 5311, White: 5920, Blue: 6464

Head Golf Pro: Moe Baranek
General Manager: Bob Skelton
Superintendent: Dave Kaminski
Architect: Andy Anderson

LA-LG-SB

Rabow Raves: Closest course to beaches.

Peridia Golf and Country Club
4950 Peridia Blvd., Bradenton
Tee Times: 753-9097, two-day advance

Directions: Off State Road 70 West of I-75

18 Holes - Par 60 - Semi-Private Course Record: 51 - Women: 2722, Men: 3334

Head Golf Pro: Gary Rehfeld
Superintendent: Ray Bartels
Architect: William Lewis

CR-LA-LG-RS

Rabow Raves: Nice sporty course, great for seniors.

Pinebrook/Ironwood Golf Club
4260 Ironwood Cir., Bradenton
www.jmeder.com/pbiwgolf

Tee Times: 792-3288, fax 798-9207; three-day advance.

18 Holes - Semi Private
Par 68 - Course Record: 53
Women: 3346, Men: 4000

Head Golf Pro: Joel King
General Manager: Joel King
Superintendent: Joe Nuzback
Architect: Dean Refram

CR-LA

Rabow Raves: Very challenging long course with 14-16 ponds, well bunkered.

River Club Golf Course
6600 River Club Blvd.,
Bradenton 34202

Tee Times: 751-4211, fax 753-0579; two-day advance.

Directions: One mile east of I-75 off State Road 70

18 Holes - Par 72 - Semi-Private Course Record: 66 - Red: 5157, White: 6102, Blue: 6614, Green: 5622, Gold: 7026

Head Golf Pro: David Erritz
General Manager: Michael Pascuzzi Superintendent: Dan Downey Architect: Ron Garl

CR-DR-LA-LG-RS

Rabow Raves: Nine miles - start to finish - of championship golf with no concurrent holes, nestled within environmentally sensitive area.

River Run Golf Links
1801 27th Street E., Bradenton

Tee Times: 747-6331, fax 749-7450; two days advance.

Directions: Exit 42 West off I-75, three miles then left on 27th St. East

© SARASOTA CONVENTION AND VISITORS BUREAU

18 Holes - Par 70 - Public
Course Record: 63 - Red: 4811, White: 5600, Blue: 6100

Head Golf Pro: Dave Beauchamp
General Manager: Dave Beauchamp
Superintendent: Mac Watson
Architect: Ward Northrup

CR-LA-SB

Rabow Raves: Reasonable rates, light fairways, ample water.

Rosedale Golf and Country Club
5100 87th St. E., Bradenton

Tee Times: 756-0004, fax 739-2308; three-day advance

Directions: Take exit 41 off I-75, go east 1/4 mile on left

18 Holes - Par 72 - Semi-Private
Course Record: 66 - Red: 5169, White: 5933, Blue: 6359, Gold: 6779

Head Golf Pro: Brad Doren
General Manager: Pat Hogan

Golf Guide

Golf Service Codes:

CR - Club Rentals
DR - Driving Range
LA - Lessons Available
LG - Lounge
RS - Restaurant

TEE SPOTLIGHT

Rosedale Golf & Country Club
5100 87th St, E,
Bradenton
756--0004

Golf Digest nominated Rosedale as "One of the best new courses in the country."

Its naturally wooded terrain, beautiful lakes and environmental preserves promises you a memorable golfing experience.

Superintendent: John Hagen
Architect: Ted McAnlis
CR-DR-LA-LG-RS

Rabow Raves: New facility, reasonable rates, challenging and popular course. Full-service clubhouse.

Timber Creek Golf Club
4550 Timber Lane, Bradenton
No Tee Times: 794-8381
Nine Holes - Par 27 - Public Total Yards: 46
General Manager: Bob Wilkins
Superintendent: Robbie Robbins
Architect: Andy Anderson
CR

Rabow Raves: Good for beginning golfers.

Village Green Golf Club
1401 Village Green Parkway, Bradenton 34209
Tee Times: 792-7171
Directions: Manatee Avenue heading west, left on Village Green Parkway at the Video Library, watch for American flag one mile on left side.
18 Holes - Par 58 - Semi-Private Course Records: 52
Head Golf Pro: Chris Watson
Superintendent: Mike Blee
Architect: Ted McAnlis
CR-LA-SB

Rabow Raves: Carts, left and right handed clubs, pull carts. Course is a real challenge for irons. Women and children welcome.

SARASOTA

Bobby Jones Golf Complex
1000 Circus Blvd., Sarasota
Tee Times: 365-4653, three days and five hours advance
Directions: Off Beneva Road between Fruitville and 17th St.
45 Holes - Public
British Course: 18 Holes - Par 72, Red: 5670, White: 6184, Blue: 5457 American Course: 18 Holes - Par 71, Red: 4326, White: 5496 Blue: 6039   Executive Course: Nine Holes - Par 30

Head Golf Pro: Paul Michaud
General Manager: Ray Grady
Architect: Vaughn Arbeiter
CA-DR-LA-LG-RS

Rabow Raves: Built in 1926 and dedicated personally by Bobby Jones. The area's most popular facility with over 155,000 rounds played here each year. Voted Best Public Golf Course - Sarasota Herald-Tribune Readers Choice Awards.

Forest Lakes Golf Club
2401 Beneva Rd., Sarasota
Tee Times: 922-1312, fax 924-7686; four days in advance
Directions: Just north of Bee Ridge Road on Beneva Road
18 Holes - Par 71- Semi-Private USGA Rating 70.8 - Course Record: 63 - Red: 5445, White: 6020, Blue: 6450
Head Golf Pro: Jay Nash
General Manager: Walter Smith
Superintendent: Gene Lanfair
Architect: Andy Anderson
CR-DR-LA-LG-RS

Rabow Raves: Great location, right in the middle of town!

Foxfire Golf Club
7200 Proctor Rd., Sarasota 34241
Tee Times: 921-7757, fax 923-8936; three days advance
Directions: Proctor Rd., just e. of I-75
27 Holes - Three nine-hole courses - Semi-Private
General Manager: Linda Talbot
Superintendent: Jim Baldwin
CR-DR-LA-RS

Rabow Raves: 27 holes, natural setting.

Gulf Gate Golf Club
2550 Bispham Rd., Sarasota 34231
Tee Times: 921-5515, three days advance.
27 Holes - Par 57/58 - Semi-Private Course Record: 50
General Manager: Joan Zahradka
Superintendent: Tom Lossman
CR-LG-RS

Rabow Raves: Nice executive course, well maintainted, island green.

Steve Rabow's Guide Book **Sports & Recreation** 169

Heritage Oaks Golf & Country Club

4800 Chase Oaks Dr, Sarasota 34241

Tee Times: 926-7600, fax 925-0795; two days advance

18 holes - Par 72 - Semi-Private
Men - 6611-6208;
Women, 5208, 4737

Head Golf Pro: Christian E. Martin
General Manager: TBA
Superintendent: Ricke Bell
Architect: Jed Azinger/Gordie Lewis
CR LA DR LG RS

Oak Ford Golf Club

1552 Palm View Rd., Sarasota 34240

Tee Times: 371-3680, fax 378-9101; 7 day advance.

Directions: East of I-75 off Fruitville Road, 81/2 miles east

27 Holes, Three nine-hole courses - Par 36 - Semi-Private
Course Record: 64/65/66
Myrtle: Red: 2346, White: 2947, Blue: 3189, Gold: 3404
Palms: Red: 2510, White: 2862, Blue: 3132, Gold: 3349
Live Oaks: Red: 2544, White: 2867, Blue: 3098, Gold: 3330

Head Golf Pro: John Kindred
General Manager: Sue Hentz
Superintendent: Jim Basey
Architect: Ron Garl
CR-DR-LA-LG-RS

Rabow Raves: Located in the middle of wetlands, this is a scenic course with plenty of wildlife. Even outside of the lounge.

Rolling Green Golf Club

4501 N. Tuttle Ave., Sarasota 34234

Tee Times: 355-6620, three days advance

Directions: Just south of DeSoto Road on Tuttle

18 Holes - Par 72 - Public
Course Record: 61 - Red: 6061, White: 6061, Blue: 6515

Head Golf Pro: Joe Mann
General Manager: Joe Mann
Superintendent: Cindy Payne
Architect: R. Albert Anderson
CR-DR-LA-RS

Rabow Raves: Friendly service, well conditioned course.

Sarasota Golf Club

7280 North Leewynn Dr., Sarasota 34240

Tee Times: 371-2431, fax 371-7589; 3 days advance

Directions: 3rd light east of I-75 off Bee Ridge Rd.

18 Holes - Par 72 - Public
Course Record: 63 - Red: 5004, White: 5900, Blue: 6300

Head Golf Pro: Duncan Clark
General Manager: Kent Pershing
Superintendent: Emilio Menendez
Architect: Andy Andersen
CR-DR-LA-LG-RS

Rabow Raves: Course has excellent fairways. All greens rebuilt in summer of 1996. Tree lined wide fairways.

Serenoa Gulf Club

6773 Serenoa Dr., Sarasota 34241

Tee Times: 925-2755, three days advance.

Directions: 3/4 miles east of I-75 off Clark Road (Exit 37)

18 Hole championship course - Par 72 - Semi-Private
Red: 4994, White: 6028, Blue: 6270

Head Golf Pro: Brian Branch
General Manager: Barbara Schmidt
Superintendent: Dan Hall
Architect: David Alden
CR-DR-LA-LG-RS

Rabow Raves: Condition of course and greens are always great. Sarasota's only Digital Caddy - automatically gives you distance to the pin.

Sunrise Golf Club

5710 Draw Lane, Sarasota 34238

Tee Times: 924-1402, fax 925-2081; three days advance.

Directions: Take exit 37 off I-75, head east for 1/4 mile, take left after second light

18 Holes - Par 72 - Semi-Private
USGA Rating 68.3 - Red: 5271, White: 5761, Blue: 6074, Gold: 6455

Head Golf Pro: Tom Zellers
General Manager: Bill Berg
Superintendent: Shane LeBout
Architect: Andy Anderson

Golf Guide

Golf Service Codes:

CR - Club Rentals

DR - Driving Range

LA - Lessons Available

LG - Lounge

RS - Restaurant

TEE SPOTLIGHT

Forest Lakes Golf & Country Club
2401 Beneva Rd., Sarasota
922-1312

Popular with major sports figures including many Hall of Famer's, this par 71 course weaves through 6,450 of Forest Lakes Country Club Estates.

Formerly host to the OTTO GRAHAM SPORTS LEGEND CLASSIC.

Golf Guide

Golf Service Codes:
CR - Club Rentals
DR - Driving Range
LA - Lessons Available
LG - Lounge
RS - Restaurant

TEE SPOTLIGHT

Serenoa Golf Club
6773 Serenoa Dr.,
Sarasota
925-2755

Director of Golf Jim Owen was the 1987 NFPGA Teacher of the Year and former Director of Golf at Longboat Key Club. Serenoa is proud to be the only course in Sarasota using DIGITAL CADDY - a computerized system that electronically measures the distance of your ball to the cup.

CR-DR-LA-LG-RS

Tatum Ridge Golf Links
421 North Tatum Rd., Sarasota 34241
Tee Times: 378-4211, four days advance.
Directions: Two miles east of I-75 off Fruitville Road, exit 39
18 Holes - Par 72 - Semi-Private
USGA Rating 71.9 -Course Record: 64 - Red: 5149, White: 6190, Blue: 6757
Head Golf Pro: Bob Keller
General Manager: Ray Cross
Superintendent: Tom Hilferty
Architect: Ted McAnis
CR-DR-LA-LG-RS
Rabow Raves: Link course, 11 ponds, lots of plantings and wildlife.

University Park Country Club
7671 Park Blvd., University Park 34243;www.universitypark/fl.com
Tee Times: 359-9999, fax 351-7778; three days advance.
Directions: 1.8 miles west of I-75 on University Parkway (Exit 40)
27 Holes - Par 72/36 - USGA Rating 71.9 - Semi-Private - Silver: 5511, Bronze: 4914, Diamond: 6951, Platinum: 6441 - Gold: 6090
Head Golf Pro: Mike Clayton
General Manager: Dale Weidemiller
Superintendent: Jeff Keech
Architect: Ron Garl
CR-DR-LA-LG-RS
Rabow Raves: School of "relaxed golf" with friendly staff.

Village Green Golf Club of Sarasota
3500 Pembrook Dr., Sarasota 34239
Tee Times: 922-9500, fax 923-0916; three days advance.
Directions: West on Pinecrest Street, off Beneva Road between Bee Ridge and Webber
18 Holes - Par 58 - Semi-Private
Course Records: 49
Head Golf Pro: Mike Toale
General Manager: Jack Binswangerr
Superintendent: Al Williams
CR-LA-LG-RS
Rabow Raves: Old, established executive course.

SOUTH SARASOTA

Calusa Lakes Golf Club
1995 Calusa Lakes Blvd., Nokomis
Tee Times: 484-8995, two days advance.
18 Holes - Par 72 - Semi Private
Course Record: 65/67 - Red: 5969
White: 6176, Blue: 6760
Head Golf Pro: Jay Hosey
General Manager: Jay Hosey
Superintendent: Phil Phelan
Architect: Ted McAnlis
CR-DR-LA-LG-RS
Rabow Raves: Championship course, challenging for all athletes.

Sorrento Par 3 Golf Course
1910 Bayshore Rd., Nokomis 34275
No Tee Times: 966-4884
Directions: Going north, first left after 661 overpass, off U.S.-41. Going south, first right before 661 overpass.
Nine Holes - Par 3 - Public - Open sunrise to sunset, 7 days/week.
General Manager: Frank Calabro
Superintendent: Frank Calabro
Architect: Andy Anderson
CR
Rabow Raves: Short course (627 yards) for quick play and no tee time waiting.

VENICE

Bird Bay Executive Golf Course
602 Bird Bay Drive W., Venice 34292
Tee Times: 485-9333, four days advance.
Directions: Bird Bay Drive, just off U.S. 41 bypass north
18 Holes - Par 56 - Semi-Private - Course Record: 51
Total Yards: 2423
CR
General Manager: Robby Robertson
Rabow Raves: Small, executive course with low prices.

Capri Isles Golf Club
849 Capri Isles Blvd.; Venice
Tee Times: 485-3371, fax 489-5167; three days advance.
Directions: Two miles east of U.S.

41 bypass on Venice Avenue
18 Holes - Par 72 - USGA Rating 68 - Semi-Private - Course Record: 64/65 Red: 5480, White: 6051, Blue: 6472
Head Golf Pro: Greg Clark
Superintendent: Mike Simpson
CR-DR-LA-RS
Rabow Raves: One of the oldest clubs in Venice, old-fashioned layout with excellent greens, challenging course.

Lake Venice Golf Club
South Harbor Blvd., Venice
No Tee Times: 488-3948
Directions: South of Venice Drive, past Venice Fishing Pier, on the left
27 Holes - Par 72/36 - Public Red: 5737/2634, White: 6302/2865, Blue: 6629/3023
Head Golf Pro: Barry Knott
General Manager: Rod Parry
Superintendent: David Knott
Architect: Mark Mahanna
CR-DR-LA-SB
Rabow Raves: Open golf, no bookings or tee-off times, open daily.

Pelican Pointe Golf & Country Club of Venice
575 Center Rd., Venice 34292
Tee Times: 496-4653, fax 493-2801; three day-advance.
Directions: Exit 35 off I-75, west on Jacaranda take second light to Center Road, about a half mile on the right side.
18 Holes - Par 72 - Semi-Private Red: 4936, White: 6022, Blue: 6614, Black: 7202
Head Golf Pro: Andy Cole
General Manager: Lou Marino
Superintendent: Andy Burmester
Architect: Ted McAnlis
CR-DR-LA-LG-RS
Rabow Raves: New, versatile course; plenty of length and enough tees for everyone.

Stoneybrook Golf & Country Club
8801 Stoneybrook Ln., Venice
Tee Times: 966-1800
Directions: South on U.S.-41, turn left on Central Sarasota Parkway, follow road one and a half miles, on the left.
18 Holes - Par 72 - Semi-Private Course Records: 64 - Red: 4984, White: 6129, Blue: 6561
Head Golf Pro: Bob Biroscak
General Manager: Bob McGinley
Superintendent: David Larson
Architect: Arthur Hills
CR-DR-LA-LG-RS
Rabow Raves: You will use every club on this challenging course.

Venice East Golf Club
107 Venice East Blvd., Venice 34293
No tee times: 493-0005, fax 493-0005
Directions: South Venice off U.S. 41 at blinking light
18 Holes - Par 3 - Public
Course Record: 54
Director of Golf: Tom Spencer
General Manager: Tom Spencer
Superintendent: Tom Tagliaferri
CR-DR-LA
Rabow Raves: Member owned, ideal for elderly players.

Waterford Golf Club
1454 Gleneagles Dr., Venice 34292
Tee Times: 484-6621, fax 483-6803; 2 days advance.
Directions: Exit 35 off I-75 to light, turn right on Venice Ave. to next light - right again to end and follow signs.
27 Holes - Par 72 - Semi Private Course Record: 65 - Red: 5242, White: 6068, Blue: 6601
Head Golf Pro: Jack McFaul
General Manager: Dave Matuszak
Superintendent: Roger Moore
Architect: Ted McAnlis
CR-DR-LA-LG-RS
Rabow Raves: Rolling terrain with plenty of lakes and fountains. Well maintained, drains quickly, cart paths cover entire course.

NORTH PORT

Sabal Trace Golf & Country Club
5456 Greenwood Ave., North Port
Tee Times: 426-2804, fax 426-3686; up to five day advance.
18 Holes - Par 72 - Semi Private

Golf Guide

Golf Service Codes:

CR - Club Rentals

DR - Driving Range

LA - Lessons Available

LG - Lounge

RS - Restaurant

TEE SPOTLIGHT

The Country Club at Jacaranda West

601 Jacaranda Blvd., Venice

493-2664

Mark Mahannh designed this 18 hole course which boasts the best tift-dwarf greens around.

Eighty four well placed bunkers add to the enjoyment and challenge.

Golf Guide

Golf Service Codes:
CR - Club Rentals
DR - Driving Range
LA - Lessons Available
LG - Lounge
RS - Restaurant

TEE SPOTLIGHT

Pelican Pointe Golf and Country Club
575 Center Rd., Venice
496-4653
Ted McAnlis designed this 18-hole course which winds thorugh nature preserves, lakes and offers the golfer a look at numerous birds and wildlife.

Championship golf which will test your skills at every hole.

Course Records: 63 - Red: 5504, White: 6250, Blue: 6681
Head Golf Pro: Jim Kelly
General Manager: Jim Kelly
Architect: Chuck Ankrom
CR-DR-LA-LG-RS

Rabow Raves: Location, location. Golf Driving Ranges and Instruction

Osprey Driving Range
235 S. Tamiami Tr., Osprey 34229
Tee Times: 966-7734
Grass tees, putting green, pro shop and golf instruction.

The David Leadbetter Golf Academy
Information: 755-1000
1-800-424-DLGA
David Leadbetter has developed an understanding of the proper swing mechanics unmatched by any other teacher in the world. His philosophies have helped Nick Price, Nick Faldo, David Frost, Larry Mize and many other reach the top of the golf world.

Gymnasiums

Arlington Park
2650 Waldemere St., Sarasota, 316-1346

Colonial Oaks Park
5300 Colonial Oaks Blvd., Sarasota, 316-1330

G.T. Bray Park
5506 33rd Ave. Dr. W., Bradenton, 749-7126

Laurel Park
509 Collins Rd., Laurel, 486-2753

Longwood Park
6050 Longwood Blvd., Sarasota, 316-1383

Newtown Community Center
1845 34th St., Sarasota, 316-1331

Newtown Estates
2800 Newtown Blvd., Sarasota, 316-1161

Woodmere Park
3951 Woodmere Park Blvd., Venice, 486-2780

Horseback Riding

Circle E Ranch
33950 SR 70 E.,
Myakka City, 322-1547

Myakka Valley Stables
7220 Myakka Valley Trail,
Sarasota, 924-8435

Schomburg Farms
2504 24th Ave E.,
Palmetto 34221, 729-2884

Wishful Thinkin' Farms
Juel Gill Rd., Myakka City, 322-1074

Ice Skating

Venice Ice Pavilion
1266 US 41 Bypass, Venice 34292; 484-0080, fax 484-3860

J.P. Igloo
5309 29th St. E., Ellenton, 34222
723-3663 fax 722-1121

Judo

Boys & Girls Club
Sarasota, 366-7769

Boys & Girls Club
Manatee, 746-4179

Kayaking

Sarasota Paddles Group
371-3784

Lawn Bowling

Bradenton Lawn Bowling Club
14th Street and 9th Ave.,
Bradenton, 792-8847

Sarasota Lawn Bowling Club
10th St. & U.S.41 316-1123
The Sarasota Club meets every Mon - Fri from 1:00 to 3:30 p.m. winter, 9:20 - 11:00 a.m. during summer.

Lawn Bowling Greens
809 N. Tamiami Tr., Sarasota, 316-1123

Parasailing

All Water Sports
1504 Stickney Pt. Rd.,
Siesta 34242, 9212754

What's Your Goal?

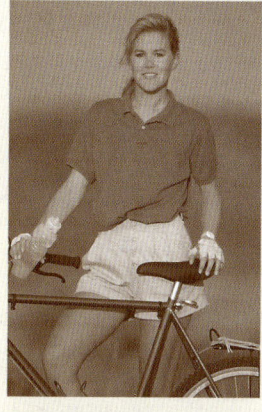

- Unique, Individualized Programs • General Fitness / Body Composition Modification
- Sport-specific Conditioning • Post-rehab Conditioning • Flexibility and ROM Training

It's safe, it's fun and it works!
All sessions conducted in the privacy of your own home or office.

Give us a try. One free session with this ad, one person per session.

Complete Body Training

PRECISION
Fitness & Wellness

Timothy S. Mullally
AFAA Certified Personal Trainer
ACSM Certified Health Fitness Instructor
941 / 730 / 4784

The World's Most Challenging Sports

BARTENDING!

Bradenton Professional School of Bartending
6815 14th St. W.,
Bradenton
Information:
758-6521

Cortez Fleet Parasail
4330 127th St. W. Cortez 34215
792-1900/794-1223

Mountain Climbing

Ted Sperling Memorial Athletic Complex at the Boys & Girls Club of Sarasota
3100 Fruitville Rd., Sarasota
366-7769

A Nicros WallSystem climbing wall, reportedly one of the best in the state, is open to climbers every Wednesday evening and Saturday mornings.

Personal Training

Precision Fitness & Wellness
739-5069

Pistol and Rifle Range

Knight Trail Park
3333 Rustic Rd., Nokomis,
486-2350

Hours: Open to the public Tuesday - Sunday 9:00 a.m. - 4:30 p.m.

Regular Firearm Safety classes taught by certified instructors; Rifle Range is equipped with 15 targets for shooting at 100 yards; Pistol Range has 50 shooting positions for 25 to 50 yard distances. Both ranges are covered and restroom facilities are provided. Shooters must provide firearms and ammunition. Cardboard, targets, ear and eye protection are sold at the range house.

Playgrounds

BRADENTON

Blackstone Park
2112 14th Ave. W., Palmetto

East Bradenton Complex
1119 13th St. E., Bradenton

G.T. Bray Park
5502 33rd Ave. Dr. W., Bradenton

Manatee Palms
65th St. and First Ave. E. Bradenton

Rose Park
Palma Sola Blvd., Bradenton

Rye Wilderness Campground
Rye Rd. and Manatee River, Brad.

Whitfield Park
Abel Elementary School, Bradenton

SARASOTA

A. B. Smith Park
241 Oak St., Sarasota

Arlington Park
2650 Waldemere St., Sarasota

Avion Park
Pompano Ave., Sarasota

Bee Ridge Park
4430 South Lockwood Ridge Rd., Sarasota

Cohen Park
1845 34th St., Sarasota

Colonial Oaks Park
5300 Colonial Oaks Blvd., Sarasota

Fruitville Park
5151 Richardson Rd., Sarasota

Gillespie Park
710 N. Osprey Ave., Sarasota

Laurel Park
509 Collins Rd., Laurel

Lido Beach
400 Ben Franklin Dr., Lido Key

Longwood Park
6050 Longwood Run Blvd., Sarasota

Newtown Estates
2800 Newtown Blvd. and 27th St., Sarasota

Nokomis Community Center
234 Nippino Trail, Nokomis

North Water Tower Park
4700 Rilma Ave., Sarasota

Orange Avenue Park
1822 N. Orange Ave., Sarasota

Pinecraft Park
1420 Gilbert Ave., Sarasota

Pioneer Park
1121 Cocoanut Ave., Sarasota

Potter Park
8587 Potter Park Dr., Sarasota

Red Rock Park
Camino Real, South of Bay Rd., Sarasota

Sevilla Park
1506 Central Ave., Sarasota

Shamrock Park
4100 West Shamrock Dr., Venice

Siesta Beach
948 Beach Road, Siesta Key

South Lido Beach
190 Taft Drive, Lido Key

35th Street Park
3530 Old Bradenton Rd., Sarasota

Turtle Beach
8918 Midnight Pass Rd., Siesta Key

Twin Lakes Park
6700 Clark Rd., Sarasota

Youth Athletic Complex
2810 17th St., Sarasota

VENICE

By-Pass Park
1101 Gulf Coast Blvd., Venice

Challenger Park
371 Olivia St., South Venice

Chuck Reiter Stadium
250 Fort St., Venice

Hecksher Park
450 West Venice Ave., Venice

Laurel Park
860 Forest St., Laurel

Service Club Park
1600 Harbor Dr., Venice

Wellfield Park
1300 Ridgeway, Venice

Woodmere Park
3951 Woodmere Park Blvd., Venice

Polo

Sarasota Polo Club
8201 Polo Club Ln.,
Sarasota 907-0000

Racquetball

MEMBERSHIP CLUBS

Bath & Racquet Club
2170 Robinhood Way, Sarasota 34231, 921-6675, fax 922-7753

Jewish Community Center
582 McIntosh Rd., Sarasota
378-5568

Sarasota Family YMCA
1075 S. Euclid Av., Sarasota 34237, 955-8194
www.sarasotaymca.org

South County Family YMCA
701 Center Rd., Venice 34292, 493-6130

Public Courts

Arlington Park
2650 Waldemere St., Sarasota, 316-1346

C.V. Walton Racquet Center
5512 33rd Ave. Dr.,Bradenton, 749-7173

Twin Lakes Park Facility
6700 Clark Rd., Sarasota, 316-1194

Running Clubs

Bradenton Runners Club
794-9039

Sailing

Bradenton Beach Sailboat Rentals
1325 Gulf Drive N., Bradenton Beach 34217, 778-4969

Enterprise Sailing Charters
Marina Plaza, Sarasota 34236, 951-1833/346-SAIL

O'Leary's Sarasota Sailing School
Island Park, 953-7505;
www.olearyswatersports.com

Spindrift Yacht Charters
410 Gulf of Mexico Drive, Longboat Key 34228, 383-7781, fax 383-2622

Scuba (See: Diving)

Shelling

Sarasota Shell Club
359-3353

Meetings 7:30 p.m. the second Thursday of every month at Mote

The World's Most Challenging Sports

BINGO!

Flamingo Bingo Tours

Venice

Information:

488-2565

Galleria Bingo

Location:

2077 Tamiami Tr. S

Venice

Information:

492-6696

Action Bingo Hall

1946 12th St., Sarasota

Information:

362-3242

Palm Plaza Bingo

4414 Bee Ridge Rd.,

Sarasota

Information:

378-1160

Sara's Bingo Bus

1903 Iowa, Bradenton

Information:

756-7026

St. Mary's All Charity

6323 14th St W.

Bradenton

Information:

753-6622

The World's Most Challenging Sports

BRIDGE!

Bradenton Bridge Center
5633 Manatee Ave. W., Bradenton
Information:
795-8982

The In-Between Bridge Club
Town N Country Plaza
Sarasota
Information:
365-7875

Marine Lab, visitors who love shelling always welcome.

Shuffleboard

Bradenton Shuffleboard Club
1525 Eighth Ave. W., Bradenton, 747-6184

Bee Ridge Park
4430 S. Lockwood Ridge Rd., Sarasota, 316-1328

Hecksher Park
450 West Venice Ave., Venice, 316-1172

Pinecraft Park
1420 Gilbert Ave., Sarasota, 316-1172

Skate Rentals

Florida Wheels Skate Center
3611 3rd. St. W., Bradenton 34205, 747-8602

Skate Port
4260 Tamiami Tr. S., Sarasota 34231, 922-1627
www.skateport.com

Skate Rinks

Florida Wheels Skate Center
3611 3rd St. W., Bradenton, 747-8602

Stardust Roller Skate Center
571 12th St., Sarasota 34237, 365-6888

Snow Skiing

Active Lifestyles
5900 Tamiami Trail S., Sarasota 34231, 923-5677, fax 924-1579

You may think this is a joke but we have one of the largest snow ski clubs in Florida. Active Lifestyles is Sarasota's only full service snow skiing shop, official headquarters for the Ski Club of Sarasota. This year they'll go to Colorodo, Switzerland, Canada, Australia and Alaska. Wax those boards, go snow, send postcards.

Soccer

COMMUNITY PROGRAMS

Englewood Youth Soccer
(Ages six-18), 474-8634

Sarasota Football Club
(Adult), 378-1400 (evenings)

Sarasota United Soccer League
377-1301

Venice Area Youth Soccer Assoc.
(Ages nine-17), 493-6465

PUBLIC FIELDS

Fruitville Park
5151 Richardson Rd., Sarasota

G.T. Bray
5506 33rd Ave. Dr. W., Bradenton

Glebe Park
998 Glebe Lane, Siesta Key

Siesta Beach
948 Beach Rd., Siesta Key

17th Street
4510 17th St., Sarasota

Twin Lakes Park
6700 Clark Rd., Sarasota

Wellfield Park
1300 Ridgewood, Venice

SCHOOLS/TRAINING

The Adidas Soccer Academy
Information: 755-1000
1-800-USA-NICK

International soccer superstar Kai Haaskivi heads a highly trained professional staff, this is an extremely competitive and physically demanding program.

Soccer Players Club
711 Cattlemen Rd., Sarasota, 379-5508

Softball

Miss Sarasota Softball
(Ages five-18), 379-1919

PUBLIC FIELDS

Arlington Park Facility
2650 Waldemere St., Sarasota, 316-1346

Bee Ridge Park
4430 S. Lockwood Ridge Rd., Sarasota, 316-1328

By-Pass Park
1101 Gulf Coast Blvd., Venice, 316-1172

Fruitville Park
5151 Richardson Rd., Sarasota, 316-1172

G.T. Bray
5506 33rd Ave. Dr. W., Bradenton, 792-9816

Laurel Park
509 Collins Rd., Laurel, 486-2753

Longwood Park
6050 Longwood Run Blvd., Sarasota, 316-1383

Miss Sarasota Softball Complex
1111 Gun Club Rd., Sarasota, 316-1172

Newtown Estates Recreation Area
2800 Newtown Blvd./Martin Luther King Blvd., Sarasota, 316-1161

17th Street
4510 17th St., Sarasota, 316-1172

Siesta Beach
948 Beach Rd., Siesta Key, 346-3207

Wellfield Park
1300 Ridgewood, Venice, 473-0243

Swimming

COMMUNITY PROGRAMS

Arlington Aquatic Complex
2650 Waldemere St., Sarasota, 316-1346

East Bradenton Recreational Complex
13th St. E. and 13th Ave. E., Bradenton, 748-4501 Ext. 3149

G.T. Bray Park Aquatic Center
5508 33rd Ave. Dr. W., Bradenton, 749-7188

Lido Beach Pool
400 Ben Franklin, Lido Key, 316-1348

Newtown Community Center
1845 34th St., Sarasota, 316-1331

Swim America Swim School/Swim Florida
925-7946

Sarasota Family YMCA
1075 S. Euclid Av., Sarasota, 955-8194

South County Family YMCA
701 Center Rd., Venice, 493-6130

PUBLIC POOLS

Arlington Aquatic Complex
2650 Waldemere St., Sarasota, 316-1346

East Bradenton Recreational Complex
13th St. E. and 13th Ave. E., Bradenton, 748-4501 Ext. 3149

G.T. Bray Park Aquatic Center
5508 33rd Ave. Dr. W., Bradenton, 749-7188

Lido Beach Pool
400 Ben Franklin, Lido Key, 316-1348

Newtown Community Center
1845 34th St., Sarasota, 316-1331

Tennis - Public Courts

BRADENTON

Bayshore Tennis Courts
34th St. W. and 54th Ave. W.

Braden River Tennis Courts
River Club Dr. and Hwy. 70

C.V. Walton Racquet Ctr
5512 33rd. Ave. Dr. W., 749-7173

Holmes Beach Tennis Courts
62nd St., Holmes Beach

Jessie P. Miller Tennis Courts
Ninth Ave. W. and 43rd St. W.

Palmetto Tennis Courts
19th St. and 14th Ave., Palmetto

SARASOTA

Arlington Park Facility
2650 Waldemere St., 316-1346, four courts with lights

The World's Most Challenging Sports

LOTTO FEVER!

Living in these lotto "loco" times makes wishing on a star seem like kids play. Truth is you have a better chance of getting struck by lightning than winning the match-six prize in the weekly Florida Lotto drawing. That's why the Lotto is often called the "Tax of Fools!"

Here's the good news: 38% of all lottery sales must go to the state's Education Enhancement Trust Fund. 50% is returned as prize money (good luck!) and the remaining 12 percent pays all expenses related to running the lottery. The Lottery Department took in more than $2 billion during its 1997 fiscal year for all games (and there are many). Grand prize money for six-number match winners is paid over 20 years, taxes are taken at payment times. And, as silly as it may be, we buy one ticket a week. Go ahead, call us fools. We figure you can't win if you don't play. The Lotto folks figure that too.

The World's Most Challenging Sports

POLITICS!

The League of Women Voters

Location:
1751 Mound St., Sarasota

Information:
365-7714

(Ed note: Not a sport for wimps.)

Colonial Oaks Park
5300 Colonial Oaks Blvd., 316-1330, two courts with lights

Fruitville Park
5151 Richardson Rd. 316-1172, two courts with lights

Gillespie Park
710 N Osprey Ave.,316-1172, three courts

Longwood Park
6050 Longwood Run Blvd., 316-1383, two courts

Newtown Community Center
1845 34th St.,316-1331, two courts with lights

Newtown Estates
2800 Newtown Blvd., 316-1161, two courts with lights

Payne Park Tennis Center
2050 Adams Lane, 954-4884, nine green clay courts with lights

Pioneer Park
1121 Coconut Ave., 316-1172, one court

Potter Park
8587 Potter Park Dr., 316-1172, four courts with lights

Riverview Tennis Courts
Riverview High School, eight courts with lights. 316-1772

Siesta Beach
948 Beach Rd., Siesta Key, 346-3207, four courts with lights

Twin Lakes Park
6700 Clark Rd., Sarasota, 316-1172. two courts

Youth Athletic Complex
2810 17th St., Sarasota, two courts with lights.

VENICE

By-Pass Park
1101 Gulf Coast Blvd., 486-2780, two courts

Hecksher Park
450 W. Venice Ave., 486-2311, six courts with lights

Laurel Park
09 Collins Rd., Laurel, 486-2753, two courts with lights.

Pinebrook Park
1251 Pinebrook Rd., 316-1172, two courts with lights.

Pine View Tennis Courts
Pine View School, 316-1172, six courts with lights.

Shamrock Park
4100 W. Shamrock Dr., 486-2706, four courts.

Woodmere Park
3951 Woodmere Pk. Blvd., 486-2780, six courts with lights.

Tennis Schools

Bollettieri Tennis Academy
755-1000/1-800-USA-NICK

Like no other tennis training center in the world, the Bollettieri Tennis Academy will help you maximize your potential and performance within your own unique style of play. With a total of 75 championship courts, the Academy is more than equipped to push you to the top of your game. Professionals who have trained at the Academy include Boris Becker, Mary Pierce, Andre Agassi, Monica Seles, Jim Courier, Pete Sampras, Petr Korda and Mark Phillippoussis. The Academy's summer camp is the largest of its kind in the U.S. and annually attracts over 6,000 camper weeks.

Trap and Skeet

Sarasota Trap & Skeet Club
488-3223

Knight Trail Park is open to the public for Trap and Skeet every Wednesday from 9 a.m. to 8:30 p.m., Friday from 9 a.m. to 1 p.m., Saturday & Sunday 9 a.m. - 4 p.m.

Volleyball

COMMUNITY PROGRAMS

Arlington Park
2650 Waldemere St., Sarasota

Bee Ridge Park Facility
4430 S. Lockwood Ridge Rd., Sarasota

Newtown Community Center
1845 34th St., Sarasota

North Jetty Park Beach
1000 Casey Key Rd., Nokomis, 486-2311

Sarasota Family YMCA
1075 S. Euclid Av., Sarasota, 955-8194

South County Family YMCA
701 Center Rd., Venice, 493-6130

PUBLIC COURTS

Arlington Park
2650 Waldemere St., Sarasota, 316-1346

Bee Ridge Park Facility
4430 S. Lockwood Ridge Rd., Sarasota, 316-1328

Fruitville Park
5151 Richardson Rd., Sarasota, 316-1172

G.T. Bray Park Gymnasium
5506 33rd Ave. Dr., Bradenton, 749-7126

Newtown Community Center
1845 34th St., Sar., 316-1331

Newtown Estates
2800 Newtown Blvd., Sar., 316-1161

N. Jetty Park Beach
100 Casey Key Rd., Nokomis, 316-1172

Siesta Beach
948 Beach Rd., Siesta Key, 346-3207

South Lido Beach
190 Taft Drive and 2201 Ben Franklin, Lido Key, 316-1172

Turtle Beach
8918 Midnight Pass Rd., Siesta, 346-3207

Venice Beach
101 The Esplanade, Venice, 316-1172

Water Sports and Windsurfing

Don and Mike's Boat and Ski Rentals

520 Blackburn Point Rd., Osprey, 966-4000

Island Style Windsurfing
2803 N. Tamiami Trail, Sarasota
954-1009

Sarasota Beach Service
383-5102

Surfing World
11904 Cortez Rd. W.,
Bradenton 34215, 794-1233

Yoga

American Yoga Association
513 S Orange Ave., Sarasota, 953-5859

Bikram's Yoga of Sarasota
1501 2nd Street, Sarasota, 954-4538
(www.bikramyogasarasota.com)

Body & Soul
1919-1/2 Adams Lane, Sarasota 34236, 955-2639

Shivan's Yoga Studio
925-9642

ana molinari...
Salon • Spa • Boutique • Gallery

Longboat Key
The Chart House Shops
201 Gulf of Mexico Drive, Suite 10
Longboat Key, Florida 34228
(941) 383-0065 • (941) 383-0225

Downtown Sarasota
52 South Palm Avenue
Sarasota, Florida 34236
(941) 365-7434 • (941) 365-1415

photography Dick Dickinson models Dawn Tunstall make-up Cheryl Poole hair Ana Molinari

The Arts

THE ART OF NATURE © BILL WEST

"Oh for a Muse of fire that would ascend the brightest heaven of invention... So wrote Shakespeare, who obviously, never spent time on the Suncoast. If he had he would have found that, like our golden sunshine, the Muses shine brightly in our hometown. We are blessed with live theater for all tastes. The classics for the hearty palate, contemporary theater for the adventurous appetite, musical comedy for a light bite, and just about everything in between. You can experience the lavish thrill of an imported New York production, or a domestic jewel created by a solid community of resident artists. It's all here, from the funky feel of off-off Broadway to the tinsel town pizzazz of Times Square. So get your ticket, take your seat, and enjoy the show."

John Scalzi came to NEWS40 in December 1995. He received his Meteorological degree from the City University of New York, and began working for WNYW's *Good Day New York.* Later he joined the National Weather Service, while teaching weather classes at City College in NYC. John completed his graduate work in Meteorology at FSU, then joined WTXL-TV in Tallahassee. He now resides in Sarasota with his wife Linda, together they enjoy seeing plays and musicals. For a our Theater Listings, see page 216.

Art Organizations

Artarget
953-2482

A not-for-profit, artist-run and member-supported organization dedicated to the exhibition of important contemporary and topical work by emerging and established professional artists who might not otherwise find a forum in the commercial marketplace. Their annual "Fly By Night" costume ball is not to be missed, featuring some of the most original and creative costumes you will ever see. Ever.

Art League of Manatee County
209 9th St. W, Bradenton 34205
746-2862, www.flnet.com/almc

For over 60 years, the Art League of Manatee County has vigorously promoted the visual arts. A nonprofit organization whose mission is to educate, stimulate and encourage participation in the arts, this vibrant group helps to define the quality of life within the community by providing a sense of cultural identity and a means of expression. Educational opportunities for adults and children, exhibitions are open and free to the public.

Fine Arts Society of Sarasota
349-1094

To stimulate appreciation of the fine arts through the permanent display of Florida artists and to provide scholarships.

Friends of Venice Art Center
390 South Nokomis Ave., Venice 34285
485-7136

Helps to raise funds and promote programs of Venice Art Center.

Manatee County Cultural Alliance
323 10th Ave. W., Suite 303, Palmetto 34221
721-0405
Arts HotLine: 745-ARTS (2787)

An independent, not-for-profit organization that serves as a sort of chamber of commerce of the arts for Manatee County. Call to be placed on their mailing list to receive their newsletter.

Women Creating Art, Sarasota-Manatee Chapter
P.O. Box 25184, Sarasota 34277
739-8250
e-mail: amyoted@msn.com or amejo@flnet.com

An organization for women actively engaged in visual arts and professions; to expand members' visibility.

The Sarasota County Arts Council
1351 Fruitville Rd., Sarasota 34236
365-5118
www.sarasota-arts.org

A private, nonprofit organization bringing together visual and performing artists and arts organizations in a partnership of business, government and the public to promote, develop and coordinate the arts in Sarasota County. Members receive discount coupons, arts information and event invitations. Gallery of local artists work open 9:00 a.m. - 5:00 p.m. Monday - Friday. This group can be held directly responsible for obtaining and maintaining Sarasota's designation as the cultural capitol of Florida.

January Festivals & Events

Latin American Art International
At Sarasota Visual Art Center January 8 - February 14.
Information 346-7509.

"Gardens of Delight" Exhibit
At Selby Gardens, featuring a collection of hand-colored reproductions of 19th century illustrations from the Garden.
January 8 - February 21.
Information 366-5731.

Carole Sparrow Music Recital
Presented by Sarasota Music Archive at Selby Public Library January 10.
Information 955-5890.

PHOTOG.

BILL WEST

8466 North Lockwood Ridge Road
Suite 149
Sarasota, Florida 34243
941.355.6664

Sarasota Visual Arts Center
707 N. Tamiami Trail, Sarasota 34236
365-2032
e-mail: svac@home.com
www.members.home.net/svac
Hours: 10:00 a.m. - 4:00 p.m. Monday - Friday;
1:00 p.m. - 4:00 p.m. Saturday - Sunday

Paintings and sculptures by local and national artists. Worthwhile classes and special events. A landmark institution, never an admission charge.

Venice Art Center
390 Nokomis Ave. S, Venice 34285
485-7136
Monday - Friday 9:00 a.m. - 4:00 p.m., Sat 10:00 a.m. - 2:00 p.m.

This wonderful (and important) community resource offering dozens and dozens of classes, some taught by world renown artists. Gallery features rotating exhibits by members and/or visiting artists. A real treasure for the Venice area - more folks from Sarasota could/should take advantage too.

Crafts

The Cutting Edge
2437 Arapaho St., Sarasota 34231
924-7907

Sewing group affiliated with American Sewing Guild meets third Monday of each month. Field trips.

Digital Fine Artists Association
P.O. Box 48798, Sarasota 34230
371-2179
www.difa.org

A not-for-profit group dedicated to sharing the knowledge and expertise of using computers to produce fine art.

Florida Suncoast Watercolor Society
2341 Tangerine Dr., Sarasota 34239
366-3355

Promotes and exhibits watercolor art work of its members.

Gulf Coast Carvers Guild
P.O. Box 31097, Sarasota 34232
922-4243

Group promotes woodcarving through exhibits, classes and lectures.

Gulf Coast Porcelain Artists
5175 Siesta Woods Drive, Sarasota 34242
349-8373
e-mail: paph@juno.com or
ruthk819@aol.com

Educates, encourages and exhibits the ancient art of china painting and porcelain art. Meets at First Presbyterian Church, Sarasota.

With the right architect or engineer...

January Festivals & Events

United Cerebral Palsy Telethon
Broadcast live on WWSB-Channel 40 from the Sarasota Main Plaza. Come join the fun ... for a good cause! January 17. Information 957-3599.

Manatee County Fair
Just say "moo!" A family-oriented fair with lots of youth exhibits and a great midway. No alcohol or games of chance. January 21 - 30. Information 722-1639.

Arts Day Downtown
In downtown Sarasota January 24. Information 365-5118.

American Jazz
The Sarasota Concert Band plus the Eddie Pawl Quintet playing special arrangements for jazz combo and concert band. VanWezel Performing Arts Center January 24. Information 955-6660.

(Virginia) Hoffman Studio of Architectural & Decorative Arts
2225 Sixth St., Sarasota 34236
365-7450
Ornamental glass, sculpture, decorative arts and custom furniture. Call for appointment.

Ikebana International, Chapter 115
P.O. Box 15677, Sarasota 34277
346-0778
Education in the art of Japanese flower arranging. Meets at Selby Gardens, Sarasota.

Woven Spirits Basketry
635 N. Tamiami Trail, Nokomis 34275
485-6730
e-mail: flasue@aol.com
www.imox.com/wovenspirit
Basketry school, supply warehouse and gallery.

Marise Art Gallery
6506 Gateway Ave., Sarasota 34231
922-7169
Offering personalized classes daily in all mediums.

Pins and Needles
390 301 Blvd. W #4B, Bradenton 34205
748-4208 or 723-9971
e-mail: nptms@aol.com
Neighborhood group of the American Sewing Guild.

Sarasota China Art Club
4760 Atlantic Ave., Sarasota 34233
924-6085 or 371-0177
Students and teachers exploring the art of porcelain decoration.

Sew What's New
966-5241
American Sewing Guild neighborhood group, 60-70 members.

Sho Fu Bonsai
602 Key Royale Dr., Holmes Beach 34217
778-9400
Development, cultivation, propagation and display of Bonsai.

Sogetsu Study Group
Community Room, Southgate Plaza, Sarasota 34239
355-0459
Encourages the study of plant and flower arrangement in Japanese style. Meets 4th Thursday of the month.

Sumi-e Society of America
4553 Lake Vista Dr., Sarasota 34233
379-4514
Encourages an appreciation of Oriental brush painting. Meets at Gulf Gate Library.

Suncoast Scribes
P.O. Box 25052, Sarasota 34277
951-0642
A group dedicated to the art of calligraphy.

Venetian Society of Basket Weavers
635 N. Tamiami Trail, Nokomis 34275
485-6730
Group educates and promotes basket making as a fine art.

Dance

American International Dance Centre/Sarasota Ballroom Dance Company
556 S. Pineapple Ave., Sarasota 34236
955-8363
Award winning dance school specializing in the American and international styles of ballroom/Latin dancing. Large modern facilities located in the charming Herald Square district of downtown Sarasota. Certified teaching faculty. Weekly dance parties. Private coaching available. Member National Dance Council of America.

Babiak Dance Ensemble
1742 Joyce St., Sarasota 34231
966-1847
e-mail: babiak1@juno.com
Presentations of international folk dances in costume; group also teaches folk dancing.

Park Dance Center
4430 Lockwood Ridge Rd. S., Sarasota 34239
5300 Colonial Oaks Blvd, Sarasota 34232
921-1206
Dance training for children and adults in ballet, tap, jazz. Exercise programs for adults and teens, "Slimmercise" for adults.

Flex Dance Studio & Boutique
3303 Bahia Vista St., Sarasota 34239
957-0070
A state-of-the-art studio with classes in ballet, tap, jazz, creative dance and acrobatics for ages three to adult, beginner to professional. Flex is home of the West Coast Dance Project, a nonprofit dance company to promote dance and provide professional experiences for aspiring young dancers. The Dance Arena is especially designed for children age three to eight, offering classes in creative movement. Kidspoint Preschool of the Arts is for ages three-and-a-half to five and provides a full curriculum plus dance and theater arts education. Kindergym offers gymnastic movement and dance. The Dancewear Boutique carries dancewear, supplies, shoes and accessories for dance training and exercise. KidDance, Inc., is a corporation for the development of creative dance concepts whose newsletter is distributed worldwide.

Florida Ballet Arts School
501 N. Beneva Rd. #700, Sarasota 34232
953-3422

the leaning tower wouldn't be.

World Design, Inc.
Architects & Engineers
(941) 755-3934

AA C 001570-EB0007666

January Festivals & Events

Anna Maria "Flavors of the Isle"
January 30.
Information 778-1541.

Baroque Bash
A truly unique event at the Ringling Musuem January 30.
Information 359-5700.

Antique Show
At Sarasota Fairground
January 30 - 31.
Information 365-0818.

Children's classes, ballet, modern, and jazz for beginners through professional.

Grapevine International Folk Dancers
5876 Clubside Dr., Sarasota 34243
351-6281
Group learns and participates in dances from around the world.

Sarasota Ballet of Florida
Information/Tickets: 359-0771/351-8000
The Sarasota Ballet of Florida is in its eighth season as a resident ballet company. The company performs most of its repertoire of world class contemporary, modern and classical ballet in its new home at the Florida State University Center for The Performing Arts, formerly known as the Asolo Center for the Performing Arts.

1999 Season:
"Madame Butterfly" (Van Wezel), January 15 - 17;
"Alice In Wonderland" (FSU), February 5 - 9;
"Apollo" (FSU), March 12 - 16;
"Swan Lake" (Van Wezel), April 9 - 11.

Sarasota Scottish Country Dancers
194 SunAire Terr., Nokomis 34275
755-6212 or 485-7488
e-mail: fmacdwied@aol.com
Weekly meetings every Thursday at 7:30 p.m. at Sarasota's Adult Recreation Club to enjoy dances of Scotland.

Design

American Society of Interior Designers
1014 East Ave., Sarasota 34237
951-6420
Continuing support for area's interior designers.

Asolo Costume Shop
5555 N. Tamiami Trail, Sarasota 34243
355-6353
Designs all costumes for Asolo productions; volunteers welcome; no individual rentals. Theaters and educational organizations only.

Asolo Scenic Studio
1337 Manhattan Ave., Sarasota 34237, Sarasota
366-7771
Designs all scenic art for Asolo productions, some construction available for outside clients.

GIO/Graphica Art & Design Resources
4976 S. Tamiami Tr., Sarasota 34231
927-2843
Art source for galleries, designers and architects.

Education and Art Instruction

Art League of Manatee County
209 9th St. W., Bradenton 34205
746-2862
www.flnet.com/almc

FLOORS BY DESIGN

With more than 25 years of combined experience, Floors by Design owners David Gruber and Scott Pintchuck know how to customize a specific look for your home or office. Choose from their selection of elegant marble, classic hardwood, natural stone flooring, carpeting, ceramic tile, window treatments* and more; you'll also find great customer service.

Carpet • Ceramic Tile • Marble • Exotic Stone • Hardwoods

**1906 Bay Road, Sarasota, FL 34239
(941) 954-8080**

* Hunter Douglass Window Treatments

Classes and workshops in a variety of media are open to the community.

Joy Bascher's North Creek Art School
2150 Cordes Way, Osprey 34229
966-4825
Fundamental art classes. Caricatures at parties. The Tropical Gallery opened in 1996 and a catalog is available.

Booker High School/Sarasota Visual and Performing Arts Center
3201 N. Orange Ave., Sarasota 34234
355-2967; X-120
A pre-professional program open to all high school students in the Sarasota County school district who are committed to an arts career. Audition required for admission, tuition is free. Five areas of discipline include art, dance, music, media (radio, television, film), theater; four theater productions, two dance productions and a variety of musical and visual performances throughout the school year.

Education Center
5370 Gulf of Mexico Dr., Longboat Key 34228
383-8811
Nonprofit center offers classes in visual arts, literature, drama, cinema, writing, music appreciation and more.

February Festivals & Events

First Friday Downtown Stroll
Wander the picturesque streets of downtown Sarasota while enjoying street performers as galleries and shops stay open late, stopping in at any restaurant of club that suits your taste whenever you need refreshment. This one is February 5 ... then do it again the first Friday of every month!
Information 951-2656.

Scottish Festival
Sarasota County Fairgrounds February 6.
Information 365-0818.

Anna Maria Island Bridge Street Fesitval
February 6 - 7.
Information 778-1541.

Friends of the Arts and Sciences
4433 Riverwood Ave., Sarasota 34231
924-5770
www.artsarasota.org

Offers watercolor work with international instructors, plus demonstrations, slide/lecture presentations, exhibitions plus extensive travel tours to nearby and faraway locations designed to increase interest in the arts and sciences. Closed July - August.

FSU/Asolo Conservatory of Professional Actor Training
5555 N. Tamiami Trail, Sarasota 34243
351-9010; X-3211 (Acting Conservatory)

Housed in the Asolo Center for the Performing Arts, this conservatory awards MFA degrees to graduate students in theater.

Hilton Leech Studio
4433 Riverwood Ave., Sarasota 34231
924-5770
Hours: 9:30 a.m. - 4:00 p.m. Monday - Friday

Internationally known school and gallery. Watercolor paintings, sculpture and photography. Offers extensive series of workshops in water color and water media. Closed June - August.

Longboat Key Adult Education Center
5370 Gulf of Mexico Drive, Longboat Key 34228
383-8811

Neighborhood center for art and education; gallery exhibits.

Longboat Key Art Center
6860 Longboat Drive S., Longboat Key 34228
383-2345

Arts and crafts education center; provides studios and galleries for exhibits.

Longwood Recreation Center
6050 Longwood Run Blvd., Sarasota 34235
316-1383

Offering a wide variety of educational and art-oriented activities including workshops and classes in copper enameling, oil, acrylic and more.

Manatee Community College
Bradenton Campus
5840 26th St. W., Bradenton
755-1511

South Campus
8000 S. Tamiami Tr., Venice
493-3504, ext. 2643

Fully accredited public community college serving both Sarasota and Manatee Counties; strong art department and art gallery.

Marie Selby Botanical Gardens
811 S. Palm Ave., Sarasota 34236
366-5731 or 366-5730
e-mail: mitchell@virtu.sar.usf.edu
www.selby.org

Periodic workshops and classes open to the public; World Orchid Center; tropical displays; Museum of Botany and the Arts.

© FRANK ATURA - RINGLING SCHOOL OF ART AND DESIGN

Marise Art Gallery
6506 Gateway Ave., Sarasota 34231
922-7169
Offering daily personalized classes in all mediums.

Mote Marine Laboratory/Aquarium
1600 Thompson Pkwy. (City Island), Sarasota 34236
388-4441
e-mail: info@mote.org
www.mote.org
Periodic workshops and lectures open to volunteers; marine/environmental research laboratory and aquarium open to the public.

Ringling School of Art and Design
2700 N. Tamiami Trail, Sarasota 34234
351-5100
www.rsad.edu
A private, four-year fully accredited college of visual arts with BFA degree programs in Computer Animation, Fine Arts, Graphic and Interactive Communications, Illustration, Interior Design. Noncredit courses, children's classes and summer art camp are also offered.

Julie Rohr Academy
4466 Fruitville Road, Sarasota 34232
371-4979
Private school for children aged two through 8th grade with strong performing arts program.

February Festivals & Events

Project Black Cinema
At the Ringling Museum
February 6 - 13.
Information 359-5700.

21st Annual Fishing College
This is angler's heaven!
February 6 - 21.
Information 745-7020.

American Express Invitational Golf Tournament
Prestancia Golf Club
February 6 - 14.
Information 800-387-9991.

Greek Glendi
Greek food, music and lots of fun. February 9 - 14.
Information 355-2616.

Mennonite Quilt & Craft Show
February 11 - 13.
Information 955-8919.

The Sarasota County Arts Council
1351 Fruitville Rd., Sarasota 34236
365-5118
www.sarasota-arts.org

A private, nonprofit organization bringing together visual and performing artists and arts organizations in a partnership of business, government and the public to promote, develop and coordinate the arts in Sarasota County.

Sarasota Garden Club
1131 Blvd. of the Arts, Sarasota 34236
955-0875

A group aiming to stimulate a knowledge of the specialized skills of gardening among amateurs, to promote the study of floral design, to cooperate with others in the beautification of our community, support and practice wise conservation measures, to fight pollution, and protect our ecology.

Sarasota Institute of Lifetime Learning (SILL)
c/o Selby Library, 1331 First Street, Sarasota 34236
365-6404

The area's absolute best winter lecture series on topics of general interest (primarily intended for retirees to widen their horizons, but younguns should not be dissuaded from participating – this really is an extraordinary event) featuring discussions and workshops led by internationally renown experts, often former ambassadors or former U.N. representatives. Sarasota series takes place at Sarasota Square East AMC Theaters (outside mall); Venice series takes place at Venice Community Center. Complete series program booklet is available at all public libraries. Well worth attending!

Sarasota Music Archive
265 S. Orange Ave., Sarasota 34236
955-5890
e-mail: smarchive@juno.com
www.sarasota-online.com/music
Hours: 10:00 a.m. - 3:00 p.m., Monday - Friday

An extraordinary collection of over 100,000 recordings, books, audio and video tapes, scores, sheet music, magazines and memorabilia Archive resources include the equipment to play every type of recording in existence. Educational services available to researchers and the community. Lectures, programs ... a priceless treasure of music.

Sarasota Visual Art Center
707 N. Tamiami Trail, Sarasota 34236
365-2032
e-mail: svac@home.com
www.members.home.net/svac

Hours: 10:00 a.m. - 4:00 p.m. Monday - Friday;
1:00 p.m. - 4:00 p.m. Saturday - Sunday

Celebrating more than 70 of supporting of the arts through education programs and exhibitions. Contemporary paintings and sculptures by local artists. A treasure.

Sumi-e Society (Oriental Brush Painters Guild)
4553 Lake Vista Drive, Sarasota 34233
379-4514

Fosters appreciation of Oriental brush painting through meetings workshops and exhibitions. Meets at Gulf Gate Library.

University of South Florida at Sarasota/New College
5700 N. Tamiami Trail, Sarasota 34243
359-4314
www.sar.usf.edu
Educational and cultural center.

Venice Art Center
390 S. Nokomis Ave., Venice 34285
485-7136
Provides educational interaction between artist and those who appreciate art. A number of day trips and overnight tours to some of Florida's interesting sites are open to the public.

Film

Sarasota's Screen Gems
We have become used to seeing movie stars in area. Tom Cruise and Nicole Kidman (*Eyes Wide Shut*) shop at Mortons - at least they did before it closed for major remodeling; Jerry Springer (*Ringmaster*) often eats at Cafe L'Europe where, thankfully, food fights are not allowed; Michael Jordon (*Space Jam*) can still be seen on occasion dunking balls on Longboat Key golf courses; author Tom Robbins (*Even Cowgirls Get The Blues*) enjoys funky antique stores in the Fruitville area...you just never know who you'll run into around here. But the Suncoast is not only home to some of the world's brightest talent, our area has also been featured on the silver screen as well. Albeit, most of the features have been more dim than stellar:

1951 — "The Greatest Show On Earth"
Directed by Cecil B. DeMille; with Charlton Heston, Betty Hutton, Cornell Wilde and a thousand local residents who earned 75 cents an hour as extras and then wildly cheered for themselves during the 1952 world premiere at what is now the Sarasota Opera House. "Blond Bombshell" Betty Hutton and "sultry" Dorothy Lamour brought their children along during filming. 100,000 people showed up for the star-studded parade scene down First Street, Central Avenue, Main Street and Orange Avenue. (Actor Jimmy Stewart played a clown but he never made it to the Suncoast, his scenes were shot in Hollywood.) A popular favorite of the day, the film went on to win an Academy Award for Best Picture besting out such worthy nominations as Stanley Kramer's *High Noon* and John Ford's *The Quiet Man*. That year's Oscarfest also featured Cecil B. DeMille receiving the monumental Irving G. Thalberg Memorial Award. Sarasota's designation as "The Greatest Place To Live On Earth" was somehow left out of the ceremony.

1980 — "Honky Tonk Freeway"
Directed by John Schlesinger; with William Devane, Jessica Tandy, Hume Cronyn and I-75, which was blown up in the film. The film, in turn, was blown up by the critics. Deservedly so.

1981 — "Sneakers"
Starring Susan Anton, Carling Bassett, Jessica Walter; and The Colony Beach & Tennis Resort on Longboat Key and St. Armands Circle – two local landmarks which, unlike this film, people still see on a regular basis. (Do not confuse this turkey with Robert Redford's semi-turkey of the same name.)

1983 — "A Flash of Green"
Directed by Victor Nunez, starring Ed Harris, Blair Brown, Richard Jordon; and Casey Key, The Waffle Shop Restaurant, Sarasota County

---

February Festivals & Events

Bluegrass Festival
Sarasota County Fairgrounds February 12 - 14. Information 365-0818.

20th Annual Terra Ceia-Rubonia Mardi Gras
Mardi Gras '70s style, complete with kazoo marching band and much more! February 13 - 14. Information 722-5048.

Spring Plant Fair
At Selby Gardens February 13 - 15. Information 366-5731.

Florida West Coast Symphony Chamber Music Concert
How very romantic! Presented by Sarasota Music Archive at Selby Public Library February 14. Information 955-5890.

February Festivals & Events

Say "I Do" Ceremony
Your chance to renew your vows at sunset on Siesta Beach. Naturally, February 14.
Information 349-3800.

Volunteer Center Giant Garage Sale
At Sarasota County Fairgrounds
February 19 - 20.
Information 365-0818.

Snowbird Art Fest
In Venice
February 19 - 20.
Information 488-2236.

Festival of the Arts
Main Street in downtown Sarasota
February 19 - 21.
Information 951-2656.

Sarasota Shell Show
She sells sea shells at Municipal Auditorium.
February 19 - 21.
Information 359-3353.

Court House and The Oaks. Based on the rare phenomenon of seeing a green flash of light just as the sun sets beyond the horizon on the Gulf of Mexico. In our lifetime we've seen the phenomenon and the movie only once.

1993 — "Seven Sundays"
French Director Jean-Charles Tacchella ("Cousin, Cousine") fell in love with the Suncoast during one of his trips to the Sarasota French Film Festival and promised to make a movie here. Staring Molly Ringwald, Rod Steiger, Thierry Lhermitte and Maurizio Nichetti; and the Riverview High Kiltie Band, marching down Main Street. The U.S. premiere at a later French Film Festival here did not evoke a similar reception as that which greeted "The Greatest Show on Earth." "Seven Sundays" was never distributed in the U.S. to theater and never made it to video … chances are it never will. The French Film Festival left too. Ce la vie.

1996 — "Great Expectations"
We all had great expectations about this modern version of the Charles Dickens classic tale, transposed to contemporary Florida and New York. Released at the end of 1997, this film brought Robert DeNiro, Ethan Hawke, Gwyneth Paltrow and Anne Bancroft to the Suncoast. Gwyneth and her then-boyfriend Brad Pitt were seen at local restaurants holding hands and smooching. (Exactly what we recommend doing in our local eateries.) Dozens of residents had the thrill of a lifetime as extras. Much of the filming took place at Ca'd'Zan on the Ringling Museum grounds and in the fishing village of Cortez.

1997 — "Palmetto"
Directed by Volker Schlendorff with Woody Harrelson and Elisabeth Shue, all made fast friends of local dignitaries (the mayor of Palmetto even got a speaking role) in this tale of trouble a-brewing. Sarasota's Gator Club was featured as were many other area hot spots. Locals went ga-ga during the shooting as the stars dined at our restaurants, showed up at movie theaters and signed scads of autographs. In keeping with the general perception of the palmetto bug (one critter actually received screen time!) the film was disgusting. If we could, we would squash it - the town of Palmetto deserves much better.

Film Programs, Projects and Festivals

Best West Florida Productions
47 S. Palm Avenue #206, Sarasota 34236
951-2378

Complete area one-stop for film, video and photography production. They not only handle everything from shoot locations to catering and accommodations, they are also fabulous to work with.

Project Black Cinema
P.O. Box 565, Sarasota 34230
359-5700

Project Black Cinema presents cutting-edge multicultural events throughout the year, culminating with the Sarasota Africana Film Festival, a seven-day festival of African cinema and cultural activities. Presented annually the third week of February, the festival is a fusion of alterntive film, exhibits, social events, guest celebrities, lectures, theater, performance, and visual arts … an exciting adventure for tourists and locals alike. Year round activities include multimedia educational training and a monthly film series.

Sarasota County Film Commission
655 N. Tamiami Tr., Sarasota 34236
957-1877
e-mail: scvb@netsrq.com
www.sarasotafl.org

Pam Kline, official county Film Commissioner, helps to find locations and contacts; her office is in the Sarasota Convention & Visitors Bureau.

Sarasota Annual Film Festival
364-9514
www.sarasotafilmfest.com

The third weekend in January is now dedicated to this new festival which includes world premieres (two films from Showtime were scheduled for the 1999 1st annual festivities), filmmaker symposiums and sneak peeks at some of the impressive work produced by Ringling and FSU students - at the Hollywood-20 Theatres.

Sarasota Film Society
P.O. Box 3378, Sarasota 34230
364-8662; Showtimes: 955-FILM
e-mail: sfsfilm@gate.net
www.filmsociety.org

On going presentations of at least 100 first-run foreign, independent, classic and rarely seen films each year from the most controversial to the most artistic, now shown in their three-screen Burns Court Cinema (506 Burns Lane, Sarasota). Sponsor of Cine-World Film Festival in November.

Movie Theaters

Our area, sophisticated well beyond its size, embraces movies. The numbers have been strong enough to warrant some significant additions to our landscape. On Memorial Day weekend in 1997, Cobb Theaters opened a 20-screen, 3,500-seat theater complex, which was to be the flagship of the corporation before the purchase by Regal, who now own it. Each individual screen in this new Downtown megaplex has stadium seating and "couch" chairs. Local skeptics lost big on this one. In 1997 Sarasota's Hollywood-20 Theaters became the most successful unit of the entire Regal chain, the second largest chain in America.

Following Regal's lead, there are now two megaplex theater/malls planned in Bradenton, just five miles apart. One will be at the Sandpile - 23 acres just east of U.S. Business 41 in downtown Bradenton - to be developed by the principles of Sarasota's Hollywood-20 complex. The other will be at Royal Palm Crossing at U.S. 301 and State Road 70, (a rumor places a Michael Jordon restaurant adjacent to later location, nice, as far as rumors go), at publication time the same owners of the Royal Palm Crossing location have announced their intent to purchase Sarasota Square Mall. Although not announced, we fully expect new theater development upgrades there as well. It's a great time for movie lovers.

Meanwhile, the Sarasota Film Society maintains a strong and loyal following as they continue to present outstanding international and independent films on their three screens at Burns Court - a significant barometer reflecting the sophistication of the community. Those who attend consider Burns Court a major treasure, for good reason.

All of this activity reinforces the important fact that our community seriously loves movies. Even Comcast Cable has expanded the number of its pay-per-view movie channels to meet the demand; we

February Festivals & Events

Cortez Fishing Festival

In fabulous Cortez

February 20 - 21.

Information 749-0280.

Performing Arts Center

February 21.

Information 955-6660.

Medieval Fair

On the grounds at Ringling Museum February 25 - 28. A truly unique experience! Information 359-5700.

Italian Feast & Festival

At Venice Airport

February 25 - 28.

Information 493-6344.

March Festivals & Events

Winter Members' Exhibit
At the Sarasota Visual Art Center February 26 - March 25.
Information 365-2032.

Design Showcase
March 1 - 28.
Information 953-4252.

22nd Annual Antique Show
A fave rave. March 3 - 4.
Information 955-0935.

"A Musical Journey"
Sarasota Concert Band at VanWezel Performing Arts Hall March 7.
Information 955-6660.

Annual Porcelain Show & Sale
February 20.
Information 953-7638.

currently have one of the highest number of such channels offered within their national system with even being been promised.

Virtually all theaters offer senior discounts, reduced prices for children and heavily discounted matinee ticket prices for everyone before 6:00 p.m.; many theaters offer weekend "midnight shows;" some theaters are dollar theaters.

BRADENTON

Bradenton Cinema 8
7150 Cortez Rd. W, Bradenton
379-6684
Major releases on eight screens.

Movies at Desoto Square
DeSoto Square Mall
303 US 301 Blvd. W, Bradenton
379-6684
Major releases on six screens.

Oakmont 8
4801 Cortez Rd. W., Bradenton
379-6684
Major releases on eight screens.

SARASOTA

AMC Sarasota Square East
Sarasota Square Mall (Outside building, east of mall)
8027 Beneva Rd. S, Sarasota
924-1383
Major releases on eight screens.

AMC Sarasota Square West
Sarasota Square Mall (Inside the mall)
8201 S. Tamiami Tr., Sarasota
924-1383
Major releases on eight screens.

Burns Court Cinema/Sarasota Film Society
506 Burns Lane, Sarasota
955-3456
eMail: sfsfilm@gate.net
www.filmsociety.org

Ongoing exhibition of more than 100 first-run foreign, independent classic and rarely seen films, presented by the Sarasota Film Society. Also the site of the Cine-World Film Festival in November each year. A true Suncoast treasure on three screens. Of particular note is "Cinema H" - weekend screenings of historic and classical films. Scheduled at publication time: "The Battleship Potemkin" (1925), Feb. 6-7; "The General" (1926), Feb. 20-21; "Le Passion de Jeanne D'Arc" (1928). March 6-7; "The Blood of a Poet" (1930) and "Un Chien andalou" (1928), March 20-21; "The 39 Steps" (1935), April 3-4; "The Magnificent Ambersons" (1942), April 17-18; "Ugestu" (1953), May 1-2; "Umberto D" (1952), May 15-16; "Breathless" (1959), May 29-30. (For more information about this series call 364-8662.)

Regal Crossing Cinema 10
Sarasota Crossing Shopping Center
5521 Fruitville Rd., Sarasota
379-6684

Major releases on 10 screens, two with six-track digital stereo.

Regal Hollywood-20 Theatres
Sarasota Main Plaza
1993 Main Street, Sarasota
379-6684

State-of-the-Art movie heaven; built in 1997 these 20 screens each have stadium seating, superior surround sound and "couch" seats. Attendence here broke national chain records. Plus, you can *always* pick up a copy of "Sarasota Downtown" (our free quarterly oversized guide to downtown and beyond) at the Hollywood-20.

Regal Parkway Cinema 8
Parkway Collection Shopping Center
6300 N. Lockwood Ridge Rd., Sarasota
379-6684
Eight screens at bargain prices.

VENICE

Regal Venetian VI
Venetian Plaza
1735 S. Tamiami Tr., Venice
493-0522
Major releases on six screens.

Film/Video Tape Rentals

You can often find the best deals in video rentals at area supermarkets where rental prices can be as low as 49 cents a night. (At press time Albertsons was running an 89 cents new release special - quite a deal.) While there are plenty of smaller "mom and pop" video stores around worth supporting, here is a list of some of the area's biggest stores which carry thousands of titles - enough to make any video junkie a happy couch potato.

BRADENTON

Barb's Video
5245 33rd St. E., Bradenton, 756-6266
3230 E. Bay Dr., Holmes Beach, 778-3325

Blockbuster Video
4951 Cortez Rd., Bradenton, 792-7551
6224 14th St., Bradenton, 755-7516
5900 Manatee Ave. W., Bradenton, 795-1118
www.blockbuster.com

Bradenton Video
7830 Cortez Rd. W., Bradenton, 792-1790
eMail: cobra1950@juno.com

Video Library
7051 Manatee Ave. W., 795-8988
5108 15th St. E., 756-0999
5608 Cortez Rd. W., 795-5518
4422 State Road 64 E., 750-6115

SARASOTA

ArgMex Video
408 Washington Blvd. S, Sarasota, 955-8604

March Festivals & Events

"Concert for Lovers"
Sarasota Concert Band performs at VanWezel The Irish tenor, live with Michael McFarlane. Presented by Sarasota Music Archive at Selby Public Library March 7. Information 955-5890.

Sarasota County Fair
Traditional county fair featuring agricultural exhibitions, arts and crafts. Midway and rides. No additional charge for entertainment.
March 12 - 20.
Information 365-0818.

St. Patrick's Day Parade
In Venice March 13.
Information 488-2236.

SpringFest '99
11th annual juried show and festival of fine arts and crafts at City Hall Park, Holmes Beach.
March 13 - 14.
Information 778-2099.

March Festivals & Events

Spring Festival
At Hunsader Farms
March 13 - 14.

Green Bridge Festival
Live entertainment, ethnic foods and popular children's scholarship art contest. March 13 - 14. Information 795-7427.

Spring Plant Fair
Selby Botanical Gardens.
March 13 - 15.
Information 366-5731.

Opera "Cavalleria Rusticana"
Presented by Sarasota Music Archive at Selby Public Library March 14. Information 955-5890.

26th Annual Telethon & Auction
Fundraising event broadcast on WWSB-Channel 40 March 14.
Information 379-2647.

ArgMex Video is the area's only exclusive Spanish language video store, specializing in Mexican films from the 1930s to early 1960s.

Blockbuster Video
4770 Tamiami Tr. S, 921-5527
8547 Tamiami Tr. S, 921-9100
3748 Bee Ridge Rd., 923-8182
3251 17th St., 952-1113
www.blockbuster.com

Lasers Edge
5541 Fruitville Rd., Sarasota
377-4419
www.lasersedgedvd.com

Network Video
21 Avenue of the Flowers, Longboat Key, 383-9328

Polish Imports
7350 S. Tamiami Tr.
923-1044
wwww.polart.com
World's largest import house of Polish products, including videos. English subtitles for many major Polish films are produced right here in Sarasota. All videos are for sale, not for rent, impressive nonetheless. Well worth a visit.

Video Library
3333 Tamiami Tr. N., 359-3309
6040 N. Lockwood Ridge Rd., 351-6961
3456 Clark Rd., 925-4570
4456 Bee Ridge Rd., 371-7626
5329 Fruitville Rd., 378-4511
4616 Cattleman Rd., 379-4368

Video Renaissance
2243 Bee Ridge Rd., Sarasota, 925-2780
The envy of bigger cities. Primarily foreign, old Hollywood and independent American and international films. Thousands of unusual titles for rent, and the owner is a walking film encyclopedia who will help you explore his world-class collection of videos. Simply amazing - titles you won't find anywhere else - a "must do" for cinephiles.

VENICE

Blockbuster Video
1647 U.S. 41 Bypass, 493-3308

Grand Video
808 Venice Ave. E., 484-0616

South Venice Video
1846 Tamiami Tr. S., 497-7700

Video Giant
478 U.S. 41 Bypass N., 484-4678

Video World of Osprey
1084 S. Tamiami Tr., 966-7777

Fountains, Outdoor Artful Spout Spots

SARASOTA

Island Park
Four dolphins frolic in a 21-jet salute to a leisurely life at sea, with colored lights at night. A $200,000 gift to the city from a restaurant which (oh what a surprise) has a great view of the fountain and whose logo just happens to include (oh, what a surprise)… guess what?

Municipal Auditorium Hazzard Fountain
Designed by Frank Martin, son of Thomas Reed Martin (who designed the auditorium), this is an electrically lit, intricately embossed fountain 11 feet in diameter with a circular water display, donated to the city in 1940 by Robert Hazzard.

Pineapple Park
Nancy Matthews' 11-foot fountain wall decorated with low-relief sculptures, surrounded by fish inlaid in the sidewalk cement.

Steigerwaldt/Jockey Fountain (aka: The Children's Fountain)
Located at Bayfront Park, downtown Sarasota, an amazing array of native Florida wildlife - all climbable - and dozens of water spouts which shoot up from the floor; a dream come true for any kid in a bathing suit and a "must do" for families with kids in the summertime. Park benches and plenty of ampitheater seating for people watching, this place is great for everyone - a long overdue and much welcome city destination for Suncoast children, beyond beaches. More please.

VENICE

Fountain Park
Vandals destroyed a sandstone fountain here in 1994. This new fountain depicts the Greek goddess of youth, Zeus' daughter Hebe, cast in iron.

BRADENTON

Bradenton City Hall
A building-side waterfall, made possible by the Department of Public Works in 1986.

Galleries

There is a good reason why the local Convention and Visitor's Bureau refers to our area "Florida's Cultural Coast": on a per-capita basis, Sarasota has the largest collection of galleries and art exhibition spaces in the Southeastern United States. The following list is represents just a few examples of the many artistic statements to be found here. (For comprehensive listings pick up a copy of *Sarasota Arts Review*, a free monthly pub, available everywhere - or call 364-5825.)

A Step Above Gallery
500 N. Tamiami Tr., Sarasota 34236
955-4477

Monday - Friday 9:30 a.m. - 6:00 p.m., Saturday 10 a.m. - 5 p.m. Original art and glass, ceramics and jewelry on the cutting edge. Affordable museum quality work shown in a contemporary setting.

A Touch of Art Gallery-Framery, Inc.
1283 S. Tamiami Tr., Sarasota 34239
951-6837

Sailor Circus
Celebrating its 50th season this year, Sarasota County students from third - 12th grades perform in this truly remarkable show. March 18 - 19, 24 - 26, April 1 - 3. Information 351-6350.

Serendipity Ball
Gala event featuring dinner, live and silnt auction, dancing and other entertainment. Benefits the American Cancer Society. March 19. Information 365-2858.

Dinner & Auction
Supporting Cardinal Mooney High School.
March 20.
Information 379-2647.

Power of the Pixel 3
An intruguing event featuring digital fine arts at Sarasota Visual Art Center
March 26 - April 8.
Information 366-2032.

Antique Show
At Sarasota County Fairgrounds
March 27 - 28.
Information 365-0818.

5403 Fruitville Rd., Sarasota 34232
379-4420
Monday - Friday 10:00 a.m. - 6:00 p.m., Saturday 10:00 a.m. - 5:00 p.m.
Lithographs and serigraphs by national artists. Many large watercolor originals; signed and numbered prints.

Ana Molinari Gallery & Salon
201 Gulf of Mexico Dr., Longboat Key 34228
383-0065 or 383-0225
52 S. Palm Ave., Sarasota 34236
365-7434/365-1415
A locally owned full service salon/gallery/boutique with three fabulous location. Art on display and for sale. Very hip, very now.

Apple & Carpenter Gallery of Fine Art
64 S. Palm Ave., Sarasota
951-2314
Monday - Saturday 10:00 a.m. - 5:00 p.m.
A fine arts and antiques business specializing in the rare and unusual. Unique in the fact that they are the only 19th/20th Century Art Gallery specializing in important paintings on Florida's Gulf Coast. This year the gallery soon celebrates its 30th Anniversary as Apple & Carpenter Gallery (founded in 1970). Connected to the art gallery is an antique gallery specializing in 18th and 19th century furniture, silver, glass and porcelain.

Art and Frame of Sarasota
1055 S. Tamiami Tr., Sarasota 34236
366-2301
www.in2art.com
Support store for local artists, large selection of supplies, frames.

Art Studios–Upstairs on Main St.
1369 Main St., Sarasota 34236
362-2003 or 954-0640
Tuesday - Friday 11:00 a.m. - 4:00 p.m.;
Saturday 10:00 a.m. - 2:00 p.m.
Featuring contemporay artwork on paper, canvas and fabric.

Art Uptown
1367 Main St., Sarasota 34236, 955-5409
Monday - Saturday 10:00 a.m. - 4:00 p.m.
Cooperative gallery features paintings, sculptures, ceramics and basketry by 32 local artists.

Baba Cool Gallery
239 Links Ave. S., Sarasota
Thurs-Sat, 11-6
Art, jewelry, clothing, in Towles Court.

Blue Dog Gallery
1958 Adams Ln., Sarasota; 952-0436
Thurs-Sat, 11-6
Ceramic murals, mosaics, in Towles Court.

Kathleen Carrillo Galleries
1945 Morrill St., Sarasota
365-9146; Thurs-Sat, 11-6
Paintings,monoprints, in Towles Court.

The Celery Barn
1945 Morrill St., Sarasota
365-9146; Thurs-Sat, 11-6

Paintings, monoprints, in Towles Court.

Chasen Galleries
16 Palm Ave., Sarasota 34236
366-4278
www.chasengalleries.com
Monday - Saturday 10:00 a.m. - 5:00 p.m.

Palm Avenue's award winning fine art gallery featuring unique canvases, sculpture. and more. Wide range of quality investment art.

Clayworks/Xcentrics Gallery
1951 Morrill St., Sarasota
954-2165; Thurs-Sat, 11-6
Unique ceramics/sculpture in Towles Court.

Coco Palm Gallery
1255 N. Palm Ave., Sarasota; 953-1122
Mon-Sat, 10-5

European and American furniture and paintings, art, antiques, estate sales, appraisals

The Collectors Wall
4976 S. Tamiami Tr., Sarasota 34231

Paintings, graphics and posters; since 1975, offfering the area's largest selection by local and internationally known artists. Custom framing to museum standards. In the Landings Shopping Center.

THE COLLECTORS WALL
FINE ART GALLERIES

PAINTINGS • GRAPHICS • POSTERS
*Since 1975, offering the area's largest selection by local & internationally known artists.
Custom Framing to Museum Standards*

927-2643
THE LANDINGS

Corbino Galleries
The Center Shops, 5350 Gulf of Mexico Drive, Longboat Key 34228
387-0822
Monday - Saturday 10:00 a.m. - 6:00 p.m.

Established in 1985, Corbino Galleries is Sarasota's leading fine arts gallery specializing in contemporary and Latin American painting and sculpture. The gallery introduces emerging artists and functions as a resource for nationally known artists associated with Sarasota such as Jon Corbino, Julio deDiego and Fletcher Martin.

Creative Framing & Gallery
2357 S. Tamiami Tr., Venice
493-2276
Monday - Friday 10:00 a.m. - 5:00 p.m.;
Saturday 10:00 a.m. - 2:00 p.m.

Local original watercolors, limited editions, fine crafts, unique shell shadowboxes. Specializing in creative work in all media, especially needlework.

Crissy Galleries
640 S. Washington Blvd. #150, Sarasota 34236
957-1110
Monday - Saturday 10:00 a.m. - 5:00 p.m.

18th-20th century American and European furniture, porcelain, paintings, sterling silver, glass and estate jewelry.

April Festivals & Events

1999 Women Creating Art Exhibit
Juried exhibit with reception. April 2 - 29 at Anna Maria Island.
Information 778-2099.

2nd Annual Florida Arts Invitational
At Sarasota Visual Art Center April 2 - May 2.
Information 349-0531.

17th Annual Orchid Ball
At Selby Gardens April 3.
Information 366-5731.

Venice Easter Egg Hunt
April 3.
Information 488-2236.

Children's Art Festival
At Ringling Museum
April 10.
Information 359-5700.

Different Strokes
22 N. Lemon Ave., Sarasota
355-2088 Mon-Sat, 10-5
Mosaics and garden art.

John Dineen Gallery
415 St. Armands Circle, St. Armands 34236
388-2992
Monday - Saturday 10:00 a.m. - 5:00 p.m.
Contemporary paintings and posters.

Jack Dowd Studio
1269 First St. #7, Sarasota 34236
952-1919
These original wood sculptures are often hysterical caricatures of sports figures and reflective of odd Americana. Also, Jack Dowd is a really cool dude.

Driftwood Galleries
6003 Cortez Rd. W., Bradenton
792-3461
Monday - Friday 9:30 a.m. - 5:30 p.m.; Saturday 9:30 a.m.-4:30 p.m.
Original paintings, crafts, prints, lighting, interior decor.

Ethno Imports
Southgate Plaza, Sarasota 34239
951-1572
Monday - Saturday 10:00 a.m. - 9:00 p.m.; Sunday noon - 5:30 p.m.
Featuring art, handicrafts and folk art from Africa, Latin America and Asia, including masks, standing figures, jewelry, baskets, pottery, ethnic clothing and gifts.

Exit Art
5380 Gulf of Mexico Dr., Longboat Key 34228
383-4099
Monday - Saturday 9:30 a.m. - 6:00 p.m.
Contemporary art gallery featuring new art wearables and fine crafts.

Florida Avenue Studios
Between 911 Central Ave. and 918 Florida Ave., Sarasota 34236
365-2054 or 964-0585
By appointment or by chance encounter. A diverse and established group of working artists' studios in historical Rosemary Court area.

Four Winds Gallery
1296 N. Palm Ave., Sarasota 34236
954-5343
Monday - Thursday 11:00 a.m. - 6:00 p.m.; Friday and Saturday 11:00 a.m. - 9:00 p.m.; Sunday 1:00 p.m - 5:00 p.m.
One of Florida's oldest Native American art galleries featuring the contemporary works of the Navajo, Zuni, Hopi and other Pueblo groups of the Southwest.

Galleria Silecchia
20 Palm Ave. S, Sarasota; 365-7414
Mon-Sat, 10-6
International collection of fine art.

Glass Reflections/Creative Concepts Galleries
53A S. Palm Ave., Sarasota

955-3839
Monday - Saturday 10:30 a.m. - 5:00 p.m. and 7:30 p.m. to 9:30 p.m.

Home decorative accessories by Susan Kutno, Murano jewelry and studio glass.

Hang-Up Gallery
45 S. Palm Ave., Sarasota 34236
953-5757
e-mail: glassue@gte.net
Monday - Friday11:00 a.m. - 5:00 p.m.;
Saturday 11:00 a.m. - 4:00 p.m.

Contemporary works of art by local and national artists.

William Hartman Gallery
48 S. Palm Ave., Sarasota 34236
955-4785
e-mail: oldink@gte.net
www.home1.gte.net/oldink/index.htm
Monday - Friday 9:00 a.m. - 5:00 p.m.; Saturday 10:00 a.m.-1:00 p.m.

Specializing in antique prints, natural history subjects and Florida landscapes.

Hilton Leech Studio
4433 Riverwood Ave., Sarasota 34231
924-5770
e-mail: hleech@juno.com
Monday - Friday 9:30 a.m. - 4:00 p.m.

Internationally known school and gallery. Watercolor paintings, sculpture and photography. Offers extensive series of workshops in watercolor and water media. Closed June - August.

Hodgell Gallery
46 S. Palm Ave., Sarasota 34236
366-1146
Monday - Saturday 11:00 a.m. - 5:00 p.m.

Contemporary fine art by regional, national, international artists

I-Sea
1920 Adams Ln., Sarasota; 358-0696
Thurs-Sat, 11-6

Paintings and 3-D images, in Towles Ctourt.

Island Gallery West
5348-E Gulf Drive N., Holmes Beach 34217
778-6648
10:00 a.m. - 5:00 p.m. Monday - Saturday

Local arts cooperative featuring paintings, sculptures, pottery, photography, American Indian beading and quilting.

Keller Ironworks
1975 Morrill St., Sarasota
747-0660; Thurs-Sat, 11-6

Functional art, in Towles Court

Kennedy Studios
1512 Main St., Sarasota
952-0358; Mon-Fri, 9:30-6; Sat 8-6

Graphics and framing.

April Festivals & Events

Opera "Die Walkure"

Presented by Sarasota Music Archive at Selby Public Library April 11. Information 955-5890.

Croquet Soirée

On the Ringling Museum grounds. April 17. Information 359-5700.

Sip & Shop

At St. Armands Circle April 18. Associated with Florida Winefest.

Florida Winefest & Auction

The third largest wine festival in the country; features exhibits, national entertainment and an auction with significant proceeds going to local charities. The best. April 21 - 25. Email to winefest@florida/winefest.org.
Internet: www.florida winefest.org.
Information 952-1109.

April Festivals & Events

Siesta Fiesta
An extravaganza of art, entertainment and fun in Siesta Village.
April 24 - 25.
Information 349-3800.

Shrine Circus
Sarasota County Fairgrounds.
April 24 - 25.
Information 365-0818.

Free Concert on Siesta Beach
By Sarasota Concert Band
April 26.
Information 955-6660.

Kokopelli Kustomware
437 Burns Court, Sarasota
362-7990; Mon-Sat, 10-5
The paint-it-yourself ceramic studio.

Lagana Galleries & Design Studios
1609 First Ave. W., Bradenton
747-2869
Call for hours or appointment.
Ceramics, calligraphy, fine prints, hand made tapestries, bedspreads, wearable art, hand crafted doll trunks, doll wardrobes, all from local artists.

The Lieberman Gallery
1881 Main St., Sarasota; 388-1530
2nd Floor - Main Plaza
Monthly exhibits of local works.

Manatee Community College Fine Arts Gallery
5840 26th St. W., Bradenton
755-1511; X-4251 or X-4225
Monday - Friday 9:00 a.m. - 4:00 p.m.
The MCC Fine Art Gallery maintains the highest standards of excellence in selecting art and artists for exhibitions and artists' lectures. Regional as well as nationally known artists are among those selected for exhibition. Other exhibitions include the Annual Art Faculty Exhibition and the annual Juried Art Student Exhibition.

The Marie Selby Botanical Gardens
811 S. Palm Ave., Sarasota
366-5731; X-10
e-mail: mitchell@virtu.sar.usf.edu
www.selby.org
Daily 10:00 a.m. - 5:00 p.m.
Museum shows wide range of botanical works in mixed media.

Mango Tree Artworks
1967 Morrill St., Sarasota
362-0481; Thurs-Sat, 11-6
Ship models/pastel paintings, Towles Court.

Marise Art Gallery
6506 Gateway Ave., Sarasota 34231
922-7169
Monday - Saturday 9:30 a.m. - 5:00 p.m.
Original oils, paintings and prints; art classes; framing and art supplies.

Mira Mar Gallery
1284 N. Palm Ave., Sarasota; 366-2093
Mon-Sat, 10-5
Fine art gallery.

Missing Link Gallery
The Shops at the Centre, 5380 Gulf of Mexico Dr., Longboat Key 34228
383-3872
October - May: Monday - Saturday 10:00 a.m. - 5:30 p.m.
June - September: Wednesday - Friday 10:00 a.m. - 5:30 p.m. or by appointment.
Specializing in authentic and antique tribal arts from all over the

world. Fine art, furnishings and antiquities.

Moore & Peters
132 S. Pineapple Ave., Sarasota 34236
955-3546
Monday - Friday 10:30 a.m. - 5:30 p.m.
Paintings by Blair Ashby, copper fountains and lighting fixtures by Joe Cooper, stonework by Richard Gudin. Custom furniture by Moore & Peters.

Paradise Gallery
1359 Main St., Sarasota 34236
366-7155
e-mail: paradise@paradisegallery.com
10:00 a.m. - 10:00 p.m. Monday - Saturday;
Summer 10:00 a.m. - 5:00 p.m., Monday - Thursday and 10:00 a.m. - 9:00 a.m. Friday - Saturday.

Largest selection of Contemporary Art in the area. Featuring works by John Lennon, Romero Britto, Charles Fazzino, Hessam, M.H. White, Harold Winer, Arnor, Huang, Jiang, Hibel, Peter Max, V.A. Porter, Schluss, John Richen, Jovan Stankis, Fred Szabries, Candace Knapp and many more. Jewelry, sculpture, serigraphs and original art.

Paradox Gallery
Southgate Plaza, Sarasota 34239
362-3715
Monday - Wednesday 10:00 a.m. - 6:00 p.m.; Thursday - Saturday 10:00 a.m. - 9:00 p.m.; Sunday 9:00 a.m. - 2:00 p.m.
Summer: Monday - Thursday 10:00 a.m. - 6:00 p.m.; Friday - Saturday 10:00 a.m. - 9:00 p.m.; Sunday 9:00 a.m. - 2:00 p.m.

Contemporary paintings, sculpture, jewelry and crafts featuring established local and regional artists including original ceramic designs by Susan Allen Griggs. Paintings and photography by Ric Miracle. Paintings by Jane Dye and Betty Hudson. Ceramics by Margaret Conte.

Micah Parker Artworks
253A Links Ave. S., Sarasota
955-7007; Thurs-Sat, 11-6
Digital fine art, in Towles Court.

Plum Door Art Studios & Gallery
1950 Adams Ln., Sarasota; 362-0960
Thurs-Sat, 11-6
Whimsical paintings, in Towles Court.

John and Mable Ringling Museum of Art
5401 Bay Shore Rd., Sarasota 34243
351-1660
www.ringling.org
Daily 10:00 a.m. - 5:30 p.m.
For more information, see page 127.

Pup Art
500 S. Pineapple Ave., Sarasota 34236
951-BARK (2275)
Tuesday - Friday 11:00 a.m. - 5:00 p.m.; Saturday 11:00 a.m. - 4:00 p.m.
A canine boutique offering gifts for dog lovers with a biting sense of humor.

Ringling School of Art and Design
2700 N. Tamiami Trail, Sarasota 34234

May Festivals & Events

Sand Sculpting Contest at Siesta Beach
Teams compete for prizes in this annual event. May 1; rain date May 2. Information 349-3800.

Pops Under the Stars
Charming outdoor concert presented by and at Manatee Community College, Bradenton. May 1. Information 753-0850.

Barefoot Beach Ball
Glitz combined with lighthearted fun ... what could be better? It also benefits Girls., Inc. May 7. Information 366-6646.

Pops Under the Stars
Charming outdoor concert presented by Manatee Community College, this one in Venice. May 8. Information 483-5988.

May Festivals & Events

Mother's Day Garden Tour
Sponsored by Children's Haven and Selby Gardens.
May 9.
Information 355-8808.

Relay for Life
An 18-hour team relay. Area businesses form teams and pitch tents on an area football field to keep the relay going through this sleep-over event. Bands and activities are also planned. Luminarias light up the night in honor or in memory of someone touched by cancer.
May 14 - 15.
Information 365-2858.

9th Annual "Evening Under the Stars" Concert
Pops concert presented at Manatee Community College and featuring the Florida West Coast Symphony.
May 15.
Information 753-0850.

359-7563
Monday - Saturday 10:00 a.m. - 4:00 p.m.
Student, faculty, local, national and international artist exhibits in mixed media. Consistently interesting.

Rick Sanders Studio
1310 Bay Rd., Sarasota 34239
364-9911
e-mail: wildartdc@aol.com
Monday - Saturday 10:00 a.m. - 5:00 p.m. or call for appointment
Original paintings and crafts, hand-blown art glass.

Santa Fe Trails Gallery
1429 Main St., Sarasota 34236
954-1972
Tuesday - Friday 10:00 a.m. - 5:00 p.m.;
Saturday 9:00 a.m. - 3:00 p.m.
Outstanding Southwestern Native American Art.

The Sarasota County Arts Council
1351 Fruitville Rd., Sarasota 34236
365-5118
www.sarasota-arts.org
Monday - Friday 10:00 a.m. - 5:00 p.m.
Gallery of local artists' works.

Sarasota Emporium
1521 Main St., Sarasota 34236
366-0954
Monday - Saturday 9:30 a.m. - 6:00 p.m.
"The biggest art show in town!" Huge inventory of posters, cards, books, calenders and original art from high-end to low-brow. Upstairs, step back into the '60s, with mood lighting, far-out clothing, incense, tapestries, candles, lava lamps, unusual gifts, extensive billiard supplies, and rock 'n' roll everything!

Sarasota Visual Arts Center
707 N. Tamiami Trail, Sarasota 34236
365-2032
e-mail: svacAhome.com
www.members.home.net/svac
Monday - Friday 10:00 a.m. - 4:00 p.m. ; Saturday Sunday 1:00 p.m. - 4:00 p.m.
Offering two large galleries and a gift shop. Exhibitions of fine art, sculpture and photos. Art instruction available. On the average 150-200 paintings are on display. Newly renovated attractive center for the Visual Arts. Admission is always free.

Selby Gallery at Ringling School of Art and Design
2700 N. Tamiami Trail, Sarasota 34234
359-7563
e-mail: selby@ringling.edu
Monday - Saturday during exhibitions (August - May) 10:00 a.m. - 4:00 p.m.
Featuring a wide range of art forms by nationally and internationally known artists, faculty and students in rotating exhibitions. The gallery also conducts other free, art-related programs, such as panel discussions, artists' presentations and symposiums.

June Simmon's Designs
68 S. Palm Ave., Sarasota; 388-4535

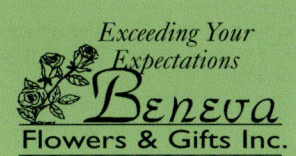

Exceeding Your Expectations
Beneva Flowers & Gifts Inc.

Our greatest asset to our customer is Beneva's commitment to quality and service. I invite you to visit our store and see some of our unique selection of exotic flowers imported directly from the Hawaiian Islands. Gourmet baskets delivered.

SARASOTA'S PREMIER FLORIST YEAR AFTER YEAR

6980 Beneva Road
Sarasota, FL 34238
Corner of Gulf Gate Dr. & Beneva Road

923-7401, 800-226-1177

Mon-Fri, 10-5; Sat, 10-4
Paintings in exhibition, exclusive jewelry.

State Street Gallery
1517 State St., Sarasota 34236
362-3767
Monday - Saturday 10:00 a.m. - 5:00 p.m.

A unique and wide range of modern and contemporary masters exhibited in a spacious recently renovated antique warehouse in downtown Sarasota.

Studio 3
1920 Adams Ln., Sarasota; 358-0696
Thurs-Sat, 11-6, Sarasota

Welded steel, 3-D collages, Towles Court.

Towles Court Art Center
1938 Adams Ln., Sarasota
Thurs-Sat, 11-6

Includes galleries:
Marge Bennett Art (955-0050)
Carol Burnett Art Gallery (362-2708)
Paddy Dugan Tile Ltd. (953-6186)
Walker Gallery (906-8039)
New World Productions (366-5520)
Claudia Porter (362--9659)
(Other art galleries in Towles Court are featured in this section of *The Guide*.)

Towles Court is an authentic Art Colony located two blocks south of the

May and June Festivals & Events

Antique Show
At Sarasota County Fairgrounds May 15 - 16.
Information 365-0818.

Casual Day '99
Sponsored by United Cerebral Palsy. May 21.
Call 957-3599 to register your company.

"In the Pink & All That Jazz"
Cocktail party at Selby Gardens benefiting the American Cancer Society and Breast Cancer Task Force. June 4.
Information 365-2858.

Venice Fine Craft Fair
Exhibitors from all over the United States.
June 12 - 13.
Information 488-2236.

Hollywood-20 Theatres on US 301, turn west on Adams or Morrill Street.

Venice Art Center
390 Nokomis Ave. S, Venice 34285
485-7136
Monday - Friday 9:00 a.m. - 4:00 p.m. , Sat 10:00 a.m. - 2:00 p.m.

This wonderful (and important) community resource offers dozens and dozens of classes, some taught by world renown artists. Gallery features rotating exhibits by members and/or visiting artists.

Women's Resource Center of Sarasota, Inc.
340 S. Tuttle Ave., Sarasota 34237
366-1700
e-mail: wrcofsar@aol.com
www.hanc.com/wrc
Monday - Friday 9:00 a.m. - 5:00 p.m.

Contemporary art by women artists.

Ziegenfuss Gallery of Fine Art
76 S. Palm Ave., Sarasota 34236
365-3266
Monday - Saturday 11:00 a.m. - 5:00 p.m.

Caters to the serious art collector and the eager novice. Many "important" local artists are shown here.

Garden Arts

American Hibiscus Society — Golby-Reasoner Chapter
7330 Westmoreland Dr., Sarasota 34243
351-1596
Meetings scheduled the second Sunday of each month.

American Hibiscus Society - Gulf Coast Chapter
200 N. Harbor Dr., Venice;
493-5836
Meetings scheduled the second Sunday of each month.

Bradenton-Sarasota Rose Society
2315 Admiral Way, Sarasota 34231
922-6006
e-mail: rosequeen@home.com
Meetings scheduled the fourth Sunday of each month (except July and August) at Sarasota Garden Club.

Florida Native Plant Society
1131 Blvd. of the Arts, Sarasota 34236
954-7526
Meetings scheduled the third Tuesday of the month, September through May.

Florida Native Plants, Inc.
730 Myakka Rd., Sarasota 34240
322-1915
e-mail: fnp@home.com
Home of Florida Native Plants, Inc., a nursery for natural gardens, growing species native to the Sarasota area since 1982. To help you pick "the right plant for the right place."

Longboat Key Garden Club
Longboat Island Chapel, Longboat Key 34228
383-3659

Meetings the last Tuesday of the month, October through April.

Manatee River Orchid Society
2107 55th Ave. W, Bradenton 34207
756-8547

Meetings scheduled the third Monday of each month at Trinity United Methodist Church, 3200 Manatee Ave. W.

Outdoor Architecture & Landscape Design
4038 Olive Ave., Sarasota 34231
923-0618

The only call you'll ever need to make to take care of all of your outdoor needs: residential and commercial design, installation and maintenance; creating stunning gardens, beautiful ponds, fountains, waterfalls and reflecting pools; stone and brick work; artistic, skilled, reliable and dependable – the very best.

Sarasota African Violet Society
2824 Wilkinson Rd., Sarasota 34231
922-5657

Meetings scheduled the third Tuesday of each month.

Sarasota Bromelaid Society
P.O. Box 1657, Tellevast 34270
748-2120
e-mail: len@mail.pcsonline.com

Meetings scheduled the second Monday of the month in the activities building, Marie Selby Botanical Gardens.

Sarasota Garden Club
1131 Blvd. of the Arts, Sarasota 34236
955-0875

Meetings scheduled the second Monday of each month, September - May.

Sarasota Orchid Society
P.O. Box 19895, Sarasota 34276
351-2483
www.clanorchids.com/sos1/htm

Meetings scheduled the first Monday of each month at Selby Botanical Gardens.

Venice Area Orchid Society
P.O. Box 443, Venice 34284
484-7840

BAMBOO © BILL WEST

July Festivals & Events

Suncoast Offshore Grand Prix

The single largest area event of the year, attracting thousands of spectators from far-flung places. Weeklong activities include a golf tournament, bed races, fishing tournament, a parade of boats, tremendous speed runs, wet pit viewing, some major parties ... and of course the world race circuit Offshore Grand Prix race itself. All proceeds from the festival go toward supporting the Suncoast Foundation for the Handicapped, Inc. Not to be missed! June 28 - July 5.

Sarasota Boat Parade & Block Party

Showcasing the powerful boats that will participate in the Offshore Grand Prix, and kicking off the event with an appropriately casual and high-spirited party. July 1.

Meetings scheduled the first Wednesday of each month at Venice Community Center. Annual show is the first weekend in February. It is spectacular.

Music

American Guild of Organists, Sarasota-Manatee Chapter
747-7194
Group promotes organ music and supports its study.

The Andrew Vincent Messina Foundation, Inc.
P.O. Box 5741, Sarasota 34277
925-8553
This wonderful children's music foundation provides music lessons and/or instruments for children who are financially unable to secure them; also supports the music therapy program at All Children's Hospital in St. Petersburg.

Barbershop Chorus of the Keys
378-1120 or 951-2087
150 local members of the Society for the Preservation and Encouragement of Barbershop Quartet Singing in America. Meets at First Baptist Church (Main St., Sarasota) every Tuesday evening.

The Bay Chorale
7402 Broughton St., Sarasota 34243
355-2235
Provides public with entertainment through music.

Bradenton Opera Guild
P.O. Box 9271, Bradenton 34206
351-5868
Opera appreciation and support. Meet first Monday of every month September - April at Congregational United Church of Christ, 3700 26th St. W, Bradenton; every meeting features live entertainment.

Cecilian Music Society
790 Manasota Key Rd., Venice 34293
493-9630
Providing monthly classical music programs at Venice United Church of Christ since 1951 on the third Thursday of each month from September to May.

Florida West Coast Symphony
709 N. Tamiami Trail, Sarasota 34236
Ticket Information: 953-4252
Celebrating its 50th anniversary in 1999! The 1999 season includes a broad range of music for every musical taste and interest; call for details. Also incorporates the Florida String Quartet, Florida Wind Quintet, Florida Brass Quintet and New Artists Piano Quartet.

Florida West Coast Youth Orchestra
709 N. Tamiami Trail, Sarasota 34236
953-4252
"The most extensive youth orchestra program of any orchestra in the country." Six youth orchestras; summer string, wind, brass and percussion programs, chamber ensemble program, scholarships and more

Gloria Musicae
954-4223

A 24-member professional vocal chamber ensemble which presents three or four concerts per season. Contracted performances upon request. Membership is by audition. Concerts conducted by guest conductors.

The Jazz Club of Sarasota
366-1552

The Jazz Club sponsors regularly scheduled concerts, jam sessions and special events throughout the year, plus educational programs in the schools and youth clubs, providing scholarships and support for a wide variety of community and cultural efforts – all this in addition to their annual Sarasota Jazz Festival every spring.

Just Kidz
6145 Roberta Dr., Englewood 34224
473-3900 or 473-1018

Community venture to interest children ages five to 15 in singing as an after-school activity. Rehearsals at the Tringali Community Center, E. Englewood, on Thursdays.

Key Chorale
P.O. Box 20613, Sarasota 34276
921-4845

Ensemble of 80 to 1000 voices performing great choral masterworks as written. Conductor, Dr. Daniel Moe.

LaMusica International Chamber Music Festival
P.O. Box 5442, Sarasota 34277
366-8450 Option 3

Two-week international chamber music festival presents concerts, workshops and special events April 6-18. Concert dates: April 8, 11, 13, 16 and 18. Daily open rehearsals, Chamber Music Colloquium, pre-concert lectures and youth activities. Bruno Giuranna, *Artistic Director*; Derek Han, *Associate Artistic Director*. Outstanding.

The Magic of Manatee Sweet Adelines
432 Spring Lakes Blvd., Bradenton 34210
751-1748

Barbershop-style singing for women. Invites women interested in barbershop singing, Tuesday evenings at Bradenton Christian School, 43rd St. W.

Manasota Theatre Organ Society
7455 Proctor Rd., Sarasota 34241
924-0674
e-mail: cpipes@aol.com

Enthusiasts of the theatre organ.

Manatee County Music Teachers Association
747-8825

Promotes music advancement within Manatee County.

Manatee Symphony Association
792-0364

Fundraising and support group for the Florida West Coast Symphony.

SARASOTA MUSIC ARCHIVE

OVER 300,000 RECORDINGS AVAILABLE OR RESEARCH, INCLUDING MUSIC IN ALL FORMATS - SHEET MUSIC TOO. REGULARALY SCHEDULED EVENTS AND SPEAKER SERIES. DAILY RECORD SALES. A "MUST DO" FOR ALL MUSIC LOVERS. AN OFFICIAL SUNCOAST TREASURE - FEATURED IN "SARASOTA DOWNTOWN."

265 S. ORANGE AVENUE
955-5890

July Festivals & Events

Powerboats at St. Armands
Your chance to get up close and personal with the spectacular boats, racers and crews that will participate in the great race. July 2.

4th of July Celebrations
Huge fireworks displays at Sarasota's bayfront, City Island, Siesta Key and Manatee River near Palmetto. Palmetto offers a day-long party (723-4570). July 4th, natch!

Selby Kids Nature & Art Day Camp
For ages 5 - 12. July-Aug. Information 366-5731.

Summer Plant Fair
Selby Gardens July 17. Information 366-5731.

Snooty's Birthday Celebration
Food, games, entertainment and a free view of Snooty in honor of this most famous area manatee. At South Florida Museum in Bradenton July 17. Information 746-4132.

The New College Slavic Vocal Ensemble
917-0881
Formed in 1993 by a visiting Russian professor, now continued by New College and USF students - group is open to participation from community residents, no prior experience in Slavic music or language needed. Emphasis on folk music from Bosnia, Bulgaria, and Russia.

Prevailing Winds
3047 Wood Pine Cir., Sarasota 34231
924-2585
Professional, versatile wind ensemble available for parties, weddings and other events, in styles ranging from light classics to easy listening, with from two to five members.

Sarasota Boys Choir
4826 S. McIntosh Rd., Sarasota
921-1344
Performing group for boys aged 7 to 14.

Sarasota Choral Society
3345 7th St., Sarasota 34237
953-4205
Community choral society presents annual performance of Handel's "Messiah," open to all.

Sarasota Chorus Sweet Adelines International
P.O. Box 18463, Sarasota 34276
921-3389
Four-part harmony (barbershop-style) chorus for women. Meets at Trinity United Methodist Church, 4150 S. Shade, Tuesday evenings.

Sarasota Concert Band
1345 Main St., Suite E, Sarasota 34236
955-6660
Now in its 45th continuous year, The Sarasota Concert Band presents "Pops" concerts in the Sousa tradition, playing music in all styles, from Beethoven to Broadway, with vocal and instrumental soloists. Forty-eight musicians comprise the full band, plus smaller ensembles ("Ragtime Band," "Reeds of Note," "Brass Five Alive"). Summer Season (July - September) in Sarasota County Parks. Winter Season held in Van Wezel Performing Arts Hall: "American Jazz" January 24, "Concert for Lovers" February 21 and "A Musical Journey" March 7.

Sarasota County Parks and Recreation Department
316-1268 or 426-4938
Offers "Sunset Serenade" series at the Venice Gazebo in the 200 block of Tampa Ave., Venice. Call for schedule.

The Sarasota Girls Choir
954-2342
Open to all girls nine to fifteen interested in learning vocal skills and performing for local organizations.

Sarasota Music Archive
265 S. Orange Ave., Sarasota 34236
955-5890
e-mail: smarchive@juno.com
www.sarasota-online.com/music
Monday - Friday 10:00 a.m. - 3:00 p.m.
An extraordinary collection of over 300,000 recordings, books, audio

and video tapes, scores, sheet music, magazines and memorabilia. Archive resources include the equipment to play every type of recording in existence. Educational services available to researchers and the community. Lectures, programs; a priceless treasure of music.

Sarasota Music Festival
709 N. Tamiami Tr., Sarasota 34236
953-4252

Internationally recognized as one of the outstanding chamber music festivals in the U.S. Often referred to as "The Tanglewood of the South," this musical celebration is the culmination of study for over 100 of the finest young musicians from the U.S. and abroad. These three weeks in June are the highlight of Sarasota's music season.

Sarasota Music Makers Organ Club
2686 Maple Loft Rd., Sarasota 34232
371-8392
Fellowship and fun for organ music lovers.

Sarasota Music Teachers Association
1667 Brookhouse Cir. #129, Sarasota 34231
966-3944
e-mail: abevon@msn.com

A professional club for music teachers that promotes performance, scholarships and other opportunities for students of members.

The Sarasota Opera Association
61 N. Pineapple Ave., Sarasota 34236
366-8450

A nationally and internationally acclaimed Sarasota Opera, marking its 40th anniversary season in 1999, this professional opera company has been lauded for its ability to bring fresh insight to traditional repertory. Brilliant reviews coupled with exciting and innovative satellite events during the season remind us why the Sarasota Opera has been hailed as "the stepping stone to the Met." The 1999 season features four full-length operas in repertory:

Bizet's "Carmen,"

Puccini's "La Rondine,"

Verdi's "Luisa Miller,"

Rimsky-Korsakov's "May Night."

In addition, the Presentation Series offers: "The Chenille Sisters" May 1

"Gone With the Wind" May 14.

The Sarasota Opera enriches the community through many outreach programs for all ages. The Apprentice and Studio Artist Programs are highly lauded for their intensive professional training. During the season, a variety of free concerts and lectures are scheduled. Sarasota Opera's ongoing philosophy: "Opera is for Everyone!"

In addition to its fine standards of artistic

SARASOTA OPERA'S DEANE ALLYN © BILL WEST

July and August Festivals & Events

Christmas in July

Sidewalk Sale

Venice downtown.

July 23 - 24.

Information 488-2236.

Bachelor Ball

One of Sarasota's most entertaining fundraising events! Date packages are auctioned off with 20 of Sarasota's most eligible bachelors. Benefits the American Cancer Society.

August 7.

Information 354-2858.

Annual Summer Children's Day

At Selby Gardens

August 7. Information 366-5731.

---

excellence and its idyllic, balmy Gulf-Side location, another of the Opera's major triumphs is its home, the beautiful history-rich Sarasota Opera House. This handsome Mediterranean Revival style building was first opened in April, 1926 as the A.B. Edwards Theater. This theater once offered the famed Ziegfeld Follies on her stage and was host to the world premiere blockbuster DeMille movie, "The Greatest Show on Earth." Later, rising young singer Elvis Presley sang here. Now fully renovated and expanded, the Opera house boasts the original chandelier from the movie "Gone With The Wind" in the lobby. The building was placed on the National Register of Historic Places in 1983.

Sarasota Opera Guild
4636 Pine Green Tr., Sarasota 34241
378-9601

Opera education, fund-raising and scholarships. Members meet third Tuesday of the month.

Sarasota Pops
Subscription and Non-VanWezel Tickets: 795-7677
VanWezel Performance Tickets: 953-3366

A 90-piece orchestra featuring musicians of all ages and all levels of experience who reside in all areas of Sarasota and Manatee Counties; four concerts each winter at VanWezel, a nice mix of symphonic works from the old masters and contemporary composers.

Sarasota Youth Opera of the Sarasota Opera Association
61 N. Pineapple Ave., Sarasota 34236
366-8450

Each year a special opera, written for and performed by youth, is selected for the Youth Opera Festival. Children aged seven to 18 are auditioned and approximately 50 are called to perform in October. A rapidly growing program, it has annually increased the number of children it reaches. Members of the Youth Opera also participate in the Opera's outreach programs. During the mainstage season, if a production has openings for children in the cast, the Youth Opera provides the singers. During the summer, the Summer Youth Opera Workshop offers advanced and beginner training The Sarasota Youth Opera Chorus meets weekly to study and perform an international repertoire.

Jonas Kamlet Library of the Sarasota Opera
61 N. Pineapple Ave., Sarasota 34236
366-8450

The Jonas Kamlet Library resources are available to all who seek information about opera. Located on the ground floor of the newly renovated Pavilion addition to the Opera Complex, the Library contains a large general collection of written material about opera singers, performances and history as well as opera librettos, music scores, recordings, and videos. Pre- and post-season video Opera Salons are presented on large screen video with surround sound. These presentations are free to the public and consist of a discussion of the opera along with the video showing.

SPEBSQUSA (Barbershop Harmony Society)
1661 Main St., Sarasota 34236
378-1120

Over 150 local men belong to this group which promotes musical four-part harmony singing.

Suncoast Chorale
493-1677 or 473-3800
70-voice chorus dedicated to production of fine music, from classical to pops choral works.

The Symphony Association of the Florida West Coast
4807 Peregrine Pt. Cir. W, Sarasota 34231
922-5195
Public support of the Florida West Coast Symphony Center.

VanWezel Performing Arts Hall
777 N. Tamiami Trail, Sarasota 34236
953-3366
See pg. 139.

Venice Area Music Teachers Association
565 Park Estates Square, Venice
Private lessons; recitals open free to public; provides scholarships.

Venice Gondoliers Barbershoppers
485-4847
International vocal organizations devoted to preserving barbershop style in both choral and quartet settings; entertains at local nursing homes, clubs and various organizations.

Venice Opera Guild
P.O. Box 2233, Venice 34284
484-0345
Promotes interest in opera, musical theater and cultural programs throughout south county. Supports and raises funds for the Sarasota Opera Association. Meetings are held the last Tuesday of every month.

Westcoast Gospel Chorus of Florida
P.O. Box 4321, Sarasota 34230
365-7543
e-mail: hlplove@aol.com
40-member gospel chorus of singers, teachers, preachers and musicians performs in concerts, workshops and seminars.

WMNF, Community Radio 88.5 FM
1210 W. Martin Luther King, Jr., Blvd, Tampa 33603
1-813-239-9663
www.wmnf.org
What radio was always meant to be, but rarely is. Volunteer programming staff changes every three hours, along with the music category. From cajun to country to celtic, from funk to punk, even in the rarified world of non-commercial radio this station is exceptional. Fundraising concerts and activities are scheduled throughout the year providing great ways to meet like minded (like-listening?) people. And you can now hear it live anywhere in the world on the web. Bumperstickers everywhere, strong support from our area helps to keep it going.

WUSF, Concert 90 (89.7 FM) and WGCU (90.1 FM)
4202 E. Fowler Ave., Tampa 33620
1-800-741-9090
www.wusf.usf.edu
While not officially a "local" station, it might as well be. Nonprofit, classical by day, jazz at night, plus news from National Public Radio. Much of the listener and corporate support for this station is derived from the Sarasota community.

September and October Festivals & Events

Venice Island Daze
September 10 - 11.
Information 433-2236.

Classic Antique Auto Show
At St. Armands Circle
September 11.

Selby Gardens Free Week
Information 366-5731.

Hillbilly Hoedown
At Sarasota County Fairgrounds
September 19.
Information 365-0818.

Downtown Fall Festival
Throughout Sarasota's charming downtown area October 9 - 10.
Information 951-2656.

11th Annual Art Festival
Visit St. Armands circle for the best combination of strolling, shopping ... and some absolutely fabulous art! Major annual festival of St. Armands featuring live music, food and judged art show; lots to see and do. October 16 - 17.

October and November Festivals & Events

Antique Show
Sarasota County Fairgrounds
October 24 - 25.
Information 365-0818.

Halloween Parade
In Venice October 30.
Information 488-2236.

Sarasota Blues Festival
Major national and regional acts perform in this all-day music and fun fest. Sarasota County Fairgrounds. November 6.
Information 365-0818.

Corvette Show
At St. Armands Circle
November 6.

Snooty Gala
Black-tie event to support education programs about manatees. November 6.
Information 746-4131.

Photography

Senior Friendship Center Camera Club
1888 Brother Geenan Way, Sarasota 34236
955-2122

Photographic instruction and hands-on participation in color and b&w photography. Meetings every Monday. Permanent photo gallery exhibiting works of Camera Club members.

Poetry

Sarasota Poetry Theater/Soulspeak
P.O. Box 48955, Sarasota 34230
366-6468
e-mail: soultalk@aol.com
www.augment.sis.pitt.edu/jms

Free workshops, readings and competitions.

Theater — Live

Asolo Theater Company
5555 N. Tamiami Trail, Sarasota 34243
351-9010 Administration
Box Office Tickets: 351-8000
e-mail: asolocenter@aol.com
www.asolo.org

Box Office Hours: Tuesday - Saturday 10:00 a.m. - 7:00 p.m., Sunday 10:00 a.m. - 6:00 p.m., Monday Noon - 5:00 p.m. Tours last about one hour. Group Rates Available; Tours are FREE

The Asolo Center for the Performing Arts includes Asolo Theater Company, a LORT Equity Theatre; FSU/Asolo Conservatory of Actor Training; Sarasota French Film Festival

Celebrating its 40th anniversary season this year, the Asolo Theater Company is the professional theater company of the Asolo Center for the Performing Arts. The Asolo presents six to eight plays annually from October through June, encompassing approximately 250 performances. The Theater Company uses national-quality actors, directors and designers to provide its subscribers and patrons with everything from world premiers to the classics in the very best of live theater. See as many as four plays in a single weekend. The 1999 season includes:

"Oh! What a Lovely War" - by Joan Littlewood, Theater Workshop and Charles Chilton, researched by Gerry Raffles - through January 29
"The Last Night at Ballyhoo" - by Alfred Uhry - through March 28
"Golden Boy" - by Clifford Odets - through February 14
"Abe Lincoln in Illinois" - by Robert Sherwood - January 15 - May 22
"The Ladies of Camellias" - by Lillian Garett-Groag - February 26 - May 21
"The Rivals" - by Richard Bransley Sheridan - March 6 - May 23
"Three Days of Rain" - by Richard Greenberg - May 12 - June 6

The Conservatory — The Florida State University/Asolo Conservatory of Actor Training is a three-year graduate program culminating in a Master of Fine Arts degree. The program was initiated in 1968, moving to Sarasota six years later to establish a permanent relationship with the Asolo Theater. Annually, the Conservatory faculty auditions more than 1,000 applicants nationwide from which a class of eight students is chosen. The conservatories are programs of Florida State University with additional scholarship and program support provided by local contributors. The 1999 season includes:

"Shaw, Shaw and More Shaw" - four one-act plays by George Bernard Shaw - January 20 - February 20
"Picasso at the Lapin Agile" - by Steve Martin - January 27 - February 28
"Kindertransport" - by Diane Samuels - March 10 - 28
"The Matchmaker" - by Thornton Wilder - April 14 - May 2
Asolo Theatre Company Production (TBA) - April 15 - May 10

Free tours of the Asolo Center for the Performing Arts are regularly scheduled on weekdays at 10:00 a.m., 10:30 a.m., 11:00 a.m. and 11:30 a.m., Monday through Saturday except during the summer and technical rehearsals between plays. In addition to getting an up-close perspective on the restored Scottish opera house which now houses the Asolo Theater Company, tour guests will also explore the backstage areas, the Asolo Conservatory of Professional Actor Training wing and the Burt Reynolds wing for Motion Picture, Television and Recording Arts. To confirm tour dates and times, or to organize a group tour, call 351-9010; X-4806.

Sarasota Visual and Performing Arts Center
Booker High School
3201 N. Orange Ave., Sarasota 34234
355-2967; X-120

Performance and visual arts high school; acceptance by audition. Call for performance schedules.

Florida Studio Theater
1241 N. Palm Ave., Sarasota 34236
366-9000
e-mail: fst2000@aol.com

Sarasota's focus on contemporary works, mainstage features contemporary works November - August. The Cabaret facility operates October - August. Sarasota Festival of New Plays features the Young Playwrights Festival (May), National Playwrights Festival (May) and Florida Playwrights Festival (July), a testing ground for Florida and national playwrights.

The 1999 season includes, on the Main Stage,
"Smoky Joe's Café" through January 16
"Gross Indecency: The Three Trials of Oscar Wilde"; Jan. 21 - Feb. 27
"Master Class"; March 4 - April 10
"Invasion of Privacy"; April 15 - May 22
 In the Cabaret, offerings include:
"Harry Who? The Music of Harry Warren" through January 23,
"A Brief History of White Music" opening February 11
 "Shakespeare's Greatest Hits: A Musical Revue" opening April 1.
Kids Comedy Club, "Write A Play" programs, seasonal reading series and performing arts classes for children and adults. FST produces touring children's theater for schools throughout Florida and the southeast U.S.

Golden Apple Dinner Theatres
Sarasota Location: 25 N. Pineapple Ave. Sarasota 34236
Sarasota Reservations: 366-5454

Venice Location: 447 U.S. 41 Bypass, Venice 34292
Venice Reservations: 484-7711

November and December Festivals & Events

Venice ArtFest '99
Judged show featuring fine artisans and craftsmen from around the country filling three solid blocks of beautiful downtown Venice. 30,000 people will attend. November 6 - 7. Information 484-6722.

Fall Plant Fair
Selby Gardens November 12 - 14.
Information 366-5731.

Antique Show
At Sarasota County Fairgrounds
November 28 - 29.
Information 365-0818.

Selby Gardens Holiday Celebration
Throughout the grounds and inside the museum. This will really spark your holiday spirit! December 1 - January 3.
Information 366-5731.

December Festivals & Events

Venice Christmas Walk
December 1.
Information 488-2236.

Annual Palm Avenue Christmas Walk
Usually held the first Thursday in December, featuring a nice mix of galleries and gifts.
Information 951-2656.

A Christmas Night at St. Armands Circle
December 3.

Selby Gardens by Candlelight
Truly spectacular! Fundraising event features thousands of luminarias, giant bromeliad tree and other delights. December 3 - 4.
Information 366-5731.

Christmas Boat Parade of Lights
Festively decorated boats parading along the waters of Sarasota Bay, draws around 50,000 spectators. Second Saturday of December.
Information 329-7672.

The quintessential Florida experience: cocktails, a delicious buffet dinner and a Broadway show. The New York Times calls it "one of the best values in the area." More than 25 years in operation. Reservations are a must. Group discounts available.

1999 Sarasota Season:
"Showboat", January 19 - March 14
"Hello Dolly", March 16 - May 9
"Phantom" May 11 - June 27
"Camelot", June 29 - September 5.

Island Players
10009 Gulf Drive, Anna Maria
778-5755

A half-century of community theater, a fun mix of lively actors and performances. This season offers:
"The Last of the Red Hot Lovers" January 15 - 31
"The Little Hut" March 12 - 28, and "Sylvia" May 7 - 16.

Manatee Players Riverfront Theater
102 Old Main Street, Bradenton 34205
Ticket and Audition Information: 748-5875
e-mail: beststage@aol.com

Home of the Manatee Players, Riverfront Theater offers interested community members a chance to participate in working productions, from performing on stage to painting sets to working backstage or in the box office, this is your chance to get involved with live theater.

Their productions reach over 21,000 audience members. Many special events are scheduled throughout the year. In 1999, the program includes:
"Cabaret" January 21 - February 7
"You Can't Take it With You" March 11 - 28
"Crazy for You" May 6 - 23.

PJ Productions
1834 Sanford Cir., Sarasota 34234
359-6717

Professional theatre for children.

The Players of Sarasota
838 N. Tamiami Trail, Sarasota 34236
Ticket Information: 365-2494

The Players, Sarasota's first performing arts company, has almost 70 years' history of producing and sponsoring musical theater, live music and other programs relating to theater and the performing arts. Open auditions for Players productions are held throughout the year. Volunteer opportunities are also available backstage and in the box office. Also, children's acting classes and very popular one-night performances of national acts on a regular basis. The Players Performing Arts School has classes in acting, voice and dance for all ages.

In 1999, see:
"Singin' in the Rain" January 21 - February 7
"Carnival" February 25 - March 14
"Big River" April 8 - 18.

The SOURCE Teen Theater
1958 Prospect St., Sarasota 34239
365-TEEN (8336)

A theater group of teen volunteers who, through the use of drama encourage their peers to make healthy decisions on important issues. Funded by Planned Parenthood of Southwest Florida.

Theatre Works
1247 First St., Sarasota 34236
952-9170
e-mail: theatreworks@aol.com

Live, professional, non-Equity stock theater in an intimate theater located in the historic Palm Tree Playhouse, presenting musicals, comedies and drama.

Venice Little Theater
140 W. Tampa Ave., Venice
488-2419

In its nearly half-century of continuous existence, Venice Little Theater has staged over 200 plays and musicals. The theater holds 286 seats and offers mainstage shows, STAGE II productions, Children's Theater productions, outreach programs, including: "The Silver Foxes" (performing group of 55 and over) "Troupe in a Trunk" (a performing group for South County Schools "Loveland Partnership" (for physically and mentally challenged students) and an outreach program for training young people in theater arts.

EYE CENTER SOUTH

Stuart A. Gindoff, O.D., F.A.A.O., F.A.C.O.P
Todd H. Morgan, O.D., F.A.A.O.
Murray L. Friedberg, M.D.
Scott E. Silverman, M.D.

Comprehensive eye care:
eye emergencies, low vision,
contact lenses and glasses.
The best!

378-EYES (3937)
Center Gate Office Park,
5540 Bee Ridge Road, Sarasota

Your Family Dentist
C. Wayne Smith, D.D.S.

922-0671
3900 Clark Road
Sarasota, Florida

when you're *serious*

about *shopping*

For over 20 years, Sarasota Square Mall has been the place to go to find everything you need for yourself, your family and your home. With our selection of stores, merchandise and great values, it's no wonder we're Sarasota's premiere shopping attraction. Seriously.

SARASOTA SQUARE MALL

Burdines, Dillard's, JCPenney, Sears and over 140 specialty shops.
Monday to Saturday 10am - 9pm, Sunday 12 noon - 5:30pm.   Tel: 922-9600
US 41 & BENEVA ROAD

VOTED *"THE BEST PLACE TO GO SHOPPING"* by the readers of The Sarasota Herald Tribune

Shopping

Shopping As An Art Form

This chapter is our salute to some of the area's unique shops, most of whom have not already been mentioned in other sections of *The Guide*. (Be sure to check out our "Unusual Finds and New Additions" section within this chapter - plenty to explore there!) This is by no means a complete list. We're sure there are plenty of other specialty shops out there just waiting to be discovered. Let us know, send your personal "finds" to: Steve Rabow's Official Guide Book, P.O. Box 15332, Sarasota, FL 34277. Look for your contributions in future editions.

Antiques and Artifact Shopping Areas

Fruitville Road Antique District
Between Central and Orange Aves. on Fruitville Rd.
Almost a dozen quality antiques shops from the wacky and weird to the stately and substantial. A great place to treasure hunt.

Gulf Gate Village Antique Village
Just southeast of Gulf Gate Mall
Numerous independent antiques stores, wide range of interests. Nice one-stop stroll.

Orange/Pineapple Shops
Between Orange and Pineapple Aves.
An established group of antique and thrift stores, all within steps of each other. Adjacent to Burns Court/Herald Square with even more shops and sites; together an important part of "Sarasota's Downtown Boom"

Venice Main Street Shopping District
Take Business 41 to Main Street
A nice collection of various antique and specialty shops, perfect for an afternoon "window shopping" stroll.

Bargain Hunting

Bargain Box
4406 Bee Ridge Rd., Sarasota 34233
371-1976
"Sarasota's premier consignment shop!" Popular bargain spot since 1965.

Designer Consignor
3639 Bahia Vista St., Sarasota
High-end, award wining consignment shop; new and nearly new sportswear, career wear, evening wear and huge selection of bridal wear. Winner of '95,'96,'97 & '98 Readers Choice Awards and '97 & '98 Best of the Best.

Fashion Exchange
3556 Clark Rd., Sarasota 34233
923-2562
Consignments and new collection of designer cocktail dresses, ballgowns, suits, bridal jewelry and accessories for all upcoming festive occasions. Call for consignment information.

Goodwill Industries - Manasota, Inc.
355-2721; fax 359-1822
15 locations in Sarasota, Manatee, DeSoto and Hardee counties

---

Say Hello to Good Buys!

Avenue Of The Flowers Shopping Center

Location: 525 Bay Isles Parkway, Longboat Key

Blue Spanish tiles cover everything, including the gas station. Retail clothing, shops, gourmet market, art gallery, Publix, and more.

Bayshore Gardens Fashion Center

Location: 1509 60th Ave. W., Bradenton

Strong emphasis on woman's fashion and accessories; restaurants; neighborhood services. Anchors: Target, Walgreens, Morrisons, T.J. Maxx.

Say Hello to Good Buys!

Beneva Village Shops

Location: Corner of Beneva and Clark Roads

Restaurants, fast food, supermarket, apparel, discount and gift shops.

Bird Bay Plaza

Location: US 41 By Pass North, Venice

Farmers Market every Saturday from 7:00 a.m.- Noon; Albee Antique & Estates (the family that founded Venice), natural foods, athletic club, fabrics and more.

offering the best shopping bargains from clothing to furniture to jewelry to electronics! Revenues support Goodwill programs such as G.E.D. classes, housing assistance, assessment and referral services, job training and job placement.

His Place
2888 Ringling Blvd., Sarasota 34237
955-1035

A "high-end" consignment store for men's clothing where you can often find Armani, Polo, Ralph Lauren and Tommy Hilfiger.

The SaBra Hadassah Shop
3750 Osprey Rd., Sarasota 34234
362-4642

Clothing, furniture, collectibles, jewelry, knick-nacks and more. We love this place. Open everyday except Saturdays and holidays. We really do.

Second Impressions
2888 Ringling Blvd., Sarasota 34237
955-1035

Amazing women's clothing consignment store featuring top-of-the-line names such as Ann Taylor, Liz Claiborne, Calvin Klein for a fraction of what you'd pay off the racks. A deal, to be sure.

The Third Street Rag
1506 Fruitville Rd., Sarasota 34236
957-0113

A nonprofit thrift store which supports the Resurrection House and homeless of Sarasota. Household goods and furniture consignment, donations of clothing. Nice.

Woman's Exchange
539 S. Orange, Sarasota 34236
955-7859

One of our very favorite places to bargain hunt! Established in 1962, The Woman's Exchange has contributed over 3 million dollars have been presented to support local arts organizations and charitable groups through sales from this award winning consignment shop. Antiques, jewelry, clothing, furniture, china, silver and much, much more. The turn-over is amazing, a must do!

Book Stores

BRADENTON

A Real Bookstore
5700 Manatee Ave. W, 34209
795-2665

Professional independent bookstore, specializing in service. Large children's room, magazine section and used hardbacks.

Books-A-Million
4225 14th St. W., 34205
748-3911; fax 746-5923

Largest bookstore in Bradenton, of epic proportions (30,000 sq. ft.) carrying everything from how-to's to who-dunnits, at prices that read like fiction. Thousands of magazines and newspapers from around the world. Hallmark card and gift shop, espresso bar. 9:00 a.m.- 11:00 p.m. everyday.

THE WOMAN'S EXCHANGE
NON-PROFIT CONSIGNMENT SHOP

ANTIQUES
JEWELRY
CLOTHING
CRYSTAL
FURNITURE
TOOLS
CHINA
COLLECTIBLES
AND MUCH MORE!

955-7859
539 South Orange Avenue
Sarasota, Florida 34236

Store Hours
Weekdays 10-4
Oct-May
Saturdays
9-1

Waldenbooks
Desoto Square Mall
747-7405

One of the world's best known bookstore chains; current hardcovers, paperbacks, magazines, tapes, calendars and more.

SARASOTA

Barnes & Noble
4010 S. Tamiami Tr. 34231
923-9907; fax 923-9510
www.barnesandnoble.com

Over 150,000 titles, progressive discounts on NY Times best-sellers. Massive music store with listening booths; extensive children's section cafe with Starbucks coffee; healthy software offerings; special bookstore events every day for all ages.

Bee Ridge Books
4104 Bee Ridge Rd 34233
377-8998

New & used books.

Book Bazaar
1488 Main St. 34236
366-1373; fax 957-3779

MICRONETICS COMPUTERS
Your One Stop Computer Store!

Micronetics Computers is the store that will offer you fast, friendly service and satisfaction guaranteed. We will build your computer according to what you need offering the best quality and lowest prices in town! Stop by and visit us soon!

**Sales • Upgrades
Service • Networking
Custom Configurations**

941-922-1588 • 941-922-1604 fax
e-mail: micronet2@msn.com

**Coral Cove Mall - Suite #6
7350 S. Tamiami Trail
Sarasota, FL 34231**

Say Hello to Good Buys!

Burns Court

Location: adjacent to Orange/Pineapple junction

Antique stores, Japanese restaurant and more, all within a 1925 Mediterranean Revival bungalow enclave; Burns Court Cinema is a wondrous 3-screen home for foreign films and independent fare.

Center Shops Of Longboat Key

Location: The center of Longboat Key

Fashion, food, apparel and gift shops in a resort setting.

---

e-mail: aparkers@aol.com

30,000 used, out of print and scarce books in all subjects.

Book Nook
3650A Webber Street 34232
922-8564

Paperback exchange, 60,000 in stock.

Books-A-Million
25 Gulf Gate Mall 34231
922-7804;fax 924-7037
www.booksamillion.com

A novel bookstore of epic proportions, carrying everything from how-to's to who-dunnits, at prices that read like fiction. Thousands of magazines and newspapers from around the world. *"We wrote the book on low prices."* 9:00 a.m.- 11:00 p.m. everyday.

Brant's Used Books
3913 Brown Ave. 34231
365-3658; fax 365-3658; e-mail: brantbks@worldnet.att.net

100,000 used, rare and collectible titles, serving Sarasota book lovers since 1956.

Campus Bookshop
6301 Tamiami Trail N. 34243
355-5252; fax 355-7584

Serving USF and New College students, open to the public. Large selection of trade books for a campus store, special orders. Computer software and disks; great "used" prices.

Coral Cove Books
7282 Tamiami Tr., Sarasota 34231
924-3848; e-maillI: jcz@gate.net
www.bibliofind.com/coralcove.html

One of the newest bookstores on the Suncoast is a treasure of rare and hard-to-get "finds" plus recent titles. Extremely reasonable prices, very friendly staff, well worth a visit.

Duck Creek Books
1962 Main Street, Sarasota
954-5575

Located upstairs in Main Bookshop, Americana, antiquarian books, autographs, bindings, manuscripts, maps and prints. Open by chance or appointment - always call ahead.

Elysian Fields
1273 Tamiami Trail S. 34239
Information: 361-3006; fax 366-4982

"Conscious living" superstore with all the trimmings – crystals, books, crystals, gifts, crystals, cassettes, crystals, videos, crystals, cards..."*To be here now, shop here often."*

Helen's Books and Comic Shop
1531 Main Street 34236
955-2989

100,000 used books, great collection of new and collector's comic books plus some records.

Learning Depot
501 Beneva Road N., Unit 520 34232

Second Largest Remainder Bookshop in the U.S. Publishers' Overstock Savings of 40%-90%

Open 7 Days a Week 9AM-11PM

Main Bookshop
1962 Main Street Sarasota

957-1919
Children's books, educational toys. Teachers' supplies.

Main Bookshop
1962 Main St. 34236
366-7653; www.mainbookshop.com

Second largest selection of publisher's overstock books in the world! We're talking huge and extraordinary - an area treasure - daily discounts range from 40-90% off retail prices, free coffee, lots of lounge areas (bring your sleeping bag and move in - owner Scott won't mind, much). Very popular. Open 9:00 a.m. to 11:00 p.m. every day.

Read All Over
2245 Bee Ridge Rd. 34239
923-1340; fax 927-2615

Large selection of national and international magazines and out of town newspapers; special book orders encouraged.

Sarasota News and Books
1341 Main St. 34236
365-6332; fax 365-6215

Area's newest independent bookstores (formally Charlie's News), certainly one of the most interesting. Significant domestic and foreign news/magazine collection, bestsellers, huge art and architecture selection plus European style cafe. Huge success due to owners Dick and Caren Lobo, who also launched the Sarasota Reading Festival.

Say Hello to Good Buys!

Charthouse Shops
Location: 201 Gulf of Mexico Drive, Longboat Key
Home of Tangerine Realty, Ana Molinari Salon, popular restaurant and boutiques.

Cortez Plaza
Location: 4425 14th St. West, Bradenton
Multi-anchored "Power Strip."

DeSoto Square Mall
Location: 303 U.S. 301 Boulevard W., Bradenton
Largest mall in Bradenton, 700,000 square feet of shopping including four major department stores, more than 100 specialty stores, six screen movie theaters, two automotive centers and restaurants.

Third Floor Books
1962 Main St. 34236
955-1978
Located on the third floor above Main Book Shop, used and rare books, books on tape, videos, sheet music, and other paper memorabilia.

Used Book Heaven
5216D Ocean Blvd 34242.
349-0067
Siesta Key's small answer to the world at large.

Waldenbooks
Sarasota Square Mall 34238
923-5229
Southgate Plaza 342339
952-1540
One of the world's best known bookstore chains; current hardcovers, paperbacks, magazines, tapes,calendars and more.

VENICE

Anderson's Paperback Book Exchange
2387 Tamiami Tr. S., Venice; 34293
900 Tamiami Tr. S., Nokomis; 34275
493-2766 (Both locations)
50,000 used paperbacks available for sales or exchange. They also accept magazines and hard-cover books in trade.

The Bookshop
241 Venice Ave. W., Venice 34283
488-1307
Strictly new books, special orders and Hallmark cards.

Delectable Delights

For those with international tastes we've collected a list of area shops which can take you around the world without ever leaving town.

A Taste of Europe
2212 Gulf Gate Dr., Sarasota 34231
921-9084 ;fax 921-9084
Imported food items (some from the Bronx) at fabulous prices. Deli and grocery. Russian and Eastern European delights, a tasty adventure.

Albritton Fruit Co.
Main Grove - 5430 Proctor Rd., Sarasota 34238
923-2573 (outside Florida call (800)237-3682); fax 925-1098
Locals love this fabulous family business - a Florida institution for over 11 decades! We figure that all visitors should be required to taunt their relatives and friends by sending fruit baskets with a requisite "wish you were here" note attached. (It gets them every time!) Albritton juice stands around town are the next best thing to picking oranges and grapefruit from your own backyard. Free samples. Not to be missed!

Alexander Catering & Cafe Spazzo
5252 Tamiami Tr. 34231
925-1498;fax 925-8390
One of the first area restaurants to include an adjacent market. Imported and domestic gourmet items to take on the go.

Wide Selection of New Books

Best Sellers Always 10% Off

Gift Books - Interior Design, Style, Art

Cards - Journals - Stationery

Complete Newstand - Domestic and Foreign

Indoor/Outdoor European-style Café

Serving Gourmet Coffee & Pastries

Wines & Beers

Steps to Theatres, Galleries, Restaurants

SARASOTA NEWS & BOOKS

1341 Main St. (corner Palm Ave.) 365-6332
Mon-Sat 7:30 am-11 pm • Sun 7:30 am-5 pm
www.sarasotanewsandbooks.com

Beers Unlimited
4428 Cortez Rd.W., Pinebrook Square, Bradenton
761-0502

Over 450 different beers (wow!), wine, cigars and more.

Bodega Sabor Latino
6170 15th St. E, Bradenton
755-2677

Fresh produce, canned foods, fresh roots and specialty Cuban sandwiches. Unusual (for the area) large collection of Latin religious candles, nice selection of magazines in Spanish too.

Berkeley Square
2236 Gulf Gate Dr., Sarasota 34231
927-2612

Teas and treasures (such as clotted cream) and a wide selection of all things British.

British Emporium
4625 Cortez Rd., Bradenton
794-6657

Pasties, puddings, chocolates, sweets, pickles, British cheese, jams, British soft drinks, bangers, curries - all imported directly from Manchester, England.

Broken Egg Market
210 Avenida Madera, Siesta Key 34242
346-2750

Siesta Key's smartest breakfast/lunch spot is also a brilliant place to

Say Hello to Good Buys!

Downtown Shops of Sarasota

Location: Main Street, Sarasota

A complete renaissance has taken place involving hundreds of intriguing stores, galleries and restaurants plus fabulous nightlife. Farmers Market every Saturday.

Fountain Court Shopping Center

Location: 6300-6700 Manatee Ave. West, Bradenton

West Bradenton's largest shopping center.

Glengary Shoppes

Location: West of U.S.41 just north of Bee Ridge Rd. Barnes & Noble (with Starbucks Cafe) and Best Buy make this mall an attractive newcomer.

pick up delicacies to go - along with an impressive array of hot sauces, syrups and condiments, many sporting a Broken Egg label. Offering "upscale" tea. A Siesta Key requirement.

Cafe Kaldi
1568 Main St., Sarasota 34236
366-BEAN; fax 366-1955
www.cafekaldi.com

Sarasota's first and only coffee company seems poised to take over the coffee loving world. The roaster is in full view within this established "hot spot" on Main Street. You simply can't imagine the number of different kinds of coffee available from around the world, all fresh roasted on premises. Large variety of loose leaf gourmet teas, custom catering available, high speed cable modem computers available, a great (really!) place for lunch too. Gift baskets a specialty.

Capt. Brian's Seafood Market
8441 N. Tamiami Tr,, Sarasota 34243
351-4492

The rule here is very simple: "The fish you buy in the market today came off the boat this morning!" Capt. Brian's defines "fresh fish." Great restaurant too, featuring world famous salad bar.

Caribbean Pie Co.
2820 Clark Road, Sarasota 34231
925-9069 ; fax 927-pies
www.caribbeanpie.com

This is the top of the mountain. Don't argue, your diet will just have to wait. Perhaps the best Key Lime pie in history. (Business for sale at publishing time - please don't change the recipe!)

Casa Italia
2080 Constitution Blvd., Sarasota 34231
924-1179

Everything you could possibly wish for from a great Italian neighborhood grocery and delicatessen. Knowledgeable proprietors will help you find your way through an amazing selection of olive oils, sauces, cured olives and fresh cheeses. Cooking classes available – if we had the time we'd sign up in a heartbeat! Large (hungry) cult following.

The Chop Shop
5906 Manatee Ave. W., Bradenton 34209
794-MEAT; fax 761-0331

For 28 years the phone number of this beloved institution has been driving local vegetarians completely nuts. Oh well. "The finest quality food products available."

Crowley Nursery & Gardens
16423 Jomar Rd., Sarasota 34240
322-0315; fax 322-0315

Edibles, oddities, vines, watergardens and exotics. Very large selection. Butterfly garden and small petting zoo for your enjoyment.

D & P Hot Stuff
308 E. Laurel Rd. Nokomis 34275
485-4164; fax 493-6061

At press time there were 164 hot sauces in stock, including the top three top rated "hottest sauces in the world." Your stomach will never forgive you, but so what. Live hot, be hot.

Delicious Fishes, Inc.
11020 MJ Road, Myakka City 34251
322-1640

Our area's only Tilapia fish farm! Seven acres of water including indoor tanks and outdoor ponds which are brimming with around a half a million Tilapia fish - a delicious Middle Eastern fresh water fish, grain fed on this family farm and sold primarily to restaurants. Individual home or office delivery of fresh, boneless filets is available for around $4.50/lb. (a steal!) depending on the market.

DeSoto Lakes Organic Farm
4180 47th St., Sarasota 34235
351-4121; fax 351-4121

Area's only organic produce farm. They will fax or mail you a copy of their harvest schedule. (During summer months they import produce from northern organic farms.) School teachers take note: class tours available upon request, ask for Bill. Produce stand open October-June; Friday 3-7:30 p.m., Saturday 8 a.m.-1 p.m.

F&D Food Market
5040 Fruitville Rd., Sarasota
371-4459

Imported Mexican and Spanish foods, Cuban sandwiches their specialty. Homemade (on premises) pork rinds every Saturday.

Fletch's Bikesenjava
1936 Hillview St., Sarasota 34239
366-7702

A full service bicylce shop and coffeebar! Fresh gourmet coffee, espresso and cappuccino in the middle of a bike store. Way cool.

The French Affair Restaurant/Market
2637 Mall Dr., Sarasota 34231
925-3414

Gallic fare including pate', goat cheese, mousse, sausage and a splendid wine collection – authentic and reasonably priced. A real find.

Gastronomia Italian Market
7119 Tamiami Tr. S, Sarasota 34231
927-8331; fax 927-9179

Another restaurant/market combo - but this one is different because it's hard to tell where the restaurant begins or where the market ends. And that's the point. A local treasure.

Geier's Sausage Kitchen
7447 Tamiami Tr., S, Sarasota 34231
923-3004

German foods, large selection. Very popular for fresh meats to-go, they have their own packing plant.

The Gourmet Market
1469 Main St., Sarasota, 34236
953-9101

Premier specialty and unique gift shoppe featuring oils, vinegars, imported cheese, pate's and an international array of fine wines.

Il Panificio
1703 Main St., Sarasota 34236
366-5570; fax 366-0326

When Nicholas Castronuovo decided to retire from his real estate

---

Say Hello to Good Buys!

Gulf Gate Mall

Location: US 41 and Clark Rd., Sarasota

After years of neglect this mall has just been purchased. Unofficial reports say that we'll see a factory outlet center evolve with some major players. Steinmart, Books-A-Million, Publx, Marshalls and Hooters stuck it out during the "dark ages" and should now reap the rewards. Stay tuned.

Say Hello to Good Buys!

The Landings

Location: South Tamiami Trail at Proctor Road

A collection of solid chain stores and nice independents. PetSmart, Pier One Imports, Circut City, Office Depot, Blockbuster Video, Gecko's - very popular restaurant and sports bars.

Midtown Plaza

Location: Bahia Vista and U.S. 41, Sarasota

Various specialty shops and restaurants in a tropical setting. Home of the world famous (and newly refurbished) Michael's On East.

Nokomis Village Shopping Center

Location: 1097 Tamiami Trail North, Venice

Huge Publix (50,000 square feet) and a major bingo hall.

---

business in New Jersey in 1989, he knew that if he didn't make his own Italian breads he'd never find them in Florida, so he opened an authentic Italian bread bakery halfway between Sarasota and St. Petersburg. So much for retiring. His breads are now some of the most popular on the Gulf coast, used by households and restaurants alike. This Italian market/restaurant on Main Street acts as the Sarasota hub for the successful operation, run by Mr. Castronuovo's grandkids.

Karl Ehmers Quality Meats & Alpine Steak House
4520 S. Tamiami Tr., Sarasota 34231
922-3797

Old world butcher shop has a large selection of USDA prime and Choice midwestern beef, pork, lamb, veal, poultry, Colorado buffalo, geese and rabbits. Karl Ehmer's internationally known German deli meats and sausage.

La Mexicana Foods, Inc.
639 10th St. E., Palmetto
723-1576

Our rule of thumb: if it's Mexican and it's in Palmetto it's probably great. True for their restaurants, true here too. Homemade chorizo, tamales, pork rinds and coming soon - homemade tortillas.

La Abjita Latin Market
2870 Ringling Blvd., Sarasota
954-6916

Authentic South American grocery store, specialties include magazines, beers you can't find anywhere else in Sarasota, imported home and food items from South America; fresh fruits and vegetables too.

La Potosina Market
2291 Ringling Blvd., Sarasota 34236
951-6938

The area's first Hispanic market; fresh produce, fresh fruit, tortillas, wide variety of chiles (poblanos, serrano, jalapeno tomatillo, guajillo) and palentas.

La Superior Bakery
412 Washington Blvd. S, Sarasota 34236
365-1619; fax 330-1169

Opened on Valentine's Day 1996, this new bakery really is an act of love for Maria and Roberto Alonso who produce extraordinary Mexican pastries and breads – baked twice daily.

The Market at the Centre Shops on Longboat Key
5370 Gulf of Mexico Dr., Longboat Key 34228
383-2887; fax 383-6425

Catering to the Longboat Key crowd with ample selections of prepared foods and baked goods. A celebration of "picnic!"

McClains of Florida Home Made Ice Cream
2301 Gulf Gate Dr., Sarasota 34231
923-6450; fax 923-6454

All homemade ice cream produced with less air than you will find in most commercial brands - more intense flavors - pints and quarts actually weigh more. You'll get hooked. "No sugar" ice cream and sorbet available too along with bags of nuts, gifts, etc. Free samples.

McClain's of Georgia Pecan & Nut Company
3511 Clark Rd., Sarasota 34231

923-6450; fax 923-6454

One of Sarasota's best kept secrets - until now. Supplys nuts, no-sugar spreads, preserves and more to some of the state's biggest fruit companies - who slap on their own labels. You can buy direct. Far superior to commercial supermarket brands, buy direct. Addictive.

Alicia Montiel Market
2268 Second St., Sarasota
917-0911

Just like visiting a supermarket in Mexico, wide range of Mexican products including domestic items, sauces, soups, sodas and tortillas - fresh fruits and vegetables too.

Morty's Bagels
24 S. Blvd. of the Presidents, St. Armands Circle, 34236
388-3811

24 varieties of homemade New York style bagels, 11 flavors of cream cheese; sandwiches and soups; fresh roasted gourmet coffee; platters made to order; gift baskets for all occasions; open 7 days at 7 a.m.!

Oriental Food & Gift Mart
2234 Gulf Gate Dr., Sarasota 34231
924-8066

Ko Cha Adams has thousands of ingredients for Oriental cooking. Food and cooking supplies from Korea, China, Japan, Thailand, Philippines and Indonesia. India too. Takeout sushi lunch. Unique on-site cooking classes available every Tuesday and Thursday, a.m. and p.m. Learn to create what you'd like. Wonderful fun, healthy too!

Pastry Art
1508 Main St., Sarasota
955-7545

6753 Manatee Ave. W, Bradenton
795-1719

Award winning European Bakery and Coffee House; tortes, desserts, pastries, cakes, cookies and party trays. The perfect beginning, middle and/or end to your day - as if you needed an excuse to go here?

Pierogi, Inc.
6611 Superior Ave., Sarasota 34231
929-0101

Lots and lots and lots and lots and lots and lots and lots of pierogis.

Sahara
1121 Tamiami Tr. S, Sarasota
954-1423

Lots of positive buzz about this restaurant/market which just opened at publication time. Middle Eastern specialties, spices and more at reasonable prices. (Opened too late to get them in the restaurant section, next year for sure - we hear very good things.)

Scandinavian Gifts
2166 Gulf Gate Dr., Sarasota
923-4313

Breads, desserts and much more - direct from Norway, Sweden, Denmark and Finland.

Scots Corner
3452 17th St., Sarasota 34231
953-6707

Say Hello to Good Buys!

Paradise Plaza

Location: U.S. 41 and Bay Road

Gift boutiques, art store, tanning den, smoke shop, health food, salon and nice book store.

Prime-Outlet

Location: Exit 43 off I-75 on 60th Ave. E, Ellenton

100 popular factory outlet stores including Saks Off 5th, DNKY, Harry & David and Sony.

Orange Avenue/ Pineapple Pointe

Location: Pineapple and Orange junction, Sarasota

A dozen or so antique and other fine shops featuring outstanding vintage clothing, furniture, glassware and a couple of great restaurants.

Say Hello to Good Buys!

The Osprey/Hillview Shops and Restaurants

Location: Osprey Ave. and Hillview Street, Sarasota

Back in 1878 this was the location of the first post office for what was then called Sara Sota, the center of the community at that time. Located just west of Sarasota Memorial Hospital; six absolutely fabulous restaurants, J.D. Ford's, Purveyors of Fine Wine and Spirits, The Tasting Room and the all new Morton's coming September.

The single malt of food shops – haggis, meat pies, sausage rolls, birdies and all things Scottish, including Irish bacon (the best!) - wonderful.

Sulters Egg Farm
6830 Richardson Rd., Sarasota 34240
371-2596; fax 378-1763

Area's only egg farm, you can buy direct from the hen. Sort of.

Swedish De-Lite
514 Central Ave., Sarasota 34236
953-4466

Specialties from Sweden including Snow Puffs, Night Puffs, Oaties and stuff that will make you say "Ya, sure, you betcha!"

Walt's Fish Market
4144 S. Tamiami Tr., Sarasota 34231
921-4605

Walt's has been here forever so marketing is minimal, in contrast to the abundance of fresh fish – they claim to sell 100,000 pounds each week! Alligator, smelt, amberjack and conch are on the menu. Cases of iced fish await your inspection.

Wong Kai Imports
5404 33rd St. E., Bradenton 34203
758-1432; fax 758-1036

Oriental grocery store featuring Chinese, Japanese, Indian, Philippine and Vietnamese foods, supplies; fresh Oriental vegetables.

Flea Markets

The Dome Flea Market
5115 State Rd. 776, Venice 34293
493-6773

Open every Friday, Saturday and Sunday from 9:00 a.m.- 4:00 p.m. Oct 1 - May 1; summer hours, Sat. & Sun. 9:00 a.m. to 4:00 p.m.;closed the month of September. 300 covered booths with 135 dealers, an institution for the past 18 years. Antiques and Collectible Warehouse on same property. Free admission and parking for all. Snack Bar on premises.

Midway Flea Market
10816 U.S. 41, Palmetto
723-6000; fax 723-9093

Front section is open seven days a week, 8:00 a.m.- 4:00 p.m. Entire market is open every Friday, Saturday and Sunday 8:00 a.m. - 4:00 p.m. Approximately 1000 spaces for vendors, 500 are covered roof and inside shopping. Four restaurants, free admission and parking.

Red Barn Flea Market
1707 1st St. E., Bradenton 34208
747-3794; fax 747-6539
www.redbarnfleamarket.com

Newly rebuilt after last year's devastating night fire (no one injured, thankfully). Over 650 booths, wide range of products and food. Open Wednesday, Saturday and Sunday. Indoor and outdoor; wild peacocks too.

Roma Flea Market
5715 15th St. E.; Bradenton
756-9036

WARNING!
Do you have Bad Water? Stains? Spots? Smell? Taste? Call The Ecowater Squad!

Free Water Testing and Estimates

- Softeners/Filters
- Reverse Osmosis
- Sodium Free Soft Water
- Aerators/Pumps
- Repairs on all makes and models
- Salt Deliver
- 10-Year Warranty Available
- Demand Operated Twin Tanks
- 24-Hour Emergency Service
- 100% Financing

Introductory Offer

$4.95*

*First 3 Months
Plus Reasonable Installation

Rent • Rent to Own • Buy
with this coupon
Not valid with other or prior purchases.
Offer expires 12/31/99.

ECOWATER
SYSTEMS

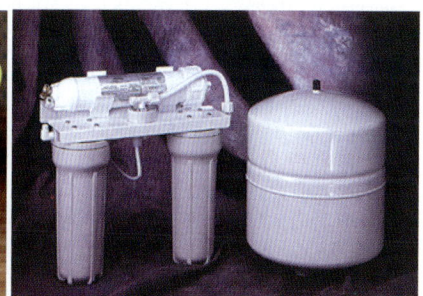

ABSOLUTE WATER CARE
Sarasota / Venice • 493-2224
Port Charlotte / Punta Gorda • 743-0111
All other areas toll free 1-877-99-WATER

Give the Ecowater squad a call. Get your water evaluated free.

Say Hello to Good Buys!

Gulf Gate Mall Village Shops

Location: Directly east of Gulf Gate Mall Located just behind Gulf Gate Mall, every shop is independent and interesting - locals love this area. Popular restaurants, gourmet food specialty shops, lots of antiques stores, fashion bargains and a brew pub. This may be one of Sarasota's best kept secrets – until now. You'll find many unique shops with a distinct international emphasis. In fact, we guess that more foreign languages are spoken here than anywhere else in the area, outside of Nick Bollettieri's Academy.

Open Saturday and Sunday from 7:00 a.m. until 5:00 p.m. with over 150 indoor booths. Free admission, free parking.

Home Essentials

Copenhagen Imports
7211 Tamiami Tr. S, Sarasota, 34231
923-2569
Fine furniture and accessories from Denmark with timeless style.

Designers Touch
3162 Bee Ridge Rd., Sarasota
922-2411
Quality custom window treatments including vertical blinds, draperies, cornice boards, top treatments, wood blinds, shutters, pleated shades and woven woods. Customer satisfaction guaranteed.

Graham Interiors
50 S. Palm Ave. Sarasota 34236
955-9495; fax 365-8906
Classic interiors for Florida lifestyles, residential, commercial, marine – by appointment.

Living Walls Furniture & Design
1311 Main St., Sarasota 34236
957-4411; fax 952-0272
Fun and exciting furnishings for the individual taste. Contemporary furniture, accessories and lighting like you've never seen before. Specializing in wall units, home entertainment systems and home offices. Complete interior design services available.

Nettle Creek
1922 Bay Rd., Sarasota 34231
366-4148; fax 365-9404
Interior Design services offered: window treatments, wall coverings, faux finishes, re-upholstery, bed coverings, furnishings, flooring, yachts & motor homes; serving Sarasota since 1978.

The Palmer House Collection
5277 Tamiami Tr. N, Sarasota
358-9939
Gwendolyn Sears, ASID and Raul Molina, Interior Display and Design emphasis "living with beautiful things." Custom interiors, antiques, chandeliers, fine furniture and upholstery.

Robinson Spry Interiors
1303 Main St., Sarasota 34236
365-2030
www.robinsonspry.com
Dan Robinson and Linda Spry have spent 30 years in the area, helping to make the transition between house and home. Consultation available for residential, commercial, renovation, new construction and yachts.

Tidmore-Henry & Associates
1014 East Ave. N., Sarasota
954-4454
Two of the area's leading lights for interior design - Robert Henry, ASID and William Tidmore, ASID. "The finest interior design, service and accessories."

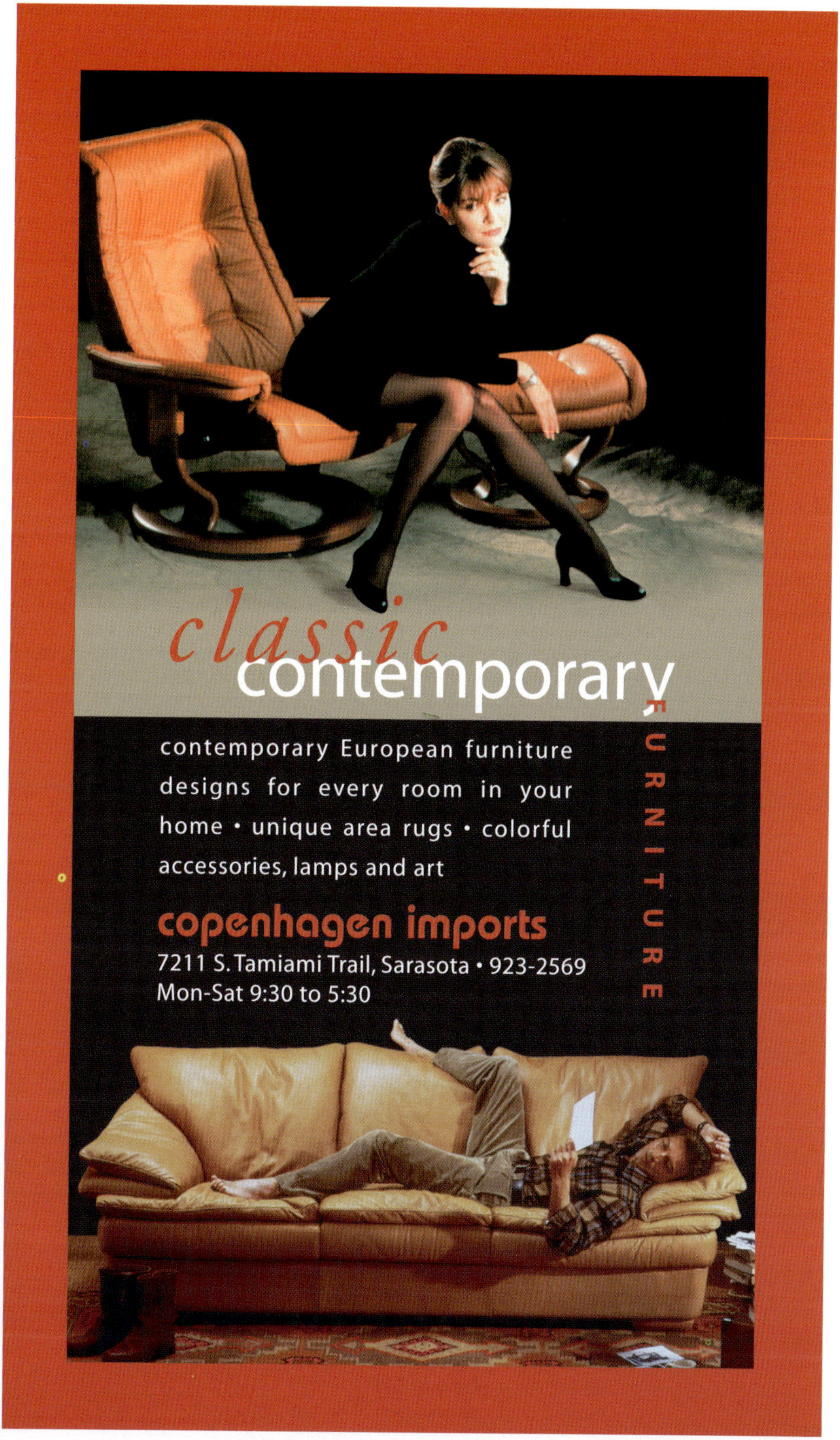

classic
contemporary
FURNITURE

contemporary European furniture designs for every room in your home • unique area rugs • colorful accessories, lamps and art

copenhagen imports
7211 S. Tamiami Trail, Sarasota • 923-2569
Mon-Sat 9:30 to 5:30

Say Hello to Good Buys

Palm Avenue

Location: Parallel to Pineapple Ave., Sarasota

Fine art galleries, antiques, boutiques, Ana Molinari salon, family owned Caragiulo's Italian restaurant and dozens of some of the most exclusive shops in the area fill this resplendent section of downtown Sarasota. Evening "Art Walks" are popular, a great place for a casual after dinner stroll.

Sally Trout
1272 N. Palm Ave, Sarasota 34236
953-4418; fax 365-4530

ASID designer Sally Trout lives for the details. By appointment only for exquisite residential and commercial interiors.

The Wallpaper Store
7350 S. Tamiami Tr., Sarasota 34231
924-3640; 925-3485

One of the largest libraries of wallcoverings and fabrics on the Gulf Coast. 2000 plus books offers over 400,000 patterns from moderately priced in-stock to exclusive designer lines with expert guaranteed installation. Plus 500,000 fabric samples, unique furniture, lamps, accessories, framed artwork, window treatments, blinds, custom bedspreads and upholstery.

Music, Music, Music

Boogie Woogie CDs
3404 Clark Rd., Sarasota 34231
921-7410; fax 927-0410
4919-B 14th St. W (US-41), Bradenton
753-8112

Area's first "no records, no tapes, only compact discs" store. You can listen to any CD before purchase on their many CD players. A good place to find "Italian" imports (outtakes and rare concert CDs) from some of your favorite popular artists, unavailable anywhere else. (Even the artists themselves don't have copies of these!)

David Braun, Piano Technician
95-PIANO

Give your piano a harmonic convergence – all tuning is done by "ear" – no electronic devices are ever used. Tuning, repair, rebuilding; the official tuner for Sarasota Opera House, Sarasota Ballet and New College/USF. Available for private residences by appointment.

City Sounds
1636 Main St., Sarasota 34236
954-7464; fax 365-1647

Area's largest collection of contemporary dance, rap and urban music on cassettes, CDs and vinyl. Owned by a very cool dude.

Daddy Kool Records
5900 S. Tamiami Tr., Sarasota 34231
921-7271; fax 92107291

Way ahead of the curve, tomorrow's hits today - owner is English D.J. who specializes in American independent and imported recordings of music on the cutting edge. Ska, Jazz and World Beat too. A "must" for anyone in love with the modern world.

Jam-A-Lot Music & More III
1864 Dr. Martin Luther King Jr. Way, Sarasota 34243
365-5695

Hip-hop/rap music that makes cars go thump-thump-thump.

Piano Services of Florida
7350 S. Tamiami Tr. Suite 4, Sarasota
924-0722; 1-800-966-2911
e-mail: contact@pianoservices.com

Over 400,000 patterns
All major lines plus designer lines of papers
Unique furniture, lamps and accessories
Framed artwork
Window treatments
Custom bedspreads
Complete decorating services
Jonathan Kendall Slentz, A.S.I.D. Allied
New home and remodeling packages
To the trade programs

THE WALLPAPER STORE
TEXTILES AND DECORATION
...where wallpaper is just the beginning!

Coral Cove Mall
7350 S. Tamiami Trail, Sarasota
Phone (941) 924-3640, Fax (941) 925-3485

www.pianoservices.com

Official piano technicians for the Van Wezel Performing Arts Hall since 1989 and one of the only restoration shops of its kind in the country, these folks are at the top of their profession. Quality tuning, repairs and restoration - on site.

Pritchard's Pianos & Organs
2108 Bee Ridge Rd., Sarasota 34239
924-1204; fax 925-2567

The largest piano and organ dealer south of Tampa - the area's only Steinway dealership. If anyone cares, (Tom Cruise, take note) we'd like a 200th anniversary limited edition delivered to our house, please. Cost: $200,000. (You can be sure that we'll say "Thank you Tom!")

Record Revival
1962 Main St. Sarasota 34236
955-1978

Located on the 3rd floor of Main Bookshop, significant collection of rare vinyl plus large selection of used CDs and tapes. Owner Fred is always looking to buy used CDs - nice jazz, soundtrack and sheet music collection too. Well worth the trip upstairs for fabulous finds.

Unusual Finds and Late Arrivals

This is where we've stuck anything/everything that doesn't seem to fit anywhere/everywhere else. But don't be mislead by this seemingly "lost puppy" category – these are, to be sure, some of the most unusual and most interesting "finds" you could possible hope for. If we were allowed to have a favorite section of *The Guide* this might very well be it. But, of course, we're not allowed to play favorites. Are we? We've also thrown in a couple of new, hot restaurants which didn't make our Restaurant Guide in time - more info on these will be included in the next edition where they properly belong - but the buzz is strong enough to warrant at least a mention here. Discoveries galore, read on.

Absolute Water Care
22 South Venice Blvd., Venice
493-2224

True to his name, this guy really cares - and what he does can change the quality of your life, at least when it comes to the water you drink, which should be lots. Free water testing/estimates; state-of-the art systems, sodium free soft water, reverse osmosis, 100% financing and 24-Hour emergency service. Best tasting water we've experienced.

Access Unlimited
5550 Bee Ridge Rd., E-4; Sarasota
371-0111

Custom web site development and hosting, direct connection high-speed (56K-V.90) nation-wide access internet service provider. The future is here - grab your (key)board - surf's up!

Advanced Audio Design
4915 S Tamiami Tr., Sarasota 34231
925-2673; fax 923-3690
www.advanced-audio.com

You walk in and are greeted by a wall-hugging ten-foot video screen. Turn the corner and there's a custom home movie theater, complete with three rows of leather recliners, a state-of-the-art interactive video computer and surround sound which is even better than what you'll find at "real" movie theaters. Free popcorn too! But there's more. Custom design, sales and installation of the absolute latest and very best in home entertainment and automation (including interior/exterior lighting right out of the 21st century, which is right around the corner. Read: theses guys are way ahead of the curve.) You'll have trouble leaving - this is way, way cool - all it takes is one visit.

Ana Molinari
201 Gulf of Mexico Dr., Longboat Key 34228
383-0065/383-0225; fax 383-5563

52 S. Palm Ave., Sarasota 34236
365-7434/365-1415

A locally owned full service salon gallery boutique with three fabulous locations to serve those who demand the very best. An elegant, cosmopolitan experience with "now" flair. Most of the News40 air talent staff have their "dos" done here, as do many others.

Angler's Repair
8208 Cortez Rd., Bradenton 34209
795-6711; www.anglersinfo.com

Fabulous custom fishing rods are made by hand. (Need we say more?) Backwater fishing guide Captain Thom Smith provides fishing rod and

---

Say Hello to Good Buys

The Plaza at Palmer Ranch

Location: U.S. 41 and Beneva Rd., Sarasota

Lots of neighborhood services and four HUGE anchor stores: Target (113,000 sq. ft.), Publix (66,000 sq. ft.) Phar-Mor and Roberds. Mega, mondo, mucho.

St. Armands Circle

Location: St. Armands Key Features many of the area's "best of the best" fashion, jewelers, specialty shops, galleries and restaurants. Italian baroque statues donated by John Ringling are scattered about the circle; Circus Ring of Fame is located on the center sidewalk.
Information: 388-1554

reel repair. Preacher Fuller builds and designs rods and has for many, many years.

Architecte Miniatura
955-5555 (Best phone number in Sarasota!); fax 365-1100;   e-mail: miniatura@webtv.net

A model building studio specializing in golf course and community site table models. The owner worked directly with Jim Henson and was responsible for the Kermit Phone. Creative, impressive, substantial, yet very, very small.

Arte Jewelers
1460 Main St., Sarasota 34236; 955-0595
www.arte/coins.com

Handmade "frames" for ancient coins? Pendants, rings, necklaces and more, all original framework for authenticated rare coins, often recovered from sunken ships then transformed (brilliantly) into personal works of art by Lorenzo Aguinsky. Visit Florida's only four-time international jewelry award winner in his very unpretentious store on Main Street. A significant find.

Artisans' World Marketplace
104 S. Pineapple, Sarasota 34236
365-5994; www.fairtradefederation.com

Nonprofit retail outlet for the world's indigenous peoples, one of the area's truly unique stores (allowing for the fact that *all* the listings in this section are truly unique.)

Robert Barnett's Rocking Horses
957-4222; fax 957-4222

Hand carved to order traditional mahogany rocking horses. International reputation, treasured heirlooms to hand down for coming generations.

Beauty & the Beads
506 S. Pineapple Ave., Sarasota 34236
952-0101

Artistic, elegant, unusual creative jewelry, beads/supplies, workshops and repairs. Fun for everyone.

Beall's
Department Stores:
935 Beneva Rd. N, Sarasota - 365-3725
6355 Manatee Ave. W, Bradenton - 761-1606
7308 Manatee Ave. W, Bradenton - 792-6691
5800 14th St. W, Bradenton - 758-1404
4125 Tamiami Tr. S, Venice - 497-6162

Outlet Stores:
3790 Tuttle Ave. S, Sarasota - 925-2511
6180 Lockwood Ridge Rd. N, Sarasota - 351-8424
5566 Cortez Rd. W, Bradenton - 792-0197
7300 Manatee Ave. W, Bradenton - 794-0981
3923 Manatee Ave. W, Bradenton - 736-3288
5834 14th St. W Bradenton - 751-5520
515 Tamiami Tr. S, Venice - 485-3530/488-6779
1757 Tamiami Tr. S, Venice - 493-9789

**INCREASE SALES
IMPROVE CUSTOMER SERVICE
EVERYDAY - ALL YEAR LONG**

Complete Web Presence Solutions

- Custom Web Site
- Development and Hosting
- Direct Connection Solutions
- High Speed Dial-Up Access
  (56K-V.90)) Nationwide access)
- Internet Service Provider

ACCESS UNLIMITED
371-0111

Your Internet Gateway to the Web

5550 Bee Ridge Road., E-4
Visit our Web Site: www.acun.com

Say Hello to Good Buys

Sarasota Crossings Shopping Center

Location: I-75 & Fruitville, Sarasota

10 screen movie theater and nice neighborhood center. Take the kids to Forget Me Not, an old fashioned homemade ice cream parlor with two colorful macaws on the premises.

Sarasota Main Plaza

Location: Main Street and Hywy 301, Sarasota

A big part of Sarasota's Downtown Boom. Home of Applebee's and the always impressive Hollywood-20 Theatres.

8240 Tamiami Tr. S, Venice - 918-9805

Not much is bigger, or more historic, than Beall's - the area's premiere locally based department store which has successfully branched out throughout Florida. But it all started here. Outlet stores offer substantial discounts, Bradenton department stores are the pride of the company, out performing most everywhere else. Local pride, local shopping - makes perfect sense to us, we go there too.

Beneva Flowers & Gifts
6980 Beneva Rd., Sarasota 34238
923-7401; 1-800-226-1177 (24-hour)

Owner Arthur Conforti may be the hardest working man in the local flower industry. Awarded the "Top 50 Award" from Teleflora - the worlds' top floral wire service - is not achieved easily. The proof is in the product and service. Specialties include exotic floral arrangements, flowers come in fresh from Hawaii. Gift baskets/balloons too.

Bennington Tobacconist
5 Fillmore Dr., St. Armands Circle
388-1562

In these evolved modern times, is it politically correct to talk about cigars or only correct if mentioned without the word "political" attached? Since 1965 the Bennington family couldn't give a hoot about what's in vogue or who's doing what to whom with their tobacco products - some of the finest in the world, mind you. The oldest retail establishment on St. Armands Circle has seen a lot, they know trends (and Presidents) come and go, but a great smoke remains great - for those who still care. And this is a great place to find some.

Blue Art Design
505 Burns Lane, Sarasota 34236
330-9300
www.snaidero.it

Provides full service design support for all architectural products displayed in showroom including Snaidero USA, California Art Tile DOMA furnishings, Abet Laminati Flooring and Con-Tech Lighting.

The Blue Parrot
1377 Main St., Sarasota, 34236
366-0813

A brand new downtown restaurant/hot spot featuring giant (10 oz burgers, romano crusted chicken and shrimp dijon; 7 draft beers and over 30 bottles, large wine list; live music. Didn't make the deadline for our Restaurant Guide - more info next edition - the word is "hot!"

Book Binders of Florida
1931 Limbus Dr., Bradenton 34243
755-3508; fax 739-6805

Have an old bible in disrepair? An 11th edition (*the* edition) Encyclopedia Britannica deserving TLC? Here's where you go to revive old friends and/or to create new ones. Books repaired and/or "inaugurated" with hand-bound craftsmanship, one by one. An impressive, surprisingly inexpensive meaningful gift to you or yours. (Here's an idea produce a collection of your "greatest hits" for your mom...maybe you'll make it back in the will.)

Burns Lane Cafe
516 Burns Court Lane, Sarasota
955-1653

Info didn't arrive in time for the Restaurant Guide this year but we

Sand, Sun, Relaxation ...ahh Vacation!

Free Gift Wrapping
In-Store Postal Service
Basic Alteration Service
Friendly Return Policy
Special Order Service

BEALLS
DEPARTMENT STORE
Simply Florida

Open Daily 9-9
Sunday 11-6

Fountain Court Center 6355 Manatee Avenue West, Bradenton #941-761-1606
Southwood Mall 5838 14th Street West, Bradenton #941-758-1404
Sarasota Commons Shopping Center 935 North Beneva, Sarasota #941-365-3725
Venice Village Shoppes 4125 Tamiami Trail South, Venice #941-497-6162

$5 off any purchase of $35 or more*

*Coupon must be presented to receive discount. Limit one coupon per customer, per visit. Cannot be redeemed for cash, applied towards existing charge balances, prior purchases or to purchase a gift certificate. Offer valid at Bealls Department Store only. Sales associate use allowance code 3. Expires January 30, 2000.

Please write hometown zip code here: _____

Say Hello to Good Buys

Sarasota Outlet Center

Location: University Parkway at I-75, Exit 40

More than 50 factory outlet stores offering brand name and designer merchandise at savings up to 70% off regular retail prices. New owners promise an exciting renovation and major additions.

Information: 359-2050

---

worth noting - located in beautiful historic house (you can dine on the porch under shady trees) just a hop, skip, jump to the Burns Court movie theaters. Thoughtful, creative cuisine, call for nightly specials.

The Chair People
3323 Central Ave., Sarasota 34236
954-2067

Yes, an entire store filled with chairs - is there a scientific term for this kind of fetish? Area's exclusive Herman Miller dealer, world famous home and office systems, many classic Eames designs still available.

Carman's Shoes
434 St. Armands Circle, St. Armands, 34236
388-3561

Carman's Shoe's has the largest collection of Onyx Line Shoes in Florida. Carman's also design features not found in any other Onyx shoe.

The Christmas Shoppee
4200 S. Tamiami Tr., Sarasota 34231
923-6084

Tired of palm trees? Perpetual sunshine getting on your nerves? It's *always* Christmas here! Fun and "cool" all year - and filled with holiday cheer for all holidays, (Easter, 4th of July and many other holidays are celebrated here with plentiful, tasteful merchandise.)

Coats of Arms by Lewiston Heraldry
101 W Venice Ave, #3, Venice 34283
486-1405

With over 30 years of experience, Edward M. (Ted) Dodds – Illuminated Manuscripter, Calligrapher and Master Heraldic Painter – has created illuminations and has personally hand painted Coats of Arms for such notables as former President Ronald Reagan and Nancy (Davis) Reagan and Mr. Frank Sheridan, CEO St. Andrews Golf Club, Scotland. His vast library contains no less than 750,000 Coats of Arms and an equivalent number of surnames, their origins and their meanings. A visit to this shop is always a warm, friendly experience.

Coral Cove Antique Gallery
7272 Tamiami Tr. S, Sarasota
927-2205

Massive antique mini-mall, open 5 nights till 8 p.m. Good stuff!

Cravats' Custom Shirts & Clothiers
Suite 222, Plaza Level, Sarasota Quay 34236
366-7780; fax 366-2874

Hank Battie does things the old world way: shirts/suits, hand tailored with care. Also accessories (ties, cuff links, straps) for the well-groomed male. Perhaps the very best mens store in the area.

J.D. Ford, Purveyors of Fine Wine & Spirits & The Tasting Room
1925 S. Osprey Ave., Sarasota 34239
362-WINE; fax 366-2052

Sarasota's premier purveyor of fine wines, spirits, beers, ales & lagers and cigars. Two fabulous wine clubs, gift baskets and wine accessories. In only its third year voted Sarasota's "Best Place to Buy Wine." The Tasting Room resembles a French bistro, with small, intimate tables and a mahogany "tasting bar" where you can sample a variety of tapanades with dipping sauces, gourmet sandwiches and exotic desserts. Amazingly popular, amazingly knowledgeable staff is reason why.

The Christmas Shoppee

An exquisite collection of unique treasures, memorable gifts and fine collectibles.

Ornaments
Silk Flowers
Handmade Wreaths
Department 56
Collectibles and Much More

4200 S. Tamiami Trail
Sarasota, Florida 34231
(941) 923-6084
Hours: M-S 10-5, Sun 12-5

Gifts for all Seasons

Fresh food at fabulous prices.

The BLUE PARROT

Lunch & Dinner 7 Days
Entertainment Nightly

366-0813
1377 Main Street
Downtown Sarasota

Say Hello to Good Buys

Sarasota Quay

Location: U.S. 41 and Fruitville Rd.

Downtown's only waterfront shopping, dining and entertainment destination. Year 'round special events including Suncoast Offshore Grand Prix Boat Parade Wet Pits and Winner's Circle Craft Festivals, Valentine's Dance, Fashion Shows and many community oriented events.

Information: 957-0120

Davirich, Inc.
7280 Tamiami Tr. S, Sarasota
926-1299

Custom crafted furniture and fine antiques. In Coral Cove Mall.

Different Strokes
22 N. Lemon Ave., Sarasota
330-0144

An inspired combination of shabby chic, garden art and mosaic art pieces. Located in the Lemon Avenue Galleria.

Dr. Hair Care
966-0333

Haircuts, perms and color in your home or office (!) - 35 years experience, licenced, bonded and insured. To our knowledge, the only one who provides this service on a full-time, on-call basis.

Eager Beaver Car Wash
Sarasota:
6449 S. Tamiami Tr., Sarasota 34231, 921-6665
1555 N. Washington Blvd., 34236, 951-7777
Bradenton: 6310 14th St. W., 34207, 753-6665
Venice: 1791 S. Tamiami Tr., 34293, 497-6665

The area's best full-service car wash serving Sarasota, Bradenton and Venice with four locations. Also offering Complete Detail Center services.

Erika B.
372 St. Armands Cir., St. Armands, 34236
388-4432

A fashion extravaganza and landmark shop on The Circle for many years; featuring Flax (regular and generous sizes), Donna Jessica, Nothing Matches, Staley Gretzinger, NiteLine, Painted Pony, K.D. Spring, Jane Yoo and Timmy Woods. Jolie and staff are tremendous.

Express It Cards & Gifts
5227 14th St. W, Bradenton
755-5005

5344 Gulf Drive, Holmes Beach 34217
779-1119; fax 779-1119

Unique gifts the lefty! "South Paw" notebooks, rulers, kitchen appliances, info books, playing cards & more. Smarter? Or aliens from another world? You decide. Discount greeting cards too.

Joseph Fanelli Antique Timepieces
60 S. Palm Ave., Sarasota
362-0303

Restored antique clocks and timepieces. Mr. Famelli was clock repair guru in NYC - John Lennon and others used him. You can too.

Fletch's Bikesenjava
1936 Hillview St., Sarasota 34239
366-7702

A full service bicylce shop and coffeebar! Fresh gourmet coffee, espresso and cappuccino in the middle of a bike store featuring cannondale and GT Bicycles. Way cool - we love this place.

Friends Jewelers
1387 Main St. Sarasota 34236
955-4956

This family jewelry store has the area's largest collection of unusual wax ring molds for mounting on display. Amazing.

The Garden Building
1501 Laurel St., Sarasota 34236
A One-Stop Pamper-Fest:

Looks by Tini Rachelle (362-2866) for haircolor, precision cuts.

Jenny's Skin Care (955-5151) European facials, peels, tinting, waxing.

Massage by Craig Hancock, LMT (330-1246) Swedish relaxation; deep tissue massage; sports massage; in-home; insurance accepted.

All Nail Review (955-8075) for the latest in nail enhancement technology, natural nail care and pedicures.

Garden Creations
4013 Cattleman Rd., Sarasota
378-2305

Area's largest selection of silk plants, flowers, trees and stone.

The Glass Slipper
653 S. Orange Ave., Sarasota 34236
951-1547; fax 954-7158; e-mail: nancywilke@home.com

Complete (read: massive) costume shop; children's costumes too. Rentals, accessories and makeup for everyone, for every occasion. Be advised, this is where you discover how bizarre your/his/her imagination really is. Fun without boundaries. Great for theme parties, official Halloween headquarters for the Suncoast.

Gulf Coast Model Railroad Shop
3222 Clark Rd., Sarasota 34231
923-9303

Choo-choooo!! A great place to take the kids (of all ages.) Four working model railroad sets are on display. Everyone loves trains.

Haps Cycle Sales
2530 17th St., Sarasota 34234
365-3442; 1-80-303-4277

Since 1948 Hap has been taking care of the area's motorcycle community with compassion, kindness and some pretty mean machines. He still rides every day - and he'll get you to join him on one of your own too.

Heart of Europe
1282 N. Palm Ave., Sarasota 34236
952-9087, fax 952-0153,
e-mail: hearte@kudos.net
www.heartofeurope.com

The only store of its kind in Florida dedicated

I do **YOUR** hair in **YOUR** home!

Dr. Hair Care
Alan Blum

Haircuts • Perms
Color • Styling
In your home or office!

35 Years Experience FL
Licensed & Insured, Bonded

966-0333

4 Convenient Locations

Sarasota • US 41 at Stickney Pt. Rd.
             • US 301 at 17th Street
Bradenton • US 41 at 63rd Avenue
Venice   • US 41 - 1 1/2 mi. North of Jacaranda Blvd.

Hours: Mon-Sat 8am - 5:30pm

We're Eager to Please!

Say Hello to Good Buys

Sarasota Square Mall

Location: 8201 S. Tamiami Tr., Sarasota

Largest shopping mall in Sarasota features four major department stores, specialty shops, fashion, major food court and 12 screen movie theaters. You can find virtually anything you are looking for at this very popular and very huge mall. Interesting activities for the whole family are scheduled weekly. Anchors: Burdines, Dillards, JC Penney, Sears, The Gap, Victoria's Secret, Toys By Nature and the ever popular destination - The Disney Store.

---

exclusively to exquisite merchandise imported from Prague, the capital of the Czech Republic (hence the name of the store); hand-blown and hand-cut glass using techniques that date back to the 13th century. Lead crystal chandeliers, Bohemian china and more. Luscious, translucent wonders.

Haven Downtown
1451 Main St., Sarasota 34236
955-1966

Extraordinary gifts for the home from the traditional to contemporary.

Helen's Books and Comic Shop
1531 Main Street Sarasota 34236
955-2989

Area's largest new and collector's comic book store for those with comic fan fever plus 100,000 used books, some records, great owner.

High-Tech Electronics
6522 Gateway Ave., Sarasota 34231
923-DISH
http://hightechelectronics.com

Family owned and operated satellite dish experts for residential and commercial use. Licensed and insured, quality and commitment; mention "Steve Rabow's Guide Book" for a special discount.

House of Maps
6603 Gateway Ave., Sarasota 34231
924-8998 ; fax 923-0047; e-mail: houseofmaps@juno.com; www.houseofmaps.com

The name says it all - map publisher of local street maps, Manatee, Sarasota and Charlotte County street map atlas, wall maps and folding maps. Custom maps available for your business. Ask for Mel.

Ioptics
510 S. Pineapple Ave, Sarasota 34236
955-5133

Sarasota's newest eyewear store became an instant hit - unlike anything else on Florida's west coast. True European design, world class artistic statements, all in a post-modern ambience. No wonder our international friends shop here, often buying six or more frames to take back to Europe where prices have become astronomical. Here, comparatively, you'll find a real deal. More importantly, you'll find a real look. The shop itself is something to look at too. Plus great music.

International Barter Exchange
1161 N. Tamiami Trail, Sarasota
P.O. Box 20188, Sarasota 34276
955-6100, ext. 22; fax 955-0151
e-mail: maryu@twp.net
www.barter-works.com

One of the most successful and ethical barter exchanges in the country, Ron and Mary Unger have built the better mousetrap. Barter Exchange is a system of exchanging goods and services which can reduce your business or personal expenses while increasing your sales and profits. It really works. But go see for yourself. And when you do be sure to tell Ron Unger "I read about IBE in Steve Rabow's Guide Book" so once you're convinced that it does indeed work you won't have to pay the $495 sign-up fee. How's that for an incentive?

Kiyoshi's
1537 Main St., Sarasota 34236
365-6544

Call & Compare! 923-DISH (3474)

LICENSED AND INSURED Save on all Satellite Dish Systems

Authorized Sales & Service

DishNetwork
Echostar
HTS
DIRECTV/USSB
RCA
Sony
Hughes
DirecPC
Panasonic
PRIMESTAR
C Band
Others Too!

Family Owned & Operated
"Expert Installation"

HIGH-TECH ELECTRONICS

VISIT OUT LOCAL SHOWROOM
6522 GATEWAY AVENUE
SARASOTA, FLORIDA 34231

Options for every Budget

Satellite Broadcasting and Communications Association
SBCA MEMBER

Residential & Commercial

Dolby Digital
Home Theater
Antennas
RV Mounts
Tripods
Portable DBS Systems
Video Surveillance
C Band Parts
Pagers / Voice Mail
Cell Phones - Primeco

WE SHIP

   Cards

Check out our "Cool" Web Site @ http://hightechelectronics.com

Shopping

Say Hello to Good Buys

Siesta Key Village
Location: Ocean Blvd., Siesta Key
Beautiful garden setting with 100 various shops, restaurants, boutiques and knick knack stores all sporting the perfect items when you are looking for that unique gift or the always necessary self-indulgent perk. And don't forget the biggest perk this area has to offer - it's just a hop, skip and a jump away from the world's "whitest, finest" sand. Especially active and great for "people watching" during season.

Sarasota's newest sushi bar, presented by downtown's old friend, master Kiyoshi - just opened, more details next edition.

Quaint-Essentials
1962 Main St., Sarasota 34236
954-1042; fax 322-9007
Located on the second floor of Main Bookshop, this antique store/booth is noteworthy because co-owner is Jeff LaHurd, author of many essential Sarasota history books. Eclectic collection has something for every taste. An explorer's delight.

Joe-Lin
5778 S. Tamiami Tr., Sarasota 34231
924-1038
Customized, handmade lamp shades and lamp repairs. All silk and hardback shades are made on the premises, duplication of your favorite shades never a problem.

King James Big or Tall
4333 Tamiami Tr. S, Sarasota 34231
922-1873
Does Michael Jordan shop here? Great looking, stylish clothes for guys with their head in the clouds and/or the serious dessert lover.

Last Flight Out
Southgate Mall 34239
917-0404; fax 917-0064
A gift store for aviators, voyagers and fellow (or sister) spirits of adventure. Unusual shirts, hats, toys and gifts, many imported from 'round the world. Notions to caress and inspire the imagination. Original, not unlike yourself. Same wonderful owners in new location at Southgate where business should soar.

Le Cigar
1345 Main St., Sarasota
36-CIGAR
Cough...cough...you mean...people really enjoy these things? (Just kidding!) Premium cigars, humidors, accessories and unique gifts. Plus, you can get downtown's only authentic shoe shine here which, by itself, is more than enough reason to visit.

Le Colonne Ristorante
22 S. Blvd. of the Presidents, St. Armands Circle, 34236
388-4284
New Italian restaurant on The Circle, family flew in direct from Sicaly, street says nothing but raves, too new to make it in our Restaurant Guide, we'll check in this year - you might consider doing the same.

Light Up Your Life
1307 Main St., Sarasota 34236
Unique, contemporary artistic and innovative European lighting.

The Magic Shop
3141 Tamiami Trail N., Sarasota 34234
358-0777; e-mail: edsmagic@aol.com
The only magic shop for professionals and amateurs on the west coast of Florida. Costumes, theatrical make-up, accessories, juggling equipment and books; friendly, helpful proprietor who will perform some of his favorite tricks right there at the store.

Maggie's Memories
1460 Main St, Sarasota 34236
Antiques, collectibles and art,

The only Big and Tall Men's Store with clothes fit for a King! Plus accessories to complete the look.

4333 South Tamiami Trail, Sarasota • 922-1873
Open Monday through Friday 9:30 - 6:00, Saturday 9:30 - 5:30

Is Your Company Eligible to Redeem This $495 Membership Coupon?

Qualifying Terms:

- Can your business currently take on additional new business?
- Can you benefit by using barter dollars to pay for your cash expenses?
- Are you seeking creative marketing tools to build your business?
- If you answered yes to any of the above, then your business qualifies to join over 600 locally active trading IBE™ members.

PROFIT THROUGH THE POWER OF EXCHANGE WITH IBE™

To redeem this $495 coupon, call Ron Unger at 955-6100, extension 22 today!
www.barter-works.com

Say Hello to Good Buys

Southbay Fashion Center

Location: U.S. 41 and Blackburn Pt. Rd., Osprey

Home to some of Sarasota's most prestigious retailers. Anchors: Jacobsen's and Ethan Allen.

Southgate Plaza

Location: Siesta Drive and U.S. 41, Sarasota

Recently renovated. The new home of Saks, William Sonoma, Gap Kids, Anne Taylor; the continuing home of Burdines, Dillards and Talbots; and the amazing new restaurant (that's even open after the mall closes) Cosimo's - not to be missed!

Venice Centre Mall

Location: Park Place and West Tampa Ave., Venice

Formally the San Marco Hotel, a white stucco marvel filled with boutiques, a cafe, beauty salon and the local headquarters for the United Way.

Merging Point Design
756-8353, fax 756-5154, www.mergingpointdesign.com
Graduates of the prestigious Ringling School of Art & Design have set up shop in Bradenton to take on the world of Web Site, Multimedia, Graphic Design and Illustration - all have a firm foundation in artistic tradition, now poised to move your important image into fast forward.

Oh My Gauze
17 N. Blvd. of the Presidents, St. Armands Circle, 34236
388-2242

5253 Ocean Blvd., Siesta Key, 34242
349-2168

The store with the incredible name features comfortable gauze clothing. Headquarters is on St. Armands Circle, additional locations can be found in Naples, FL and Lake Geneva, WI.

Picasso's at the Grotto
443 Burns Court, Sarasota 34236
362-9006

This artist haven is open noon-midnight, serving lite bites and desserts which will change your perspective on life itself. (Art, with fork.)

Pamaro Shop
North Store: 7782 N. Tamiami Tr., Saraosta
355-5619

South Store: 4586 S. Tamiami Tr., Sarasota
923-3299

Florida's largest dealer in Henry Link fine furnishings. Famous furniture names here include Acacia, Alexvale, Basset, Bob Timberlake, Craftmaster, Habersham Plantation, Seaside Retreat, Weekend Retreat and lots more - thousands of items. Both locations are landmarks.

Polish Imports
7350 S. Tamiami Tr., Sarasota 34231
923-1044, www.polart.com

The largest importer of Polish goods in the world now presents their first retail store in Sarasota. Unique wood carvings, folk dolls, wallhangings, crystal and much more, for much less than you expect.

Rhapsodies
4787 Swift Rd., Sarasota
923-2377

A gift and gourmet basket superstore, for all occasions. Substantial, unique, impressive. This is where to go when the response you are looking for is nothing less than "wow!" - you'll get it.

RUM International, Inc.
4134 Gulf of Mexico Dr., Longboat Key, 34228
955-7505
www.rowvirusboats.com

Exclusive U.S. importer of Virus Open Water Rowing Boats along with other equally impressive products - some with worldwide rights.

Sarasota Toy Company
1905 S. Osprey Ave.
362-1122

Brand new, independent, locally owned toy chest filled with everything that any kid not hooked on video will really love. (If hooked, unglue - pry if necessary - child's eyes from video set and take here.

Sarasota Vault Depository
640 Washington Blvd., Sarasota 34236
954-9003

The most secure building in the state of Florida is located downtown. Private, secured individual vaults and deposit boxes - all sizes including walk-in vaults; 24-hour armed guard; anonymous accounts.

Seascape Aquarium
2162 Gulf Gate Dr., Sarasota 34231
922-0914, fax 921-4745

Hand crafted custom aquariums made to order, up to 2000 gallons; tropical and marine fish and invertebrates from 70-80 countries of the world. Fish, small animal and reptile exhibits. Great for kids.

Shrode Jewelers
1433 Main St., Sarasota 34236
365-4234; fax 365-4286

A local favorite. Since 1936 five generations of families have been served by Shrode Jewelers – one of the area's most popular places for fine craftsmanship. Custom work and repairs are done on premises with meticulous detail and care. Wide array of important figurines and exclusive distributor of many "name" collectibles. This store sparkles.

POLISH IMPORTS

- Wood Carvings
- Folk Dolls
- Wallhangings
- T-shirts & Hats
- Handpainted Dishware & Pottery
- Crystal
- Videos & CDs
- Books & Maps
- Translation Software & more!

CORAL COVE MALL
7350 S. Tamiami Trail
Sarasota, Florida 34231
(941) 923-1044

For a free catalog call:
(941) 927-8873

Visit our web catalog:
www.polart.com

SHRODE JEWELERS

Founded in 1936, Shrode is Sarasota's oldest jeweler. Shrode offers the finest in unique jewelry, diamonds, crystal and porcelain, expert watch and jewelry repair and custom jewelry design.

Winner : Sarasota Herald-Tribune Reader's Choice Award for best jewelry store.

1433 Main Street • (941) 365-4234

Say Hello to Good Buys

Venice Pines Plaza

Location: Jacaranda Blvd. and Center Rd., Venice

98,000 sq. ft. of blue tile accents and atmosphere, nice neighborhood offerings surrounded by golf course community.

Venice Main Street

Located in the heart of this historic community, The Avenues of Downtown Venice (Tampa, Venice, and Miami) offer personal service, local ownership, unique architecture and a true sense of community to enhance your shopping experience along palm lined avenues.

Venice Village Shops

Location: 4115 Tamiami Trail South, Venice

48 neighborhood stores, 3 restaurants and more, in a relaxed contemporary, "Florida life" setting.

Swim Mart
3898 S. Osprey Ave., Sarasota 34239
365-2428; fax 365-2428

Florida's largest, biggest, grandest, finest, hippest, most ultra massive collection of swimwear for women, men and children. Sunglasses too. The only place to go before the beach!

Tennis Look
465 John Ringling Blvd., St. Armands Circle,
388-2002

Full line of womens, mens and childrens tennis clothing and accessories. Unique tennis theme cards and gifts too. Lob one for the Gipper.

Ten Thousand Villages
3737 Bahia Vista St., Sarasota 34232
362-2729; fax 365-6329; e-mail: bwloop@home.com

The sights, sounds and textures of intriguing creations handcrafted by skilled artisans from 30 countries. A "one-world" shopping adventure, to be sure. Even better, shopping here makes a significant difference!

Victorian Garden Florist
539 S. Washington Blvd., Sarasota 34236
362-7116

One of the area's most creative, artful, floral arrangers. One trip inside will tell you that romance is spoken here fluently. Loyal following.

Jack Vinales Antiques
539 Pineapple Ave. S., Sarasota 34236
957-0002

There are many, truly wonderful, antique stores in our area – but none like this. Specializing in 20th century design masterpieces, this store was "raided" by the prop department for the HBO series "From the Earth to the Moon." (They paid cash.) Shop featured in 1/98 edition of Southern Living Magazine and, it seems, continually in the local press.

Vintage Motor Co. of Saraosta
2836 Tamiami Tr., Sarasota 355-6500

The single most impressive used-car store in Florida.

William Harris Rock Shop
1118 Snead Ave., Sarasota 34237
366-6608; fax 366-4890

Five warehouses full of rocks. Everything from a 200 lb. amethyst to a polished lapis bead necklace to million year old fossils. Jewelry, stone-age antiquities and Mr. Harris himself who makes up for the cold nature of his wares with overflowing warmth and knowledge. Not fancy (wear your digging boots) but a recommended adventure to be sure. You'll see things here you won't see anywhere else. Honest.

Wet Noses
472 John Ringling Blvd., St. Armands Circle
388-DOGS; www.wetnoses.com

Unique gifts or pets and the people who love them; greeting cards, clothing, beds, personalized bowls, gourmet treats, collars and leashes.

Wild Birds Unlimited
7382 Tamiami Tr. S, Sarasota 34231
922-1388

Unlimited nature gifts and backyard feeding specialist; birdseed, feeders, birdbaths, optics, windchimes, binoculars and more.

Native Shopping

World's Largest Selection of Swimwear

Name Brand Sale Suits Up To

70% OFF

Swimwear as low as $11.99!

Millions of swimsuits to choose from!

Guaranteed lowest prices!

Over 127 manufacturers in stock with sizes available for the whole family!

FREE
BEACH TOWEL OR
12 OZ. ALOE LOTION
MINIMUM $20 PURCHASE
ONE COUPON PER PERSON.
WE HONOR ALL COMPETITORS' COUPONS.

SWIM MART

Open Sunday 10am - 5pm
Monday - Saturday 9:30am - 8pm
3898 S. Osprey Ave. 365-2428
New Store in Prime Outlets - Ellenton 721-8924

Food, Wine & Fun

ON FLORIDA'S GULF COAST

Michael's On East

- Voted one of Florida's Top 20 restaurants for eight consecutive years. (Florida Trend magazine, 1992-1999)

- Inspired Continental Menus • Impeccable Service • Plush, Swirling New Design

- EastSide Bar & Lounge for entertainment & late night fun.

- Enjoy our FREE Happy Hour Buffet of Tapas-style treats, from 5-7 p.m. Monday-Friday.

1212 East Avenue South • Midtown Plaza • Sarasota
(941) 366-0007

Michael's Seafood Grille & The Down Under Jazz Club

- Executive chef John Mancini charts a new course for Sarasota's favorite seafood restaurant. Come taste what's new!

- Award-winning seafood, steaks, pastas and chops served in a casually sophisticated waterfront setting.

- Sarasota's best live jazz and a casual, dockside menu at the adjacent Down Under Jazz Club. Enjoy our FREE Happy Hour buffet weekdays from 4 to 7 p.m.

- The "After Dark" disco at Michael's Seafood Grille - Wed.-Sat. nights from 10:30 p.m. Voted Sarasota's favorite place to go dancing!

214 Sarasota Quay • Sarasota • (941) 951-2467

Visit our web site at www.bestfood.com.
Voted one of the top ten restaurant web sites in the United States.

Restaurants

Our Area Restaurants

Welcome to the only comprehensive *Restaurant Guide* on the Suncoast. We think you'll be impressed by the range and quality of offerings available. Much like just about everything else on the Suncoast, the number of truly wonderful restaurants is disproportionate to the actual size of our community - world class dining, it's here in abundance.

The Listings
It takes equal parts guts, gumption and gumbo to open a restaurant!
Everyone has good days. Everyone has bad days. Lives and livelihoods are presented to you daily, tableside. (One person's "Scream" is another persons "Gone With The Wind" - we'll trust you to know your personal tastes.) Remember, ours is an *Exploring Guide* - while we are respectful of professional critical evaluation our comments are generally reflective of what the restaurants themselves want you to know about their services and specialties. Also, we strive to give primary focus on local flavor - we tend to shy away from "cookie cutter" national chains. Unlike most of the "guides" you'll find in newspapers and magazines, the restaurants included here are not determined exclusively by advertising participation.

One thing is for sure, there are enough good restaurants in the area to please almost every culinary taste. Since ours is an area which depends largely on visitors and retirees you can bet that going out to eat has been elevated to a way of life around here. Eat, enjoy, live well.

Tipping
Tipping is not a city in China!
Customs in other countries may differ but here in the United States our waitstaff depend primarily on tips to survive. Please remember to tip your waiter/waitress: 15% of the bill is standard. 20% for outstanding service. To not leave tip is a serious insult, please be considerate.

Early Bird Specials
The best bargain in town!
Specifically designed for the retirement/fixed income crowd, Early Bird Specials are usually a third to half off the regular menu prices, plus they often include extras like a beverage and dessert. You do not have to be a senior citizen to take advantage of Early Bird Specials, you only have to show up at the restaurant early - usually between 4-6 p.m. You'll find notations of which restaurants offer Early Bird Specials in this section.

Reservations / Changes
Reservations are recommended whenever possible!
Year-by-year there are more changes in this section than in any other part of *The Guide* - nothing changes as quickly as the restaurant scene. If you can make reservations do so, calling ahead is always a good idea anyway, even out of "Season."

Getting Listed
Help us help you!
Is your favorite eatery missing from our current list or do you know of a new restaurant which is opening in the near future? Please send us the details (name of restaurant, address, phone number and the name of who to contact) and we'll do the rest. Restaurants are never charged to be included in The Guide.

Send information to:

Steve Rabow's Guide Book; P.O. Box 15332, Sarasota, FL 34277 or rabow@acun.com

---

Key to Restaurant Listings

AX
American Express

CB
Carte Blanche

DC
Diners Club

DS
Discover

MC
Master Card

VS
Visa

LC
Local Checks are OK with proper I.D.

$
Under $7 lunch, under $12 dinner.

$$
Mostly $7 - $12 lunch, mostly $12 - $20 dinner.

$$$
Mostly $12 and over lunch, mostly $20 and over dinner.

Price categories are based on an average cost per person not including beverages, tax or tip.

All Star Steakhouse & Sports Bar
3611 1st St. East, Bradenton 34208
747-3595, fax 750-8641
Lunch & Dinner - 7 days
Locally Owned - 5 Years
$$; AX/DS/MS/VS
Full Bar
House Specialties: Steaks

Alley Cat Cafe
1558 4th St., Sarasota
954-1228, fax 955-6118
Lunch - Mon-Sat, Dinner - Tues-Sat
Locally Owned - 5 Years
$$; AX/DC/MS/VS/DS/LC
Full Bar
House Specialties: Sea Bass, naturally-raised lamb and veal.
Other Points of Interest: Charming cafe tucked away in cluster of old Florida cottages. Inside seating with wonderful collection of antiques. Outside seating under beautiful oak trees and garden.
Most Popular Item: Chilean Sea Bass topped with sauteed blue crab finished with lemongrass, coconut milk, chili oil.

Alpine Steak House at
Karl Ehmer's Quality Meats
4520 Tamiami Tr. S., Sarasota
921-3798
Lunch & Dinner - Mon-Sat
Locally Owned - 24 Years
Early Bird Specials
$; MS/VS/LC
Beer/Wine Only
House Specialties: Sauerbraten with potato dumplings and red cabbage; prime rib.
Other Points of Interest: Old fashioned butcher shop and steak house under one roof. Customers can order right out of meat case. Nice imported beer selection.
Most Popular Item: Steaks

Althea's
220 Miami Ave. West, Venice 34285
484-5187, fax 483-3388
Breakfast - 7 Days
Lunch & Dinner - 7 Days
Locally Owned - 6 Years
$; DS/MC/VS/DC/LC
Full bar
House Specialties: Fresh seafood, Maine lobster, vegetarian specials.
Other Points of Interest: American cuisine with a European flair.
Most Popular Item: Fresh seafood.

Andiamo
533 14th St. West, Bradenton 34205
746-3114
Lunch - Mon-Fri, Dinner - Mon-Sat
Early Bird Specials
Locally Owned- 5 Years
$$; AX/MC/VS
Full bar
House Specialties: Veal, Pasta, Chicken, Seafood, Steaks, Italian.
Other Points of Interest: Fine dining in a casual atmosphere. Live music Fri.-Sat. Catering available, take out/delivery.
Most Popular Item: Grouper Francais.

Anna Maria Oyster Bar
100 Bay Blvd. South, Anna Maria 34217
778-0475
Lunch & Dinner - 7 Days
Locally Owned - 17 Years
$; AX/DS/MC/VS
Full Bar
House Specialties: Live Maine Lobster, Fresh Gulf Grouper and Key West Pink Shrimp, Pasta, Steamer Pots, Alaskan King Crab Legs. All you can eat fish.
Other Points of Interest: Located 741' out in Tampa Bay on the historic Anna Maria City Pier. Dolphins jump and play while you enjoy dinner inside or outside on the deck with guitar, tropical entertainment.
Most Popular Item: Fresh Grouper sandwich.

Anna Maria Oyster Bar Landside
6906 14th St. West, Bradenton 34207
758-7880, fax 751-9478
Lunch & Dinner - 7 days
Early Bird
Locally owned - 1 Year
$$; AX/DS/MC/VS/LC
Full Bar
House Specialties: Live Maine Lobster, Alaskan King Crab Legs, Gulf Grouper, Key West Pink Shrimp, Pasta Skillets, Steamer Pots, Grouper Sandwiches and all you can eat fish specials.
Other Points of Interest: Land-locked version of the original Anna Maria Oyster Bar where they replaced the five "playful porpoises" with a full bar. Complete menu is available for take out. Live entertainment.
Most Popular Item: Grouper sandwich.

Anthony's Italian Deli
1812 S. Osprey Ave. , Sarasota 34239
365-2998, fax 365-7905
Lunch - Mon-Fri
Locally owned - 13 Years
$; DS/MC/VS/AX/LC
No Liquor Served
House Specialties: All natural, no preservatives. Daily specials, usually Italian lasagna, eggplant and sausage dishes. Authentic Italian espresso will get you going.
Other Points of Interest: U.S. Chef Open Silver and Bronze winner for his tiramisou. Popular with hospital/medical district employees; loved by locals; great for lunch/dinner takeout.
Most Popular Item: Lasagna.

Back Bay Steakhouse
1700 S. Tamiami Trail, Sarasota 34293
493-0254, fax 497-5608
Dinner - 7 Days
Early Bird Specials

BEACH BISTRO

Surfside

Anna Maria Island • 778-6444

- Zagat: "Best Food on the Gulf Coast"
- Florida Trend: Top 20 Restaurants Golden Spoon
- Wine Spectator: Award of Excellence

Key to Restaurant Listings

AX American Express

CB Carte Blanche

DC Diners Club

DS Discover

MC Master Card

VS Visa

LC Local Checks are OK with proper I.D.

$ Under $7 lunch, under $12 dinner.

$$ Mostly $7 - $12 lunch, mostly $12 - $20 dinner.

$$$ Mostly $12 and over lunch, mostly $20 and over dinner.

Price categories are based on an average cost per person not including beverages, tax or tip.

Locally Owned - 1 Year
$$; AX/DS/MC/VS
Full bar
House Specialties: Steak, Ribs, Seafood.
Other Points of Interest: Banquet/private party room. Jack Fanning's "Shadows" performs Fri-Sat. Voted #1 steaks in Venice area.
Most Popular Item: Prime Rib.

Bangkok Restuarant
4791 Swift Rd., Sarasota 34231
922-0703
Lunch - Mon-Fri, Dinner - 7 Days
Locally Owned - 7 Years
$; AX/ DC/DS/MC/VS/ LC
Beer/Wine only
House Specialties: Authentic Thai cooking, seafood combos, Thai curries.
Other Points of Interest: Fabulous food, very reasonable prices. Beautiful newly-expanded dining room, Readers choice for "Best Thai in Sarasota" 5 years in a row. Popular with locals all year long. Family owned and operated. Ask Boon for "Sticky Rice!"
Most Popular Item: Pad Thaia.

The Banyan Cafe
5401 Bay Shore Rd., Sarasota 34234
359-3183, fax 359-0541
Lunch - 7 Days
Locally Owned - 5 Years
$; MS/VS/LC
Full Bar
House Specialties: Cuban Black bean soup, salads, overstuffed sandwiches, daily chef specials, sumptuous desserts and low-cal specials.
Other Points Of Interest: Located on the grounds of Ringling Museum, surrounded by banyan trees. Romantic setting with indoor garden and southern verandah. Locally Managed by Orange Blossom Catering.
Most Popular Item: Salad Nicoise.

Barnacle Bill's Seafood
3634 Webber St., Sarasota
923-5800, fax 926-0221
Lunch - Mon-Sat, Dinner -7 days
Locally Owned -
$$; AX/DC/DS/MS/VS/DS/LC
Full Bar
House Specialties: Fresh seafood. Gulf grouper, snapper, haddock, halibut, salmon, mahi, stone crab in season, Ipswich clams, crab cakes, homemade Key Lime pie.
Other Points of Interest: Look before you buy. Fresh seafood from the market fish case. Bill says: "Absolutely Sarasota's finest fresh seafood."
Most Popular Item: Crab cakes.

Bart's Bayside
230 Sarasota Quay, Sarasota 34236
359-3183, fax 955-4626
Lunch & Dinner - 7 Days
$$; AX/DC/DS/MS/VS/LC
Full Bar
House Specialties: Shrimp Bradley,

coconut shrimp.
Other Points Of Interest: Newly remodeled beautiful handpainted aquatic murals abound. Waterfront view, outside seating. Accessible by boat. Private dining area available. Runner-up "Best Entree" in Taste of Sarasota for Nutty Grouper. Owner is former NBA player.
Most Popular Item: Nutty Grouper.

Beach Bistro
6600 Gulf Dr., Holmes Beach 34217
778-6444, fax 778-6573
Dinner - 7 Days
Locally Owned - 13 Years
$$$; AX/CB/DC/DS/MC/VS/LC
Full Bar
House Specialties: Bouillabaisse, rack of lamb with port and rosemary demiglaze and mint pesto drizzle, Roast duckling. Award-winning desserts including chocolate truffle terrine *(which is Kimberly's favorite!)* One of Florida's most highly acclaimed restaurants.
Other Points Of Interest: Restaurant is surfside, gorgeous views right on the water! 1998 Zagat's Florida Gulf Coast Guide "Best Food" and "Best Waterfront Dining". 1998 Golden Spoon (a top-twenty award). No smoking.

Beach Cafe Bar & Restaurant
431 Beach Road, Sarasota 34242
349-7111
Dinner - Mon-Sat, Early Bird
Late night menu in bar
Locally Owned - 17 Years
$$; MC/VS/LC
Full Bar
House Specialties: Veal scallopini, grouper Oscar, lamb, duckling, dover sole and pasta.
Other Points Of Interest: Live music Thursday-Saturday in the lounge.
Most Popular Item: Fresh seafood.

Beach House Restaurant
200 Gulf Dr. North
Bradenton Beach 34217
779-2222, fax 778-7385
Lunch & Dinner - 7 Days, Early bird,
Locally Owned - 4 Years
$; AX/CB/DC/DS/MS/VS
Full Bar
House Specialties: Clam bake, Fresh fish, stuffed snapper.
Other Points of Interest: Directly on the beach. Nightly sunset contest. Volleyball courts. Call ahead for preferred seating for inside dining only.
Most Popular Item: Beach Nut Grouper.

Beef O'Brady's
5942 34th St. W., Bradenton 34210
755-4046
Lunch & Dinner - 7 Days
Locally Owned - 3 Years
$; DS/MC/VS/LC
Beer/Wine Only
House Specialties: Watterson sandwich, Reubens and salads.

Other Points of Interest: Family sports pub with 2 big screen TVs and 12 smaller TVs. Happy Hour for beer 4 to 7 p.m. every day.
Most Popular Item: Wings, wings!

Bein's & Joffrey's Deli & Coffee House
1345 Main St., Sarasota 34236
953-JAVA, fax 954-8488
1995 Main St., Sarasota 34236
906-9500, fax 906-9502
Breakfast, Lunch, Dinner - 7 days
Locally owned - 3 Years
$; AX/DC/DS/MC/VS
Beer/Wine only
House Specialties: Soups (including matzo ball), rye bread, hoagie rolls, bagels, cookies and scones baked in-house; white albacore tuna; turkey pastrami and regular hot pastrami; cakes, pies and muffins
Other Points of Interest: Catering, gift baskets, coffee merchandise/gifts. Outdoor seating and sofas in the store, games and puzzles.
Most Popular Item: Corned beef on rye.

Bella Roma Italian Restaurant
5239 Ocean Blvd., Siesta Key 34242
349-0995
Dinner - 7 days in season
Early Bird Specials
Locally Owned - 7 Years
$$; AX/DC/DS/MC/VS
Beer/Wine Only
House Specialties: Pasta, Veal, Fresh Seafood.
Other Points Of Interest: Small romantic atmosphere.
Most Popular Item: Risotto ai porcini.

Bellini Ristorante
1551 Main St., Sarasota 34236
365-7380, fax 924-0726
Lunch - Mon-Fri, Dinner - Mon-Sat
Locally Owned - 10 Years
$$; AX/CB/DC/MC/VS/AX/DC
Beer/Wine Only
House Specialties: Homemade pasta and desserts. Linguine Pescatora, veal chops. Piedmonte, Lombardy and Veneto regional cuisine.
Other Points Of Interest: Very popular with downtown business lunch crowd, evening is reserved for romantics. Owner is warm and wonderful.
Most Popular Item: Veal chops.

Benedicts
375 US 41 By-Pass, Venice 34292
485-7057
Breakfast & Lunch - 7 days,
Dinner - Mon-Sat
Locally Owned
$; AX/CB/DC/DS/MC/VS/LC
Beer/Wine Only
House Specialties: Cheese smashed browns, homemade crabcakes, comfort foods, Friday night all-you-can-eat fish fry.
Other Points of Interest: Former owner of Broken Egg on Siesta Key is just as charming and witty as ever, food is just as fabulous too. Patio dining.
Most Popular Item: Potato crusted brunch pie.

Better Bagels
4854 S. Tamiami Tr., Sarasota 34231
924-0393, fax 924-0358
Breakfast & Lunch - 7 Days
Locally Owned - 13 Years
$; No Credit Cards
No Liquor Served
House Specialties: Not just for breakfast anymore! They have challah bread, pizza soup, sandwiches for lunch.
Other Points Of Interest: Winner "Tasters Choice Award Best Bagel"
Most Popular Item: Anything on a bagel.

The Big Kitchen
3800 Clark Road, Bldg. M
Sarasota 34233
925-3675, fax 923-0414
Lunch & Dinner - 7 days
Locally Owned - 1 Year
$$; AX/DC/DS/MS/VS/DS/LC
Full Bar
House Specialties: All bread and desserts baked on premises. Authentic Jewish sourdough rye bread and their own unique flat bread. Lunch features unique and large sandwiches; dinner features fresh seafood and many unusual entrees.
Other Points of Interest: Site of McCurdy's Comedy Club on Thursday, Friday and Saturday evenings. Full dinner menu and bar service is available before and during the shows. Finalist as "Best New Restaurant" 1998. Decor is funky and features kitchen motif with original art by Sarasota artists.
Most Popular Item: Portobello New York Strip Steak.

Bijou Cafe
1287 1st St., Sarasota 34236
366-8111, fax 366-7510
Lunch - Mon-Fri, Dinner - Mon-Sat, (7 nights/week during season)
Locally Owned - 12 Years
$$$; AX/CB/DC/MC/VS
Full Bar
House Specialties: Certified black Angus beef, plmmes gratin dauphinois, roast duckling, crab cakes, lamb shanks, shrimp piri-piri.
Other Points Of Interest: Centrally located in downtown Sarasota in the historic theatre and arts district. Charming intimate and romantic decor. Critic's Choice: "Most Favorite Restaurant In Area." Zagat Survey: "Most popular, most romantic and best continental cuisine." Very popular for very good reasons.
Most Popular Item: Pommes Gratin Dauphinois.

Bistro 41
7252 S. Tamiami Tr., Sarasota
923-4511

Lunch - Mon-Fri, Dinner - Mon-Sat
Locally Owned - 5 Years
$$; AX/CB/DC/DS/MC/VS
Beer/Wine Only
House Specialties: European country style cuisine. Fresh seafood, pasta, beef, lamb, veal, duck.
Other Points of Interest: A French bistro with an Italian accent and a new American attitude. One of the area's most respected and most innovative menus.

Blase Cafe
5263 Ocean Blvd., Sarasota 34242
349-9822
Breakfast, Lunch & Dinner - Tues-Sun
Locally Owned - 2 Years
$$; No credit cards accepted/LC
Full Bar
House Specialties: Pan seared tuna, filet mignon, portabello demi-glaze, Equidorian esciuiche, New Orleans omelette, Andouline sausage and shrimp, Spinach Provencal with shrimp.
Other Points of Interest: Outdoor seating in a garden-like setting.
Most Popular Item: Snapper Camino Real.

Blue Dolphin Cafe
470 John Ringling Blvd.
Sarasota 34236
388-3566
Breakfast & Lunch - 7 days
Locally owned - 1 Year
$; MC/VS/LC
Beer/Wine only
House Specialties: Chicken Fajita wrap, Belgian waffles
Most Popular Item: Chicken Fajita wrap.

The Boardroom Cafe
1819 Main St., Sarasota 34236
954-3370
Breakfast & Lunch - Mon-Fri
Locally Owned - 2 Years
$; MC/VS/LC
House Specialties: Gourmet stuffed sandwiches, 11 different salads, daily soups and specials.
Other Points Of Interest: Cafe is located on the first floor of Sarasota City Center, next to a 50' "waterfall".
Most Popular Item: Chicken chutney.

The Boathouse
1000 Boulevard Of The Arts
Sarasota 34236
953-1234, ext. 1365
Lunch & Dinner - 7 days
Early Bird, Late Night
$; AX/CB/DC/DS/MC/VS
Full Bar
House Specialties: Steaks, coconut shrimp, Grouper Reuben, honey barbeque baby back ribs.
Other Points Of Interest: Great menu for picky eaters; vegetarian and children's menus. Located right on the Hyatt Basin Marina with a great view of the water. Boat access from Marker 12 in the ICW.
Most Popular Item: Grouper Reuben.

Bob's Boathouse Restaurant
1310 Old Stickney Pt. Rd.,
Sarasota 34242
312-9111
Lunch - 7 Days
Dinner - 7 Days
Early Bird; Late Night Menu
$$; AX/DS/MC/VS
Full Bar
House Specialties: Fresh fish.
Other Points Of Interest: Unique quonset hut setting on the waterfront. Two boats available upstairs for on-board dining - eat onboard and overlook the restaurant w/birds-eye view; "hot rocks" table-side cooking, tiki hut bar & swimming pool. 200 ft. of dock space arriving soon. Huge, fun for everyone! Music/dancing nightly.
Most Popular Item: Planked salmon.

Briandi's
202 S. Tamiami Tr., Nokomis 34285
488-9511
Dinner - 7 Days
Locally Owned - 9 Years
$$; MC/VS
Beer/Wine Only
House Specialties: Italian dinners, veal, chicken and seafood.
Other Points Of Interest: Family style atmosphere.
Most Popular Item: Big 13 Layer lasagna.

Bridge Tender Inn
135 Bridge St., Bradenton Beach 34216
778-4849
Lunch & Dinner - 7 Days
Locally Owned - 6 Years
$; MC/VS/AX/DS/LC
Full Bar
House Specialties: Steaks and seafood. Prime Rib Tuesday nights. Crab cakes.
Other Points Of Interest: Overlooking Sarasota Bay, indoor or patio dining; Happy Hour 11:30 a.m.-6 p.m. 7 days, Sunday Brunch, Boat Accessible.
Most Popular Item: Salmon.

British Open Pub
8579 S. Tamiami Tr., Sarasota 34238
927-1022
Lunch & Dinner - Mon-Sat
Locally Owned - 4 Years
$; MC/VS
Beer/Wine Only
House Specialties: Wellington Specials, Fish and chips, Cornish pasty, chicken mushroom pie, and gourmet pizza.
Other Points of Interest: Very nice atmosphere; voted No. 1 British Pub.
Most Popular Item: Prime Rib Sandwich.

The Broadway Bar
1044 N. Tamiami Tr., Sarasota 34236
953-4343
Lunch - Mon-Sat, Dinner - 7 Days
Locally Owned - 44 Years

Key to Restaurant Listings

AX
American Express

CB
Carte Blanche

DC
Diners Club

DS
Discover

MC
Master Card

VS
Visa

LC
Local Checks are OK with proper I.D.

$
Under $7 lunch, under $12 dinner.

$$
Mostly $7 - $12 lunch, mostly $12 - $20 dinner.

$$$
Mostly $12 and over lunch, mostly $20 and over dinner.

Price categories are based on an average cost per person not including beverages, tax or tip.

$; No Credit Cards/LC
Full Bar
House Specialties: Antipasto salad. pizza.
Other Points Of Interest: Oldest Italian restaurant in Sarasota. A landmark. Tiles came from former John Ringling residence; former upstairs was reportedly a house of ill repute.
Family dining with a casual atmosphere.
Most Popular Item: "Best Pizza In Town."

Broadway Cafe
5629 Manatee Ave. West
Bradenton 34209
794-5066
Breakfast & Lunch - 7 Days
Dinner - 7 Days
Locally Owned - 8 Years
$; DS/MC/VS
No Liquor Served
House Specialties: Leg of lamb, baked salmon.
Other Points Of Interest: Large menu selection, home cooking, inexpensive breakfast.
Most Popular Item: Roast turkey.

The Broken Egg
210 Avenida Madera, Siesta Key 34242
346-2750
Breakfast & Lunch - 7 Days
Locally Owned - 13 Years
$; AX/CB/DC/DS/MC/VS/LC
Beer/Wine Only
House Specialties: Gourmet breakfast and lunch. Generous portions. Outstanding homemade desserts. Fresh squeezed juices.
Other Points Of Interest: Friendly owner. On premise bakery. Outdoor dining. Great to-go meals too. Catering available. "A must do on Siesta Key!"
Most Popular Item: Incredible Hash browns.

Buccaneer Inn
595 Dream Island Rd.
Longboat Key 34228
383-5565, fax 387-9705
Lunch & Dinner - 7 Days
Breakfast buffet Sat & Sun
Early Bird Specials in season
Locally Owned - 4 Years
$$; AX/DS/MC/VS
Full Bar
House Specialties: Prime rib, fresh seafood, pastas.
Other Points of Interest: Live music and dancing 7 nights a week. Tropical location overlooking sleepy lagoon, since 1957. Gift shop and boutique. Kids menu.
Most Popular Item: Fresh seafood.

Bud's Restaurant, Barbara's Too!
789 US 41 By-Pass, Venice 34292
485-6092
Breakfast & Lunch - Mon-Sat
Locally Owned - 4 Years
$; No Credit Cards/LC
No Liquor Served
House Specialties: Daily specialty omelets, stuffed cabbage.
Other Points Of Interest: Low prices. Everything made fresh daily.
Most Popular Item: Meatloaf platters.

Cactus Steak House
1185 US 41 By Pass S., Venice 34292
484-5191
Lunch - Mon- Fri, Dinner -7 days
Late Night - Fri & Sat
Locally Owned - 8 Years
$$; AX/DS/MC/VS
Full Bar
House Specialties: Wild onion, steaks, chicken and ribs cooked over a natural wood fire. Mexican dishes. Seafood - swordfish, salmon, grouper.
Other Points Of Interest: "Great fajitas and margaritas"
Most Popular Item: Steaks.

Cafe Amici
5802 Longwood Run Blvd.
Sarasota 34243
355-4517
Lunch - Tues-Fri, October to May
Dinner - 7 days
Locally Owned - 1 Year
$; AX, DS, MC, VS, LC
Beer/Wine only
House Specialties: Veal Melanzane, Penne Caprese.
Other Points of Interest: Praised in review by Sarasota Herald-Tribune.
Most Popular Item: Fettuccine Amici.

Cafe Baci
4001 S. Tamiami Tr., Sarasota 34231
921-4848
Lunch - Mon-Fri, Dinner - 7 Days
Early Birds
Locally Owned - 6 Years
$$; AX/CB/DC/DS/MC/VS
Full Bar
House Specialties: Veal piccata, lasagna verde, chicken francese and gnocchi.
Other Points Of Interest: Northern Italian cuisine. Fifth generation restaurant. Everything is prepared to order, freshness, superior quality and variety. Pasta made fresh on premises. Award-winning wine list. Lounge featuring live entertainment.
Most Popular Item: Veal dishes.

Cafe Barrister
1900 Main St. #107, Sarasota 34236
362-4314
Breakfast & Lunch - Mon-Fri
Locally Owned - 5 Years
$; AX/MC/VS/LC
No liquor served
House Specialties: Cuban, "The Judge," "The Hostile Witness."
Most Popular Item: "Best Club in town!"

Cafe Campestre
3164 Bee Ridge Rd., Sarasota 34239
923-5356
Lunch - Mon-Sat, Dinner - 7 Days
Locally Owned - 14 Years

The Broken Egg
A Piece of Work

Casual Dining
In a Relaxed Atmosphere
Serving Breakfast & Lunch Daily

Siesta Key Village
210 Avenida Madeira
Sarasota, Florida 34242
(941) 346-2750

Key to Restaurant Listings

AX
American Express

CB
Carte Blanche

DC
Diners Club

DS
Discover

MC
Master Card

VS
Visa

LC
Local Checks are OK with proper I.D.

$
Under $7 lunch, under $12 dinner.

$$
Mostly $7 - $12 lunch, mostly $12 - $20 dinner.

$$$
Mostly $12 and over lunch, mostly $20 and over dinner.

Price categories are based on an average cost per person not including beverages, tax or tip.

$; MC/VS
Beer/Wine Only
House Specialties: "Uchepos" - Authentic Aztec dish. Fajitas, chile relleno and seafood enchiladas. Steak Tampiquena. Homemade hot tamales, enchiladas verdes, vegetarian dishes, sopapillas.
Other Points Of Interest: Authentic Mexican cooking. Family owned and operated. "Jalisco" style cooking. Friendly atmosphere. Smoke-free.
Most Popular Item: Chile relleno.

Cafe Kaldi
1568 Main St., Sarasota 34236
366-2326, fax 366-1955
e-mail: kofewhse@gte.net
www.cafekaldi.com
Breakfast, Mon-Sat, Lunch, Mon-Fri, Late night (desserts)
$; AX, DS, MC, VS, LC
No liquor served
House Specialties: Surprisingly wonderful sandwiches (curry chicken salad, rare roast beef and cheese, more); Sarasota's only coffee roaster - gourmet Coffees roasted in store (35 varieties/60 flavors); Espresso/Cappuccino; specialty coffee drinks; signature baked goods; "two-hands" sandwiches; soups as a meal, natural fruit smoothies, granitas.
Other Points of Interest: In-store roasting of coffees, coffee tastings in season. Cyber cafe featuring Comcast cable modem high-speed access; at publication time Cafe Kaldi coffee is being made available at Marshal's department stores nationwide!
Most Popular Item: Double Ghirardelli Chocolate Cafe Mocha.

Cafe Lido
700 Ben Franklin Dr., Sarasota 34236
388-216, fax 388-31751
Breakfast, Lunch & Dinner - 7 days
Locally Owned - 3 years
$$; AX/CB/DC/DS/MC/VS
Full Bar
House Specialties: Fresh seafood and Certified Angus Beef prepared with regional ingredients and cooked Floribbean style.
Other Points of Interest: Outside patio dining surrounded by lush landscaping. Inside restaurant features a cozy, intimate atmosphere with a small lounge. Tiki Bar sits directly on the beach and offers a poolside menu until 8 p.m. with complimentary finger foods daily from 4:30 to 7.
Most Popular Item: Goombay Banana Grouper.

Cafe L' Europe
431 St. Armands Circle
St. Armands 34236
388-4415, fax 388-2362
e-mail: leurope@ix.netcom.com
www.cafeleurope.net
Lunch - Mon-Sat, Dinner - 7 Nights
Locally Owned - 25 Years
$$$; AX/CB/DC/MC/VS/DS
Full Bar
House Specialties: fresh seafood, prime meats.
Other Points Of Interest: World class dining in an atmosphere of European elegance. Carl Steger entertains at the piano Tuesday through Sunday evenings. Winner of 1998 DiRona Award.
Most Popular Item: Brandied duckling.

Cafe of The Arts
5230 N. Tamiami Tr., Sarasota 34234
351-6477, fax 351-0675
Breakfast - 7 Days, Lunch - Mon-Sat
Dinner - Tues-Sat, Sunday Brunch
Locally Owned - 7 Years
$$; AX/DS/MC/VS/LC
Full Bar
House Specialties: L'immigrant sandwich, bouillabaisse, rack of lamb, duck l'orange.
Other Points Of Interest: Beautiful views of lush wooded property; 2-3 fresh seafood specials daily. "Best French Restaurant" last 5 years.
Most Popular Item: Veal Francaise.

Cafe on the Bay
2600 Harbourside Dr.
Longboat Key 34228
383-0440
Breakfast, Lunch & Dinner - 7 Days
Locally Owned - 3 Years
$$; AX/MC/VS
Full Bar
Most Popular Item: "Mixed Grill" - salmon, tuna and swordfish.

Captain Curt's Crab & Oyster Bar and The Backroom Saloon
1200 Old Stickney Point Rd.
Siesta Key 34242
349-3885, fax 346-0910
Lunch & Dinner - 7 Days
Locally Owned - 4 Years
$; AX/DS/MC/VS
Full Bar
House Specialties: Cajun Grouper, baby back ribs, Indiana-style pork tenderloin.
Other Points Of Interest: Live entertainment nightly in Backroom. Takeout available. Amazing Key Lime pie
Most Popular Item: Cajun Grouper.

Captain Eddie's Seafood Restaurant & Oyster Bar
107 Colonia Ln. East, Nokomis 34275
484-4623, fax 484-0805
Lunch & Dinner - Mon-Sat
(closed Monday April-December)
Locally Owned - 15 Years
$; MC/VS
Beer/Wine Only
House Specialties: Fresh local sea food from our own boats.
Other Points Of Interest: Nominatee "Best of the Best" 2 times. Voted bes seafood Venice Gondolier Reader 1997. Won "Best Seafood Where the

Locals Really Eat", 1997; Play underwater videos made by Capt. Eddie. *Most Popular Item:* Rock shrimp.

Caragiulo's Italian Restaurant
69 S. Palm Ave. , Sarasota 34236
951-0866, fax 365-2239
e-mail: jcrest@aol.com
Lunch - Mon-Fri, Dinner - 7 Days
Locally Owned - 10 Years
$$; AX/CB/DC/DS/MC/VS
Full Bar
House Specialties: Chicken basilico, veal marsala, Pappardelle Alla Portanesca, gourmet pizzas, Caesar salad. Fresh seafood specials.
Other Points Of Interest: Cigar bar. Located in the heart of the Theater District. Open for lunch and dinner. Classic Italian movie posters and photos adorn the walls. Patio dining. Hugely popular with locals year 'round. Live music in Lounge Sat. and Sun.
Most Popular Item: Gourmet pizza and Caesar salad.

Caroline's on the Bay
Seafood Grille & Bar
482 Blackburn Pt. Rd., Osprey 34229
966-7431, fax 966-6393
Lunch - Tues-Sun, Dinner - 7 days
Locally Owned - 30 years
$$; AX, MC, VS
Full bar
House Specialties: Fresh seafood, steaks, pasta.

Cafe Amici
Affordable Italian
"Homemade" Specialties

Loved by locals and friends alike. The very definition of a festive trattoria casual and family dining. This hidden treasure offers variety of classical regional italian specialties and wine.

LUNCH • DINNER • CATERING

355-4517
Billy Stearns Tennis Center
5802 Longwood Run Blvd.
University Pkwy. 2 traffic lights W. from I-75 (exit 40)

• Sarasota's Only Daily Custom Coffee Roaster
• Kaldi Signature Bakery • Custom Catering • Soups From Scratch
• Two fisted Sandwiches • Gift Baskets
• Surf the Internet

• More than 40 fresh roasted coffees from around the world
1568 Main Street   Sarasota   366-2326
www.cafekaldi.com

Café Kaldi **BRING THIS AD IN FOR 10% OFF ANY WHOLE BEAN COFFEE**

Other Points of Interest: Great view of Casey Key Marina and intracoastal waterway. Boat accessible at Marker 33 in the ICW. Gift shop, kayak rentals, boat rentals.
Most Popular Item: Osprey crab cakes.

Carrabba's
1940 Stickney Point Rd., Sarasota 34231
925-7407, fax 925-7103
Dinner - 7 days
$$; AX/DC/DS/MC/VS
Full Bar
House Specialties: Thrill of the Grill. All food cooked over oak and pecan wood. Gourmet pizzas cooked in wood burning oven.
Other Points of Interest: Wood-burning pizza oven; wood-burning grill; open kitchen. Happy hour every day 4-7.
Most Popular Item: Speedino Di Mare

Cattle Company Cafe
6706 14th St. W., Bradenton 34207
758-5643
Lunch & Dinner - 7 Days
Locally Owned - 24 Years
$; MC/VS
No Liquor Served
House Specialties: Steaks, broiled chicken, seafood, 50 item salad bar.
Other Points of Interest: Banquet facilities available.
Most Popular Item: Soup & salad bar.

Cedars Cafe
545 Cedars Ct., Longboat Key 34228
383-7863, fax 383-5534
Lunch - Tues-Sat, Dinner - Wed-Sat
Early Bird Specials, Sunday Brunch
Locally Owned - 9 Years
$$$; AX/MC/VS/LC
Full Bar
House Specialties: Fresh Florida seafood, Rack of Lamb, roast duck, filet mignon and fresh seafood.
Other Points Of Interest: Located pool side, beautiful outdoor setting. "Casual Florida dining." Six wine dinners per year, call for schedule.
Most Popular Item: Grilled Veal Chops with Morel Sauce.

Charley's Crab
420 St. Armands Circle
St. Armands 34236
388-3964, fax 388-1058
Lunch & Dinner - 7 Days
Early bird specials
Locally Owned - 18 years
$$; AX/CB/DC/MC/VS/LC
Full Bar
House Specialties: Six to eight fresh fish daily, home made pasta dishes, crab cakes.
Other Points Of Interest: Votes "Best Outside Cafe," live piano player lunch and dinner. Unique banquet room.
Most Popular Item: Jonah lump crabcakes.

THE BEST SEAFOOD MEALS & DEALS IN TOWN!

Family Restaurant
Children's Menu
Seafood
Specialty Items:
Grouper &
Baby Back Ribs

CRAB & OYSTER BAR
Siesta Key, Florida

Open Daily
Hours 11 am - 'Til
Sunday Noon - 'Til
Happy Hour 4-6 pm

Captain Curt's Backroom Saloon
Enjoy Entertainment Nightly, Featuring Live Music, Karaoke & Satelite TV for Sports Fans and Gift Shop

1200 Old Stickney Pt. Road & Midnight Pass Rd.
Siesta Key ■ 349-3885

Key to Restaurant Listings

AX
American Express

CB
Carte Blanche

DC
Diners Club

DS
Discover

MC
Master Card

VS
Visa

LC
Local Checks are OK with proper I.D.

$
Under $7 lunch, under $12 dinner.

$$
Mostly $7 - $12 lunch, mostly $12 - $20 dinner.

$$$
Mostly $12 and over lunch, mostly $20 and over dinner.

Price categories are based on an average cost per person not including beverages, tax or tip.

The Chart House
201 Gulf Of Mexico Dr.
Longboat Key 34228
383-5593, fax 383-5879
Dinner - 7 Days, Early Bird Specials
$$$; AX/CB/DC/DS/MC/VS
Full Bar
House Specialties: Aged beef, salad bar, fresh fish.
Other Points Of Interest: Wonderful view of New Pass. Unique decor and architecture.
Most Popular Item: Prime rib.

Chef Caldwell's
20 Adams Drive. S.
St. Armands Circle 34236
388-5400, fax 388-4021
Lunch - Mon-Sat, Dinner - 7 Days
Locally Owned - 5 Years
$$; AX/DC/DS/MC/VS
Beer/Wine Only
House Specialties: Roasted duckling, grilled veal chop, grouper Grenobloise, key lime pie, chocolate ganache.
Other Points Of Interest: Originator of Heart healthy dining; former Colony/Michael's Executive Chef now very successful on his own, with wife Jean.
Most Popular Item: Pecan crusted snapper.

Chef Paul's
4900 N. Tamiami Tr., Sarasota 34234
365-5976
Breakfast & Lunch - 7 Days
Locally Owned - 12 Years
$; AX/DS/MC/VS/LC
No liquor served
House Specialties: Area's best Eggs Benedict. grilled Reuben, homemade soups, steak & eggs.
Most Popular Item: Eggs Benedict.

The Chelsea Grill
1991 Main St., Sarasota Main Plaza
Sarasota 34236
362-0808, fax 362-7868
Lunch - Mon-Fri, Dinner 7 days
Locally Owned - 2 Years
$$; AX/DS/MC/VS
Full Bar
Other Points of Interest: New owner did not have time to talk with us, we'll try again for the next edition.

Chez Andre
5406 Marina Dr., Holmes Beach 34217
778-5320
Breakfast - Tues-Sun,
Lunch -Tues-Sun, Dinner - Thur-Sun
Locally Owned - 10 Years
$$; MC/VS
Beer/Wine Only
House Specialties: Bakery fresh croissants. Dinners: venison, game, quail and duck; fresh Seafood, veal.
Other Points Of Interest: Bakery and breakfast items available for take-out. Florida Magazine Fine Dining Award (1995).
Most Popular Item: Sweetbreads.

China Blossom Restaurant & Lounge
15 Avenue Of The Flowers
Longboat Key 34228
383-9533
Lunch - Mon-Sat, Dinner - 7 Days
Locally Owned - 13 Years
$; AX/DS/MC/VS/DS
Full Bar
House Specialties: Chicken, lobster, beef, shrimp, fish and vegetables in a wide variety of presentations.
Other Points Of Interest: Only Chinese restaurant on Longboat Key. Many combination specials. Free delivery anywhere on Longboat Key.
Most Popular Item: General Tso Chicken.

The China Palace
5131 14th St. West
Bradenton 34207
755-3758, fax 756-3650
Lunch & Dinner - 7 Days
Locally Owned - 18 Years
$$; AX/DC/DS/MC/VS
Full Bar
House Specialties: Crispy duck, beef steak Wor Bars. Bird's nets dishes, butterfly shrimp, sizzling noodle, tea smoked duck, flaming duck, Peking duck (24 hour notice).
Other Points Of Interest: You feel like you're in China in this authentically decorated restaurant. Winner of Sarasota "Best of the Best" for 6 years. Winner of Reader's Preference.
Most Popular Item: Sweet & sour chicken.

China Pavilion
8383 S. Tamiami Tr., Sarasota 34238
925-8383, fax 925-3758
Lunch - Mon-Fri, Dinner - 7 Days
Locally Owned - 12 Years
$; AX/DS/MC/VS
Full Bar
House Specialties: General Tso's chicken, seafood with garlic sauce.
Other Points Of Interest: Casual dining.
Most Popular Item: General Tso's chicken.

Christellie's Italian Restaurant
5718 Cortez Rd. West, Bradenton 34210
792-4195
Lunch & Dinner - Mon-Sat
Early Bird Specials
Locally Owned - 15 Years
$; AX/DS/MC/VS
Beer/Wine Only
House Specialties: Pasta and Pizza.
Other Points Of Interest: Family-style home cooked Italian food.
Most Popular Item: Veal Parmesan.

Churchill's Bar & Restaurant
1816 S. Osprey Ave., Sarasota 34239
951-0990, fax 954-6064
e-mail: playrugby1@aol.com
Lunch - Mon-Fri, Dinner - Mon-Sat
Late Night Menu
Locally Owned - 3 Years
$; AX/DC/DS/MC/VS/LC
Beer/Wine only

House Specialties: Homemade soups, salads, finest chargrilled dishes. Fresh fish dishes, spinach & artichoke, steak, mushroom and Guiness Pie, hummus, chicken curry, Chicken leg & tarragon pie, scallops picatta, pasta dishes, Shrimp Vera Cruz.
Other Points of Interest: Churchill automobiles and memorabilia; caters to vegetarians; "to go" menu; catering available; happy hour every day; great selection of beer and wines.
Most Popular Item: Fresh snapper specials.

Chutney's Etc. International Cafe
1944 Hillview St., Sarasota 34239
954-4444, fax 954-4444
Lunch - Mon-Fri, Dinner - Mon-Sat
Locally Owned - 11 Years
$; MC/VS/LC
Beer/Wine Only
House Specialties: Hummus, Poabayhandosh, Falafel. Vegetarian specials, curries, tandoori.
Other Points of Interest: Catering, take-out, vegetarian menu. Award-winning ethnic cuisine. Creative Indian/Middle Eastern menu; Ashwin and Denise work hard to create memorable meals.
Most Popular Item: Indian curries and vegetarian specialities.

Ciao! Italia
5370 Gulf of Mexico Dr.
Longboat Key 34228
383-0010
Lunch & Dinner - 7 Days
Locally Owned - 3 Years
$; AX/ MC/VS/LC
Beer/Wine Only
House Specialties: Antipasta, shrimp Fra Diavolo, Chicken cacciatore, Gourmet Pizza.
Other Points Of Interest: Quality with casual atmosphere on Longboat Key. Bistro setting.
Most Popular Item: Veal Marsala.

City Pizza
6645 Midnight Pass Rd.,
Siesta Key 34242
349-4490
Lunch -Mon-Sat, Dinner - 7 Days
Locally Owned - 10 Years
$; AX/DS/MC/VS
Beer/Wine Only
House Specialties: Pizza and pasta dishes, Frank's friendly personality.
Most Popular Item: Pizza.

Coach & Horses British Pub
6240 N Lockwood Ridge Rd.
Sarasota 34243
358-1353, fax 358-1353
4921 Cortez Rd. West,
Bradenton 34210
795-4575, fax 358-1353
Bayshore Shopping Center
6152 14th St. West, Bradenton 34207
758-4646, fax 358-1353
Lunch & Dinner - 7 Days
Locally Owned - 3 Years

$; AX/DS/MC/VS
Beer/Wine Only (Full bar at Bayshore Gardens location)
House Specialties: Certified Angus beef specials, gourmet pizza, Indian curries, "the best" chicken wings.
Other Points of Interest: 14 beers on draught (12 imported). Large bottled beer selection. Authentic cozy British pub atmosphere.
Most Popular Item: Fish & chips.

Coasters Seafood Company
1500 Stickney Point Rd.
Sarasota 34231
923-0500, fax 926-0315
Lunch & Dinner - 7 days
Late Night menu
Locally Owned - 4 Years
$$; AX/DC/DS/MS/VS
Full Bar
House Specialties: Oyster Cargot, lobster quesadillas, Chesapeake Bay salad, shrimp etouffe, steamed cherrystone clams, broiled seafood platter, live Maine lobster, Alaskan king crab legs.
Other Points of Interest: Located on the intracoastal waterway, offers indoor dining or on the waterfront deck. Live music on weekends and steel drum music on weekend afternoons. Happy hour daily. Tropical drink specials.
Most Popular Item: Maryland lump crabcakes.

Key to Restaurant Listings

AX
American Express

CB
Carte Blanche

DC
Diners Club

DS
Discover

MC
Master Card

VS
Visa

LC
Local Checks are OK with proper I.D.

$
Under $7 lunch, under $12 dinner.

$$
Mostly $7 - $12 lunch, mostly $12 - $20 dinner.

$$$
Mostly $12 and over lunch, mostly $20 and over dinner.

Price categories are based an average cost per person not including beverages, tax or tip.

Cock 'N Bull Pub
1468 Main St., Sarasota 34236
316-9300
Dinner - 7 days, Early bird specials
Locally Owned - 2 Years
$$; CB/DC/DS/MC/VS/LC
Full Bar

The Colony Bistro
1620 Gulf Of Mexico Dr.
Longboat Key 34228
383-5558, fax 383-7549
Breakfast -Mon-Sat, Dinner 7 days
Locally Owned - 30 Years
$$; AX/DC/DS/MC/VS
Full Bar
House Specialties: Veal meat loaf, beef brisket (Buffalo, NY recipe!)

The Colony Dining Room
1620 Gulf Of Mexico Dr.
Longboat Key 34228
383-5558, fax 383-7549
Breakfast & Lunch Mon-Sat
Dinner 7 days
Locally Owned - 29 Years
$$$; AX/DC/DS/MC/VS
Full Bar
House Specialties: Roast Colorado Rack of Lamb, pan roasted American red snapper.
Other Points Of Interest: Located on the Gulf of Mexico; DiRona Award winner; Wine Spectator's Award of excellence.
Most Popular Item: Crispy fried lobster tail.

Columbia Restaurant
411 St. Armands Circle, St. Armands
388-3987
Lunch & Dinner - 7 Days
Early Bird Specials/Late Night
Locally Owned - 38 Years
$$; AX/CB/DC/DS/MC/VS
Full Bar
House Specialties: 1905 salad. Steaks and seafood.
Other Points Of Interest: A landmark in Tampa and Sarasota. Nightclub with live entertainment located right next door, on beautiful St. Armands Circle. Music/dancing every Thurs.-Sun.
Most Popular Item: Crab claws and Paella.

Corkscrew Deli
4982 S. Tamiami Tr., Sarasota 34231
925-3955, fax 926-0066
Breakfast & Lunch - Mon-Sat
Locally Owned - 4 Years
$; AX/CB/DC/DS/MC/VS/LC
No liquor served
House Specialties: Some of the best sandwiches in Sarasota. Really.
Other Points of Interest: Tastefully decorated. A great place for a quick, informal lunch. A secret no more.
Most Popular Item: Combo Salad.

Cosimo's Brick Oven
201 Southgate Plaza, Sarasota 34239
363-0211, fax 363-0411
Lunch & Dinner - 7 days
$; MC/VS
Full bar
House Specialties: Wood-fired gourmet pizzas, grilled veal chop with wild mushroom Madeira sauce, hot crab appetizer, grilled chicken penne.
Other Points of Interest: Exclusive, affordable wine list; original artwork throughout; cigar friendly (bar only). One of the area's best new restaurants (opened 1998). Open late, even after mall closes. Great staff, great food, great portions - a new favorite.

The Country Buffet
5415 14th St. West, Bradenton 34207
727-8410
Lunch & Dinner - Wed-Sun
Locally Owned - 5 Years
$; No credit cards accepted/LC
No liquor served
House Specialties: Chicken, meatloaf, chicken-n-dumplings, clam chowder.
Other Points of Interest: Good home cooking; recipes from the Heartland of America. Senior discounts.
Most Popular Item: Fried and baked chicken.

Crab Trap I
5611 US 19, Palmetto 34222
722-6255, fax 729-4788
Crab Trap II
4815 Memphis Rd., Ellenton 34222
729-7777
Lunch - Mon-Sat, Dinner - 7 Days
Locally Owned - 25 Years
Early Bird Specials
$$; DS/MC/VS
Full Bar
House Specialties: Maryland-style crab dishes including crab cakes, Imperial and stone crab. 120 item menu.
Other Points of Interest: Both locations on the water. Great decor. Florida Trend "Top 20" for over 20 years consecutively.
Most Popular Item: Crab Cakes.

Crow's Nest Marina Restaurant & Tavern
1968 Tarpon Center Dr., Venice 34285
484-9551
Lunch & Dinner - 7 Days
Late Night menu in Tavern
Locally Owned - 22 Years
$$; AX/DS/MC/VS
Full Bar
House Specialties: Stone crab in season, mussels, Ipswich clams, grouper, mahi mahi, salmon, fresh and creatively prepared.
Other Points Of Interest: Venice's waterfront landmark since 1976. Overlooking the marine and intracoastal waterway. Casual fine dining upstairs. Wine Spectator Award of Excellence for the 450+ selection wine list! Downstairs tavern features a raw bar, late night menu and live entertainment several nights a week.

**Winner - A Taste of Sarasota
First Place - Best Entree**

Open Later than Mall Hours

Wood-Fired Pizza
Specialty Salads
Signature Pasta
Homemade Desserts
Full Bar

Hours
Monday-Thursday
11am - 10pm; bar 'til 11pm

Friday and Saturday
11am 'til 11pm;
bar 'til midnight

Sunday
Noon 'til 8pm; bar 'til 9pm

TRATTORIA & BAR

201 Southgate Plaza
Across from Dillards,
corner of US 41 and Siesta Drive
363-0211

Key to Restaurant Listings

AX American Express

CB Carte Blanche

DC Diners Club

DS Discover

MC Master Card

VS Visa

LC Local Checks are OK with proper I.D.

$ Under $7 lunch, under $12 dinner.

$$ Mostly $7 - $12 lunch, mostly $12 - $20 dinner.

$$$ Mostly $12 and over lunch, mostly $20 and over dinner.

Price categories are based on an average cost per person not including beverages, tax or tip.

Most Popular Item: "Gunther Gebel Williams" Filet Mignon.

Cuisine De France
7449 Manatee Ave. West
Bradenton 34209
792-3782
Lunch - Tues-Sun, Dinner in season, call first.
Locally Owned - 17 Years
$$; MC/DS
Beer/Wine Only
House Specialties: Specialty egg dishes, chicken salad, fresh baked breads, croissants.
Other Points Of Interest: Authentic French atmosphere.
Most Popular Item: Chicken salad with fresh fruit.

Cuoco Matto Ristorante
1603 N. Tamiami Tr.
Sarasota 34236
365-0000, fax 362-7878
Lunch & Dinner - 7 Days
Locally Owned - 2 Years
$; AX/CB/DC/DS/MC/VS
Full bar
House Specialties: Seafood. Meats and pizza in wood-burning oven.
Other Points of Interest: Newly expanded, open kitchen, relaxed family atmosphere, authentic Italian cuisine.
Most Popular Item: Capellini Shrimp.

D. Coy Duck's Bar and Grille
5410 Marina Dr., Holmes Beach 34217
778-5888
Lunch & Dinner - 7 Days
Locally Owned - 6 Years
$; No Credit Cards/LC
Full Bar
House Specialties: Prime Rib, grouper, chicken salad, BBQ ribs and wings.
Other Points Of Interest: Entertainment Mon.-Sat. night featuring jazz and contemporary music. Old time booths, theme nights each week: Monday, Home cooking; Tuesday, Mexican; Wednesday, Greek.
Most Popular Item: Prime Rib.

Da Ru Ma Japanese Steak & Seafood
318 Sarasota Quay, Sarasota 34236
951-2440
Dinner - 7 Days, Early bird specials
Locally Owned - 5 Years
$$; AX/DC/DS/MC/VS
Full Bar
House Specialties: Sushi bar, lobster Nippon.
Other Points Of Interest: Teppan-yaki grill, cooks at table. Sushi bar with chef. Also serving seafood, steak and chicken. Gift shop.
Most Popular Item: Filet mignon.

Daiquiri Deck & Cafe Gardens
5250 Ocean Blvd., Siesta Key 34242
349-8697, fax 346-3904
Lunch & Dinner - 7 Days
Locally Owned - 14 Years

$; AX/DS/MC/VS
Full Bar
House Specialties: Over 20 frozen drink flavors and combinations. Charbroiled grouper, snapper, chicken and hamburgers. Conch fritters and California-style pizza and tropical fruit salads.
Other Points Of Interest: a casual "after the beach" atmosphere and outdoor dining on the deck in the heart of Siesta Village. Great spot for people watching. Famous for its beautiful staff and true island hospitality.
Most Popular Item: "The Bushwacker," a frozen daiquiri made with Kahlua, dark rum, coconut and cream.

David Michaels
328 John Ringling Blvd. S.
Sarasota 34236
388-4429, fax 388-4326
Lunch & Dinner - Mon-Sat
Locally Owned - 4 Years
$$; CB/ DC/DS/MC/VS/LC
Beer/Wine Only
House Specialties: Unique salads, Ahi tuna steak seasoned with Asian spices, fire roasted and served with passion fruit cracked pepper glaze.
Other Points of Interest: One of the Florida Trend "Top 200" restaurants in Florida. Patio dining in good weather.
Most Popular Item: Beefalo.

DeFina's Restaurant
1965 Tamiami Tr. South, Venice 34293
493-8499
Dinner - Mon-Sat
Locally Owned - 14 Years
$; AX/DS/MC/VS/LC
Beer/Wine Only
House Specialties: Baby back ribs, shrimp scampi, steak dinners.
Other Points Of Interest: Family owned. Italian cuisine. Fresh home cooking daily.
Most Popular Item: Chicken Parmesan.

Demetrio's Pizzeria
4410 Tamiami Tr. South, Sarasota
922-1585
Lunch & Dinner - 7 Days
Locally Owned - 18 Years
$; DS/MC/VS
Beer/Wine Only
House Specialties: Pizza. Greek salad, pasta.
Other Points Of Interest: A Sarasota landmark for great pizza and Greek food. Takeout available.
Most Popular Item: Pizza.

Demetrios Seafood & Steakhouse
6331 S. Tamiami Tr., Sarasota 34231
921-3648
Dinner - 7 days
Locally Owned - New
$; DS/MC/VS
Full bar
House Specialties: Lobster, seafood and steaks.
Most Popular Item: Lobster.

Der Dutchman Restaurant
3713 Bahia Vista, Sarasota 34232
955-8007, fax 955-5665
Breakfast - Mon-Sat
Lunch & Dinner - Mon-Sat
$; MC/VS/DS /LC
No Liquor Served
House Specialties: "Amish Kitchen Cooking" - full soup and salad bar, roasted turkey, meatloaf, Amish style roast beef, real mashed potatoes, homemade pies and desserts.
Other Points Of Interest: Breakfast buffet and an "in-house" bakery. Takeout available on all items. Friendly atmosphere, plus a Victorian gift shop. Don't miss the homemade pies here!
Most Popular Item: Broasted chicken.

Dirty Moe's Seafood & Spirits
7423 Manatee Ave. West
Bradenton 34209
798-3876, fax 758-9485
Lunch & Dinner - 7 Days
Late Night Menu
Locally Owned - 4 Years
$; AX/MC/VS/LC
Full Bar
House Specialties: Fresh seafood, daily specials, steaks, ribs.
Other Points of Interest: "Best of the Best" in 1997 for entrees and appetizers. Live Entertainment and Karaoke, Early bird specials. Snow Crab & lobster specials on weekends. Late night menu available til 1:30 AM. Catering and takeouts available.
Most Popular Item: Grouper sandwich.

Down Under Jazz Club
214 Sarasota Quay, Sarasota
951-2467
Lunch & Dinner - 7 Days
Locally Owned - 1 Year
$; AX/MC/VS
Full Bar
House Specialties: Quesadillas, fried Maine calamari, Shrimp Wellington, grilled chicken club, burgers, soups and salads.
Other Points of Interest: Tropical casual lunches and dinners served indoors or outside by the bay, live entertainment daily and "Sarasota's favorite happy hour!" Right on the water.
Most Popular Item: Grilled Grouper Reuben.

The Dragon Chinese Restaurant
1204 Stickney Point Rd.
Siesta Key 34242
349-5885
Dinner - 7 Days
Locally Owned - 7 Years
$; MC/VS/DS
Beer/Wine Only
House Specialties: Cantonese, Hunan and Szechuan cooking.
Other Points of Interest: Take-out Service for dinner; free delivery.

of Sarasota, Florida
Located in **Pinecraft**
The Amish Settlement of Sarasota

New Restaurant August '99
Banquet Facilities seats up to 300

- Try our All You Can Eat Soup & Salad Bar
- We specialize in Broasted Chicken, Roast Beef, & Real Mashed Potatoes
- Visit our Bakery & Gift Shop
- All Menu Items Available for Carry-Out
- Handicap Access to all Areas
- Open Monday - Saturday 6 am-8 pm
- Closed Sundays

3713 Bahia Vista   (941) 955-8007
• Fax (941) 955-5665 • Bakery (941) 365-9279
www.derdutchmanfl.com

Key to Restaurant Listings

AX
American Express

CB
Carte Blanche

DC
Diners Club

DS
Discover

MC
Master Card

VS
Visa

LC
Local Checks are OK with proper I.D.

$
Under $7 lunch, under $12 dinner.

$$
Mostly $7 - $12 lunch, mostly $12 - $20 dinner.

$$$
Mostly $12 and over lunch, mostly $20 and over dinner.

Price categories are based on an average cost per person not including beverages, tax or tip.

Most Popular Item: Cashew Chicken.

Dry Dock Waterfront Grill
412 Gulf Of Mexico Dr.
Longboat Key 34228
383-0102, fax 383-9130
Lunch -Mon-Sat, Dinner - 7 Days
Locally Owned - 10 Years
$$; AX/MC/VS/LC
Full Bar
House Specialties: Casual lunch and dinner menu features grouper sandwiches, chargrilled burgers and steaks, crab cakes, peel-n-eat shrimp, lobster, salads and fresh seafood.
Other Points Of Interest: Casual waterfront dining on Sarasota Bay. "Located at the premier marina on Florida's West Coast." Outdoor patio.
Most Popular Item: Grilled grouper dinner.

Durhams Continental Dining
6290 N. Lockwood Ridge Rd.
Sarasota 34243
358-0447, fax 358-0548
Dinner - 7 days
Early Bird Specials/Happy Hour
Locally Owned - 4 Years
$$; AX/DS/MD/VS
Full Bar
House Specialties: Filet Oscar, Wiener Schnitzel, true Maryland-style Crabcakes, Snapper Largo.
Other Points of Interest: An ambiance of soft lights and warm woods create an understated elegant atmosphere with big band and swing background music. Vegetarian selections available. Happy hour daily.
Most Popular Item: Veal Oscar

Dutch Haus Family Restaurant
1247 S. Beneva Rd., Sarasota
954-4287
Breakfast, Lunch & Dinner - Mon-Sat
Locally Owned - 6 Years
$; AX/DS/MC/VS
No Liquor Served
House Specialties: Amish peanut butter homemade pies, cakes, cobblers, sweet rolls, home-cooked meals, ham loaf, meatloaf, chuck roast.
Other Points Of Interest: Awarded "Best Dinner Under $10."
Most Popular Item: Meatloaf.

Dutch Oven
6518 Gateway Ave., Sarasota 34234
921-6778
Breakfast - 7 Days
Lunch - 6 Days
Sunday Brunch
$; NC/LC
No Liquor Served
House Specialties: Amish homestyle cooking, prepared to your order. Real mashed potatoes every day. stuffed cabbage, beautiful salad plates.
Other Points Of Interest: The restaurant has been serving homemade food for more than 20 years. WE know our clients by name. Vegetarian menu available. Take-out.
Most Popular Item: Homemade meatloaf with real mashed potatoes and gravy.

El Adobe
4023 Tamiami Tr. South
Sarasota 34231
921-7476, fax 923-7600
Lunch & Dinner - 7 Days
Locally Owned - 25 Years
$; AXCB//DC/DS/MC/VS
Full Bar
House Specialties: Mexican cuisine; Carne Ortega-filet mignon stuffed with mild pepper cheese.
Most Popular Item: Carne Ortega.

El Greco Cafe
1592 Main St., Sarasota 34236
365-2234, fax 365-4942
Lunch & Dinner - Mon-Sat
Locally Owned - 9 Years
$; MC/VS
Beer/Wine Only
House Specialties: Lamb, Moussaka, Dolmades, Spanakopita, Gyros, Greek salad, baklava
Other Points Of Interest: Consistently voted "Best of the Best" Greek Restaurant in Sarasota Magazine and Sarasota Herald Tribune, for good reason.
Most Popular Item: Lamb shanks.

Empress Gardens Restaurant
6090 Lockwood Ridge Rd.
Sarasota 34243
359-3658
Lunch & Dinner - 7 days
Early Bird Specials
Locally Owned - 9 Years
$; AX/DS/MC/VS
Full Bar
House Specialties: Empress chow mein, Szechuan shrimp, Thai cuisine.
Other Points Of Interest: Sarasota Herald Tribune Readers Choice "Best Runner Up Chinese Restaurant."
Most Popular Item: Orange Chicken.

Euphemia Haye
5540 Gulf Of Mexico Dr.
Longboat Key 34228
383-3633, fax 387-8336
Dinner - 7 Days, Late Night Menu in Hayloft Dessert Bar & Lounge
Locally Owned - 23 Years
$$$; CB/DC/MC/VS/DS
Full Bar
House Specialties: Roast duckling, pepper steak.
Other Points Of Interest: Golden Spoon Award, Florida Trend, 6th year. DiRona Awards. Live entertainment 7 nights. Cigars available. Extensive wine list. Dining By Candlelight Award (America's 200 Most Romantic Restaurants). Very popular.
Most Popular Item: Roasted duckling.

The Expedition Co. Bar & Grill
997 Venice By Pass North
Venice 34292
485-6393, fax 483-4013
Breakfast - 7 Days
Lunch & Dinner -Mon-Fri
Locally Owned - 17 Years
$; MC/VS; Full Bar
House Specialties: Seafood. Shrimp scampi, ribs, pasta. Great breakfast.
Other Points Of Interest: Fun for the family, plenty for kids to see. Newly remodeled - safari type atmosphere.
Most Popular Item: St. Louis style ribs.

Fandango International Cafe
5148 Ocean Blvd.
Siesta Key 34242
346-1711, fax 379-2072
Lunch & Dinner - 7 Days
Locally Owned - 11 Years
$$; DS/MC/VS
Beer/Wine Only
House Specialties: Hummus, jerk grouper, lamb kabob. Extensive variety of vegetarian foods and salads from different countries. "Wonderful and very exotic."
Other Points Of Interest: Upbeat atmosphere. Live jazz by nationally known jazz artists. Outdoor dining available. "Best of Best" - Middle Eastern Vegetarian and Caribbean Food.
Most Popular Item: Jerk Chicken.

Fifty's Diner
3737 Bahia Vista St., Sarasota 34232
953-4637, fax 365-0809
Lunch & Dinner - Mon-Sat
Early Bird Specials
Locally Owned - 5 Years
$; DS/MC/VS/LC
No Liquor Served
House Specialties: Full menu, on site baking, cooking from scratch. Always have Mom's Meatloaf. Daily specials. Great soup.
Other Points of Interest: Lots of 50s memorabilia and gift shop. Saturday night Kruz-in (car club). Tues. night is "Bike Nite"; Totally clean and smoke free. Family owned and operated. Old fashioned "Farmers Market" every Sat. morning.
Most Popular Item: Pot roast.

First Watch
8383 S. Tamiami Tr., Sarasota
923-6754
1395 Main St., Sarasota 34236
954-1395, fax 957-3597
www.firstwatch.com
Breakfast & Lunch -7 Days
Locally Owned -11 Years
$; AX/DS/MC/VS/LC
No Liquor Served
House Specialties: Pancakes, omelettes, breakfast skillets, lunch specialty sandwiches and salads.
Other Points Of Interest: Downtown location good meeting spot for business people or friends. The South Trail locale offers waterfront/outdoor dining.
Most Popular Item: Blueberry Pancakes.

Flying Bridge Restaurant
482 Blackburn Point Rd.
Osprey 34229
966-7431, fax 966-6393
Lunch & Dinner - 7 Days
Early Bird Specials
Locally Owned - 30 Years
$; AX/MC/VS
Full Bar
House Specialties: Fish-n-chips and Snapper Margarita.
Other Points Of Interest: Family owned. Great view of intracoastal waterway. Boat accessible at Marker 33 in the ICW. Outdoor dining, kayak rentals, boat rentals, gift shop.
Most Popular Item: Fresh fish.

Forest Lakes Restaurant
2401 Beneva Rd., Sarasota 34232
921-7979, fax 924-6497
Lunch - 7 days, Dinner - Tues-Sat
Sunday Brunch, Early Bird Specials
Locally Owned - 2 Years
$; AX/DS/MC/VS
Full Bar
House Specialties: Cedar plank seafood specialties, prime rib, steaks.
Most Popular Item: Cedar planked salmon with dill crust.

Dutch Oven

Amish Homestyle Cooking

Monday-Friday 7 am-2 pm
Saturday 7:30 - Noon (breakfast only)
Closed Sundays

Affordable catering for all occasions
The Joyet Family - proprietors

**6518 Gateway Avenue
Sarasota, FL 34231
921-6778
(located behind Gulf Gate Mall)**

Great Food · Great Spirits · Great Fun
Something for Everybody!!

Gecko's Grill & Pub "At the Landings"
4870 S. Tamiami Tr. · 923-8896 · fax 923-8545

Sarasota's Most Popular Meeting Place and Sports Center. Pro Bar Staff. Great Happy Hour. Giant Margaritas. Famous Fishbowls. Buckets of Beer. American Pub Food with a Twist of Gourmet. 10 TVs and Big Screen. Special Events Nightly. Giant Burritos. Tender Rubens. French Dip. 1/2 lb Burgers. Lots of Salads. Blackened Fish. Blackened Chicken. Red Beans & Rice and More!

Gecko's Grill & Pub "Twelve Oaks Plaza"
7228 55th Avenue East · 727-8988

NEW LOCATION! A Sarasota Tradition Opens in Bradenton. Great Dining Experience. Pro Bar Staff. Tender Juicy Prime Rib. Pork Marsala. Homemade Meat Loaf. Real Mashed Potatoes. Giant Cobb Salad and More!
At State Road 70 and I-75 (Exit 41B) in Twelve Oaks Plaza.

Red Barn Bar
2058 Bee Ridge Rd. (Across from Southgate)
922-7855

One of Sarasota's Original Cocktail Lounges. Best Value on Cocktails, Beer & Wine. Play Pool, Darts, and Foosball. Open 365 Days! It's the greatest in small town neighborhood bars. Come in and join the fun.

Wild·Eats Grille & Market "Paradise Plaza"
3800 S. Tamiami Tr. (Behind Publix, Facing Osprey Ave.) · 954-1330

Sarasota's Healthier Fare Alternative! Serving Vegetarian, Vegan and Traditional Cuisine For the Healthy Mind, Body and Spirit. Warm, Friendly, Relaxing, Smoke-Free. Outside Patio Seating Available. Market Entrees and Takeout Menu Selections Available. Beer & Wine. Breakfast · Lunch · Dinner

Four Fabulous Fun Filled Places all owned by a great group of Sarasota's Finest.

Francoise et Henri
1359 Main St., Sarasota 34236
951-1510, fax 952-1504
Lunch - Mon-Fri, Dinner - Mon-Sat
Late Night Menu (in season)
Locally Owned - 2 Years
$$$; AX/CB/DC/DS/MC/VS
Full Bar
House Specialties: Dover sole, rack of lamb, bouillabaisse, Coq au Vin, beef bourgoignon, chocolate souffle, crepes Suzette.
Other Points of Interest: Authentic French chateau decor, fireplace, secluded booths, private dining room. 2nd floor location (use the elevator).
Most Popular Item: Dover sole.

French Affair
2637 Mall Dr., Sarasota
925-3414
Lunch & Dinner - Mon-Sat
Dinner 7 days during Summer months
Locally Owned - 17 Years
$; MC/VS/LC
Beer and Wine Only
House Specialties: Daily French specials (this is the real thing!) based on owner and chef's artistic mood! (see?)
Other Points Of Interest: Outstanding everything, including select wines at reasonable prices; a real find!!
Most Popular Item: Bouillabaisse.

Gastronomia Restaurant
7119 S. Tamiami Tr., Sarasota 34232
927-8331, fax 921-9179
Lunch - Mon-Sat, Dinner - 7 days
Locally Owned - 3 Years
$; AX/CB/DC/DS/MC/VS
Beer and Wine Only
House Specialties: Osso buco, spaghetti carbonara, proscuitto and melon, Caesar salad.
Other Points Of Interest: "Best of the Best" 1998 - Best Italian Restaurant. Also finalist for best caterer and best wine list. Expanded menu for 1999.
Most Popular Item: Osso buco.

Gecko's Grill & Pub
4870 S. Tamiami Tr., Sarasota
923-8896
7228 55th Ave. East (12 Oaks Plaza)
Bradenton 34203
727-8988
e-mail: eventsandmore@msn.com
Lunch & Dinner - 7 Days
Locally Owned - 7 Years
$; AX/DC/DS/MC/VS/LC
Full Bar
House Specialties: Monster burgers, killer burritos, mounded salads, great wings and buckets of cold beer, giant margaritas.
Other Points Of Interest: (Sarasota location) Comedy show Sundays at 9:30

Gastronomia
RESTAURANT & CATERING
**7119 South Tamiami Trail
at Buccaneer Plaza, Sarasota**

927-8331

Opening in 1999 Two New Locations:
*University Pkwy at Lockwood Ridge
*Main St. at Links Ave.

Voted Best Italian Restaurant '96, '97 & '98

284 Restaurants Steve Rabow's Guide Book

Key to Restaurant Listings

AX
American Express

CB
Carte Blanche

DC
Diners Club

DS
Discover

MC
Master Card

VS
Visa

LC
Local Checks are OK with proper I.D.

$
Under $7 lunch, under $12 dinner.

$$
Mostly $7 - $12 lunch, mostly $12 - $20 dinner.

$$$
Mostly $12 and over lunch, mostly $20 and over dinner.

Price categories are based an average cost per person not including beverages, tax or tip.

---

p.m., blues Monday 11 p.m.; Wed Happy Hour Trivia; Thursday band open mike nite; Friday DJ. Cigar friendly. Hugely popular happy hour. (Bradenton) Sarasota's favorite place to meet has come to Bradenton. Pro bar staff, great food and sports bar all in one.
Most Popular Item: Ultimate chicken sandwich.

Giorgio's Ristorante
2085 Siesta Dr., Sarasota 34239
366-5366, fax 349-3587
Dinner, 7 days.
Locally Owned - 4 Years
$$; AX/CB/DC/ DS/MC/VS
Beer/Wine Only
House Specialties: Fresh pasta, veal, seafood, chicken
Other Points of Interest: Located across from Southgate Mall; warm ambience is due to Max the owner. He will make you feel like a star, every visit special.

Golden Apple Dinner Theater
25 N. Pineapple Ave., Sarasota 34236
366-5454, fax 364-9100
Lunch - Sat (in season) & Sun
Dinner - Tues-Sun
Locally Owned - 28 Years
$$$ (includes dinner and a show); AX/DC/DS/MC/VS/LC
Full Bar
House Specialties: Prime rib, Chef Ray's famous garlic mashed potatoes.
Other Points of Interest: A full evening's entertainment under one roof. Cocktails, candlelight dining and a professional Broadway show. "One of the best values in the area" - NY Times.
Most popular item: Prime rib.

Gulf Drive Cafe
900 Gulf Dr. North
Bradenton Beach 34217
778-1919, fax 778-1975
Breakfast, Lunch & Dinner - 7 Days
Locally Owned - 18 Years
$; MC/VS/DS/LC
No Liquor Served
House Specialties: Belgian waffles, fresh spinach and feta cheese omelettes, fresh fish, pasta dishes, apple walnut pie, peanut butter creme pie. Daily breakfast, lunch and dinner specials, fresh roasted coffees, espresso and cappuccino.
Other Points Of Interest: Waterfront dining, outdoor patio for dining. Large spacious windows to view the outside. Impressive view, delicious food.
Most Popular Item: Fresh grilled fish.

Harry's Continental Kitchens
525 St. Judes Dr., Longboat Key 34228
383-0777, fax 383-3029
Lunch & Dinner - 7 Days *(closed Monday in summer)*, Sunday Brunch
Locally Owned - 20 Years
$$; AX/ MC/VS/LC
Beer/Wine Only
House Specialties: Fresh local fish, seafood, roast duck, domestic lamb chops.
Other Points Of Interest: Florida Trend top 200 Award '97-98; Wine spectator Award '97-98. Catering small to large parties. Gift baskets and gourmet take out. Loyal Longboat crowd.
Most Popular Item: Harry's crab cakes.

Hemingway's
325 John Ringling Blvd.
St. Armand's 34236
388-3948, fax 388-4002
Lunch & Dinner - 7 Days
Early Bird Specials, Late Night
Locally Owned - 11 Years
$$; AX/CB/DC/DS/MC/VS
Full Bar
House Specialties: Lahvash - Armeniana cracker bread smothered with havarti cheese. toppings available. St. Armands salad, beef melt, focaccia, prime rib, Key West pepper steak, pecan snapper; St. Kitts chicken florentine, Hemingways seafood chowder.
Other Points Of Interest: Six different decors throughout the year. Hemingway "look alike" contest. The only area restaurant to serve Passover Dinner. Outdoor seating. Children's menu. "Christmas In July" each year is a Suncoast Treasure - not to be missed.

Hillview Grill
1920 Hillview St., Sarasota 34239
952-0045, fax 366-8753
Lunch - Mon-Fri, Dinner - Mon-Sat (Sunday October to May)
Locally Owned - 10 Years
$$; AX/DS/MC/VS Full Bar
House Specialties: Fresh fish, homemade pastas, daily specials.
Other Points Of Interest: Casual neighborhood restaurant with strong California influence. Excellent preparations of fresh fish. Excellent wine list Excellent service. Okay, everything here is excellent. Sidewalk dining area
Most Popular Item: Chef's daily fresh fish selections - you can't go wrong.

Hob Nob Drive-In Restaurant
1701 N. Washington Blvd.
Sarasota 34234
955-5001
Breakfast, Lunch & Dinner - 7 Days
Locally Owned - 41 Years
$; No Credit Cards/LC
Beer/Wine Only
House Specialties: Fresh snapper, chicken wings, hot dogs.
Other Points Of Interest: "Coldest draft beer in town." Sarasota's oldest drive-in. Featured on the Food Network who said "Wow! - what a find! Featured on Steve Rabow's Suncoast Treasures who said "Wow! - what a find!" See a continuing theme here?
Most Popular Item: Hob Nob Burger

Honey-Crust Pizza
160 North East Shopping Plaza
Sarasota 34235
957-3919
Lunch & Dinner - Mon-Sat
Locally Owned - 16 Years
$; No Credit Cards/LC
No Liquor Served
House Specialties: Greek salad, gyro, subs, spinach pizza; unique and very popular pizza - secret is in the crust.
Most Popular Item: Pizza

Hot Diggity Dog
5666 Swift Rd., Sarasota 34231
922-8018
Lunch - Mon-Sat, Dinner Mon-Fri
Locally Owned - 28 Years
$; No Credit Cards/LC
Beer/Wine Only
House Specialties: Hot Diggity Dog: Coney Island style hot dog. Cheese steak sandwiches, California/Mex burritos, Greek gyros, great burgers and lots of warm attention from "Mom!"
Other Points Of Interest: Monthly live comedy on Friday (call for dates). Delivery available ($10 minimum.)
Most Popular Item: Coney Island Hot Dog.

Hungry Fox
419A St. Armands Circle
St. Armands 34236
388-2222
Breakfast & Lunch - 7 Days

French Affair

Intimate French Bistro

LUNCH ≈ DINNER
Award Winning Catering
Gourmet Food to Go

11 am - 4 pm Lunch
5-8:30 Dinner
CLOSED SUNDAY

925-3414
2637 Mall Drive
Behind Gulf Gate Mall

Propriataire – Alain Mons
Chef – Didier Guedras

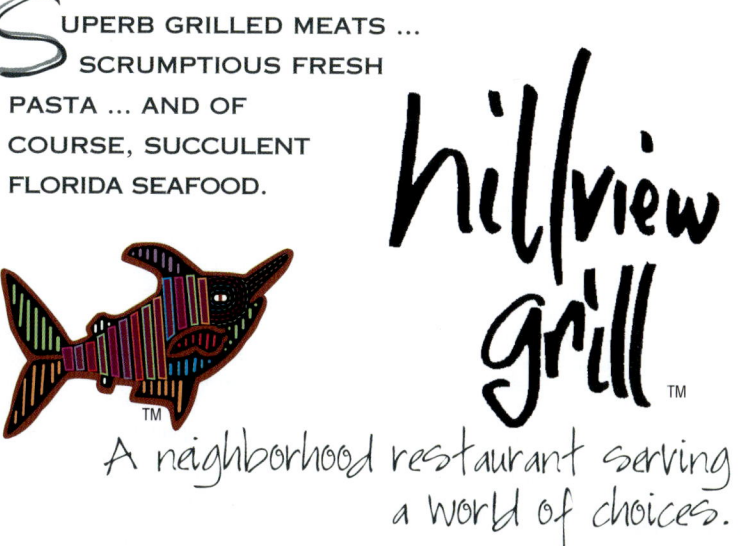

CHARGRILLED NEW ZEALAND RACK OF LAMB • FETTUCINE PRIMAVERA • BLACK BEAN CAKES

SUPERB GRILLED MEATS ... SCRUMPTIOUS FRESH PASTA ... AND OF COURSE, SUCCULENT FLORIDA SEAFOOD.

hillview grill™

A neighborhood restaurant serving a world of choices.

1920 HILLVIEW ST. • SARASOTA, FL 34239 • (941) 952-0045

LUNCH MONDAY-FRIDAY, DINNER NIGHTLY FROM 5:00 • COMPLETE BAR

JAMBALAYA • GROUPER PICCATA • JAMAICAN "JERKED" CHICKEN

FILET MIGNON • CASHEW CHICKEN • EGGPLANT LOBSTER ROULADE

Restaurants — Steve Rabow's Guide Book

Key to Restaurant Listings

AX — American Express

CB — Carte Blanche

DC — Diners Club

DS — Discover

MC — Master Card

VS — Visa

LC — Local Checks are OK with proper I.D.

$ — Under $7 lunch, under $12 dinner.

$$ — Mostly $7 - $12 lunch, mostly $12 - $20 dinner.

$$$ — Mostly $12 and over lunch, mostly $20 and over dinner.

Price categories are based on an average cost per person not including beverages, tax or tip.

Dinner - Mon-Sat
Early Bird Specials, Sunday Brunch
Locally Owned - 14 Years
$; AX/DS/MC/VS
Beer/Wine only
House Specialties: Cajun, salads, fresh fish.
Other Points Of Interest: Beautiful view overlooking St. Armands Circle. Wonderful Sunday brunch with complementary champagne or Bloody Mary. Outdoor dining available.
Most Popular Item: Aged Angus beef.

IL Panificio
1703 Main St., Sarasota 34236
366-5570, fax 366-0326
Lunch & Dinner - 7 Days
(open to 6:30 p.m.)
Locally Owned - 4 Years
$; No Credit Cards/ LC
House Specialties: Pizza, calzones, fresh baked breads and cappuccino.
Other Points Of Interest: Italian market in restaurant-right out of New York. A touch of "Little Italy." Deli, gourmet gifts. "Best cappuccino in town."
Most Popular Item: Pizza.

Isabelle's Eatery
6836 Gulf of Mexico Dr.
Longboat Key 34228
383-0689, fax 383-0136
Breakfast & Lunch - 7 Days
Locally Owned - 2 Years
$; LC/No Credit Cards
No Liquor Served
House Specialties: Eggs Rancheros. Homemade biscuits, salads and sandwiches. Country Benedict (biscuits, sausage, & gravy).
Other Points Of Interest: Located in Whitney Beach Plaza. Waterfront; outdoor seating available.
Most Popular Item: Eggs Benedict.

Ivo's Italian & Continental Cuisine
2605 Gulf of Mexico Dr.
Sarasota 34228
383-8898, fax 383-0182
Dinner - Tues-Sun
Locally Owned - 17 Years
$$; AX/DC/MC/VS/LC
Beer/Wine Only
House Specialties: Caesar salad, whole dover sole, duckling with chestnut stuffing, rack of spring lamb, osso buco, prime veal, fresh pastas.
Other Points Of Interest: Wonderful personalized service, famous (because it's the best) table side Caesar salad, location at the Four Winds Resort on Longboat Key. Simply great.
Most Popular Item: Whole dover sole.

J & J Barbecue
2620 9th St. West, Bradenton 34205
746-6683, fax 746-4714
Lunch & Dinner - Tue-Sat
Locally Owned - 18 Years
$; VS/MC/AX/LC
Beer Only
House Specialties: BBQ everything and homemade desserts.
Most Popular Item: Ribs.

J. Ryan's on the Grill
8389 S. Tamiami Tr., Sarasota 34238
923-3200, fax 927-7248
Lunch & Dinner - 7 Days, Late Night
Locally Owned - New
$$; AX/CB/DC/DS/MC/VS
Full Bar
House Specialties: Stone cooked fish, steaks, chicken, chops.
Other Points Of Interest: Upscale, innovative American dining with exhibition kitchen; catering; pizzas on the grill; take-out; vegetarian items available; gourmet American cuisine. Area's only stone grill. This place rocks.
Most Popular Item: Stone cooked fish.

Javier's Restaurant
6621 Midnight Pass Rd., Siesta Key 34242
349-1792, fax 349-4152
Dinner - Tue-Sat, Early Bird Specials
Locally Owned - 6 Years
$$; AX/MC/VS
Beer/Wine Only
House Specialties: Shrimp Peru Empanadas, grilled lamb chops ceviche, filet mignon, Papa's Rellenos pork piccata, yuck frita, tamales, roas duck, chicken en spiral, fajita quesadilla, Bananas foster, flan de coco, strawberries Acapulco.
Other Points Of Interest: New taste will tantalize you, or enjoy traditiona American favorites. South American "accent" will introduce you to dishe found nowhere else in the area. A tropical-plant-filled room transport you for a special dining experience.
Most Popular Item: Peruvian seafood paella.

J.P. Crawdad's Oyster Bar
1485 Tamiami Trail S., Venice 3428
484-3515, fax 485-9169
Lunch Mon-Sat, Dinner 7 days
Locally Owned - 7 Years
$; AX/DS/MC/VS
Full bar
House Specialties: Kansas-City bee freshly cut. Cajun cuisine: crawfis boil, crawfish and shrimp Etoufee.
Other Points Of Interest: Located o intracoastal with waterfront view Takeout available. Life entertainmer Thurs-Sat. Monday blues band. Sun day Karaoke.
Most Popular Item: Freshly cut steaks

Joto Japanese Steak House
7971 N. Tamiami Tr., Sarasota 3424
351-4677
Dinner - 7 Days
Locally Owned - 15 Years
$$; AX/DC/MC/VS
Full Bar
House Specialties: Tempura, stir-fry teriyaki and Teppan-yaki.

Other Points Of Interest: All food is prepared at your table. The restaurant has two dining areas, one for table cooking, and The Garden Room featuring sushi bar and traditional Japanese cuisine.
Most Popular Item: Steak and shrimp.

Kevin's Country Cafe
1578 Main St., Sarasota 34236
951-2483
Breakfast - Mon- Fri, Lunch - Sun-Sat
Locally Owned - 2 Years
$; DS/MC/VS
No Liquor Served
House Specialties: Chicken, jalapeno bagels, country club sandwiches.
Other Points of Interest: Downtown location. Deli and bakery.
Other Points of Interest: Sunday Brunch
Most Popular Item: Charred chicken salad.

Key West Grill
900 Venetian Bay Blvd., Venice 34292
488-0588, fax 495-9111
Lunch & Dinner - 7 days
Early Bird Specials
$; AX/DC/DS/MC/VS/LC
Full bar
House Specialties: Mesquite wood burning grill and "Island blackening."
Other Points Of Interest: Very unique and tropical atmosphere.
Most Popular Item: Blackened mahi-mahi.

Key West Willy's
107 Gulf Drive S.
Bradenton Beach 34217
778-7272
Lunch & Dinner - 7 Days
Early Bird Specials, Late Night
Locally Owned - 8 Years
$; DS/MC/VS
Full Bar
House Specialties: Grouper and steak.
Other Points Of Interest: Old Florida Key West atmosphere; nightly entertainment and fabulous sunset views.
Most Popular Item: Oysters on the half shell.

La Terrazza Ristorante
5157 Ocean Blvd., Siesta Key 34242
349-8646
Dinner -Tues-Sun
Locally Owned - 12 Years
$$; MC/VS/AX/DS
Beer/Wine Only
House Specialties: Northern Italian specialties including veal, pasta and fresh fish. All breads and desserts made on premise. Daily specials.
Other Points Of Interest: Extensive wine list. Enclosed, a/c terrace. One-block from Siesta Beach.
Most Popular Item: Sauteed Red Snapper with a Citrus Relish.

Landmark Restaurant and Grill
133 S. Tamiami Tr., Venice 34285
485-0668
Lunch & Dinner - 7 days

simply...

The soul of Europe in the heart of Longboat Key
As always, come and enjoy our specialties including
Caesar Salad, Dover Sole, Duckling Mistral and
Rack of Lamb, all served tableside. Fresh Pasta and
exceptional Osso Buco when available.
Available for private parties. Reservations suggested.

Ivo's
ITALIAN & CONTINENTAL CUISINE
Adjoining Four Winds Resort on Gulf of Mexico Drive
2605 Gulf of Mexico Drive, Longboat Key ■ **(941) 383-8898**

Il Panificio

ITALIAN BREAD AND PIZZA.
THE QUALITY OF LIFE.

PIZZA • FOCACCIA
STROMBOLI • CALZONE
CAPPUCCINO BAR
FULL BAKERY
ITALIAN MARKET
ITALIAN DELI
SPECIALTY BREADS
SIGNATURE BREADS
WHOLESALE AND RETAIL
CATERING FOR ALL OCCASIONS

FAMILY OWNED AND OPERATED
MAIN STREET LOCATION
1703 MAIN STREET
SARASOTA, FLORIDA 34236
OPEN 7 DAYS
TEL 366-5570 FAX 366-0326

Key to Restaurant Listings

AX
American Express

CB
Carte Blanche

DC
Diners Club

DS
Discover

MC
Master Card

VS
Visa

LC
Local Checks are OK with proper I.D.

$
Under $7 lunch, under $12 dinner.

$$
Mostly $7 - $12 lunch, mostly $12 - $20 dinner.

$$$
Mostly $12 and over lunch, mostly $20 and over dinner.

Price categories are based on an average cost per person not including beverages, tax or tip.

Early Bird Specials
Locally Owned - 2 Years
Grill - $; Dining Room - $$
AX/DC/DS/MC/VS
Full Bar
House Specialties: Rack of lamb, prime rib.
Other Points of Interest: Beautifully decorated dining room. "Best Steakhouse in Venice," "Best Burger in Venice." Live entertainment 5 days a week. Takeout available. Vegetarian menu available upon request.
Most Popular Item: Prime rib.

Lantern Restaurant
3126 1st Street W., Bradenton 34208
746-5350
Lunch & Dinner Mon-Sat
Locally Owned - 20 Years
$; MC/VS
Beer/Wine Only
House Specialties: Chicken Chop Suey, stuffed chicken wings.
Other Points of Interest: Good portions at great prices.
Most Popular Item: House fried rice.

Le Petit Jardin Cafe
218 West Tampa Ave., Venice 34285
485-4449
Breakfast & Lunch Mon-Sat
Dinner- Tue-Sat (November-April)
Locally Owned - 23 Years
$; AX/DS/MC/VS/LC
Beer/Wine Only
House Specialties: Homemade crepes, quiche and desserts.
Other Points Of Interest: Bistro style restaurant located in historical building. Small, clean, warm and cozy atmosphere. Everything homemade.
Most Popular Item: Quiche of the day.

Leverock's Seafood House
12320 Manatee Ave. West
Bradenton 34209
794-8900
www.leverocks.com
Lunch & Dinner - 7 Days
Early Bird Specials
Locally Owned - 7 Years
$; AX/DC/DS/MC/VS
Full Bar
House Specialties: Onion Crusted Salmon and Seafood Martinique. Fresh Florida Seafood. Clam chowder. Pies made on premises.
Other Points Of Interest: Beautiful waterfront view. Free docking for boats. In operation in St. Petersburg since 1948. Call ahead seating.
Most Popular Item: Onion Crusted Salmon.

Little Bavaria
1262 Jacaranda Blvd., Venice 34292
492-5366
Lunch - Tues-Sat, Dinner - Tues-Sun
Locally Owned - 7 Years
$; MC/VS
Beer/Wine Only
House Specialties: German specialties, sauerbraten, Weiner schnitzel and sausage plate.
Other Points Of Interest: Authentic home cooked German foods. Bavarian lodge setting, comfortable and intimate. Very clean. Takeout available.
Most Popular Item: Sauerbraten.

Lonestar Steakhouse
4705 Cortez Rd. W., Bradenton 34210
794-0828
7575 S. Tamiami Tr., Sarasota 34231
927-2233
Bradenton: Lunch & Dinner - 7 Days
Sarasota: Dinner only - 7 Days
$$; AX/DC/CB/DS/MC/VS
Full Bar
House Specialties: Mesquite grilled steaks, chicken, salmon, shrimp.
Other Points of Interest: Fresh hand-cut meats daily. Homemade salad dressings and desserts. Texas road house decor with genuine Southwest regional artifacts. Buckets of peanuts on your table, and shells on the floor. Fun atmosphere with singing and dancing waitstaff. 2 for 1 in the bar from 11 a.m. to 7 p.m.
Most Popular Item: Rib eye steak and 9 oz. Filet Mignon.

Lynches Landing
4000 Gulf of Mexico Dr.
Longboat Key 34228
383-0791, fax 383-0792
Lunch - Mon-Sat, Dinner - 7 Days
Late Night
Locally Owned - 12 Years
$; AX/CB/DC/DS/MC/VS
Full Bar
House Specialties: Cork cottage pie, corned beef and cabbage, baby back ribs, fresh fish, live Maine lobster, steak.
Other Points Of Interest: Irish decor with a fantastic view of the Gulf. Great sunsets. Six-piece Dixieland jazz band every Wednesday. Live Irish music Fri.-Sat. Vegetarian menu available. Takeout available. Free transportation to and from hotels on Longboat Key.
Most Popular Item: Cork cottage Pie.

Main Bar Sandwich Shop
1944 Main St., Sarasota
955-8733
Lunch - Mon-Sat
Locally Owned - 40 Years
$; MC/VS/LC
Beer/Wine Only
House Specialties: Variety of sandwiches and salads.
Other Points Of Interest: Started by a circus family, circus memorabilia and entertainment autographs on walls.
Most Popular Item: Famous Italian sandwich

Mama Leones
1266 Jacaranda Blvd., Venice 34285
496-9148, fax 497-7564
Lunch & Dinner - 7 Days
Locally Owned - 5 Years
$; AX/MC/VS

Beer/Wine Only
House Specialties: Pizza and pasta.
Other Points Of Interest: Nice, family atmosphere. Located in Venice Pines Shopping Center.
Most Popular Item: Veal dishes.

Mama Onesti
3728 N. Tamiami Tr., Sarasota 34234
355-4099
Lunch - Mon-Fri, Dinner -7 days
Locally Owned - 17 Years
$; AX/MC/VS, Full Bar
House Specialties: Snapper Livionise, Fish, Veal Saltimbocca, Veal Marsala.
Other Points Of Interest: Italian Market theme with open kitchen. Full lounge with free pizza buffet. Newly expanded banquet facilities. Great pizza, wonderful specials, kids welcome, nice selection of single malt.
Most Popular Item: Veal Marsala.

Manhattan Bagel Company
4065 S. Tamiami Tr., Sarasota 34231
927-9440, fax 927-9240
Breakfast & Lunch - 7 Days
Locally Owned - 3 Years
$; No credit cards accepted
No Liquor Served
House Specialties: "Best Bagels in Sarasota," deli sandwiches, wrap sandwiches.
Most Popular Item: Bagels with lox and cream cheese.

Manhattan Bagel
5917 Manatee Ave., Bradenton
794-0336, fax 794-5529
Breakfast & Lunch - 7 days
Locally Owned - 2 Years
$; AX/DS/MC/VS/LC
No Liquor Served
House Specialties: Fresh baked bagels. Hot breakfast sandwiches. Dozens of different cream cheese spreads and huge deli lunch sandwiches.
Most Popular Item: Dozen bagels to go.

Mar Vista Pub & Restaurant
760 Broadway St. (Marker 39)
Longboat Key 34228
383-2391, fax 387-4317
Lunch & Dinner - 7 Days
Locally Owned - Many Years!
$$; AX/DC/DS/MC/VS
Full Bar
House Specialties: Seafood specials nightly - all fresh fish.
Other Points Of Interest: Casual atmosphere and the finest in food and courteous service.
Most Popular Item: Grouper sandwich or any fresh catch.

Marie's Italian Kitchen
5767 S. Beneva Rd., Sarasota
923-1000
Lunch Mon-Fri, Dinner - Mon-Sat
Locally Owned - 1 Year
$;AX/DS/MC/VS
Beer/Wine
House Specialties: Chicken Marsala, Chicken Marengo, Veal Zingara,

Paglia e Fieno, Veal Saltimbocca, Chicken Cacciatora.
Other Points of Interest: New restaurant receiving plenty of raves - catering/Take-Out/Vegetarian Menu available. Looks (and tastes) like a winner!
Most Popular Item: Portobello and chicken over fettucini.

Marina Jack Restaurant
2 Marina Plaza, Sarasota 34236
365-4232, fax 957-1291
Lunch & Dinner - 7 Days
Late Night Menu in Lounge
Locally Owned - 28 Years
$$; MC/VS
Full Bar
House Specialties: Fresh grilled Florida fish, Angus beef, lump crab cakes, herbed group, Black & Blue tuna (blackened and seared).
Other Points Of Interest: Waterfront location. Voted "Best Waterfront Restaurant" for last several years. Vegetarian meals available. Live entertainment, takeout available.
Most Popular Item: Key West Snapper

Marina Jack II Dinnerboat
2 Marina Plaza, Sarasota 34236
366-9255, fax 957-1291
Lunch - In season, Dinner - Wed-Sun
Locally Owned - 30 Years
$$$; MC/VS
Full Bar

Key to Restaurant Listings

AX
American Express

CB
Carte Blanche

DC
Diners Club

DS
Discover

MC
Master Card

VS
Visa

LC
Local Checks are OK with proper I.D.

$
Under $7 lunch, under $12 dinner.

$$
Mostly $7 - $12 lunch, mostly $12 - $20 dinner.

$$$
Mostly $12 and over lunch, mostly $20 and over dinner.

Price categories are based on an average cost per person not including beverages, tax or tip.

House Specialties: Prime Rib and fresh seafood.
Other Points of Interest: Two hour cruise on Sarasota Bay. Vegetarian menu available.
Most Popular Item: Prime Rib.

Mario's Italian Restaurant
6240 S. Tamiami Tr., Sarasota 34231
921-3684
Lunch - Mon-Fri, Dinner -7 Days
Early Bird Specials
Locally Owned - 17 Years
$; AX/DS/MC/VS/LC
Full Bar
House Specialties: Linguine with clam sauce. New York style pizza and lasagna.
Other Points Of Interest: Italian and New York murals on wall. Warm family restaurant.
Most Popular Item: Spaghetti.

The Marker IV Oyster Bar
459 N. Tamiami Tr., Venice 34292
484-0344
Lunch & Dinner - 7 Days
Locally Owned - 10 Years
$; AX/DS/MC/VS
Full Bar
House Specialties: Grouper sandwiches, seafood platters, peel-and-eat shrimp.
Other Points Of Interest: "We serve more than oysters and seafood!" Located next to Fisherman's Wharf on Intracoastal – beautiful water view. Casual atmosphere. Boat accessible. Covered outdoor dining, live entertainment, football games (a great Monday Night Football spot). Voted #1 for a beer and #1 for chicken wings.

Maureen
5350 Gulf of Mexico Dr.
Longboat Key 34228
383-7774
Dinner - Tues-Sat
Locally Owned - New
$$; AX/DC/DS/MS/VS
Full Bar
House Specialties: Osso Buco, bouillabaisse, fish stews, tournedos royale, filet mignon crowned with lump crabmeat.
Other Points of Interest: Martini bar, dressy casual, international menu with influences of Thai, regional Italian, French, Contemporary. Owned and operated by the chef. "We apologize that we cannot accommodate small children." Hip, cool, on Longboat!
Most Popular Item: Osso buco.

Mediterraneo
1970 Main St., Sarasota 34236
365-4122
Lunch - Mon-Fri, Dinner - 7 days
Late Night
Locally Owned - 3 Years
$$; AX/DC/MC/VS
Full Bar

House Specialties: Veal chop Milanese with arugola and fresh tomatoes.
Other Points of Interest: Authentic Italian atmosphere and decor (beautiful photographs of Italy); some of the area's best pizzas and salads; broad Italian wine selection; very popular with downtown and theater crowd, located across from Hollywood-20. Fluent Italian spoken by everyone here.
Most Popular Item: Fresh pasta and tiramisu.

Mel-O-Dee Restaurant
4685 N. Tamiami Tr., Sarasota 34234
355-5768
Breakfast, Lunch & Dinner - 7 Days
Brunch daily until 2 p.m.
Locally Owned - 42 Years
$; DS/MC/VS/LC
No Liquor Served
House Specialties: Home cooked meals. Beef stew, steaks, turkey and REAL mashed potatoes.
Other Points Of Interest: Homemade blueberry muffins with each meal. Homemade soups. Great shakes!
Most Popular Item: Turkey dinner.

The Melting Pot Fondue Restaurant
1055 S. Tamiami Tr., Sarasota
365-2628
Dinner - 7 Days
Locally Owned - 14 Years
$$; AX/MC/VS
Beer/Wine Only
House Specialties: Traditional European style fondue - cheeses, chocolates, oil and broth styles. Beef, chicken and seafood.
Other Points Of Interest: "The fondue craze of the past has become a fun experience of the present."
Most Popular Item: Center cut filet and lobster.

Michael's On East
1212 East Ave., Sarasota
366-0007
Lunch - Mon-Fri, Dinner - 7 Days
Locally Owned -10 Years
$$$; AX/DC/MC/VS
Full Bar
House Specialties: Grilled Black Angus, filet of beef w/wild mushroom ragout, bowtie pasta, oak-roasted rack of lamb, seared Chilean Sea Bass.
Other Points of Interest: Five consecutive years Golden Spoon Award, one of Florida's Top 20 Restaurants, Zagat Survey Gulf Coast's most popular restaurant; Sarasota's only AAA Four-Diamond restaurant. Full-service catering and ballroom facilities; weekend jazz; cigar friendly; very popular.
Most Popular Item: Louisiana lump crab cakes w/roasted potatoes, seasonal vegetables and Gulf Coast remoulade.

Michael's Seafood Grille & Down Under Jazz Bar
214 Sarasota Quay, Sarasota 34236

951-2467, fax 954-3641
www.bestfood.com
Lunch - Sat-Sun, Dinner - 7 Days
Early Bird Specials
Locally Owned - 2 Years
$$; AX/DC/DS/MC/VS/LC
Full Bar
House Specialties: Soft shell crab, crab cakes, baby Maine lobster, fried calamari, steamed live lobster and grilled and fried lobster tails.
Other Points of Interest: Waterfront location, live entertainment 7 nights and dancing. Nightly specials. Happy hour Mon-Fri. with free buffet. Outdoor dining on the water. Two menus. Late night food.
Most Popular Item: Sauteed Chilean Sea Bass with roasted garlic, tarragon and lemon cream.

Midnight Pass Pub
8865 Midnight Pass Rd.
Siesta Key 34242
349-2280, fax 349-0346
Lunch & Dinner - 7 Days
Locally Owned - 11 Years
$; AX/MC/VS
Beer/Wine Only
House Specialties: Pizza, wings, burgers, fish sandwiches, burgers and ribs. Home of the Chocolate Key Lime Pie.
Other Points of Interest: Newly remodeled (again). Now offering bike, boat, kayak and wave runner rentals. Full service marina. Happy hour 4-6. Brand new game room.
Most Popular Item: Burgers.

Miller's Dutch Kitchen
3401 14th St. West, Bradenton 34205
746-8253
Lunch & Dinner - Mon-Sat
Locally Owned - 17 Years
$; MC/VS
No Liquor Served
House Specialties: Baked chicken and dressing, roast beef, cabbage rolls, meatloaf - all home cooked food.
Other Points Of Interest: 20 different kinds of pies, Amish style cooking. Smoke-free environment. Big gift shop.
Most Popular Item: Peanut butter pie.

Millie's
3900 Clark Rd., Sarasota 34238
923-4054
Breakfast & Lunch - Wed-Sun
Locally Owned - 11 Years
$; No Credit Cards/LC
No Liquor Served
House Specialties: Homemade everything. No sugar pancakes, homemade syrup, German Apple Pancakes.
Other Points Of Interest: Country inn interior, furnished with antiques. Charming and friendly waitstaff.
Most Popular Item: Stuffed French toast.

Mim's Healthy Gourmet
301 S. Pineapple Ave., Sarasota 34236
364-8561, fax 957-3247
Breakfast, Lunch & Dinner - Mon-Fri
Locally Owned - 5 Years
$; AX/DS/MC/VS/LC
Full Juice Bar, No Liquor Served
House Specialties: Indian curries, Dahl, flavored hummus, largest variety of gourmet vegetarian food in town.
Other Points Of Interest: Outdoor patio dining, a lot of organically grown foods. Will cater to all special diets.

Mr. Wong's Wok & Grill
8330 S. Tamiami Tr., Sarasota 34238
966-3689, fax 966-0067
Dinner - 7 Days
Locally Owned - 14 Years
$; AX/DS/MC/VS
Full Bar
House Specialties: Authentic Chinese cuisine and grill food.
Other Points Of Interest: Voted best Chinese restaurant in Sarasota for 5 years in a row. Take out. Delivery in limited area.
Most Popular Item: Beef Szechuan

Mona Lisa Italian Restaurant
4989 Ringwood Meadow
Sarasota 34235
377-6562
Lunch - Wed-Fri, Dinner - 7 Days
Locally Owned - 15 Years
$$; AX/MC/VS/DC/LC
Beer/Wine Only

EAT. DRINK.
BE ITALIAN.

MEDITERRANEO
Contemporary Italian Cuisine

1970 Main Street, Sarasota
(941) 365-4122

Key to Restaurant Listings

AX
American Express

CB
Carte Blanche

DC
Diners Club

DS
Discover

MC
Master Card

VS
Visa

LC
Local Checks are OK with proper I.D.

$
Under $7 lunch, under $12 dinner.

$$
Mostly $7 - $12 lunch, mostly $12 - $20 dinner.

$$$
Mostly $12 and over lunch, mostly $20 and over dinner.

Price categories are based on an average cost per person not including beverages, tax or tip.

House Specialties: Traditional Central Italian cuisine.
Other Points Of Interest: Intimate lakeside setting in the Meadows, open to the public. Space for private parties up to 45. Full menu includes chicken, steaks, seafood, lamb chops.
Most Popular Item: Veal specialties.

Moore's Stone Crab Restaurant
800 Broadway, Longboat Key 34228
383-1748
www.stonecrab.com
Lunch & Dinner - 7 Days
Locally Owned - 30 Years
$$; AX/DS/MC/VS/LC; Full Bar
House Specialties: Stone crabs and fresh seafood.
Other Points Of Interest: Waterfront with dock space for restaurant diners. Oldest restaurant in Manatee County. Children friendly. Takeout available.
Most Popular Item: Stone Crabs.

Morel Restaurant
3809 S. Tuttle Ave., Sarasota 34239
927-8716
Dinner - Tues-Sat
Locally Owned - 43 Years
$$; AX/MC/VS
Beer/Wine Only
House Specialties: Pan seared Veal Loin Chops, Rack of Lamb, Porcini-crusted tuna, and daily specials.
Other Points of Interest: Inspired traditional cuisine in warm and intimate bistro atmosphere. Truly casually elegant. Facilities for private parties and small, in home gatherings. Zagat Guide "don't miss" - a major "wow!"
Most Popular Item: Hoisin and maple glazed Chilean sea bass.

Munroe's on First Street
1296 First St., Sarasota 34236
316-0609, fax 316-0611
Lunch - Mon-Fri, Dinner - Mon-Sat
Locally Owned - 2 Years
$$; AX/DC/DS/MC/VS
Full Bar
House Specialties: Regional American cuisine, Batter-fried Lobster Tail, Maryland Style Crabcakes, and Veal Chop. Selected wine menu.
Other Points Of Interest: Intimate dining downstairs, vintage tavern upstairs with entertainment. Historical building in the Theater District. Catering available. Seriously wonderful. Outdoor dining.
Most Popular Item: Maryland Style Crabcakes.

Napoli's Italian Restaurant & Grill
5242 Ocean Blvd., Siesta Key 34242
346-2352
Lunch & Dinner - 7 Days
Locally Owned - 36 Years
$; AX/MC/VS/LC
Beer/Wine Only
House Specialties: Veal and chicken cacciatore. Stuffed shells. Lasagna and pizza.
Other Points Of Interest: Newly remodeled outside patio dining overlooking Siesta Village. Great for people watching.
Most Popular Item: Lasagna.

Nature's Way Cafe
1572 Main St., Sarasota 34236
954-3131
Breakfast & Lunch - Mon-Sat
Locally Owned - 5 Years
$; No Credit Cards/LC
No Liquor Served
House Specialties: Vegetarian favorites. Gardenburgers and veggie sandwiches.
Other Points Of Interest: Southern Californian cuisine. Light and airy. Non-smoking environment.
Most Popular Item: Chicken walnut raisin salad.

Nellie's Deli, Market & Catering
3688 Webber St., Sarasota 34231
921-4571, fax 925-3469
e-mail: nelliedeli@home.com
www.nelliesdeli.com
Breakfast - Mon-Fri, Lunch - Mon-Sat
Locally Owned - 18 Years
$; AX/DC/DS/MC/VS/LC
Beer/Wine Only
House Specialties: New York style deli with gourmet market, wine boutique, Jewish style, gourmet dinners to go.
Other Points Of Interest: "Best of the Best" Award 1994-1998. Reader's Choice Award 1992-1997.
Most Popular Item: Nellie's Overstuffed Sandwiches

New China Restaurant
1083 N. Tamiami Tr., Nokomis 34275
484-8662
Lunch - Mon-Fri, Dinner - Mon-Sat
Locally Owned - 10 Years
$; MC/VS
Beer/Wine Only
House Specialties: Very large menu featuring Szechuan and Hunan style cooking.
Other Points Of Interest: "Fat menu, thin waist."
Most Popular Item: Szechuan dishes.

Nicki's West 59th Restaurant
1830 59th St. W., Bradenton 34209
795-7065
Lunch - Mon-Sat, Dinner - 7 days
Early Bird Specials
Late night menu in Lounge
Locally owned - 6 Years
$; MC/VS/DS/AX
Full Bar
House Specialties: Roasted Leg of Lamb, lamb shanks, fresh seafood, Duck, Chateaubriand, Saganaki and Veal Diane prepared table side.
Other Points of Interest: Entertainment nightly. Full service catering available. Banquet facilities, parties of 50 or less.
Most Popular Item: Champagne Snapper.

Nicky's Italian Pizza
1522 Main St., Sarasota 34236
366-6429
Lunch & Dinner - Mon-Sat
Locally Owned - 6 Years
$; LC
Beer/Wine only
House Specialties: Pizza, Pasta, Veal, Chicken.
Other Points Of Interest: Real Italian chef from Italy (of course!)
Most Popular Item: Veal Carginale.

Ntinos Pizzeria & Restaurant
660 S. Tamiami Tr., Venice 34285
485-4474
Breakfast, Lunch & Dinner - 7 Days
Locally Owned - 19 Years
$; No Credit Cards/LC
Beer/Wine Only
House Specialties: Greek salad with home made dressings, excellent corned beef hash for breakfast (leanest around).
Other Points of Interest: Voted "Best Pizza in Venice" several years in a row. Very popular with the locals. Lines out the door during seasosn.
Most Popular Item: Homemade pizza.

Oaks Open Pit BBQ
6112 S. Tamiami Tr., Sarasota 34231
922-7778
Lunch - Mon-Sat, Dinner - 7 days
Locally Owned - 21 Years
$; No Credit Cards/LC
Beer/Wine Only
House Specialties: Barbecued ribs, seafood, shredded pork and chef salads. Now serving smoked fish - Mahi Mahi.
Other points of Interest: "All you can eat" specials. Full service catering. Private room available.
Most Popular Item: Shredded Pork Dinner.

O'Brien's Irish Pub & Eatery
5917 Manatee Ave. West
Bradenton 34209
794-1141
Lunch & Dinner - Mon-Sat
Late Night Menu
Locally Owned - 2 Years
$; MC/VS/LC
Beer/Wine Only
House Specialties: Irish entrees and beers.
Other Points of Interest: Full menu available for take out, catering. Live entertainment on Fridays and Saturday evenings. Pub setting. Awesome desserts! "#1 Pub" Bradenton Herald. Taste of Manatee dessert winner for carrot cake.
Most Popular Item: Mulligan Beef Stew.

Oberlins Restaurant
1158 N. Washington Blvd.
Sarasota 34236
953-4787
Breakfast, Lunch & Dinner - 7 Days
Locally Owned - 28 Years
$; DS/MC/VS
Full Bar
House Specialties: 10 breakfast specials. Belgian malted waffles. Daily lunch specials. U.S. Choice prime rib and steaks, broasted fish and chicken.
Other Points Of Interest: Family restaurant with home cooked meals.
Most Popular Item: Broasted fish and chicken.

Old Hickory Restaurant
5100 N. Tamiami Tr., Sarasota 34234
355-8757
Dinner - Tues-Sun
Early Bird Specials
Locally Owned - 31 Years
$; MC/VS
Full Bar
House Specialties: Ribs, bbq, steak
Other Points Of Interest: Wood burning pit.
Most Popular Item: Sirloin steak.

The Old Salty Dog
5023 Ocean Blvd., Siesta Key 34242
349-0158
1601 City Island Rd., City Island 34236
388-4311
801 Blackburn Pt. Rd., Osprey 34292
966-6094
Lunch & Dinner - 7 Days
Locally Owned - 12 Years
$; MC/VS
Beer/Wine Only
House Specialties: "Old Salty Dog" - beer batter deep fried 1/4 pound hot dog. Traditional English fish-n-chips.
Other Points Of Interest: Old Florida with a touch of English pub. Waterfront patio and inside dining. Fine British ales. City Island location is one of Sarasota's best kept secrets.
Most Popular Item: Fresh Grouper sandwich.

Oma Pizza and Restaurant
201 Gulf Dr. North
Bradenton Beach 34217
778-0771
Lunch & Dinner - 7 Days, Late Night
Locally Owned - 17 Years
$; MC/VS/LC
Beer/Wine Only
House Specialties: Homemade pizza, lasagna and veal marsala.
Other Points Of Interest: Italian Atmosphere. Directly across from beach.
Most Popular Item: Lasagna.

100° East Chinese Grill & Noodle Company
1991 Main St., Sarasota Main Plaza
Sarasota 34236
366-EAST, fax 906-1395
Lunch & Dinner - 7 days
Locally Owned - New
$$; AX/DC/MS/VS/DS/LC
Full Bar
House Specialties: Mongolian grill, Pad Thai Noodle Dish, Curry Noodle Dish, Cantonese Lo Main as well as

Key to Restaurant Listings

AX
American Express

CB
Carte Blanche

DC
Diners Club

DS
Discover

MC
Master Card

VS
Visa

LC
Local Checks are OK with proper I.D.

$
Under $7 lunch, under $12 dinner.

$$
Mostly $7 - $12 lunch, mostly $12 - $20 dinner.

$$$
Mostly $12 and over lunch, mostly $20 and over dinner.

Price categories are based on an average cost per person not including beverages, tax or tip.

---

several specialty coffee drinks from the bar.
Most Popular Item: The Mongolian feast.

Ophelia's on the Bay
9105 Midnight Pass Rd.
Siesta Key 34242
349-3776, fax 349-3328
Dinner - 7 Days
Locally Owned - 10 Years
$$; AX/DS/MC/VS/DC
Full Bar
House Specialties: Fresh native seafood.
Other Points of Interest: "Most Romantic Restaurant" Sarasota Mag/WWSB. Bayfront ambience, dockside patio overlooking tropical water garden and sweeping vista of Little Sarasota Bay.
Most Popular Item: Cedar roasted salmon.

The Original Front Burner
3542 S. Osprey Ave., Sarasota 34239
957-1214, fax 954-1946
Lunch - Mon-Fri, Dinner - 7 Days
Locally Owned - 6 Years
$$; AX/CB/DC//DS/MC/VS/LC
Beer/Wine Only
House Specialties: Gourmet pizza, rack of lamb, grilled tuna, baby bay scallops.
Other Points of Interest: Gourmet food in a comfortable setting. A favorite with locals.
Most Popular Item: Potato crusted grouper.

The Original Oyster Bar
7250 S. Tamiami Tr., Sarasota 34231
924-2829, fax 922-2836
Lunch & Dinner - 7 Days
Locally Owned - 39 Years
$; No Credit Cards/LC
Full Bar
House Specialties: Stuffed flounder, clam chowder and crab cakes. Grouper dinners. Specializing in seafood but also serves delicious prime rib.
Other Points Of Interest: This is the area's oldest seafood restaurant, founded in 1958. Daily specials. Happy Hour from 3-7 pm.
Most Popular Item: Stuffed flounder.

Osteria
29 N. Blvd. of Presidents
St. Armands 34236
388-3671, fax 388-3672
Dinner - 7 Days
Locally Owned -15 Years
$$$; AX/CB/DC/DS/MC/VS
Full Bar
House Specialties: Authentic Northern Italian food. Seafood.
Other Points Of Interest: Grand piano with singing Maitre'd. Intimate and romantic atmosphere. Piano bar on weekends.
Most Popular Item: Lobster tail Osteria

Ozzie
6559 Gateway Ave., Sarasota 34231
921-4389
Dinner - Tues-Sun
Locally Owned - 4 Years
$; AX/MC/VS/DS/DC
Beer/Wine Only
House Specialties: Cajun cuisine. Steaks, Seafood, Chicken, Vegetarian dishes.
Other Points of Interest: Nice atmosphere, cozy dining. 40 item menu. Moderately priced wine list.
Most Popular Item: "Shrimp to Die For" and "Smashed Chicken."

Pattigeorge's (also called P.G's)
4120 Gulf Of Mexico Dr.
Longboat Key 34228
383-5111, fax 387-6454
Dinner - Tues-Sun
Locally Owned - New
$$$; AX/DC/DS/MC/VS/LC
Full Bar
House Specialties: Miso glazed Chilean sea bass, bone-in filet mignon, pako crusted Longboat Roll.
Other Points Of Interest: Artistic desserts, innovative appetizers, "Fine Coastline Cusine" - international costal emphasis. Hottest spot on Longboat Key, credit belongs to owner Tommy Klauber - everything he touches is monumental. Boat Accessible.

Paddy's Sports Bar & Grill
2604 Manatee Ave. East
Bradenton 34208
747-7276
Lunch & Dinner - 7 Days
Locally Owned -9 Years
Early Bird Specials, Late Night
$; AX/DS/MC/VS/LC
Beer/Wine Only
House Specialties: Prime rib, subs
Other Points of Interest: Irish flavor, 5 TVs, jukebox, pinball, pool tables, darts, sports bar.
Most Popular Item: Philly steak sub.

Panda Inn
5209 33rd St. East, Bradenton 34203
757-5773, fax 751-4974
Lunch & Dinner - Tues-Sun
Early Bird Specials
Locally Owned - 4 Years
$$; AX/DS/MS/VS
Full Bar
House Specialties: Oyster Cargot, lobster quesadillas, Chesapeake Bay salad, shrimp etouffe, steamed cherrystone clams, broiled seafood platter, live Maine lobster, Alaskan king crab legs.
Other Points of Interest: On the intracoastal waterway, indoor dining or on waterfront deck. Live music on weekends, steel drum music on weekend afternoons. Happy hour daily. Tropical drink specials.
Most Popular Item: Maryland lump crabcakes.

Papa Nick's Pasta & Pizza
75 S. Beneva Rd., Sarasota 34237
365-5559
Lunch & Dinner - 7 Days
Locally Owned - 7 Years
$; MC/VS Beer/Wine Only
House Specialties: Greek food. Pasta.
Other Points Of Interest: Family atmosphere. Everything is freshly made on premises.
Most Popular Item: N.Y. Style Pizza.

Park Grille & Cafe
7661 Park Blvd., University Park 34201
359-2995, fax 756-3066
Lunch - Mon-Sat
Sunday Brunch
$; DS/MC/VS
Full Bar
Other Points Of Interest: Finalist "Sar. Mag./WWSB Best Sunday Brunch" award; lakeside setting; banquet facilities.

Pasta E Basta
1991 Main St., Sarasota Main Plaza, Sarasota 34236
957-3317, fax 957-6481
Lunch - Mon-Fri, Dinner - Wed-Mon
Locally Owned - 2 Years
$; AX/CB/DC/DS/MC/VS
Beer/Wine Only
House Specialties: Full Italian menu including veal, fresh seafood, chicken, pasta, home made foccacia bread.
Other Points of Interest: Located near Hollywood-20 Theaters; full catering available. Lunch buffet featuring pasta, salads in addition to full menu - great for lunch on the go, great value too.
Most Popular Item: Penne Ortolana.

The Pasta House
530 US 41 By Pass South, Venice 34292
484-6171
Dinner - 6 Days (closed Tues)
Locally Owned - 11 Years
$; AX/DS/MC/VS
Beer/Wine Only
House Specialties: Osso Buco, Portofino Sauce, Beef Braciola.
Other Points Of Interest: Authentic Northern Italian cuisine. Cafe-like family atmosphere.
Most Popular Item: Beef Braciola.

Patches Family Restaurant
501 Venice Ave. East, Venice 34293
484-6713
Breakfast & Lunch - Mon-Sun
Dinner - Mon-Sat
Locally Owned - 7 Years
$; MC/VS
Beer/Wine Only
House Specialties: Prime rib and roast chicken, lamb shanks, fish & chips.
Other Points Of Interest: Family oriented. Homemade specials and baked goods. AAA approved.
Most Popular Item: Fish & chips.

Patricks Restaurant
1400 Main St., Sarasota 34236
952-1170
Lunch & Dinner - 7 Days
Late Night, Sunday Brunch
Locally Owned - 14 Years
$; AX/MC/VS
Full Bar
House Specialties: Award-winning burgers, steaks, pastas, gourmet pizza.
Other Points Of Interest: Located in the heart of Downtown Sarasota, serving "The Best" burgers in town with upscale sports bar. Open 11 a.m. until midnight, 7 days a week.
Most Popular Item: Award-winning burgers.

Peaches
3201 Manatee Ave. W., Bradenton 34205
747-2894
5702 Cortez Rd. W., Bradenton 34210 794-5140
6057 26th St. W., Bradenton 34207
727-0443
Breakfast & Lunch - 7 Days
Locally Owned - 9 Years
$; No Credit Cards or checks
No Liquor Served
House Specialties: Peaches and cream coffee cake. Omelettes.
Other Points Of Interest: Vegetarian items. Everything homemade.
Most Popular Item: Chicken Salad with fresh fruit.

Pelican Alley
1009 Albee Rd. West, Nokomis
485-1893
Lunch - 7 Days (November-May)
Dinner - 6 Days (closed Tues)
Late Night - Fri & Sat
Locally Owned - 19 Years
$; AX/CB/DC/DS/MC/VS
Full Bar
House Specialties: Grouper sandwiches and incredible seafood chowder. Fresh seafood combos and mixed grill.
Other Points Of Interest: Located on Intracoastal waterway. Casual dining. Takeout available. Outdoor dining, kid friendly.
Most Popular Item: Seafood chowder.

Pelican Pointe Golf & Country Club
499 Derbyshire Dr. (off Center Rd.)
Venice 34293
496-9463, fax 493-2801
Lunch - Mon-Sat, Dinner - Thurs-Fri
Sunday Brunch
Locally Owned - 4 Years
$; AX/DS/MC/VS; Full Bar
House Specialties: Quiche, Crepes, Veal, Seafood.
Other Points of Interest: Daily and nightly specials. Complete wine list and drink specials. Available for private parties and corporate functions.
Most Popular Item: Seafood crepes.

Key to Restaurant Listings

AX
American Express

CB
Carte Blanche

DC
Diners Club

DS
Discover

MC
Master Card

VS
Visa

LC
Local Checks are OK with proper I.D.

$
Under $7 lunch, under $12 dinner.

$$
Mostly $7 - $12 lunch, mostly $12 - $20 dinner.

$$$
Mostly $12 and over lunch, mostly $20 and over dinner.

Price categories are based on an average cost per person not including beverages, tax or tip.

Phillippi Creek Village Oyster Bar & Restaurant
5353 S. Tamiami Tr., Sarasota 34231
925-4444
Lunch & Dinner - 7 Days
Late Night - Fri-Sat
Locally Owned - 9 Years
$; MC/VS
Full Bar
House Specialties: Full service seafood. Oyster pot. Oysters served raw or broasted; blackened and baked fish; everything is fresh.
Other Points Of Interest: Located on the water, families welcome, boat accessible, outdoor dining available, voted "Best Oyster Bar in Town" (Sarasota Herald-Tribune) for 6 years. "Best Raw Bar Seafood Restaurant" for 1998. A local tradition.
Most Popular Item: Grouper sandwich.

Piazza Napoli
3535 Fruitville Rd., Sarasota 34237
365-0280
Lunch & Dinner - 7 Days
Locally Owned
$; AX/CB/DC/DS/MC/VS/LC
Beer/Wine Only
House Specialties: Homemade pizza and calzones, meatballs.

Piccirilli's Italian
6713 14th St. W., Bradenton 34207
758-4491
Dinner - Tue-Sun
Locally Owned - 21 Years
$$; MC/VS
Full Bar
House Specialties: Chateaubriand, veal, pasta, steaks and seafood.
Other Points Of Interest: Warm, traditional Italian setting. Table side preparation.
Most Popular Item: Owner says: "Everything is good."

Polpo Mario Restaurant
3131 Clark Rd., Sarasota 34231
925-0226
Dinner - Tues-Sun
Locally Owned - 2 Years
$$; AX/DC/CB/DS/MC/VS
Beer/Wine Only
House Specialties: Homemade pasta, Northern Italian cuisine, seafood specialties.
Other Points Of Interest: Fine dining. Small intimate dining room. Italian specialties. "Outstanding restaurant!" Open kitchen. Takeout available.
Most Popular Item: Grouper Livornese.

Poki Joe's Cafe
6614 Superior Ave., Sarasota 34231
922-5915
Lunch - Sun, Dinner - Tue-Sun
Sunday Brunch
Locally Owned - 18 Years
$; AX/MC/VS
Beer/Wine Only
House Specialties: BBQ baby back ribs. Black Forest Mushroom Pasta.
Other Points Of Interest: Based on 1930s, 40s and 50s eras, the music is wonderful. Very casual. Full service catering. Largest selection of beer in the area, including many varieties of micro-brewed beer. Late night Blues party Fri./Sat. nights.
Most Popular Item: Baby back ribs.

Pontillo's Pizzeria
6592 Superior Ave., Sarasota 34231
921-0990, fax 922-0362
Lunch - Mon-Sat, Dinner - 7 days
Locally Owned - 1 Year
$; LC
Beer/Wine Only
House Specialties: Oyster Cargot, lobster quesadillas, Chesapeake Bay salad, shrimp etouffe, steamed cherrystone clams, broiled seafood platter, live Maine lobster, Alaskan king crab legs.
Other Points of Interest: Located on the intracoastal waterway, offers indoor dining or on the waterfront deck. Live music on weekends and steel drum music on weekend afternoons. Happy hour daily. Tropical drink specials.
Most Popular Item: Maryland lump crabcakes.

Pops Tropicgrille
112 Circuit Rd., Venice
488-3177
Breakfast, Lunch & Dinner - 7 Days
Locally Owned - 6 Years
$; DS/MC/VS/LC
Full Bar
House Specialties: Pop's Special Breakfast. Cajun grilled chicken sandwich. Ribs and shrimp combo plate. Prime rib.
Other Points Of Interest: Children's menu; outdoor seating on the intracoastal waterway; gift shop stocked with items from local artisans. Entertainment on weekends.
Most Popular Item: Cajun Grouper sandwich.

Portbello
1538 Stickney Pt. Rd., Sarasota 34231
927-9600
Lunch & Dinner - 7 Days
Locally Owned - 3 Years
$$; AX/DS/MC/VS
Beer/Wine Only
House Specialties: Zuppa Dipesce, Ravioli Aragosta, Finfish & Shellfish, Rigatoni Alla Vodka, Dry Dock Selections
Other Points of Interest: Beautiful "New England" waterfront location, catering/take out/vegetarian menu available; chef/owner was a personal favorite of Frank Sinatra for many years.

Poseidon Restaurant
3454 Gulf of Mexico Dr.
Longboat Key 34228
383-2500, fax 383-3094
Dinner - 7 Days

Locally Owned - 4 Years
$$$; AX/CB/DC/DS/MC/VS
Full Bar
House Specialties: Fresh seafood; lobster, grouper, salmon, tuna, swordfish, crab, steaks, chops, & pasta.
Other Points of Interest: Waterfront dining. Monday night lobster specials. Great wine list, wonderful dishes. Pianist Tues-Sat.
Most Popular Item: Cedar planked pompano or salmon.

Primo! Ristorante
8076 Tamiami Tr., Sarasota 34243
359-3690, fax 359-1045
Dinner - 7 Days, Early Bird Specials
Locally Owned - 11 Years
$; AX/CB/DC/DS/MC/VS/DC
Full Bar
House Specialties: First wood-fire pizza in town. Prime veal, homemade pasta, fresh seafood, grilled meats, homemade desserts.
Other Points of Interest: European atmosphere with homemade Italian food. Casual family atmosphere. Rooms available for weddings, meetings and entertaining.
Most Popular Item: Spaghetti Sorrento.

Rico's Pizzeria
1902 Bay Rd., Sarasota 34239
366-8988, fax 365-2046
6447 Gateway Ave., Sarasota 34231
92-9604
5131 N. Tamiami Tr., Sarasota 34243
358-9958, fax 358-9959
Dinner - 7 Days, Early Bird Specials
Locally Owned - 2 Years
$; AX/DC/MC/VS/DC
Beer/Wine only
House Specialties: Seafood pasta, Philly steak & cheese, lasagna, grilled chix salad.
Other Points of Interest: Homey atmosphere with a New York attitude. Family owned and operated.
Most Popular Item: White pizza.

Rizzo Brother's Italian Restaurant
5120 Manatee Ave. West
Bradenton 34209
747-3360
Dinner - 7 Days
Locally Owned - 9 Years
$; DS/MC/VS/AX
Beer/Wine Only
House Specialties: Italian specialties. Fresh seafood. Veal Marsala, pizza and white pizza.
Other Points of Interest: Romantic bistro-style restaurant. Very comfortable.
Most Popular Item: Seafood Genovese.

Roadhouse Grill
5051 14th St. W., Bradenton 34207
755-0999, fax 727-9635
Lunch & Dinner - 7 Days
$; AX/DC/CB/DS/MC/VS
Full Bar
House Specialties: Steak, chicken, ribs, seafood, salads, sandwiches.
Other Points of Interest: Old fashioned steak house and saloon. Barrels of peanuts around for patrons to munch. Steaks are hand cut daily. Exhibition style cooking. Family oriented. TV with 60" screen.
Most Popular Item: Choice Sirloin.

Roessler's Flight Deck Restaurant
2033 Vamo Way, Sarasota 34238
966-5688, fax 966-4077
Lunch - Sun, Dinner - 7 Days
(closed Monday in summer)
Locally Owned - 20 Years
$$; AX/DC/DS/MC/VS
Full Bar
House Specialties: Daily specials, tableside presentations such as Steak Diane and Banannas Foster.
Other Points Of Interest: Family owned and operated in area for 20 years. Live entertainment on Fri. and Sat.
Most Popular Item: Steak Diane prepared tableside.

Rosebuds
2215 S. Tamiami Tr., Osprey 34229
918-8771, fax 918-0463
Dinner - Tues-Sun, Early bird specials
Locally Owned - 3 Years
$$; AX/MS/VS
Full Bar
House Specialties: Black Angus steaks, fresh seafood, veal, chicken, sauted dishes.
Other Points of Interest: Voted one of Sarasota's most romantic restaurants. Decor is beautifully decorated with roses, cherry wood mahogany, french doors and an up-north feel like Chicago or New York. Cigar smoking in lounge only.
Most Popular Item: Black Angus steaks,

Rotten Ralph's East Side
Manatee Ave. E., Braden River Plaza
Bradenton
746-3097
Lunch & Dinner - 7 Days
Locally Owned - 10 Years
$; DC/MC/VS/DS
Full Bar (Anna Maria); Beer/Wine Only at Bradenton location.
House Specialties: British style fish and chips, steamer pots - steamed shellfish with vegetables in a big pot. Homemade Key Lime Pie.
Other Points Of Interest: "On the Water!" Outside covered deck and outside dining, marina atmosphere. Full menu available from 11 a.m. to 9 p.m.
Most Popular Item: British Style Fish & Chips.

Saga Japanese Steakhouse
8383 S. Tamiami Tr., Sarasota
924-2800
Dinner - Tues- Sun
Locally Owned - 5 Years
$$; AX/CB/DC/DS/MC/VS
Beer/Wine Only

Key to Restaurant Listings

AX
American Express

CB
Carte Blanche

DC
Diners Club

DS
Discover

MC
Master Card

VS
Visa

LC
Local Checks are OK with proper I.D.

$
Under $7 lunch, under $12 dinner.

$$
Mostly $7 - $12 lunch, mostly $12 - $20 dinner.

$$$
Mostly $12 and over lunch, mostly $20 and over dinner.

Price categories are based on an average cost per person not including beverages, tax or tip.

House Specialties: Teppan Yaki style dining and Sushi bar.
Other Points of Interest: Chef owner really cares about customer satisfaction. Different specials offered daily.
Most Popular Item: Filet Mignon and Shrimp combination.

Sage
1371 Main St., Sarasota 34236
954-2226, fax 366-6452
e-mail: melsage@gte.net
Dinner - Mon-Sat
Locally Owned - 1 Year
$$; AX/DC/DS/MC/VS
Beer/Wine Only
House Specialties: Blackened beef carpaccio, Polynesian steamed clams, lobster & tobiko ravioli, crisp potato fried prawns, grilled ostrich, buffalo, baked cod, cornish hen
Other Points of Interest: Downtown near the Opera House and theaters. Takeout available. Private lunch parties available. Warm friendly atmosphere. Jazz music. Voted "Best New Restaurant '97", Sarasota Magazine. District and Theatre District.
Most Popular Item: Lobster & Tobiko Ravioli with Lime Ginger Sauce.

Saltwater Cafe
1071 N. Tamiami Tr., Nokomis 34275
488-3775, fax 488-099
e-mail: ssaltwater@aol.com
Breakfast, Lunch & Dinner - 7 days
Late Night Menu, Early bird specials
Locally Owned - 2 Years
$$; AX/CB/DC/DS/MC/VS
Full Bar
House Specialties: Fresh seafood, steaks, pasta, pizza, desserts.
Other Points of Interest: Area's largest variety of great seafood and landfood. Menu with over 300 items. Live entertainment weekends. Outstanding food in a relaxing atmosphere. Family-owned.
Most Popular Item: Live Maine lobster.

Sammy's
1526 Main St., Sarasota 34236
330-1266, fax 330-1956
Breakfast & Lunch - 7 days
Dinner Fri & Sat
Locally Owned
$; DS/MS/VS
Beer/Wine Only
House Specialties: New England style cooking & beer batter fish & chips. Codfish cakes, New England Clam Chowder, clam fritters, Philly cheese steak sandwich, New York grilled Reuben.
Other Points of Interest: 70's-80's theme games, albums, 8-tracks. Relaxed atmosphere. Brings you back to your recent past.
Most Popular Item: Carne Espetada.

Sand Dollar Rooftop Restaurant
233 Ben Franklin Dr., Sarasota 34236
388-5555, fax 388-4321
Breakfast - 7 days, Lunch - Mon-Sat
Dinner - 7 days
$$; AX/CB/DC/DS/MS/VS
Full Bar
House Specialties: Oyster Cargot, lobster quesadillas, Fresh local seafood and chargrilled steaks.
Other Points of Interest: Saturday evening seafood buffet. Champagne Sunday brunch. Spectacular view of the Gulf of Mexico from our rooftop location. Private rooms available for banquets and special events.
Most Popular Item: Fresh local seafood.

Sandbar Restaurant
100 Spring Ave., Anna Maria 34216
778-0444
Lunch & Dinner - 7 Days
Locally Owned - 19 Years
$$; AX/DC/DS/MC/VS
Full Bar
House Specialties: Seafood. "Chicken Anna Maria." Golden snapper sandwich.
Other Points Of Interest: Since 1911 this has always been a restaurant, just not the same one. Dine inside or outside on the beach. Live music. Amazing view and great sunsets. Tropical drinks. Very popular spot.
Most Popular Item: Fresh fish.

Santa Fe Steakhouse
5451 Fruitville Rd., Sarasota 34232
378-0595, fax 378-5762
Lunch & Dinner - 7 Days
Locally Owned - 7 Years
$; AX/DC/MS/VS/LC
Full Bar
House Specialties: Ribs and steaks cooked over oak/pecan wood fire pit. Great value and super variety. Authentic Southwestern recipes.
Other Points Of Interest: Southwestern motif. Catering available.
Most Popular Item: BBQ ribs.

Sarasota Ale House
3800 Kenney Dr., Sarasota 34232
378-8888, fax 378-8899
Lunch & Dinner - 7 days
Late Night Menu, Early bird specials
$; AX/DC/MS/VS
Full bar
House Specialties: Lobster Manila, All you can eat snow crab, Prime Rib, Seafood, steaks, pasta, ribs.
Other Points of Interest: Sports theme: 36 draft beers. 36 TV's. All major sporting events.
Most Popular Item: Baby back ribs.

The Sarasota Bread Company
208 Southgate Plaza, Sarasota 34239
957-2200, fax 957-0447
e-mail: summerhouse@aol.com
www.sarasotarestaurants.com
Breakfast, Lunch & Dinner - 7 days
Locally Owned - 1 Year
$$; AX/MS/VS
Beer/Wine Only

House Specialties: Satay plate, Memphis pork barbeque, oven-roasted vegetable Pannini, Greek salad, Mushroom and brie omelette, Thai chicken, roast leg of lamb, tiramisu torte, Creme Brulee tart.
Other Points of Interest: A working bakery, European style cafe and a gourmet marketplace featuring imported olive oils, cheeses and wines. Gourmet to-go meals, sides, platters and desserts are available daily and special orders are taken. Artisan breads and pastries are baked daily.
Most Popular Item: Rack of lamb.

Sarasota Brewing Co.
6607 Gateway Ave., Sarasota 34231
925-2337
Lunch & Dinner - 7 Days
Late Night; Locally Owned - 10 Years
$; AX/CB/DC/DS/MC/VS
Full Bar
House Specialties: Handcrafted beer, wings, homemade soups, tempting desserts.
Other Points Of Interest: Area's first brewery. A "Cheers" oriented sports bar. Fun atmosphere with big-screen TV. Happy hour 3-6p.m. and 10 p.m. to closing.
Most Popular Item: Beer and burgers.

Saulina's Pizza
8428 Lockwood Ridge N., Sarasota 34243
355-7050
Lunch & Dinner - 7 days
Locally Owned - 7 Years
$; AX/DS/MC/VS/ LC
Beer/Wine Only
House Specialties: Eggplant parmesan, veal parmesan.
Other Points Of Interest: "People come from all over Manatee, Sarasota and Venice to eat our pizza!" Homemade dough.
Most Popular Item: Pizza.

Scalini
1000 Blvd. Of The Arts
Sarasota 34236
953-1234, ext. 1288
Breakfast - 7 Days, Dinner - Tues-Sat (Sunday and Monday for pre-Van Wezel performances), Sunday Brunch
$$; AX/CB/DC/DS/MC/VS/LC
Full Bar
House Specialties: Theatre goers menu (Van Wezel Season), Seasonal Buffet Menu.
Other Points Of Interest: Award winning (Sarasota Herald Tribune) Champagne Sunday Brunch.
Most Popular Item: Costaletta D'Agnello al Rosemarino (broiled lamb chops with rosemary mint glaze).

Seafood Shack
4110 127th St. West, Cortez 34215
794-1235, fax 794-8119
Lunch & Dinner - 7 Days
Locally Owned - 26 Years
$; AX/DS/MC/VS

Full Bar
House Specialties: Fresh red snapper. Blackened seafood and steaks.
Other Points Of Interest: Located on Intracoastal waterway, come by boat or by car. Second story main dining room. Two restaurants here, one strictly for lighter menu - sandwiches. Paddle boat sightseeing cruises include dinner discount in restaurant.
Most Popular Item: African lobster.

Seagrape Restaurant
2050 Ben Franklin Dr., Sarasota 34236
388-3694, fax 388-1938
e-mail: halfmoon@ix.netcom.com
www.halfmoon-l.doksy.com
Breakfast, Lunch & Dinner - 7 days
Locally Owned - 9 Years
$$; AX/DC/DS/MC/VS/LC; Full Bar
House Specialties: Seafood, nightly specials.
Other Points of Interest: Beach deck dining on the Gulf of Mexico. Beautiful contemporary setting.
Most Popular Item: Grouper Piccata

Serenoa Golf Club
6773 Serenoa Dr., Sarasota 34241
925-2755, fax 922-6142
Lunch - 7 Days
Locally Owned -8 Years
$; AX/MC/VS/ LC
Full Bar
House Specialties: Sandwiches, burgers chicken breast sandwiches and

Join us in the
SAND DOLLAR
Rooftop Restaurant
Overlooking the sparkling Gulf of Mexico

Weekend Seafood Buffet $19.95

Sunday Brunch $17.95

Early Dining Specials from $8.95

Please see our dining discount in the Coupon Savings section.

Reservations are recommended.
Please call 388-5555 ext. 3332

Holiday Inn
Lido Beach
Just a short stroll from St. Armands Circle

Key to Restaurant Listings

AX American Express

CB Carte Blanche

DC Diners Club

DS Discover

MC Master Card

VS Visa

LC Local Checks are OK with proper I.D.

$ Under $7 lunch, under $12 dinner.

$$ Mostly $7 - $12 lunch, mostly $12 - $20 dinner.

$$$ Mostly $12 and over lunch, mostly $20 and over dinner.

Price categories are based on an average cost per person not including beverages, tax or tip.

---

homemade soups.
Other Points Of Interest: View of the lake and golf course.
Most Popular Item: Club sandwiches.

The Serving Spoon
1825 S. Osprey Ave., Sarasota 34239
366-1277
Breakfast & Lunch - 7 Days
Locally Owned - 7 Years
$; AX/DS/MC/VS/LC
No Liquor Served
House Specialties: Breakfast burrito and chicken peanut pasta salad. Fresh pastries, great pancakes, omelettes du jour. Homemade soup. Low calorie salads.
Other Points Of Interest: Diverse menu.
Most Popular Item: Breakfast burrito.

Shake Pit
3801 Manatee Ave. West
Bradenton 34205
748-4016
Lunch & Dinner - 7 Days
Locally Owned - 38 Years
$; No Credit Cards/LC
No Liquor Served
House Specialties: Shakes-"best shakes, hamburgers, chicken cheese, and BLT." Homemade ice cream actually made on premises.
Other Points Of Interest: Burgers made fresh every day. Monthly specials shown on marquee. Landmark for 38 years. Well-loved by locals.
Most Popular Item: Burgers.

Shaner's
3440 Clark Rd., Sarasota 34231
925-4551, fax 927-6460
Lunch - Mon-Sat, Dinner - 7 Days
Locally Owned - 7 Years
$; AX/DS/MC/VS
Full bar
House Specialties: Pizza, burgers, Chicken Caesar salad, Chicken Parmigiana sandwich and Philly Cheese steak sandwich.
Other Points Of Interest: Locally owned by an ex-baseball player. Sports bar. Family style restaurant. Daily lunch and dinner specials.
Most Popular Item: Thin crust Pizza.

Shangri-La Restaurant
5828 Bee Ridge Rd., Sarasota 34233
378-5585
Lunch - Mon-Sat, Dinner - 7 Days
Locally Owned - 8 Years
Early Bird Special
$; DS/MC/VS
Beer/Wine Only
House Specialties: Hunan and Cantonese cooking. Seafood and steak dishes.
Most Popular Item: Early Bird Combination Specials.

Sharky's On the Pier
1600 Harbor Dr. South, Venice 34285
488-1356
Lunch & Dinner - 7 Days
Late Night - Fri-Sat
Locally Owned - 11 Years
$; DS/MC/VS/AX
Full Bar
House Specialties: Fresh fish - daily catch. Great Lakes perch (in season), ribs, steak, shrimp.
Other Points Of Interest: Voted "Best of the Best" at Taste of Sarasota 1997. Located "Smack Dab on The Gulf," large outdoor tiki bar & deck serves up tropical frozen drinks and a light beach menu. Inside dining offers a full menu of entrees, outstanding service and a gulf view.
Most Popular Item: Gulf Max.

Shells Seafood Restaurants
7253 S. Tamiami Tr., Sarasota 34231
924-2568, fax 924-2458
8200 East Bay Dr., Holmes Beach 34217
778-5997
Dinner - 7 Days
Late Night - Fri & Sat
Locally Owned - 12 Years
$; AX/DS/MC/VS
Full Bar
House Specialties: Award-winning shrimp pasta and clam chowder plus many different great seafood items. Chicken and steak tool.
Other Points of Interest: Voted #1-12 years running in Sarasota Herald Tribune Readers Choice. Takeout available.
Most Popular Item: Shrimp Pasta.

Shogun Japanese Steak House & Seafood Restaurant
1219 Venice Bypass S., Venice 34292
485-8746
Dinner - 7 Days
Locally Owned - 8 Years
$$; DS/MC/VS
Beer/Wine Only
House Specialties: "Shogun Special" - lobster, shrimp and filet mignon.
Other Points Of Interest: All dinners served Hibachi style, table side.
Most Popular Item: Filet & Shrimp.

Shooters Waterfront Cafe USA
7150 N. Tamiami Tr., Sarasota 34237
355-3357, fax 355-4149
Breakfast, Lunch & Dinner - 7 days
Early Bird Specials, Sunday Brunch
Locally Owned - 1 Year
$$; AX/DS/MC/VS
Full Bar
House Specialties: Pasta, seafood, steaks, salads, Sunday Brunch.
Other Points of Interest: Waterfront, boat access, live entertainment, tiki bar.
Most Popular Item: Steaks.

Siam Orchid
4141 S. Tamiami Tr., Sarasota 34231
923-7447, fax 365-7304
Lunch - Mon-Fri, Dinner - 7 nights
Locally Owned - 9 Years
$; AX/DC/MC/VS/DS
Beer/Wine Only
House Specialties: Seafood Thai style,

Thai style vegetarian dishes.
Other Points Of Interest: Award winning - too many to list. Catering and takeout available. A local favorite.
Most Popular Item: Whole fish.

Sign of the Mermaid
9707 Gulf Dr., Anna Maria 34216
778-9399
www.manatee-online/mermaid.com
Dinner - 6 Days (closed Tuesday)
Locally Owned - 7 Years
Early Bird, Sunday Brunch
$$$; VS/MC/ LC
Beer/Wine Only
House Specialties: Charred rare tuna, Shoa Mei dumplings. Bouillabaisse. Rack of Lamb.
Other Points Of Interest: A lovingly restored island cottage (moved to Anna Maria from St. Petersburg by barge in the early 1900's) with antiques and comfortable seating for 39 people. An eclectic/adventuresome menu. Please bring your own bottle (no corkage fee). All entrees are prepared to order.
Most Popular Item: Charred rare tuna.

Silver Star Restaurant
180 N. Lime Ave., Sarasota 34237
365-5051
Breakfast, Lunch & Dinner - 7 Days
Locally Owned - 18 Years
$; No Credit Cards
Beer/Wine Only

House Specialties: Greek and American cuisine. Gyros, Spinach pie, Moussaka, Pastitsio. Daily specials. Fish and meatloaf.
Other Points Of Interest: Home baked pies; serve 70-item breakfast menu all day long.
Most Popular Item: Gyros.

Snook Haven Restaurant & Fish Camp
5000 Venice Ave. East, Venice 34292
485-7221, fax 484-3637
Lunch & Dinner - 7 Days
Locally Owned - 9 Years
$; MC/VS
Beer/Wine and some pre-mixed liquor drinks.
House Specialties: Burgers, ribs, chicken, seafood, grouper, gator and shark bites.
Other Points Of Interest: Located on wild and scenic Myakka River. Deck hanging over edge of river, all tables have view of river. Entertainment nightly, 5-9 p.m. Sunday afternoon country and western band plus BBQ. Old Florida atmosphere. Supposedly some of the original Tarzan films were shot here. Canoe, pontoon and fishing boat rentals. Tour boat rides Fri, Sat & Sun at 3 p.m.
Most Popular Item: Burgers and chicken wings.

Soul Food Kitchen
616 10th St. E., Bradenton 34208
750-8484

Sharky's
on the Pier

- Fresh Seafood
- Lunch and Dinner Daily
- Casual Dining Inside or Out
- Live Entertainment.

"Smack Dab on the Gulf" at the Venice Fishing Pier

1.4 Miles South of Venice Ave.
488-1456

Key to Restaurant Listings

AX American Express

CB Carte Blanche

DC Diners Club

DS Discover

MC Master Card

VS Visa

LC Local Checks are OK with proper I.D.

$ Under $7 lunch, under $12 dinner.

$$ Mostly $7 - $12 lunch, mostly $12 - $20 dinner.

$$$ Mostly $12 and over lunch, mostly $20 and over dinner.

Price categories are based on an average cost per person not including beverages, tax or tip.

Breakfast, Lunch & Dinner - Tues-Sun
Locally Owned - 18 Years
$;LC
No Liquor Served
House Specialties: Short Ribs, Oxtails, Neckbones, Chitlins, Black-eyed Peas, Collard Greens and Daily Specials.
Other Points of Interest: Authentic Southern Soul Food that "fills you up, makes you strong!" Oldest soul food restaurant on the Suncoast. Catering available; very popular with local clientele. Friendly, all welcome.

South Beach Cafe
1991 Main St., Sarasota Main Plaza, Sarasota 34236
906-2049, fax 362-4675
Breakfast, Lunch & Dinner - 7 Days
Locally Owned - 2 Years
$; DS/MC/VS/LC; No Liquor Served
House Specialties: Fresh baked bagels and gourmet pizza. 15 flavors of coffee at our coffee bar.
Other Points of Interest: Located right next to Hollywood-20 Theaters, South Beach Miami decor; large coffee bar.

The Sports Page Bar & Grille
1319 Main St., Sarasota 34236
365-0469, fax 365-0288
Lunch & Dinner - 7 Days, Late Night
Locally Owned - 10 Years
$; MC/VS/AX/DS/DC
Full Bar/Package service available
House Specialties: Nachos, burgers, wings, home made soups and daily specials.
Other Points Of Interest: Great location. Interesting sports pictures, memorabilia. Pool tables. Kitchen open until 1:30 a.m., bar until 2:30 a.m. daily.
Most Popular Item: Chicken wings.

Stockyard Steakhouse
4041 Cattleman Rd., Sarasota 34233
378-9699, fax 378-9779
Lunch & Dinner - 7 Days
Early Bird Specials/Late Night/
Locally Owned - 6 Years
$$; AX/MC/VS
Full Bar
House Specialties: USDA Prime steaks - "the only steakhouse in Sarasota to offer this ultimate quality."
Other Points Of Interest: 1998 Sarasota Herald Tribune Readers choice Awards: Best Steakhouse, Best dinner under $10, Best early bird, Best all-around restaurant, Best burger, Best bar, Best happy hour, Best power lunch. Kids eat free - one per adult entree.

Strudels 'N Cream Cafe & Bakery
1660 Ringling Blvd., Sarasota 34236
954-7775, fax 379-3587
Breakfast & Lunch - Mon-Fri
Locally Owned - 8 Years
$; No credit cards accepted/LC
Full Bar
House Specialties: Pastries, French bread, muffins.

Subconscious
1303 N. Washington Blvd.
Sarasota 34240
954-4281, fax 954-9371
Lunch - Mon-Sat
Locally Owned - 10 Years
$; No credit cards accepted/LC
No Liquor served
House Specialties: Cuban sandwich, hoagies, fresh soups, Buffalo wings.
Most Popular Item: Cuban Sub.

Sugar & Spice Family Restaurant
4000 Cattlemen Rd., Sarasota 34233
342-1649, fax 342-0334
Lunch & Dinner - Mon-Sat
Locally Owned - 14 Years
$; DS/MC/VS
No Liquor Served
House Specialties: Roasted turkey and dressing. Homemade soups, sandwiches, complete entrees and irresistible homemade pies and cakes.
Other Points Of Interest: Wholesome food with a friendly feeling of down home hospitality. Colorful Amish style quilts hanging from wooden rafters may be purchased.
Most Popular Item: Roasted turkey.

Sullivan's Irish Pub & Grill
501 N. Beneva Rd., Sarasota 34237
(in courtyard at Town & Country Plaza)
954-7709
Lunch & Dinner - 7 Days
Locally Owned - 9 Years
$; DC/MC/VS
Full Bar
House Specialties: Cottage pie, Reuben sandwiches and other Irish specialties.
Other Points Of Interest: 17 beers on draft. Irish pub decor and atmosphere. Nightly entertainment, with Irish folk music. Jazz on Sunday evenings. Happy Hour 2-7 p.m.
Most Popular Item: Chicken and mushroom pie.

The Summerhouse Restaurant
6101 Midnight Pass Rd.
Siesta Key 34242
349-1100, fax 346-1755
e-mail: summerhouse@aol.com
www.summerhouserestaurant.com
Dinner - 7 Days, Early Bird Specials
Sunday Brunch, Late Night
Locally Owned - 17 Years
$$$; AX/CB/DC/DS/MC/VS
Full Bar
House Specialties: Macadamia nut shrimp, sashimi, roast quail, baked salmon en croute, tournedos rossini, veal oscar, heavenly homemade desserts.
Other Points Of Interest: Lush tropical gardens, glass-walled dining room. Outdoor dining available year round. Happy hour and live entertainment nightly in Treetop Lounge.
Most Popular Item: Tournedos Rossini.

Sunset Grill
110-112 Circuit Rd., Nokomis 34275
488-3177, fax 484-9071
Breakfast - Sun, Lunch & Dinner - 7 Days
Locally Owned - 1 Year
$$; AX/DS/MC/VS/LC
Full Bar
House Specialties: Steamship pot, ribs and shrimp combo plate, breakfast raft (potatoes loaded with a variety of toppings) Cajun grilled chicken sandwich.
Other Points Of Interest: Fresh fish market, 175 seat of waterfront with deepwater dockage. Outdoor seating as well as indoor. Gift shop. Entertainment Wed.-Sun. - reggae, parrot-heads welcome. Boat accessible at Marker 10 at Nokomis Beach Bridge.

The Sunset Grille
4711 Gulf of Mexico Dr.
Longboat Key 34228
383-2451, fax 383-7979
Breakfast, Lunch & Dinner - 7 Days
Locally Owned - 10 Years
$$; AX/CB/DS/DC/MC/VS
Full Bar
House Specialties: Specializing in steaks, we offer chef's specialties 7 days and nights per week.
Other Points Of Interest: Newly renovated. Casual al fresco lunch and dinner under our banyan tree with a view of the Gulf of Mexico.
Most Popular Item: Shrimp Portofino.

Surfrider Restaurant
6400 Midnight Pass Rd.
Siesta Key 34242
346-1199
Dinner - Tue-Sat, Early Bird Specials
Locally Owned - 10 Years
$$; AX/MC/VS
Beer/Wine Only
House Specialties: Garlic shrimp primavera, pasta Jambalaya, BBQ ribs, pasta athena, gorgonzola shrimp, blackened scallops, Caribbean chicken, steaks, margarita shrimp, chicken supreme, scallops casino, seafood pot, snickers surprise, Siesta sunshine tart, Brandy Alexander cheesecake.
Other Points Of Interest: An original Florida beach house, very romantic and unique. The beautiful Gulf of Mexico is just 100 yards from the patio. Stroll the beach, then savor fresh, lively tastes, generous portions and reasonable prices. "Come eat where Bette Davis used to live!"
Most Popular Item: Siesta Key Shrimp.

Tai Ping Chinese Restaurant
150 Shopping Ave., Sarasota 34237
(Ringling Shopping Center)
366-0508
Lunch & Dinner - Mon-Sat
Locally Owned - 5 Years
$; MC/VS
Beer/Wine only
House Specialties: Tai Ping crispy noodle w/lobster, scallops, shrimp, pork & chicken in golden brown sauce over crispy noodles.
Other Points of Interest: Good food and friendly service in attractive surroundings - unusually good Chinese food, a great find.
Most Popular Item: Orange peel chicken.

The Tasting Room
1925 S. Osprey Ave., Sarasota
362-WINE
Lunch & Dinner - Mon-Sat
Locally Owned - New
$$$; AX/MC/VS
Full Bar
House Specialties: Mixture platters of innovative "finger food", homemade desserts; specialty drinks including Martinis and single malt Scotch.
Other Points of Interest: Liquor store, walk-in humidor, temp. controlled fine wine room, cigar friendly, indoor/outdoor dining; very hip clientele. One of the area's unique hot spots.
Most Popular Item: Special Martini.

Tex Mex Cafe and Saloon
1756 Honore Ave., Sarasota 34235
371-4500
2615 Mall Dr., Sarasota 34231
925-4500, fax 925-7503
Lunch & Dinner - 7 Days
Locally Owned - 6 Years
$; AX/MC/VS
Full Bar (Honore Ave. only); Beer/Wine Only (Mall Drive)
House Specialties: Southwestern specialties such as fajitas, quesadillas, burritos, tamales and margaritas.
Other Points of Interest: Authentic Southwestern red and green chile sauces. Fabulous Margaritas. Happy Hour 4-7 PM daily. Karaoke Thurs-Sat 9:15 p.m.
Most Popular Item: Sweet Texas Fire Quesadillas.

Thai Garden Restaurant
7804 S. Tamiami Tr., Sarasota 34231
922-0032, fax 921-1310
Lunch & Dinner - 7 Days
$; AX/DC/DS/MC/VS
Beer/Wine Only
House Specialties: Authentic Thai food, stir fry, crispy duck, curries.
Other Points of Interest: Unique decor, warm, excellent food, very neat and clean, fresh food, beautiful setting, good service.
Most Popular Item: Duck's Special.

Theresa's Family Restaurant
608 14th St. W., Bradenton 34205
747-7066
Breakfast & Lunch -Mon-Fri & Sun
Locally Owned - 12 Years
$; DS/MC/VS/DS
Beer/Wine Only
House Specialties: Deli featuring full line of high end products. Homestyle

Key to Restaurant Listings

AX
American Express

CB
Carte Blanche

DC
Diners Club

DS
Discover

MC
Master Card

VS
Visa

LC
Local Checks are OK with proper I.D.

$
Under $7 lunch, under $12 dinner.

$$
Mostly $7 - $12 lunch, mostly $12 - $20 dinner.

$$$
Mostly $12 and over lunch, mostly $20 and over dinner.

Price categories are based on an average cost per person not including beverages, tax or tip.

cooking with healthy alternatives.
Other Points of Interest: Large local clientele. Low calorie and vegetarian items available. Takeout available.
Most Popular Item: Cheese Blintzes.

Thro-Doughs Pizza Forum
19A North Blvd. of the Presidents
Sarasota 34236
388-2882
Lunch & Dinner - 7 Days
Locally Owned - 10 Years
$; No Credit Cards
Beer/Wine Only
House Specialties: Stromboli, spaghetti and Calzone.
Other Points Of Interest: Right on St. Armands Circle. Indoor seating as well as takeout. Hand-tossed, homemade sauce, great pizza. Non-smoking restaurant.
Most Popular Item: Pizza.

Tia Panchas
4222 26th St. West, Bradenton
755-4222
Lunch - Mon-Sat, Dinner - Mon-Sat
Locally Owned - 1 Year
$; AX/VS/MC/DS
Beer/Wine Only
House Specialties: Homemade authentic Mexican food, black bean soup, chili rellenos, fajitas.
Other Points Of Interest: "Best Sangria in town, 100% homemade!"
Romantic, cozy setting.
Most Popular Item: Mexican pizza.

Tommy Bahama
300 John Ringling Blvd., Sarasota 34236
388-2888
Lunch & Dinner - 7 days
Locally Owned - 2 Years
$$; AX/MC/VS
Full Bar
House Specialties: Island inspired cuisine.
Other Points of Interest: Full line of Tommy Bahama men and women's weekend wear clothing available.
Most Popular Item: Pollo Island Pasta.

Tony's Place
6051 Manatee Ave. W., Suite E
Holmes Beach 34217
778-5440
Lunch & Dinner - Mon-Sat
Early Bird Specials
Locally Owned - 3 Years
$; MC/VS/LC
Beer/Wine Only
House Specialties: Home cooked Italian food.
Other Points of Interest: Italian motif. Freshly remodeled. Will prepare special dishes upon request. Take-out and delivery available.
Most Popular Item: Eggplant Parmesan

Trolley Station
3550 Clark Rd., Sarasota 34231
923-2721, fax 923-2722
Locally Owned - 19 Years
$; MC/VS; Full Bar

House Specialties: Chicago ribs, homemade soups and salad bar featuring oven-hot bread.
Other Points Of Interest: Winner: "Best Hamburger" -Sarasota Herald-Tribune. The 9th largest user of Angus beef in United States. Nice mix of antiques and interurban trolley car memorabilia. Casual dining.
Most Popular Item: Jumbo hamburgers.

Tropical Thai Restaurant
4304 14th St. W., Bradenton 34207
758-6390, fax 758-6390
1420 Main St., Sarasota 34236
364-5775
Lunch & Dinner - 7 Days
(Bradenton closed Mondays)
Early Bird Specials
Locally Owned - 6 Years
$; AX/DS/MC/VS
Beer/Wine Only
House Specialties: Thai Food.
Other Points Of Interest: Take-out and banquet facilities available. Lunch buffet in Bradenton every day.
Most Popular Item: "Fancy Duck" and Snapper with chile sauce.

Tudor Rose
3676 Webber St., Sarasota 34232
923-3096
Lunch & Dinner - Mon-Sat
(7 Days in Season)
Locally Owned - 2 Years
$; MC/VS/DS
Beer/Wine Only
House Specialties: English fish and chips, steak and mushroom pie, chicken royal, chicken and mushroom pie and cottage pie, curries.
Other Points Of Interest: Traditional English pub with memorabilia from pubs in England. Nine British draft beers and a selection of ciders. All dishes home cooked from scratch. Play Trivial Pursuit every Thursday night; Karaoke on Friday night. Live soccer via satellite. Smoke extractors for your comfort.
Most Popular Item: Fish & Chips.

Turtles Restaurant
8875 Midnight Pass Rd.
Siesta Key 34242
346-2207, fax 346-3125
Lunch & Dinner - 7 Days
Early Bird Specials, Late Night
Locally Owned - 12 Years
$$; AX/DS/MC/VS
Full Bar
House Specialties: Snapper New Orleans, salmon pasta.
Other Points Of Interest: Romantic casual waterfront dining. Entertainment seasonal.
Most Popular Item: Snapper New Orleans.

Two Senoritas
1355 Main St., Sarasota 34236
366-1618
Lunch & Dinner - 7 Days, Late Night
Locally Owned - 4 Years
$; AX/MC/VS/DS/LC

Full Bar
House Specialties: Fajitas, Carne Asada, Chile Relleno, Flautas
Other Points Of Interest: Authentic Mexican food, great homemade salsa.
Most Popular Item: Chicken Enchilada.

Valenti's Restaurant
1200 Venice Ave. East, Venice 34293
484-1888
Lunch - Mon-Fri, Dinner - 7 Days
Locally Owned - 9 Years
$; DS/MC/VS/LC
Beer/Wine Only
House Specialties: Chicken cacciatore, shrimp, scallops, veal marsala
Other Points of Interest: Simple. Italian. Friendly with great food.
Most Popular Item: Veal.

Villa Capri
4500 S. Tamiami Tr., Sarasota 34231
921-3337
Lunch & Dinner - 7 Days
Locally Owned - 5 Years
$; AX/DS/MC/VS/LC
Beer/Wine Only
House Specialties: Veal Milano, Ziti, Filet Di Pomadoro.
Other Points Of Interest: Take out, lunch delivery and catering. Amazingly great New Jersey-style Italian fare, you'll be one of the family here.
Most Popular Item: Chicken Francese.

FAMILY OWNED SINCE 1975

VOTED 1ST PLACE:
• Best Meal under $10 • Best Homemade Dessert
955-7771
3434 BAHIA VISTA STREET
BREAKFAST • LUNCH • DINNER

AMISH HOME COOKING IN A HURRY!
925-7437
CORNER OF BENEVA & GULF GATE DR.
Next to Speedway
LUNCH AND DINNER 11 AM - 8 PM

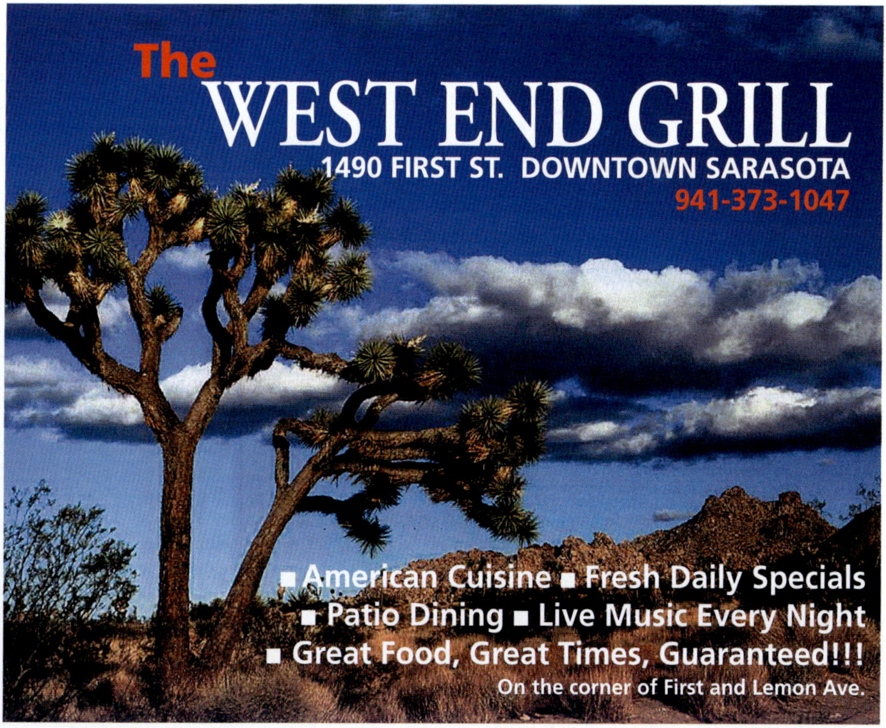

The WEST END GRILL
1490 FIRST ST. DOWNTOWN SARASOTA
941-373-1047

■ American Cuisine ■ Fresh Daily Specials
■ Patio Dining ■ Live Music Every Night
■ Great Food, Great Times, Guaranteed!!!
On the corner of First and Lemon Ave.

Key to Restaurant Listings

AX
American Express

CB
Carte Blanche

DC
Diners Club

DS
Discover

MC
Master Card

VS
Visa

LC
Local Checks are OK with proper I.D.

$
Under $7 lunch, under $12 dinner.

$$
Mostly $7 - $12 lunch, mostly $12 - $20 dinner.

$$$
Mostly $12 and over lunch, mostly $20 and over dinner.

Price categories are based on an average cost per person not including beverages, tax or tip.

The Waffle Shop Restaurant
210 Shopping Ave., Sarasota 34237
(Ringling Shopping Center)
955-1456
Breakfast & Lunch - 7 Days
Dinner - Friday (November - April)
Locally Owned - 56 Years
$; No Credit Cards/LC
House Specialties: Waffles and omelettes, great burgers, all-you-can-eat Fish Fry on Friday.
Other Points Of Interest: This is the oldest restaurant in Sarasota.
Most Popular Item: Omelettes

Walt's Fish Market & Oyster Bar
4144 S. Tamiami Tr., Sarasota 34231
921-4605
Lunch & Dinner - 7 Days
Locally Owned - 34 Years
Early Bird Specials
$; MC/VS/DS/LC
Full Bar (beer/wine only at S. Tr. location)
House Specialties: Fresh, fresh, fresh fish. Alligator and stone crabs in season.
Other Points Of Interest: Voted "Best of the Best" Seafood Restaurant.
Most Popular Item: Blackened fish.

The Waterfront Restaurant
7660 S. Tamiami Tr., Sarasota 34231
921-1916
Dinner - 7 Days, Late Nights - Fri-Sat
Locally Owned - 12 Years
$$; MC/VS
Full Bar
House Specialties: Steak, lobster tails and grilled fish. Daily specials.
Other Points Of Interest: Steaks and seafood. Homemade beer rolls with dinner. Located in South Point Mall .
Most Popular Item: Lobster Tail and Steak.

The West End Grill
1490 1st St., Sarasota 34236
373-0157, fax 373-0209
Lunch & Dinner - 7 days, Early bird specials, Late night menu
Locally Owned - 1 Year
$; AX/DC/DS/MC/VS/LC
Full bar
House Specialties: Homemade soups, imported and domestic beers.
Other Points of Interest: Located on the corner of 1st and Lemon Ave. Built in the 1920s, on the historical register. Cigar friendly. Live music 7 days a week. Patio. Great atmosphere.
Most Popular Item: Philly steak sandwich.

Wild-Eats Grille & Market at Paradise Plaza
3800 S. Tamiami Tr., Sarasota 34231
954-1330
e-mail: eventsandmore@msn.com
Breakfast & Lunch - 7 days
Dinner Mon-Sat
Locally Owned - 2 Years
$; AX/DC/DS/MC/VS
Beer/Wine only
House Specialties: Red Flannel Hash breakfast burrito, Portabello everything, Caesar Wrap; veggie melt; eggplant crepes; avocado Reuben, scrambled tofu.
Other Points of Interest: Let your tastebuds run Wild. Serving vegetarian, vegan and traditional cuisine for the healthy mind, body & spirit. Warm, friendly, relaxing and smoke-free. Cheery and serene setting. Outside patio seating available. Takeout available.
Most Popular Item: Veggie burger.

Woody's BBQ
5864 Bee Ridge Rd., Sarasota 34233
378-9874
3142 53rd Ave. E., Bradenton 34209
755-1446
Lunch & Dinner - 7 Days
Locally Owned - 5 Years
$; MC/VS; Beer/Wine Only
House Specialties: Baby Back Ribs, smoked chicken and turkey, pork, sandwiches, salads, homemade desserts and salad dressings..
Other Points of Interest: Winner '95 Best of the Best BBQ from Sarasota Magazine, and finalist in '95 Reader's Choice Best BBQ. Offering "all you can eat" specials. Take-out, delivery and catering.
Most Popular Item: Baby back ribs.

Yoder's
3434 Bahia Vista St., Sarasota 34239
955-7771
Breakfast, Lunch & Dinner - Mon-Sat
Locally Owned - 23 Years
$; No Credit Cards/LC
No Liquor Served
House Specialties: Amish home cooking. Over 20 homemade pies daily.
Other Points Of Interest: Well-known and loved by locals. Winner: "Best Dinner Under $10" WWSB/Sar. Mag.
Most Popular Item: Baked chicken and pot roast with vegetables.

Yoder's Express
6986 S. Beneva Rd., Sarasota 34238
925-7437
Breakfast, Lunch & Dinner - Mon-Sat
Locally Owned - 3 Years
$; LC/ No credit cards
No Liquor Served
House Specialties: Amish home cooking. Daily specials, sandwiches, salads, and 20 varieties of pies.
Other Points of Interest: Carry-out or dine. "The Fast Food of Home Cooking."
Most Popular Item: Mom's Meatloaf.

Yoshino
417 Burns Ct., Sarasota 34236
366-8544
Dinner - 6 days, closed Tuesday
Locally Owned - 10 Years
$$; Beer/Wine Only
House Specialties: Sushi, fresh seafood, duck and chicken.
Other Points Of Interest: "At home atmosphere" - small rooms and intimate sushi bar.
Most Popular Item: Shasha Mi Sushi.

HELP!

Is your favorite eatery missing from our current list or do you know of a new restaurant which is opening in the near future?

Please send us the details – name of restaurant, address, phone number and the name of whom to contact – we'll do the rest.

Restaurants are *never* charged to be included in *The Guide*.

Send new information to:
Steve Rabow's Guide Book
P.O. Box 15332
Sarasota, FL 34277

For advertising rates:
(941) 927-1771

LISTINGS BY CUISINE

American Traditional
All Star Steakhouse
Banyan Cafe
Beach Cafe Bar & Restaurant
Beef O'Brady's
Benedicts Restaurant
Big Kitchen Restaurant & Bar
Blue Dolphin Cafe
Bob's Boathouse
Buccaneer Inn
The Daiquiri Deck &
  Cafe Gardens
Cafe on the Bay
Candlelight Restaurant
Chef Paul's
Cock 'N Bull Pub
The Colony Bistro
The Country Buffet
Crab Trap I & II
Dry Dock
Fifty's Diner
First Watch
Gecko's Grill & Pub
Golden Apple Dinner Theater
Gulf Drive Cafe
Hemmingway's
Hob Nob
Hot Diggity Dog
Kevin's Country Cafe
Lynches Landing
Marina Jack Dinner Boat
Mel-O-Dee
Midnight Pass Pub
Millie's
Oberlin's
Old Hickory
Paddy's Sports Bar & Grill
Park Grill & Cafe
Patches Family Restaurant
Patricks
Peaches
Pelican Pointe
Pops Tropicgrille
Roadhouse Grill
Rosedale Golf & C.C.
Sammy's
Sarasota Ale House
Sarasota Brewing Co.
Serenoa Golf Club
Shooters
Snook Haven
Sports Page
South Beach Cafe
Strudel's N Cream
The Summerhouse
Theresa's Family Restaurant
Trolley Station
Waffle Shop

The West End Grill
Wild Eats Grille & Market

Amish
Der Dutchman
Dutch Haus Family Restaurant
Dutch Oven
Millers Dutch Kitchen
Sugar & Spice
Yoders
Yoders Express

Buffet
The Country Buffet
Forest Lakes Restaurant
Park Grill

Barbeque
J&J Barbeque
Old Hickory
The Oaks Barbeque
Santa Fe Steakhouse
Surfrider Restaurant
Woodys

British Isles
Churchills
The Coach & Horses British
  Pub & Restaurant
Cock 'n Bull Pub
Lynches Landing Bar & Grill
O'Brien's Irish Pub
Paddy's Sports Bar
Rotten Ralph's
Sullivan's

Cajun/Creole
Beach Cafe
Hillview Grill

Caribbean
Cafe Lido
Cafe on the Bay
Daiquiri Deck and Cafe Gardens
Hillview Grill
Javier's Restaurant
Key West Grill
Mar Vista Pub & Restaurant
Surfrider Restaurant

Chinese
100º East Chinese Grill
  & Noodle Co.
China Blossom
China Palace
China Pavilion Restaurant
The Dragon
Empress Gardens
Lantern
Mr. Wong's Wok & Grill
New China
Panda Inn
Shangri-La
Tai Ping

Continental
Althea's
Banyan Cafe
Beach Bistro
Beach Cafe Bar & Restaurant
Big Kitchen Restaurant
The Bijou Cafe
Blase Cafe
Cafe L'Europe
Cafe Lido
Chef Caldwell's
Churchill's Bar & Restaurant
The Colony Dining Room
Crab Trap I & II
Durham's
Euphemia Haye
Forest Lakes Restaurant
Gecko's Grill & Pub
Harry's Continental Kitchen
Hemingway's
Ivo's Continental
Mar Vista Pub & Restaurant
The Melting Pot
Munroe's
Nicki's West 59th ST. West
Ophelia's
Portobello
Roessler's
The Sand Dollar
Sarasota Bread Co.
Seagrapes
The Summerhouse

Eclectic
Alley Cat Cafe
Big Kitchen
The Bijou Cafe
Bistro 41
Blase Cafe
Cafe Kaldi
Cafe on the Bay
Cafe Venice
Carmichael's
Euphemia Haye
Hillview Grill
J. Ryan's
Javier's Restaurant
Maureen
Michaels On East
Morel
The Original Front Burner
Pattigeorge's

Sage Restaurant
Sign of the Mermaid
St. Armands Bread Co.
Surfrider Restaurant
The Tasting Room

Fondue
The Melting Pot

French
Cafe of the Arts
Chez Andre
Chez Daniel
Cuisine de France
Durham's
Francoise et Henri
French Affair
Le Petit Jardin
Cuisine de France

German
Alpine Steakhouse
Little Bavaria

Greek
Chutney's
Demetrio's
El Greco Cafe
Fandango
Ntino's
Silver Star

Indian
Chutney's
Mim's

Italian
Andiamo
Anthony's Italian Deli
Bella Roma
Bellini Ristorante
Broadway Bar
Cafe Amici
Cafe Baci
Cafe L'Europe
Caragiulo's
Carrabba's
Christellie's
Ciao! Italia
Cosimo's
Cuoco Matto
DeFina's
Gastronomia
Giorgio's
Ivo's Italian & Continental
La Terrazza
Mama Leones
Mama Onesti
Marie's

Mario's
Mediterraneo
Mona Lisa
Napolis
Nick's Italian
Ntino's
Oma
Osteria
Pappa Nicks
Pasta E Basta
Pasta House
Pattigeorge's
Piazza Napoli
Portobello
Primo! Ristorante
Rico's
Rizzo Bros.
Saulina's
Scalini
Tony's Place
Valenti's
Villa Capri

Japanese
Da Ru Ma
Joto
Saga
Shogun
Yoshino

Jewish Deli
Better Bagels
Bein's & Joffrey's
Corkscrew Deli
Manhattan Bagel
Nellie's Deli

Mexican
Cafe Campestre
Cisco & Pancho
El Adobe
Javier's
Tex/Mex Cafe
Tia Panchas

Natural Foods/Vegetarian
Mim's
Wild Eats Grill & Market

Nouvelle American
Alley Cat Cafe
Beach Cafe
Bistro 41
Blase Cafe
Candlelight Restaurant
Carmichael's
Cedars Cafe
The Colony Dining Room
David Michael's

Hungry Fox
Javier's Restaurant
Michael's On East
Morel
Munroe's
Ophelia's on the Bay
Patrick's
Pattigeorge's
Sage Restaurant

Oyster Bar
Anna Maria Oyster Bar
Anna Maria Oyster Bar Landside
Crow's Nest
Captain Curt's
Captain Eddie's
J.P. Crawdads
  Marker 4 Oyster Bar
  The Original Oyster Bar
  Phillippi Creek Oyster Bar

Pizzaria
  Broadway Bar
  Caragulio's
  Carrabbas
City Pizza
Cosimios
Demitrios
Honey Crust Pizzeria
Mama Leones
Nicki's Italian Pizza
Oma
Pappa Nicks
Pontillo's
Primo!
Pizza World
Rico's Pizzeria
Rizzo Bros.
Saulina's Pizza
Thro-Dough Pizza

Seafood
Althea's
Anna Maria Oyster Bar
Backbay
Barnacle Bill's Seafood
Bart's Bayside
Beach House
Bob's Boathouse
Captain Brian's
Captain Curt's Crab & Oyster Bar
Captain Eddie's Seafood Rest.
Caroline's
Charley's Crab
Chart House
Coasters Seafood Co.
Crab Trap I & II
Crow's Nest
Dirty Moe's Seafood & Spirits

Dry Dock
Expedition Co.
Flying Bridge
Hillview Grill
J.P. Crawdad's
Key West Willy's
Leverock's
Marina Jack Restaurant
Marker 4 Oyster Bar
Mar Vista Pub & Restaurant
Michael's Seafood Grill
Moore's Stone Crab
Old Salty Dog
Original Oyster Bar
Pattigeorge's
Pelican Alley
Phillipi Creek
  Oyster Bar
Poseidon
Rosebud
Rotten Ralph's
Saltwater Cafe
Seafood Shack
Seagrape
Sharky's on the
  Pier
Shells
Sunset Grill
Sunset Grille
Surfrider Restaurant
Turtle's Restaurant
Walt's
The Waterfront Restaurant

Spanish
Javier's
Sammy's

Steakhouse
All Star Steakhouse
Alpine Steak House
Backbay Steakhouse
Cattle Co. Cafe
Chart House
Chelsea Grill
Demetrio's
J.P. Crawdad's
Joto Steakhouse
Key West Willy's
The Landmark
Lonestar
Rosebud
Santa Fe Steakhouse
Sarasota Ale House
Sega Steakhouse
Shogun
Stockyard Steakhouse

Tex-Mex
Tex-Mex Cafe & Saloon
West End Grill

Thai
100º East
Bangkok Restaurant
Empress Garden
Siam Orchid
Thai Garden

LISTINGS BY SERVICES

Boat Access Available
Anna Maria Oyster Bar
Bart's Bayside
Bob's Boathouse
Buccaneer Inn
Cafe on the Bay
Caroline's
Coasters Seafood Co.
Crows Nest
Da Ru Ma
Dry Dock
Michael's Seafood Grill
Flying Bridge
J. P. Crawdad's
Marker 4 Oyster Bar
Marina Jack
Mar Vista Pub & Restaurant
Ophelia's on the Bay
Pattigeorge's
Summerhouse
Sunset Grill
Turtle's Restaurant

Catering Services
Alley Cat Cafe
Alpine Steak House
Althea's
Andiamo
Anthony's Italian Deli
Bangkok Restaurant
Banyan Cafe
Barnacle Bills's Seafood
Beach Cafe
Beach House
Beef O'Brady's
Bein's & Joffrey's
Bella Roma
Better Bagels
Big Kitchen
Blase Cafe
Blue Dolphin Cafe
Cafe Kaldi
Cafe L'Europe
Cafe Lido
Cafe on the Bay

Captain Brian's
Caroline's
Cedars Cafe
Charley's Crab
Chart House
Chef Caldwell's
Chez Daniel
China Blossom
China Palace
Churchill's Bar
Chutney's
Coasters Seafood Co.
The Colony Dining Room
The Colony Bistro
Crows Nest
Cuoco Matto
David Michael's
DeFina's Restaurant
Dirty Moe's Seafood
Durham's Continental Dining
Dutch Oven
El Greco Cafe
Fandango
Flying Bridge
Forest Lakes Restaurant
Harry's Continental Kitchen
Hillview Grill
Key West Willy's
Lantern
Mama Onestl
Manhattan Bagel
Mario's
Mar Vista Pub
Michael's Seafood Grill
Mim's
Munroe's
Nellie's Deli
New China
Original Front Burner
Pasta E Basta
Portobello
Ricco's Pizzeria
Sammy's
Sand Dollar Rooftop Cafe
Santa Fe Steakhouse
Siam Orchid
Sports Page
Summerhouse
Thai Garden
Tony's Place
Trolley Station
Walt's
The West End Grill

Cigar Room Available
Althea's
Bart's Bayside
Caragiulio's
Chelsea Grill

Cosimo's
Cuoco Matto
Gecko's Grill & Pub, North
Rosebud
Saltwater Cafe

Dinner Theater
Golden Apple

Gourmet Takeout Available
Alley Cat Cafe
Alpine Steak House
Althea's
Andiamo
Anthony's Italian Deli
Bangkok Restaurant
Banyan Cafe
Bart's Bayside
Beach Cafe
Beach House
Beef O'Brady's
Bein's & Joffrey's
Bella Roma
Better Bagels
Big Kitchen
The Bijou Cafe
Blase Cafe
Buccaneer Inn
Cafe Kaldi
Cafe L'Europe
Cafe Lido
Cafe on the Bay
Captain Brian's
Coaster's Seafood co.
Capt. Eddie's
Caragiulo's
Caroline's
Cattle Co. Cafe
Charley's Crab
Chef Caldwell's
Chef Paul's
Chelsea Grill
Chez Andre
Chez Daniel
China Blossom
China Palace
China Pavilion
Christellie's
Churchill's Bar & Restaurant
Coach & Horses Pub
The Colony Dining Room
The Colony Bistro
Cuisine De France
Cucco Matto
Da Ru Ma
David Michael's
DeFina's
Der Dutchman
Dirty Moe's Seafood

Dry dock
Durham's Continental Dining
El Adobe
El Greco
Empress Gardens
Fandango
First Watch
Flying Bridge
Francoise et Henri
Gastronomia
Gecko's Grill & Pub
Gulf Drive Cafe
Harry's Continental Kitchen
Hob Nob
Honey Crust
Hot Diggity Dog
The Hungry Fox
Javier's Restaurant
J.P. Crawdad's
Key West Grill
Key West Willy's
The Landmark
Lantern
Le Petite Jardin
Mama Leones
Mama Onesti
Manhattan bagel
Marina Jack
Mario's
Melting Pot
Midnight Pass Pub
Millie's
Mim's
Mr. Wong's Wok & Grill
Nellie's Deli
New China
O'Brien's Irish Pub
Old Hickory
100° East Chinese Grill
Original Front Burner
Paddy's Sports Bar & Grill
Pasta E Basta
Patrick's
Portobello
Primo! Ristorante
Rico's Pizzeria
Roessler's
Rotten Ralph's
Sage
Saltwater Cafe
Sarasota Ale House
Sarasota Bread Co.
Saulina's Pizza
South Beach Cafe
Summerhouse
Sunset Grill
Surfrider Restaurant
Tai Ping
Theresa's

Thro-Dough's
Tony's Place
Trolley Station
Walt's
West End Grill
Wild Eats Grill & Market

Kid Friendly
Alley Cat Cafe
Alpine Steak House
Althea's
Andiamo
Augies
Bangkok Restaurant
Banyan Cafe
Bart's Bayside
Beach Cafe
Beach House
Beef O'Brady's
Bella Roma
Better Bagels
Big Kitchen
Blase Cafe
Bob's Boathouse
Cafe Kaldi
Captain Brian's
Captain Curt's
Coasters Seafood Co.
Captain Eddie's
Caragiulo's
Carolines
Carrabba's
Cattle Co. Cafe
Charley's Crab
Chef Caldwell's
Chef Paul's
Chelsea Grill
Chez Andre
China Blossom
Christellie's
Ciao! Italia
City Pizza
The Colony Dining room
The Colony Bistro
Cosimo's
The Country Buffet
Cuoco Matto
Da Ru Ma
DeFina's
Dirty Moe's
Dry Dock
Dutch Oven
Empress Gardens
Expedition Co.
Fandango
Fifty's Diner
First Watch
Flying Bridge
Gecko's Grill & Pub

Gulf Drive Cafe
Hemingway's
Honey Crust
The Hungry Fox
J.P. Crawdad's
Key West Grill
Key West Willy's
The Landmark
Lynches Landing
Mama Leone
Mama Onesti
Manhattan Bagel
Mario's
Marker 4 Oyster Bar
Mar Vista Pub & Restaurant
Michael's Seafood Grill
Midnight Pass Pub
Millie's
Nellie's Deli
New China
O'Brien's Irish Pub
Old Hickory
Ophelia's on the Bay
Pasta E Basta
Trolley Station
Walt's
West End Grill
Wild Eats

Private Rooms
Althea's
Bart's Bayside
Beach Bistro
Beach House
The Bijou Cafe
Blue Dolphin Cafe
Cafe L'Europe
Cafe Lido
Coasters Seafood
Caragiulo's
Caroline's
Cattle Co. Cafe
Cedars Cafe
Charley's Crab
Chez Daniel
China Blossom
China Pavilion
Christellie's
Colony Dining Room
Cuoco Matto
David Michaels
DeFina's Restaurant
Fandango
First Watch
Flying Bridge
Francoise et Henri
Harry's Continental Kitchen
Hillview Grill
Key West Grill

Key West Willy's
The Landmark
Mama Onesti
Marina Jack Dinner Boat
Mario's
Michael's Seafood Grill
Roessler's
Rosebud
  Sand Dollar
    Sunset Grill
      Surfrider Restaurant
        Turtle's

Michael's On East
Michael's Seafood Grill
Morel
Munroe's
Ophelia's on the Bay
Original Front Burner
Pattigeorge's
Pops Tropicgrille
Portobello
Roessler's
Rosebud
Rotten Ralph's Waterfront
Sage
Saltwater Cafe
Sand Dollar Rooftop Restaurant
The Summerhouse
Sunset Grill
Surfrider Restaurant
Wild Eats Grill & Market

Romantic Setting
  Alley Cat Cafe
    Althea's
      Banyan Cafe
Bart's Bayside
Beach Bistro
Beach Cafe
Beach House
Bella Roma
The Bijou Cafe
Blase Cafe
Bob's Boathouse
Cafe L'Europe
Cafe Lido
Cafe on the Bay
Cafe Venice
Candlelight Restaurant
Caroline's
Cedars Cafe
Chart House
Chelsea Grill
Chez Daniel
China Blossom
China Palace
Ciao! Italia
Colony Dining Room
Colony Bistro
Cuoco Matto
Da Ru Ma
David Michael's
DeFina's Restaurant
Durham's Continental Dining
Empress Gardens
Fandango
Francoise et Henri
Giorgio's
Harry's Continental Kitchen
Hungry Fox
Javier's
The Landmark
Lynches Landing
Mama Leone's
Mama Onesti
Marina Jack
Mar Vista Pub
Melting Pot

Sunday Brunch
Althea's
Blase Cafe
Blue Dolphin Cafe
Chef Paul's
Chez Andre
The Colony Dining Room
Demetrio's
Dutch Oven
First Watch
Forest Lakes Restaurant
Harry's Continental Kitchen
Hungry Fox
Mim's
Ophelia's
Park Grill & Cafe
Patrick's
Roessler's
Rotten Ralph's
Saltwater Cafe
Summerhouse
Sunset Grill
Turtle's Restaurant

Waterfront View
Alley Cat Cafe
Anna Maria Oyster Bar
Bart's Bayside
Beach Bistro
Beach House
The Boathouse
Bob's Boathouse
Buccaneer Inn
Cafe on the Bay
Coasters Seafood Co.
Caroline's
Chart House
China Palace
Colony Dining Room

Steve Rabow's Guide Book Restaura

Trap I & II
's Nest
u Ma
Dock
Watch
g Bridge
Drive Cafe
lle's Eatry
rawdad's
WestGrill
West Willy's
hes's Landing
na Jack
ker 4 Oyster Bar
Vista Pub & Restaurant
ael's Seafood Grill
ight Pass Pub
e's Stone Crab
alty Dog
elia's on the Bay
Grill & Cafe
george's
obello
essler's
ten Ralph's
d Dollar
Grape
enoa Gulf Club
rky's on the Pier
oters
ok Haven
set Grill
set Grille
frider Restaurant
tle's Restaurant

Ophelia's on the Bay
Pattigeorge's
Roessler's
The Summerhouse

e Dinners
Cat Cafe
e Steak House
acle Bill's Seafood
Bijou Cafe
Venice
iulo's
ne's
rs Cafe
ea Grill
Daniel
Italian
er's Seafood Co.
y Dining Room
no's
's Nest
Moe's Seafood & Spirits
ock
ois et Henro
ew Grill
a Onesti
na Jack
oe's

...DY FOR 2000

...*The Guide* is completely updated - it is our goal to provide the ...t comprehensive resource for residents, newcomers and tourists ... annual basis. To be included in our listings for the year 2000...

...iness, group or event is currently being cited in *The Guide*:

... You will be contacted by our Research Department requesting ...luled changes and updates. All listings should provide your ...ame, Address (including Zip Code), Phone Number, Fax Number, ...Internet Address. If you have not been contacted by September 30, ...e call us at 927-1771.

...iness, group or event is not currently included in *The Guide*:

...me your information, there is no charge to be listed within most ...of *The Guide*. For the year 2000 (9th edition) there will be a $50 ...or listings in the following sections: Shopping, Real Estate, Health ...ith the exception of area hospitals), Legal/Financial Services and ...modations. (This fee will allow us to continue to upgrade The *Guide* ... readers while expanding the range of participants from the commu-... complimentary copy of *The Guide* will be provided for individuals/ ...esses who have been charged for their listings, the $50 listing fee will ...aived for individuals/businesses who provide *The Guide* with advertis-...support.) Again, the overwhelming number of listings in *The Guide* will ...tinue to be provided at no charge.

...request a 2000 Guide Book New Information Submission Form:

...ease call 927-1771. Be sure to provide us with your Name, Phone and Fax ...umber when you call. All submissions must be in writing.

To submit new information for the 2000 Guide Book (9th Edition):

> Steve Rabow's Guide Book
> P.O. Box 15332
> Sarasota, FL 34277

A contact name and phone number must be included with all submissions.

Other Publications From Rabow Communication Arts:

> Sarasota Downtown Quarterly Guide
> Sarasota Family YMCA Quarterly Guide
> Die Freundliche Seite Floridas (Annual German Guide
> to Florida's West Coast)

For a copy of these publications send $3.00 s/h per title to:

> Rabow Communication Arts
> P.O. Box 15332
> Sarasota, FL 34277

Be sure to include your name, address, telephone number and which publication you are requesting. We will send you the most current edition.

To Request Current Advertising Rates: 927-1771

Guide Book 2000 (9th Edition) Ad Deadline: October 15, 1999